European Values at the Turn
of the Millennium

European Values Studies

The European Values Studies is a series based on a large-scale, cross-national and longitudinal research program. The program was initiated by the European Value Systems Study Group (EVSSG) in the late 1970s, at that time an informal grouping of academics. Now, it is carried on in the setting of a foundation, using the (abbreviated) name of the group (EVS). The study group surveyed basic social, cultural, political, moral, and religious values held by the populations of ten Western European countries, getting their work into the field by 1981. Researchers from other countries joined the project, which resulted in a 26-nations data set. In 1990 and 1999/2000, the study was replicated and extended to other countries. By now, almost all European countries are involved in one or more waves of the study, including those in Central and Eastern Europe. This series is based on the survey data collected in this project. For more information see: www.europeanvalues.nl.

VOLUME 7

European Values at the Turn of the Millennium

edited by

Wil Arts
and
Loek Halman

BRILL

LEIDEN · BOSTON

2004

This book is printed on acid-free paper

Library of Congress Cataloging-in-Publication Data

European values at the turn of the millen[n]ium/Wil Arts, Loek Halmal [editors]
    p. cm. — (European values studies, ISSN 1568-5926; v. 7)
    Includes bibliographical references and index.
    ISBN 90-04-13981-8 (pb. : alk. paper)
    1. Social values—Europe. 2. Civil society—Europe. 3. Family—Europe.
4. Work—Europe. 5. Europe—Religion. I. Arts, Wilhelmus Antonius, 1946–
II. Halman, Loek. III. European values studies (Leiden, Netherlands); v. 7.

HM681.E87 2004
303.3'72'094090511—dc22

2004054400

ISBN 90 04 13981 8
ISSN 1568-5926

PRINTED IN THE NETHERLANDS

PART THREE: RELIGION AND MORALITY

Chapter Eleven
Religious beliefs and practices in contemporary Europe
LOEK HALMAN & VEERLE DRAULANS

Chapter Twelve
Normative orientations towards the differentiation between
religion and politics
LOEK HALMAN & THORLEIF PETTERSSON

APPENDICES

ACKNOWLEDGMENTS

This book was a long time coming. The first drafts and ideas of most chapters were discussed in a European Values workshop in Leuven, Belgium, in December 2001. Many of these preliminary chapters were more or less completed by the end of 2002. Some other chapters were presented at a European Values workshop in Tilburg, the Netherlands, at the Tilburg University Anniversary Conference 'Sustainable ties in the information society', in March 2003. That it took longer than intended, is mainly due to the fact that the editors were too occupied with other activities, such as the preparation and production of the sixth volume in this series on European Values. We are grateful to those who have contributed to this book, and who were so kind to wait patiently. Everything comes to those who wait!

We are also grateful to Jaak Billiet from the Catholic University of Leuven, and the Scientific Research Community 'Methodology of Longitudinal and Comparative Research into Social and Cultural Change' of the Fund for Scientific Research—Flanders (Belgium), for their help in organizing the December 2001 meeting in Leuven. Without their generous support, the Leuven meeting could not have been organized. The same applies to Tilburg University and its Faculty of Social and Behavioral Sciences who supported and helped to organize the Tilburg workshop. It goes without saying that the EVS Foundation was as always the unseen force behind both workshops.

The analyses reported in this book could not have been performed, if Zentralarchiv in Cologne, in close collaboration with Tilburg University, had not provided the collaborators with the updated data from the most recent wave of surveys carried out in Europe in 1999/2000. Without their generous help and support, the empirical analyses could not have been performed.

Also, we would like to express our thanks to Kees Boos of the Faculty of Social and Behavioral Sciences of Tilburg University for his indispensable help during the closing phases of the project.

Last but not least, we would like to thank Regine Reincke and Joed Elich of Brill International Publishers for their confidence in this project.

Tilburg, July 2004
Wil Arts & Loek Halman

CHAPTER ONE

EUROPEAN VALUES AT THE TURN OF THE MILLENNIUM: AN INTRODUCTION

Wil Arts & Loek Halman

1 Introduction

Cross-national value research has prospered in the last few decades. We owe this flourishing especially to the fact that a great number of major comparative datasets have been made available since the 1970s, and new statistical methods of analysis and their related software have been developed. These 'blessings' have given a new impetus to cross-national value research. Gauthier (2002) is even of the opinion that, because of the before mentioned developments, cross-national research has entered a new era. It is a tempting prospect to deal in this introduction with all the achievements, promises, and problems of cross-national value research at the turn of the millennium. For brevity's sake we will, however, only have a furtive glance at the history of 'general' comparative sociology and give a succint account of the methodological debate about 'general' comparative cross-national research. We will next allocate slightly more room for the state of affairs in cross-national value research. Finally, we will delineate the plan of this book.

2 A short history of comparative sociology

Comparative sociology, in the narrow sense of the term, has a long pedigree. It was already at the core of early and even proto-sociology. The founding fathers of sociology, such as Ferguson and Millar in eighteenth century Scotland, and Comte and Tocqueville in nineteenth century France, utilised cross-national, cross-cultural and cross-societal comparisons to make all-embracing causal inferences and to put their comprehensive theories to an empirical test. They did this, however, in a rather loose and unsystematic way. It was John Stuart Mill who introduced greater rigour in the mid-nineteenth century by showing in his *System of Logic* (1843) that the comparative method in social science was simply an application of the experimental method of the natural sciences to the ready-made cases of sociology. But he also showed that this method had some severe limitations compared to the experimental method that natural scientists use in laboratories.

Although the classical sociologists of the turning of the nineteenth to the twentieth century were not as presumptuous as the founding fathers, they too used the comparative method but in a more refined way. In criticism of Mill, Émile Durkheim concluded, that if comparison was carried out with true precision and control and yielded correlations (rather than invariant causal connections), it could qualify as a quasi-experimental method. The way to proceed, according to Durkheim, was to abstract the relevant variables and to establish measures and objective indices for them, controlling for other influences, adducing statistical correlations, and so on. 'We have only one way to demonstrate that a given phenomenon is the cause of another, viz., to compare the cases in which they are simultaneously present or absent, to see if the variations they present in these different combinations of circumstances indicate that one depends on the other'. Thus, for Durkheim, 'the comparative method is the only one suited to sociology' (Durkheim, [1895] 1964: 125).

A rather different method of comparison to that used by Durkheim is to be found in the work of Max Weber ([1922] 1988). His method consisted not so much in isolating factors or variables whose operations could be observed in a large number of cases, as in analysing many concrete features of different societies. He did this in order to show how characteristics which are in some respects similar from one case to another are also in other important respects different, in so far as they are affected by other features of the unique historical configuration of which they are part. The way to proceed, according to Weber, was making qualitative assessment of relevant historical evidence in terms of its meaningful significance (cf. Mitchell, 1968: 33–36).

Notwithstanding the fact that the comparative method has been at the core of sociological inquiry from the origin of sociology as a distinct discipline up to and including the era of the classics, later on the comparative approach moved into the background for several decades. A laudable exception is Sorokins (1927) work on social mobility that uses the comparative method thoughtfully. In those years mainly international organisations appear to have devoted much effort to the comparison of countries.

After the Second World War, however, the comparative approach gained new importance, emphasis and practitioners. This turn is attributed to several developments since then, such as changes in 'the world social structure—the invention of the United Nations and UNESCO, the emergence of new, self-conscious societies, and a growing sense of interdependence of societies (. . . .) the new resources provided by the computer, the systematic use of field interviews, the cross-cultural survey, methodical schedules of observation, and the growing collaboration of research teams drawn from around the world have all played a part' (Marsh, 1967: V; see also: Warwick & Osherson, 1973: 5–6).

In spite of these new developments, in comparative sociology still two main cross-national research traditions, following Durkheim and Weber, can be distinguished: a qualitative case-oriented approach, in which a comprehensive examination of cases is given preference over generality, and a quantitative variable-oriented one, in which generality is given preference over complexity (Ragin, 1989: VIII–XI). The former approach is today especially applied in the field of historical sociology and policy research. The latter one is mainly used to explore and test explanatory ideas originating from general and theoretical sociology. The cross-national value research findings discussed in the chapters of this book belong to this latter tradition.

3   *Quantitative variable-oriented comparative cross-national research*

Before switching from the history of comparative sociology to the discussion of the value research projects, of which this paper renders accounts, we must have recourse to a more or less precise classification of types of comparative research. As Melvin Kohn mentioned in his 1987 ASA Presidential Address, four types of cross-national research can be identified (Kohn, 1987: 714–716):

1. Studies in which the nation or the country is the object of study. The investigator(s) is (are) mainly interested in the understanding of the particular country(ies).
2. Studies in which the nation or country is the context of study.

Here the aim of the researchers is to test 'the generality of findings and interpretations about how certain social institutions operate or about how certain aspects of social structure impinge on personality'.
3. Studies in which the nation is the unit of analysis. Such studies focus primarily on the understanding 'how social institutions and processes are systematically related to variations in national characteristics'.
4. Studies in which nations are components of larger international systems: transnational studies.

The chapters of this book can all be located within the second category of studies where nations or countries are the higher-order contextual units of analysis and where these units are treated as a set of variables. In all of them it is supposed that the characteristics of these higher-order units are the 'causes' of certain characteristics of lower-order units, in cross-national value research more particularly, individual attitudes, values, judgements, and propensities to act. It is also assumed, however, that there is a great likelihood that third factors intervene between the presumed causes and effects. In all of the chapters the data are analysed by using multivariate quantitative methods.

To sum up: the chapters included in this book are looking, firstly, for theoretical explanations of how the values and principles that people cherish and the attitudes they hold are systematically related to characteristics of the nation-states researched and, secondly, are using the quantitative tools of mainstream sociology to test those explanations empirically.

4   *Cross-national value research in action*

The five comparative cross-national research projects mentioned in this section, which inquire into the cultural statics and dynamics of contemporary societies, are successively the International Social Survey Programme (ISSP), the International Social Justice Project (ISJP), the Religious and Moral Pluralism (RAMP) project, the European Social Survey (ESS), and the European Values Study (EVS) and World Values Surveys (WVS).

4.1 *International Social Survey Programme (ISSP)*

ISSP is a consortium of research teams from various countries whose joint interest is in studying cross-national differences and similarities in social attitudes. It started in 1983 when SCPR, London, secured funds from the Nuffield Foundation, Oxford, to hold meetings to further international collaboration between existing surveys—the General Social Survey, conducted by NORC in the USA, the British Social Attitudes Survey, conducted by SCPR in Britain, the Algemeine Bevölkerungsumfrage der Sozialwissenschaften, conducted by ZUMA in West Germany, and the National Social Science Survey, conducted by ANU in Australia. Prior to this, NORC and ZUMA had been collaborating bilaterally since 1982 on a common set of questions. The four founding members agreed to (1) jointly develop modules dealing with important areas of social science, (2) field the modules as a fifteen-minute supplement to the regular national surveys (or a special survey if necessary), (3) include an extensive common core of background variables and (4) make the data available to the social science community as soon as possible.

The standard procedure today is that identical annual multi-national survey modules are collectively designed. They are developed by appointed subcommittees and pre-tested in various countries. The annual plenary meeting of the ISSP then adopts the final questionnaire. ISSP questions need to be relevant to all countries and expressed in an equivalent manner in all languages. In the mean time modules have been fielded about the role of government (1985, 1990, 1996), social networks (1986), family and changing gender roles (1988, 1994, 2002), social inequality (1987, 1992, 1999), work orientations (1989, 1997), religion and religious beliefs (1991, 1998), the environment (1993, 2000), and national identity (1995, 2003). Since 1983, the ISSP has grown to (in 2003) 37 nations: the founding four—Australia, Germany, Great Britain and the United States—plus Austria, Brazil, Bulgaria, Canada, Chili, Cyprus, Czech Republic, Denmark, Finland, Flanders, France, Hungary, Ireland, Israel, Italy, Japan, Latvia, Mexico, Netherlands, New Zealand, Norway, Philippines, Poland, Portugal, Russia, Slovakia, Slovenia, South Africa, Spain, Sweden, Switzerland, Taiwan and Venezuela. (For information on ISSP, see: http://www.issp.org). Participating national surveys employ some standard methodological conventions in order to avoid 'artefactual' differences in the results. For instance probability-based sampling techniques are required. In most countries the questionnaire is a supplement to a regular (mail, telephone or personal interview) survey, in others it forms a separate survey. Collections of ISSP research are *inter alia* Jowell, Witherspoon & Brook (1989), Becker, Davis, Ester & Mohler (1990) and Jowell, Brook & Dowds (1993). The datasets can be downloaded from internet and are also available on CD-rom.

The ISSP marks several new departures in the area of cross-national research. First, the collaboration between organisations is not ad hoc or intermittent, but routine and continual. Second, while necessarily more circumscribed than collaboration dedicated solely to cross-national research on a single topic, the ISSP makes cross-national research a basic part of the national research agenda of each participating country. Third, by combining a cross-time perspective with a cross-national perspective, two powerful research designs are being used to study societal processes.

4.2   *International Social Justice Project (ISJP)*

The ISJP is a collaborative cross-national survey programme that seeks to generate a comparative picture of popular perceptions of economic and political justice in advanced industrialised nations (cf. Kluegel, Mason & Wegener, 1995). The ISJP includes surveys of people from five of the world's most influential capitalist democracies (Great Britain, Japan, Netherlands, USA and West Germany) and eight post-communist countries (Bulgaria, Czechoslovakia, East Germany, Estonia, Hungary, Poland, Russia and Slovenia) comprising the large majority of the population of Central and Eastern Europe. The study started in 1989 when the first core group of this project met in London, in conjunction of the meeting of the International Studies Association. The survey was fielded, with one exception, in the summer of 1991.

The goals of the project are both descriptive and theoretical. On the descriptive side of the ISJP agenda is the aim to generate a comparative picture of popular perceptions of economic and political justice in advanced industrialised nations. The researchers were fortunate to begin this study prior to the velvet revolutions in Central and Eastern Europe of 1989. Therefore they set as one of their goals to provide baseline data for the study of social change in this region. The results also give a comparative picture of popular views of justice in some major capitalist democracies. Although there has been

The research project evoked widespread interest in many other European and non-European countries, where colleagues and research institutions joined the project and used the original EVS questionnaire. In this way comparable surveys became available outside Western Europe, i.e. in the Scandinavian countries, Hungary, Malta, the Soviet Union, the United States, Canada, Chile, Argentina, Japan, South Africa, Australia and New Zealand. The resulting study was the largest comparative research project ever carried out enabling the analysis of differences and similarities in basic values and attitudes among populations of 26 societies around the globe. The 1981 data has been deposited at the ESRC Survey Archive at the University of Essex.

Apart from a large series of books on the findings for individual countries, several comparative studies were published by Stoeztel (1983), Harding, Phillips & Fogarty (1986), Halman, Heunks, de Moor & Zanders (1987), Halman (1991), Inglehart (1990).

In order to explore the dynamics of values change, a repeat survey was necessary. A second wave of surveys was designed and pretested during the eighties and launched in 1990. The new wave of surveys, however, was designed not only to monitor changes in Europe, but also to compare the value orientations of Western Europeans with the values of people in Central and Eastern European countries. The design of the questionnaire built on findings from the 1981 surveys and was coordinated by a Steering Committee consisting of some initiators of the project and some new members. The second wave of surveys was conducted in 1990 in almost all European countries including Switzerland (in 1989, using the pre-test EVS questionnaire) and Austria as well as many Central and Eastern European countries (again minus Greece), and in Hungary, Czech Republic, Slovakia, Poland, Bulgaria, the Baltic States, and the former German Democratic Republic the survey was conducted for the first time by associated research teams. The 1990 surveys in Europe were coordinated by the Institut für Demoskopie in Allensbach, Germany, while Ron Inglehart (University of Michigan Ann Arbor USA) organized and/or coordinated the surveys in non-European countries. Data from the 1990 surveys have been deposited at Steinmetz archive in Amsterdam and are also available from the ICPSR survey data archive at the University of Michigan. For the results and more information on the EVS 1990 study we can refer to many publications (see also: www.euro-peanvalues.nl), for instance Barker, Halman & Vloet (1992), Ashford & Timms (1992), Ester, Halman & de Moor (1994), Halman & Vloet

(1994), Nicolás & Inglehart (1994), De Moor (1995), Halman & Nevitte (1996), Ester, Halman & Rukavsihnikov, (1997), Inglehart, (1997), Halman & Riis (1999, 2003).

To further explore the dynamics of value change in Europe, and probe more deeply into their causes and consequences, a third wave has been launched and fieldwork has been conducted in 1999 or 2000 throughout Europe (see Halman, 2001). In order to prepare the questionnaire five research or working groups (4 substantive and 1 methodological group) have been established. The four substantive research groups covered the four main domains in the questionnaire: religion and morality, society and politics, primary relations, work and leisure. The main tasks of these substantive research groups were: the development of theories and concepts as well as to suggest concrete items to be included in the questionnaire of 1999. The work within these substantive groups built on the experiences from the two previous waves and an important limiting condition was of course that in order to trace value change about 75% of the questions had to remain the same, using exactly the same wording and answercategories as in the previous waves. Several items were proposed tapping new issues such as solidarity, democracy, gender roles, non-traditional religiosity, social capital (the 1999 questionnaire as well as the questionnaires from 1981 and 1990 can be downloaded from the EVS home page: www.europeanvalues.nl).

In 1999/2000 the survey was carried out in all Western European countries, except for Norway and Switzerland, but including Greece and Turkey and also including almost all Central and Eastern European countries. Exceptions here are Albania, Yugoslavia, and Bosnia & Herzegovina. The 1999/2000 European Values Study is coordinated from Tilburg University. The survey data are processed in Amsterdam (NIWI, Netherlands Institute for Scientific Information Services, NIWI), Cologne (ZA, Zentralarchive) and Tilburg (WORC, the Work & Organization Research Centre of Tilburg University) and a pooled file including all 33 countries is deposited at and available from Zentralarchive in Cologne (www.gesis.org/en/data_service/topics/50-CD-ROM/index.htm).

Since EVS is not grounded on a single overarching theory or theoretical perspective, the participants in the project use the data to test very different theories and perspectives. Some of the researchers focus on values and value changes in specific domains, e.g., religion, morality, politics, others use the data to test their theories and hypotheses on current phenomena, e.g., democracy, social capital and solidarity (see e.g., Arts, Hagenaars & Halman, 2003).

The EVS project was the cradle of the World Values Survey. Ronald Inglehart from the University of Michigan has made every effort to get the 1990 survey done in countries other than those participating in the European Values Study. Researchers from nearly 40 societies involved in the 1990 world-wide values project met in Spain in 1993 to evaluate the results of the first two waves of surveys. According to the participants, coherent patterns of change were observed from 1981 to 1990, with a wide range of key values. To explore these changes and probe more deeply into their causes and consequences, the WVS group agreed to carry out surveys in 1995 and 2000. The 1995 World Values Survey carried out a wave of research in a large number of Western and non-Western countries (see: www.worldvaluessurvey.org). They aim at a better coverage of non-Western societies and analyzing the development of a democratic political culture in the emerging democracies.

The World Values Survey questionnaire retains those items that gave the most significant results from the 1981 and 1990 surveys, replicating about 60 per cent of the 1990 questionnaire. The additional space made available was used to probe more deeply into key topics, particularly democratization and global change. The WVS project explores the hypothesis that mass belief systems are changing in ways that have important economic, political and social consequences (Inglehart, 1990, 1997, 2003a, 2003b). It does not assume either economic or cultural determinism: findings to date suggest that the relationships between values, economics and politics are reciprocal, with the exact nature of the linkages in given cases being an empirical question, rather than something that can be determined a priori.

The data from the 1999/2000 European Values Study surveys have been pooled with data from the 2000 World Values Surveys and deposited at international data archives (see Inglehart, Basanez, Diez Medrano, Halman & Luijkx, 2004). This pooled dataset will enable researchers to make global comparisons of basic human values.

5 *What such projects reveal*

As we have mentioned in the introduction, Gauthier (2002) has aired the opinion that comparative research has entered a new era. Hosts

of new cross-national datasets have become available, and new statistical methods of analysis have given a new impetus to comparative
research. She does not answer the question, however, of what the
results of the research have been. To give a provisional and partial
answer to this question we will have a look at some of the results
of the above discussed value research projects.

At the most abstract level the outcomes of these projects show
that structural similarities between countries cohere with similarities
in value orientations. Intrinsic country-specific characteristics, however,
produce cross-national *dis*similar value patterns. The outcomes of the
discussed comparative value research projects show, in other words,
that countries have some things in common (institutional arrangements,
cultural influences, economic developments) that lead to more or less
similar value patterns, but also that the resemblances are sometimes
rather limited. Countries and their populations remain often highly
unique in many ways. There is not one unique trajectory of cultural
change. The results of these analyses challenge the idea that changes
in society 'spring from one underlying condition, such as the emergence
of a certain kind of attitude or motivation, an alteration in the basis
forms of production, or a revolution in communications' (Tilly, 1984:
45). That does not alter the fact, however, that the characteristics
of today's nation-states appear to be an important source for differences in people's attitudes, values and propensities to act. That is a
straightforward statement, but it leaves some important questions
unanswered. What do we mean when we say that nations, countries
or states are important determining factors for the understanding
and explanation of differences as well as similarities in values, attitudes and beliefs? Concepts like 'nation', 'state', 'country' cover a
wide variety of qualities which all may contribute to a varying degree
to the interpretation and comprehension of the differences and similarities. The problem comparative sociology is confronted with is to
argue or decide which characteristics can be regarded sources of
such differences and similarities. Referring to countries, nations, or
states without defining or explaining what features should be taken
into account, hardly adds new information to the observation that
there appear to be differences and similarities. The problem is, however, that it is hardly been thoroughly examined or theorised what
these features are or can be. As such, notions like country, nation,
and state are merely 'black boxes' hiding many features, which might
and will be important. The enormous amount of (survey) data avail-

Jorge Vala, Marcus Lima and *Diniz Lopes* explore in their contribution the feelings of prejudice in countries that have a tradition of immigration and in countries that have recently moved from being an emigration society towards being an immigration society. They also try to explain prejudice and feelings of solidarity towards immigrants from a number of personal characteristics, including egalitarian and meritocratic value orientations. The results of their analyses reveal that the differences between emigrant countries and new immigrant countries are rather small, but they also reveal that positional characteristics but also egalitarian versus meritocratic orientations are important attributes to understand varieties in prejudice and solidarity towards immigrants.

In Part Two the main focus shifts to issues related to the domains of work and family life. It is obvious that both life spheres are important for most Europeans. Most Europeans are living in and/or have families and most of the Europeans spend significant parts of their lives working. The importance is also revealed in the surveys from the European Values Study. More than 80% of the Europeans consider family very important while large majorities consider work very important (58%) or quite important (33%) (see Halman, 2001: 7–8).

It is often argued that modernization processes have fundamentally changed the structure and function of the family. For some these changes indicate the breakdown of the family, the decline of family life and in fact the crisis of family. Others have argued that it is far too early to conclude that family life will not survive. They refer to the continued support and expressed need for close intimate relationships as evidence for the survival of the family.

James Georgas, Kostas Mylonas, Aikaterini Gari and *Penny Panagiotopoulou* focus on this intruiging topic and they start with the observation that the definitions of family are changing nowadays and that several types of family can be distinguished. A leading hypothesis in their contribution is that family values and attitudes differ in the different cultural regions in Europe. They explore the associations between family values and attitudes on the one hand and demographic and cultural variables on the other hand. One of the main conclusions from their analyses is that although there are differences in family values between European countries, these differences appear rather modest.

Family is also the topic that is tackled by *Leen Vandecasteele* and *Jaak Billiet*. They are interested in the social background of marriage success factors and the developments over time of the impact of such factors. Although it is often argued that social background factors are decreasingly important attributes of orientations with respect to marriage success factors, the analyses reveal that level of education, age and religious involvement still are important explanatory factors for these orientations. Just as the Greek contributors to this volume conclude in their chapter, Vandecasteele and Billiet do not find big differences between countries in this respect nor do they find big differences in effects of these attributes over time. The authors interpret the results as evidence that in the age of reflexive modernization, collective entities are still important. Such collective entities have not lost their power.

The chapter of *Malina Voicu* not only focuses on family life but also on work. She investigates the impact of policies on the values of work and family. Especially policies for women support will affect not only the degree to which women take part on the labor market, but also orientations towards women's position in society. Voicu investigates if there is indeed a relationship between policies aiming at facilitating women to enter the labor market and sharing household tasks between partners on the one hand and gender value orientations on the other. She does not consider this relationship in causal terms, but merely in terms of linkages. She observes remarkable differences between European countries not only with regard to these gender value orientations but also in policies. She also finds that similar policies are associated with similar orientations and that similar social and economic contexts have similar value orientations.

Hans de Witte, Loek Halman and *John Gelissen* investigate work orientations in Europe at the end of the twentieth century and formulate hypotheses concerning individual and contextual factors that are derived from modernization theory and the notion of scarcity. Multi level analysis is used to test these hypotheses. The results indicate that the differences in work orientation are mainly due to individual, as opposed to contextual variables. Especially individual characteristics are associated with an intrinsic work orientation. These associations mostly confirm their hypotheses. And intrinsic work orientation is also associated with post-materialism and with a self-oriented value (as opposed to conformity), as hypothesized. As far as the differences between the European countries are concerned, it appeared that the intrinsic work orientation was not associated with the level of prosperity, or the level of unemployment within a given country.

In Part Three the main focus is on religion and morality. It is almost commonplace to state that Europe is a secularized society, meaning that the importance of religion has diminished both in society and for the individual. A large body of literature has developed yielding evidence that religion in general and churches and church leaders in particular have lost their once dominant and prominent position in contemporary Europe. Analyses of the previous EVS data collected in 1981 and 1990 demonstrated remarkable similarities and differences in the religious and moral profiles of European societies. Such differences seem to indicate that there is not one unique trajectory of religious change but that the trajectory has many faces and did not advance in all European societies in a similar speed and pace.

These differences and similarities in European trajectories of (religious) change are further explored in the chapter of *Veerle Draulans* and *Loek Halman*. In particular they investigate whether the differences in religious profiles can be attributed to longstanding cultural and religious traditions and/or can be explained from cultural modernization processes such as economic development, individualization and globalization.

Loek Halman and *Thorleif Pettersson* investigate contemporary linkages between religion and politics or more in particular people's views on whether religion should have an impact on politics or not from three theoretical perspectives: a modified secularization approach, a new paradigm in the sociology of religion, and notions on the impact of peoples' value orientations. Several hypotheses are formulated and in a multi-dimensional design, the impact of people's values, their socio-economic background, and a number of country characteristics are analysed simultaneously. The analyses reveal that traditional values are conducive to a negative view on the differentiation between religion and politics, while a civic orientation generates a positive view. The younger, the higher educated, and males appear more positive. Positive attitudes towards differentiation between religion and politics is more prevalent in more secularized societies while pluralism in the religious and political sectors appears favourable to the acceptance of a closer relationship between religion and politics.

The contribution of *Ola Listhaug* and *Kristen Ringdal* deals with a topic that is closely related to religion, namely morality. More specifically, they address the issue of civic morality in stable, new and half hearted Democracies. They argue that a strong sense of civic morality is important for the development of a well functioning society and as such civic morality is important for the former Soviet societies. In order to make the transformation from dictatorship to democracy successful, civic morality has to be very strong. However, the results of their analyses do not support the idea that civic morality is highest in Central and Eastern European countries. In fact it does not differ much from levels found in Western countries. As a consequence the authors cannot find strong correlations between political performance and civic morality. What seems to matter are cultural and social variables, such as age and religiosity, particularly in these former Soviet states. Nevertheless, the main conclusion from their analyses is that civic morality does not differ much across political systems and generally remains at a high level.

The question of who is religious in the former Soviet States and who is not, is investigated by *Larisa Titarenko*. In her contribution she investigates whether gender differences and other social and demographic characteristics have an impact on religious orientations in these former Communist societies. Although she confined the analyses to former Soviet States, she finds striking differences in levels of religiosity in these countries. The growth of spirituality or religiosity in certain parts can be attributed to the collapse of the Soviet empire and reflects a kind of social and economic deprivation, the psychological discomfort as a result of uncertainties and the failure of Soviet beliefs in general. She finds evidence for her claim that women will be more religious than men, and this is confirmed in all countries. As such, the social profile of the religious people in Eastern Europe does not differ much form the social profiles of the Western religious people.

The chapters in this book seem to demonstrate that Europe is still far from a homogenous part of the world. Not only are there significant differences between Eastern and Western European societies, also within these two blocks of countries there are often wide differences and sometimes unexpected similarities. It means that Western Europe despite the unification processes taking place within the European Union has not yet resulted in a homogenous culture. As such, the observation of Bailey (1992: 13), based on the 1990 data, is still valid. Europe is a geographical unit but it is also an area of wide diversity in values and practices and a fascinating variation of social arrangements. In another context we characterized Europe's values profile as the Cultural diversity of European Unity (Arts, Hagenaars & Halman, 2003). The chapters in this book are another demonstration of this diversity in unity.

References

Arts, W., J. Hagenaars & L. Halman (eds.) 2003. *The Cultural Diversity of European Unity. Findings, Explanations and Reflections from the European Values Study*. Leiden-Boston: Brill.

Ashford, S. & N. Timms 1992. *What Europe Thinks. A Study of Western European Values*. Aldershot: Dartmouth.

Bailey, J. 1992. Social Europe: Unity and diversity—An introduction. Pp. 1–16 in J. Bailey (ed.), *Social Europe*. London & New York: Longman.

Barker, D., L. Halman & A. Vloet 1992. *The European Values Study 1981–1990*. London: Gordon Cook Foundation.

Becker, J.W., J.A. Davis, P. Ester & P. Mohler 1990. *Attitudes in Inequality and the Role of Government*. Rijswijk: Sociaal en Cultureel Planbureau.

Borre, O. & E. Scarbrough (eds.) 1995. *The Scope of Government*. Oxford: Oxford University Press.

De Moor, R. (ed.) 1995. *Values in Western Societies*. Tilburg: Tilburg University Press.

Dobbelaere, K. & O. Riis 2003. Religious and moral pluralism: Theories, research questions, and design. Pp. 159–172 in R.L. Piedmont & D.O. Moberg (eds.), *Research in the Scientific Study of Religion Volume 13*. Leiden, Boston: Brill.

Durkheim, E. [1895] 1966. *The Rules of Sociological Method*. New York: The Free Press.

Ester, P., L. Halman & R. de Moor (eds.) 1994. *The Individualizing Society. Value Change in Europe and North America*. Tilburg: Tilburg University Press.

Ester, P., L. Halman & V. Rukavishnikov 1997. *From Cold War to Cold Peace*. Tilburg: Tilburg University Press.

Gauthier, A.H. 2002. The promises of comparative research. *Journal of Applied Social Science Studies* 122: 5–39.

Halman, L. 1991. *Waarden in de Westerse Wereld*. Tilburg: Tilburg University Press.

—— 2001. *The European Values Study: A Third Wave*. Tilburg: EVS, WORC, Tilburg University.

——, F. Heunks, R. de Moor & H. Zanders 1987. *Traditie, Secularisatie en Individualisering*. Tilburg: Tilburg University Press.

—— & A. Vloet 1994. *Measuring and Comparing Values in 16 Countries of the Western World*. Tilburg: WORC.

—— & N. Nevitte (eds.) 1996. *Political Value Change in Western Democracies*. Tilburg: Tilburg University Press.

—— & O. Riis (eds.) 1999. *Religion in Secularizing Society*. Tilburg: Tilburg University Press.

—— & O. Riis (eds.) 2003. *Religion in Secularizing Society*. Leiden-Boston: Brill.

Harding, S., D. Phillips & M. Fogarty 1986. *Contrasting Values in Western Europe*. London: MacMillan.

Inglehart, R. 1990. *Culture Shift in Advanced Industrial Society*. Princeton, NJ: Princeton University Press.

—— 1997. *Modernization and Postmodernization*. Princeton: Princeton University Press.

—— (ed.) 2003a. *Human Values and Social Change. Findings from the Values Surveys*. Leiden-Boston: Brill.

—— (ed.) 2003b. *Islam, Gender, Culture, and Democracy: Findings From The World Values Survey and the European Values Survey*. Willowdale, Ontario, Canada: De Sitter Publications.

——, M. Basanez, J. Diez Medrano, L. Halman & R. Luijkx 2004. *Human Beliefs and Values in Global Perspective: A Cross-cultural Sourcebook*. Mexico City: Siglo XXI.

Jowell, R., S. Witherspoon & L. Brook (eds.) 1989. *British Social Attitudes: Special International Report*. Aldershot: Gower.
——, L. Brook & L. Dowds (eds.) 1993. *International Social Attitudes, the 10th BSA Report*. Aldershot: Gower.
Kaase, M. & K. Newton (eds.) 1995. *Beliefs in Government*. Oxford: Oxford University Press.
Klingemann, H.D. & D. Fuchs (eds.) 1995. *Citizens and the State*. Oxford: Oxford University Press.
Kluegel, J.R., D.S. Mason & B. Wegener (eds.) 1995. *Social Justice and Political Change. Public Opinion in Capitalist and Post-Communist States*. New York: Aldine de Gruyter.
Kohn, M.L. 1987. Cross-national research as an analytic strategy. *American Sociological Review* 52: 713–731.
Layder, D. 1994. *Understanding Social Theory*. London: Sage.
Marsh, R.M. 1967. *Comparative Sociology*. New York: Harcourt, Brace & World, Inc.
Mason, D.S., J.R. Kluegel with L. Khakulina, P. Mateju, A. Orkeny, A. Stoyanov & B. Wegener 2000. *Marketing Democracy. Changing Public Opinion About Politics, the Market, and Social Inequality in Central and Eastern Europe*. Lanham, MD: Rowman & Littlefield.
Mitchell, G.D. (ed.) 1968. *A Dictionary of Sociology*. London: Routledge & Kegan Paul.
Nicolás, J.D. & R. Inglehart (eds.) 1994. *Tendencias mundiales de cambio en los valores sociales y políticos*. Madrid: Fundesco.
Niedermayer, O. & R. Sinnott (eds.) 1995. *Public Opinion and Internationalized Governance*. Oxford: Oxford University Press.
Ragin, C.C. 1987. *The Comparative Method*. Berkeley: The University of California Press.
Sorokin, P.A. 1927. *Social and Cultural Mobility*. New York: Harper.
Stoetzel, J. 1983. *Les valeurs du temps présent: une enquête européenne*. Paris: Presses Universitaires de France.
Svallfors, S. 1995. Preface. Pp. 7–9 in S. Svallfors (ed.), *In The Eye of the Beholder*, Stockholm: The Bank of Sweden Tercentenary Foundation.
Tilly, C. 1984. *Big Structures, Large Processes, Huge Comparisons*. New York: Russell Sage Foundation.
Tyriakan, E.A. 1991. Modernisation: Exhumetur in Pace. Rethinking Macrosociology in the 1990s. *International Sociology* 6: 165–180.
Van Deth, J.W. & E. Scarbrough (eds.) 1995. *The Impact of Values*. Oxford: Oxford University Press.
Warwick, D.P. & S. Osherson 1973. Comparative analysis in the social sciences. Pp. 3–41 in D.P. Warwick & S. Osherson (eds.), *Comparative Research Methods*, Englewood-Cliffs, N.J.: Prentice-Hall, Inc.
Weber, M. [1922] 1988. *Gesammelte Aufsätze zur Wissenschaftslehre*. Tübingen: J.C.B. Mohr (Paul Siebeck).
Wegener, B. (ed.) 2000. Special Issue: Social Justice Beliefs in Transition. Eastern and Central Europe 1991–1996. *Social Justice Research* 13, No. 2.

CHAPTER TWO

EUROPEAN VALUES CHANGES IN THE SECOND AGE OF MODERNITY

Wil Arts & Loek Halman

1 *Introduction*

When, in the late 1970s, the European Values Study was designed the most important question to be empirically addressed was whether the modernizing process and its underlying pattern of structural and cultural changes would lead to convergence of value orientations among the individual European nation states.[1] Or would lasting forms of divergence sooner characterize Europe at the turn of the millennium? If, on the whole, a common, albeit it in details varying European value system can be observed in contemporary Europe, so went the follow-up question, what are then the more detailed differences and similarities among societies, and what have been the particular changes and continuities in the course of time?

Numerous books, articles and papers have appeared since the early 1980's reporting on the analyses of the various waves (1981, 1990, 1999) of the EVS surveys. They succeeded in clearly delineating the changing value patterns of the populations of a great number of European countries. What these cross-national and longitudinal empirical explorations suggest is firstly that Europeans, in spite of a common cultural heritage that has left an unmistakable imprint on them, are far from homogeneous in their value patterns. Furthermore, the findings help to convince social scientists that over time changes in value patterns, both in the long and in the short run, are far from negligible.

Describing cross-national and over time continuities and varieties in value orientations is one thing, explaining and interpreting them

---

[1] An earlier slightly different version of this paper has been published in the *Festschrift* for Alexandra Kasińska-Kania, *Kultura, Osobowość, Polityka*, Warzawa: Wydawnictwo Naukowe SCHOLAR, 2002.

theoretically is something quite different. The EVS is definitely in
need of better explanations and interpretations. This is the impression one obtains if one leafs through the major books and articles
that ensued from the EVS-project. The current theoretical predica-
ment of cross-national value research in general and EVS in particular has been aptly described by Svallfors (1995: 7): 'In recent
years, the comparative study of values and opinions has gathered
new momentum. For a long time, such studies were hampered by
the lack of adequate data, and the imagination or researchers was
sometimes allowed to run too far in advance of empirical evidence.
Since the early or mid-eighties, several large-scale collaborative research
projects have been launched. The situation today sometimes seems
like the complete opposite from what it was twenty years ago: we
are now rich on data, while qualified analysis and interpretations lag
considerably behind.'

   What we aim to do in this paper is to make a fresh attempt to
improve on this annoying state of affairs. Before we will proceed to
do some 'qualified analyses' using the EVS-data we will, however,
first take a close look at the 'interpretations' and make an assessment of what theoretical sociology has achieved as far as it concerns
the actual and potential impact of modernization theory on the EVS.

2   Theoretical perspectives

At first glance the theoretical perspectives used in the EVS are numerous. A closer look at the theoretical ideas incorporated in the EVS,
however, leads to the conclusion that explanations and interpretations
have been based, most of the time, on insights from modernization
theory. The crucial theoretical notion within this comprehensive cross-
national research project has, for a long time, been that the most
important development in recent European history has been the transition from tradition to modernity, aptly dubbed by Polanyi ([1944],
1957): 'the great transformation'. The core idea is that in modern
societies, rational decision-making and co-ordinating mechanisms such
as markets and states have eclipsed traditional communities. The history of economic, political and social life in modern societies is generally presented as consisting of two main periods. While the first
era involved the expansion of markets into pre-existing communities

in the nineteenth century, the twentieth century saw the interventionist state imposing itself upon the new market economy (Streeck & Schmitter, 1985: 120). The important and distinctive features of this transformation from traditional to modern society are often sketched by referring to a whole range of sub-processes such as industrialization, urbanization, democratization, secularization, bureaucratization, and professionalization.

2.1 *Towards instrumentalism and individualism?*

The transition from tradition to modernity, the theory assumes, has had far reaching consequences for the value patterns that Europeans cherish today. As a result of the transition Europeans increasingly have an ethos characterized by instrumentalism and individualism.

One of the central hypotheses of the EVS-project postulates that as societies advance economically and technologically, an individualization process will occur and the values of their populations will increasingly shift in the direction of an individualistic ethos. The process called individualization refers to the growing autonomy of individuals in modern societies that puts a strain on their relationships to institutions. One of the consequences of individualization is that people are increasingly developing their own patterns of values and norms that tend increasingly to differ from institutionalized value systems. The pursuit of self-actualization and personal happiness is at the center of value development and norm selection within an individualistic ethos.

Another of the pivotal hypotheses of the project is that as countries advance economically and technologically, the value patterns of their populations will increasingly become rationalized. In the first stage of the rationalization process—especially taking place in developed agrarian societies—the cultural shift is one from tradition to substantive rationality. In the second stage—occurring in industrial societies—there is a cultural shift from substantive to instrumental rationality. Instrumentalization refers to the growing propensity of individuals in modern times to think in terms of goal and means, in terms of effectiveness and efficiency instead of in terms of traditional or substantive values. Modern individuals will bring their moral considerations more and more into conformity with practical reason.

2.2   *Modernization theory revisited*

In order to gain an understanding of the assumed and observed processes of the individualization and the instrumentalization of value systems, most researchers in the EVS group interpreted these processes against the background of a more encompassing process, that of the modernization of European societies.

In the boldest and most informative, but therefore also most vulnerable version of modernization theory the crucial independent variable in the causal model is the industrialization process. The argument is as follows. Due to the industrialization process the division of labor has increased in all European countries in the last two centuries. The emergence and spread of national and international markets has continued and even accelerated. Further commercialization of economic life has taken place. There has been a general enlargement of economic scale. Economic growth has seemed to drag on endlessly. The number of persons working in agriculture has continually decreased.

Intrinsic in the industrialization process is, according to modernization theory, an irreversible commitment to technical and economic rationality. The logic of industrial society imposes technical and economic rationality not only on the work place but also on all other spheres of society in a gradual but unremitting and persuasive way. Thus it enforces features that are functionally consistent with rationality and undermines those that are not. As a result all industrial societies will be brought on to convergent developmental paths. The place a particular society starts from, and the route it follows, are likely to affect its features for many years. However, all industrializing societies will respond to the inherent logic of industrialism itself. Consequently, any differences between industrial societies should eventually disappear as economic development continues.

Why should the modernization process in general and industrialization in particular lead to an ethos of individualism and instrumentalism? The answer is that it is the force of industrial circumstances, the inherent logic of industrialism that persuades people to adhere to particular opinions, ideas and values. Since this force is the same for everyone, and similar in strength, consensus originates from it. The underlying theory is simple (Inkeles, 1960). It is assumed that people have experiences, develop attitudes, and form values in response to the forces or pressures which their environment creates. The theory holds that, within broad limits, the same situational pressures, the same framework for living, will be experienced as similar and will generate the same or similar response by people from different countries. The core proposition is as follows: In so far as industrialization, urbanization and the development of large-scale bureaucratic structures and their usual accompaniments create a standard environment with standard, institutional pressures for particular groups, to that degree they should produce relatively standard patterns of experiences, attitudes, and values.

2.3   *Changing values*

One of the problems, however, the researchers working within the context of the EVS had to solve was that the modernization process was theoretically considered to be a long-term trend spanning centuries rather than decades. The data from the EVS, for a long time spanning only one decade and now covering nearly two, therefore offer insufficient information to test the predictions derived from modernization theory. 'Alas, nothing can be done about it! We have to abandon the hope of a comprehensive explanation of the findings of the European Value Study and be satisfied with partial and tentative explanations of certain statistical regularities.' This was the hasty and pessimistic conclusion of some of the researchers.

Other researchers, more optimistic by nature, were of the opinion that there was a viable solution at hand that could salvage the original goal. Certainly not the best solution, but perhaps a second best one. Twenty years ago not all European societies were, nor are they today, 'mature' industrialized societies. Neither has the industrialization process proceeded in the time period 1981–1999 to the same degree in all European societies. Therefore countries can be classified according to their level and pace of industrial development. The time-span of development becomes much wider than the nearly twenty years period of the EVS. By using modernization indicators for the countries studied and doing cross-sectional analyses it becomes possible to test predictions derived from modernization theory. But now it is not the data, but the theory that has failed. The pivotal assumption that technological and economic advance was the fuelling force appeared to be highly questionable. The case of the United States and, to a lesser extent, that of Canada called the hypotheses into question that as countries advance economically and technologically, the values of

their populations increasingly shift in the direction of individualization and instrumentalization.

Most researchers within the EVS group accepted defeat. Bailey
(1992), for example, argued that what is needed is a theory that
explains more cross-national variations than modernization theory
allows. Because different variants of modernization theory have stressed
technological determinism in one way or another, they leave no room
for the impact of other nation specific situations and developments.
De Moor (1994) likewise stated that modernization theory is far too
general to explain the dynamics of change in the various value domains
and the changes in each domain in the different countries. According
to him, instead of modernization theory empirically founded middle-
range theories were needed. Others, however, were still unconvinced.

What did they propose to do? Ronald Inglehart (1977, 1990) suggested that at least two amendments are necessary if value researchers
want to continue working with modernization theory as their paradigm. The first amendment is that we must not focus all our attention on long-term developments, but that we also need to take into
consideration short-term changes, such as the different phases of the
business cycle, and short time events, such as wars and revolutions.
They too have an impact on people's values. The force of favorable
or unfavorable circumstances influences people's value orientation.
The impact of circumstances is not only temporary, but also in certain stages of the life cycle permanent. Children at an impressionable
age, i.e., in their formative years, will later remember those developments and events vividly and act according to these lasting impres-
sions. He added to this observation the remark that value changes take
place largely through intergenerational population replacement. Cultural
shifts will therefore be more visible if we look at younger cohorts.
As a result of these deliberations he advanced both a socialization
hypothesis and a scarcity hypothesis to modify and improve modernization theory. Furthermore, he argued that we must take much more
notice of the difference between life cycle, period, and cohort effects.
The socialization hypothesis for example refers to a cohort effect,
whereas the scarcity hypothesis refers to a period effect.

The second amendment Inglehart (1997, 2000) has proposed rests
on the assumption that nowadays we have arrived at a new stage in
the history of humankind, that of post-modernity or post-industrialism.
This new stage is not only accompanied with new technological
developments (information and communication technology, biotech-

nology) and economic changes (globalization of markets, flexibility of work), but it also brings new values, particularly post-materialistic rather than materialistic ones.

2.4 Death and resurrection of modernization theory

For many theoreticians and researchers Inglehart's improvements came too late and did not go far enough to rescue modernization theory. Immanuel Wallerstein (1979) argued already before the start of the EVS that modernization theory was dead and that we should allow it to rest in peace. Others assigned the same dismal fate to value research and theory. Michael Hechter (1992, 1993, 1999) interpreted the answers within contemporary main stream social science to questions such as 'Do values matter?' and 'Should values be written out of the social scientist's lexicon?' The answer to the first question was negative and to the second affirmative. Fortunately, however, Hechter himself argues convincingly that skepticism about value theory and research might today no longer be warranted.

In recent years, however, modernization theory has been making a remarkable comeback. The reason for this revival is that a number of social scientists have come to the conclusion that recent history can best be interpreted as a process of ongoing modernization. Both Giddens (1990, 1991, 1994, 1998, 2000) and Beck (1992, 1994, 1999, 2000), for example, have argued that because of current trends and changes in the modernization process modernity has entered a new phase. Increasingly, the simple modernity that is characteristic for industrial societies has been replaced by the reflexive modernity of a post-industrial age. Instead of producing greater certainty and control the attempts at planned societal change have resulted in what Giddens calls 'manufactured uncertainty'. Owing to this uncertainty, Beck characterizes today's European societies as risk societies.

Modernization theory also owes its revival to the transformation process of post-communist countries in Eastern Europe (Arts et al., 1999). Some authors even proclaim that modernization theory 'has recorded the long-term developments within the Eastern European area (. . .) long before they were empirically verifiable' (Müller, 1992: 111). In the 1950s and the 1960s modernization theorists predicted a convergence of East and West determined by the logic of industrialism. One of their theses was that convergence would only become visible at the institutional level later on, although they already saw signs of convergence then. They were of the opinion that, in spite of severe ideological conflicts, a very broad consensus between East and West was discernible at the deeper level of fundamental values.

3   Reflexive modernity

Both Giddens and Beck argue, so we have mentioned before, that due to the forces that the process of modernization has unleashed, modernity has now entered a new phase, that of reflexive modernity. Instead of producing greater certainty and control by eliminating external risks, attempts at planned societal change have resulted in internal, self-inflicted risks and therefore in manufactured uncertainty. This uncertainty is the unanticipated by-product of molding the social and natural worlds to human purposes through institutional arrangements aiming at technical and social engineering. Such intervention in nature with technical means and in society via the institutions of the welfare state has changed societal circumstances in a fundamental way.

3.1   From simple to reflexive modernity

Giddens identifies three developments that have given the rise of manufactured uncertainty its momentum. Firstly, *globalization* or the steadily spreading intertwining of the consequences of human action across an ever-growing time-space span has diminished our capacity to control our lives. Our day-to-day activities are increasingly influenced by events taken place at the other side of the world. Conversely, local lifestyle habits have taken on global consequences. The result of the globalization process is increased uncertainty of how to cope with rather new and far away high consequence risks, such as overpopulation, environmental disasters, armed conflict and unfamiliar diseases. Second, uncertainty has also increased because of the emergence of a *post-traditional* social order. In a cosmopolitan world, tradition has lost its authority as ways of arranging life are no longer predefined but open to discussion and subject to free choice. These two developments result in social relations being distanced from traditional and localized contexts of interaction. Third, this leads to the emergence of a coping strategy with a high level of *reflexivity*, i.e., an ability to use one's own responsibility as much as possible in order to find solutions to the social problems one meets in late modern society.

As 'the reflexivity of modern social life consists in the fact that social practices are constantly examined and reformed in the light of incoming information about those very practices, thus constitutively altering their character' (Giddens, 1992: 38), late modernity displays an increasing dislocation between knowledge and control. Giddens argues that modernization, by influencing human relationships and institutions, has changed the nature of trust. In the process of modernization all localized contexts of interaction with built-in trust have gradually lost their efficacy. Although people are increasingly faced with and dependent upon abstract systems, Giddens emphasizes the significance of active trust in post-traditional relationships. Active trust 'in contexts ranging from intimate personal ties right through to global systems of interaction', in Giddens' (1994: 186) view, is the foundation on which new forms of solidarity are built.

Giddens' analysis shows a remarkable resemblance to Beck's ideas (1992; 1994). This German sociologist contends that in the ongoing process of modernization the contours of modern industrial society are dissolving and giving way to a new developmental phase in modern society: risk society. With the notion of risk society, Beck argues that the adverse side-effects of modern industrial society have come to threaten its achievements as distributional conflicts over 'goods' are being overshadowed by conflicts over the distribution of 'bads'. The same political and economic institutions that accompany the creation of such risks, have distanced people from the basic certainties that traditional parameters of industrial society had to offer while failing to provide mechanisms for monitoring and protecting against risks. Beck argues that traditional models of conducting and arranging life have lost their obligatory and embedded nature and have been replaced by individualized models based on welfare state regulations. Rather than a matter of free choice, individualization is painted as a compulsion to construct one's own biography with its commitments and networks under the conditions and models of the welfare state, such as the educational system, the labor market, etc. (1994: 14). Even models of marriage and family have become a matter of decision making. While traditional models 'constricted the scope of action . . . they also obligated and forced the individuals into togetherness' (ibid., 15), today people can choose from a number of models, whereby the togetherness is broken up. People must rely on themselves to stage their own biographies. They have to face the turbulence of a global risk society without having recourse to traditional commitments and ties. Therefore risks become personalized and self-confronting. In this sense, Beck argues that modernity has become reflexive.

Such developments tend to transform the nature of solidarity, according to Beck (1992), as the transition from class to risk society is accompanied by a change of values, one in which positive change aiming at the ideal of equality is substituted for a defensive utopia heralding the value of safety. As a consequence, a social epoch arises with the emergence of a risk society in which solidarity against need gives way to solidarity against anxiety. Because capabilities and re- sources to deal with risks are unequally distributed among individuals, new social segmentations and conflicts have arisen. Traditional social categories have dissolved while commitments and networks are in a state of flux; unknown and unintended consequences in risk society may strike anyone. In a sense, Beck argues, 'there are no others'.

3.2   *Risk assessment*

In a risk society individuals are continuously confronted with a plu- rality of options coupled with uncertainty. They develop an attitude of risk assessment and a future-oriented calculation of the past and present. They create and adopt new lifestyles to cope with the man- ifested uncertainty rather than adhering to the traditional behavioral patterns of former generations (Mills, 2000). But coping with uncer- tainty in this way might lead to adopt a life strategy through which the development of stable identities is hard to attain. Since there is a reflexive understanding of the future risks involved in any action, taken at any time, a person may either opt for postponement of important life biography decisions or opt for 'flexible' solutions where one always has the possibility of 'opting out'.

The other side of risk is trust and according to Giddens (1991) trust is involved in decisions with long-term implications for the future, like marriage, emigration, and divorce. Trust is a way of coping with risk but because of modernization there is a breakdown of *ontologi- cal security* as Giddens has pointed out. In a modern world trust itself has become increasingly fragile, because of which the investment in trusty relationships will be postponed, or made less binding, by allow- ing more transitions between one status (job or marriage) and another. The 'crisis of trust' not only involves human, interpersonal relationships but also the way people view and treat institutional linkages and commitment. Modern institutions are and need to be more adaptable and less binding than in the past.

4 Research questions

The expositions of Beck and Giddens about the so-called second age of modernity have been received with a storm of applause in the media, but have also encountered caustic critique by some scholars. Dingwall (1999) for example raises objections against the fact that empirical evidence rarely figures in their arguments. He sets the virtues of empirical research against the vices of Grand Theory. Goldthorpe (2001) and Münch (2002) do more or less the same. They argue that research findings call the validity of Beck's and Giddens's Grand Theory, that stresses the historically unprecedented nature of contemporary developments and their discontinuity with the past, in question. There is hardly evidence for their far-reaching claim that we are witnessing today a historical disjunction and the beginning of a new epoch.

In the following sections of this paper we aim to steer a course between the Scylla of uncritical praise and the Charybdis of harsh rebuke. We will cherish the virtues of empirical research without sacrificing the heuristics of Grand Theory. Although Beck's and Giddens's expositions of the social effects of reflexive modernization have not been molded into explanatory theories from which testable hypotheses can be derived, they do not have a metaphysical nature. They have both attributed at least some of the predicted social effects to empirically identifiable social processes. This opens the possibility to use their Grand Theory as a source of conjectures and expectations, i.e., as a heuristic device.

The question we want to address in this paper is firstly whether we can derive hunches and guesses, conjectures and expectations from Beck's and Giddens's Grand Theory that are potentially fruitful for acquiring an insight into the what, how and why of value change in contemporary Europe. Second, we want to empirically test whether these conjectures and expectations make empirical sense if and when we confront them with the data of the consecutive waves of the EVS.

5 Conjectures and expectations

Using Beck's and Giddens's Grand Theory of Reflexive Modernization as a heuristic devise, in other words as a set of orienting statements, we can derive more concrete expectations, i.e., hypotheses, regarding differences between European countries at a certain point in time and, more specifically, at the turn of the millennium. Furthermore, we can derive from their theory hypotheses concerning the cultural conse-quences of the development of those countries in the last few decades. The crucial assumptions used by us for deriving hypotheses from the theory of reflexive modernization are as follows. First, European countries can be ordered and clustered according to how far the modernization process has proceeded. Second, European countries can be clustered according to which ideal type of welfare state they best approximate. Applying the former assumption, the first hypothesis is as follows: *The further a contemporary European country has proceeded on the road to reflexive modernity, that is the more it has solved the visible problem of creating wealth and combating poverty, the more it has come to face the invis-ible problems of risk and trust.* The second hypothesis applies not only the first assumption, but also follows from the fact that Giddens (1998) supports Inglehart's thesis of the rise of post-materialism in advanced affluent democracies. This hypothesis holds that *the more affluent a European country and the longer its democratic pedigree, the more its population will cherish post-materialist values.* The third hypothesis applies the latter assumption, it asserts that *the modernization process throws mature welfare states sooner into a value crisis, than immature ones.* Regarding the mature welfare states one could hypothesize that *social-democratic and liberal welfare states will be more vulnerable as far as the value crisis is concerned than corporatist welfare states.* The reason why this should be the case is that corporatist welfare states facilitate the collective repre-sentation of interest better that the social democratic and liberal ones.

To which predictions do these hypotheses lead? First concerning Europe today. In north-western Europe people are more uncertain of how to cope with the consequences of manufactured risks, than they are in continental Europe, and in continental Europe they are more uncertain than in the Mediterranean countries and in the post-communist countries of Central and Eastern Europe. The same reg-ularity applies to the degree of interpersonal and institutional trust and post-materialism. Regarding the changes in the last few decades, people's feelings of loosing control of their lives have become stronger in all European countries. Their interpersonal and institutional trust has also continuously declined, whereas post-materialism has been on the rise.

6   *Data and measurements*

The analyses cover almost the whole of Europe. All European countries, except for Turkey, Norway, and some former Yugoslavian countries are included. The comparisons in time include also Norway for
the 1981–1990 comparisons. These longitudinal trends over the last
twenty years are confined to Western European countries, while the
1990–1999 comparisons are made on a larger number, but not all,
countries. The 1990 survey included the following East Central
European countries: East Germany, Poland, Czechoslovakia, Slovenia,
Hungary, Bulgaria and the Baltic States.[2]

We focus on issues of risk and uncertainties and particularly the
way these issues shape and have shaped people's opinions on trust,
feelings of control over life, and post-materialism.

In order to tap the idea that people *control* their own lives, people were asked to indicate on a 10-point scale whether they feel they
have completely free choice and control over their lives.[3]

Trust is divided in interpersonal and institutional trust. *Interpersonal
trust* is measured by a single question asking whether or not most
people can be trusted. Unfortunately, the EVS questionnaire did not
contain a more elaborate measurement of interpersonal trust. Therefore,
we had to confine our measurement to this single question with only
two response categories: 1 = most people can be trusted; 2 = can't
be too careful.

The degree of *institutional trust* has been measured by adding the
responses to the question, how much confidence do you have in: the
church, the armed forces, the education system, the press, trade unions,
the police, parliament, civil service. Factor analyses demonstrated
that a fairly reliable scale can be constructed combining the responses
to these items. Scores were calculated based on this factor analysis.

The commonly used indicators developed by Ronald Inglehart (1977;

---

[2] Romania was also included, but the data was not adapted to the international
codings at the time of these analyses.
[3] The question wording was: Some people they have completely free choice and
control over their lives, and other people feel that what they do has no real effect
on what happens to them. Please use the scale to indicate how much freedom of
choice and control you feel you have over the way your life turns out? 1 = none
at all; 10 = a great deal).

1990; 1997) measure *materialism* and *post-materialism*. People were asked
to indicate their first and second choice from four different goals for
society for the next ten years. Two of the items are indicative of the
materialist view, two of the post-materialist. The materialist goals are
maintaining order in the nation; fighting rising prices. The two post-
materialist alternatives are giving people more say in important government decisions; protecting freedom of speech. Depending upon
their first and second choices, people can be placed in 4 categories,
ranging from pure materialists (both materialist options are preferred)
to pure post-materialists (both post-materialist options are preferred).
The groups between these two contain people who prefer a materialist
and a post-materialist goal. This group is the mixed group. An index
can be constructed to classify countries. This index is simply the
result of subtracting the percentage of materialists in a country from
the percentage of post materialists. The more positive the score, the
more post-materialist a country; the more negative, the more post-
materialistic a country is.

7   *Analyses and results*

Most of our analyses are confined to macro level data, e.g., comparing
country means or percentages. These comparisons are visualized in
a number of plots. Cluster analysis is applied to investigate whether it
makes sense to divide European countries along the lines previously
discussed.

7.1   *Control over life*

The lowest levels of control are, contrary to the predictions, found in
Central and Eastern European countries. But even in post-communist
Europe we cannot speak of a lot of people experiencing a lack of
control. Only a minority of the citizens of European countries suffers
from 'existential uncertainty' in the sense that they have the feeling
that they have no control over their lives. On the 10-point scale, where
1 indicates 'no control' and 10 means 'a great deal of control', the
percentages with score 1 to 3 are limited to around 10% and in north-
western Europe often much less. Generally speaking, people in North-
Western European countries feel they have control over the way

their lives turn out. According to the theory of reflexive modernity, lack of control should be prevalent in North-Western Europe.

If we take a closer look at country-specific outcomes it is not easy to see an overall pattern let alone to give an informative interpretation of that pattern. Central and Eastern Europeans appear somewhat more inclined than others to state that they have no control over their lives. This is particularly true for people in the former Soviet states Russia, Ukraine and Belarus. One could argue that this is a clear case of transition anomie (Arts et al., 1995). But even in these countries there are as many or more people who feel they have a great deal of control over their lives. People in Iceland, but also in Denmark, Sweden and the UK state that they control their lives. However, people in Austria, West Germany and Malta also hold this opinion. The Dutch, but also people in Belgium and France are less convinced that they have a great deal of control over their lives. Surprisingly, people in Croatia and Slovenia are rather optimistic in this respect. People in these countries are even more positive than the Dutch or Belgians, and also more than people in other Mediterranean countries. No sensible interpretations of these findings come to mind.

Figure 2.1   Percentages of respondents saying that they have no control (1–3) and a great deal of control (8–10) over their lives

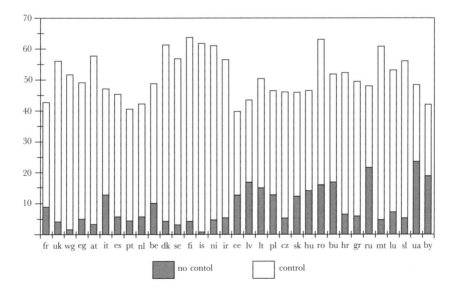

A cluster analysis may show some overall pattern with regard to control over life. An analysis on country means reveals four clusters of countries in Europe. It is evident from these results that the prediction concerning the grouping of countries is only partially confirmed. West Germany and Austria were expected to form a cluster with other continental European countries, but appear to be close to the North-Western countries. Malta, as a Mediterranean country, is also part of this cluster. On the other side, low levels of control are found in post-communist societies, and particularly in those societies that were part of the former Soviet Union. Lithuania appears closer to other post communist societies than to Russia. French people seem to resemble people in Central and Eastern Europe, which is of course contrary to our expectation.

7.2 *Interpersonal trust*

Trust in other people is, generally speaking, not very high in Europe. Most people, and in most countries large majorities, are of the opinion that one cannot be too careful in dealing with other people. In Portugal, and in Romania, about 9 out of every 10 respondents share this opinion. Whereas the high level of Portuguese distrust is rather exceptional in Western Europe, the widespread distrust in Romania is less exceptional in Central and Eastern Europe. Generally, levels of interpersonal trust are lower in these post-communist societies than in Western European societies. In Western Europe, four countries deviate clearly from the general trend, the Netherlands, Denmark, Sweden and Finland. These are the only four countries where majorities of the people say that other people can be trusted. And these were the countries in which according to reflexive modernization theory trust should be low!

The pattern is not as anticipated, but is rather the mirror image of the expected one. The highest levels of interpersonal trust can be found in the North-Western countries, followed by continental European countries, which in turn score higher than Mediterranean countries. Least confidence in other people is found among people in post communist societies. People struggling to solve the visible wealth problem seem to be people who are also struggling to face the invisible problem of trust.

Figure 2.2   Percentages of people who trust other people and percentages saying that one cannot be too careful

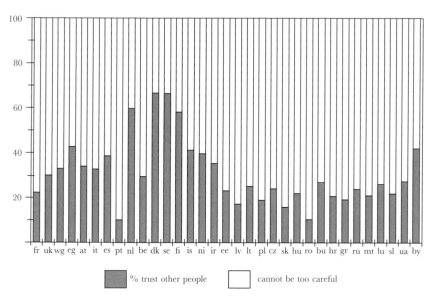

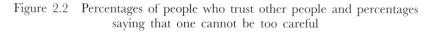

7.3   *Institutional trust*

The pattern is less clear with regard to institutional trust. High levels of institutional trust are again found in north-western Europe, with the exception of Great Britain. Resembling high levels of institutional trust are found, however, in Malta, Spain and Luxembourg. Polish people appear to trust the institutions in their country to a large extent. Least trusted are the institutions in Greece and the Czech Republic. Czechs differ from their former fellow citizens, the people in Slovakia, who appear to have much more trust in the institutions of their country. Generally speaking, however, the institutions are least trusted in Central and Eastern European countries.

A cluster analysis reveals five clusters of countries. Iceland, Ireland, Malta, Denmark and Finland form a cluster with the highest levels of trust. The Czech Republic, Greece, Bulgaria and Romania form a cluster with the lowest levels of trust. The three other clusters fall between these two extremes. It appears that Portugal, Luxembourg, Austria, the Netherlands, Sweden and Poland have much in common

Figure 2.3   Mean scores on confidence in institutions

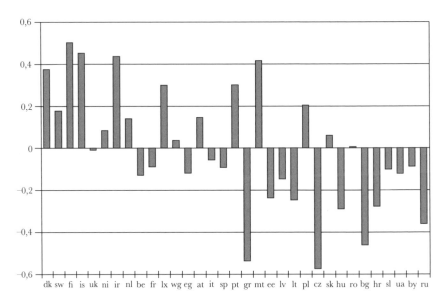

with regard to institutional trust. Furthermore, Western and Eastern European countries appear to resemble each other to a large extent as well. Again, no sensible interpretation of these findings comes to mind.

7.4   *Post-materialism*

The percentages of materialists are highest in post-communist countries, which confirms the expectation that these societies would be least post-materialistic. However, there are some exceptions, such as Croatia and Slovenia, where materialism is as low as in many western European countries. In fact, the percentage of post-materialists is higher in these former Yugoslavian countries than in Finland, Iceland, France and other Western countries. The largest percentages of post-materialists are not found in the north-western European countries, but in Austria and Italy, both representing two different European regions: Austria is part of continental Europe, Italy is a Mediterranean European society. So, a clear division in regions as was expected does not appear.

This conclusion also follows from the cluster analysis. Sweden, Croatia, Italy, the Netherlands and Austria appear most post-materialistic, whereas many eastern European countries, and Bulgaria, Hungary and Russia in particular appear least post-materialistic.

Figure 2.4 Percentages of materialists and postmaterialists in Europe

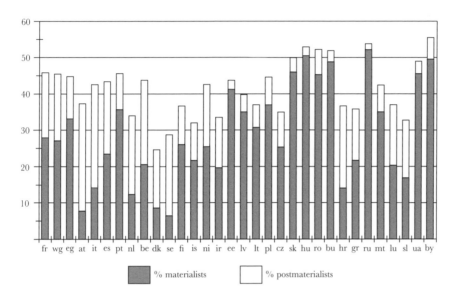

% materialists   % postmaterialists

7.5 *Overall pattern*

What overall pattern emerges from these analyses? The answer is found in a cluster analysis of the country scores on the four indicators. The results are only partially clear. Denmark, Sweden, Finland and the Netherlands are one cluster of countries with apparently highly similar positions on the four indicators. So, the North-Western European pattern deviates clearly from the rest of Europe. The Netherlands appears to be part of the Nordic group, while Iceland is not. Iceland comes closest to Northern Ireland, Spain, East Germany and Belarus, a group of countries whose connection is not apparent. Austria, West Germany, Italy, Ireland, Bulgaria, Ukraine, Luxembourg and Belgium appear to be closer to each other than to all the other countries. This again is a cluster whose connection is unclear.

Portugal and Romania appear as one cluster, which will be mainly due to the exceptional low degrees of interpersonal trust in these countries. However, in the second step of the clustering procedure these countries are close to the other Central and Eastern European countries. This large cluster of countries not only includes Central and Eastern European countries. In addition to Portugal, France, and Malta belong to this cluster. It is difficult to interpret the results of this cluster analysis. What is revealed is that the expected division

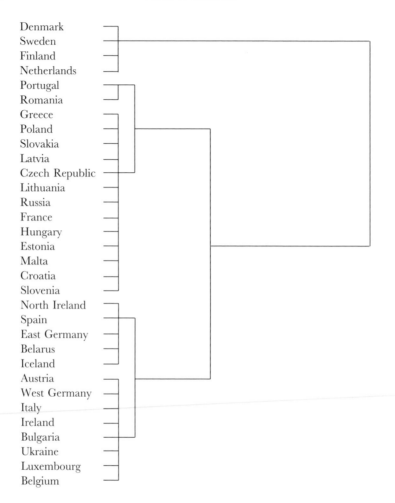

Figure 2.5   The cluster structure of the countries based on the 4 indicators

of European societies does not appear in these analyses. Only the North-Western pattern is as expected.

7.6   *Trajectories of change*

The expectation derived from reflexive modernization theory is that throughout Europe, people have, in the last few decades, gradually lost control over their lives. From Figure 6 it becomes clear that there is not much evidence that such a development has occurred.

On the contrary, in most countries a growing number of people hold the opinion that they gained control over their lives. Evidence for a decline can be found in some Central and Eastern European countries, e.g., the three Baltic States, Slovakia and Hungary, and also in Finland. In these countries the feeling that people control their lives declined during the 1999s while in Bulgaria, Poland, East Germany and Slovenia, control has increased (sharply) from 1990 to 1999.

In Italy and particularly Northern Ireland, control over live increased mainly during the eighties while it hardly changed during the nineties, whereas in West Germany, the Netherlands, Denmark, Iceland and Ireland, the largest increase in control took place during the nineties. Thus, the expectation that control is on the decline cannot be substantiated from such figures.

Trust is also assumed to be on the decline in Europe. However, the trend is not always in the direction of decline, and if decline occurs, it is far from uniform. The decline in interpersonal trust seems mainly

Figure 2.6   Shifts in locus of control between 1981 and 1990, and between 1990 and 1999

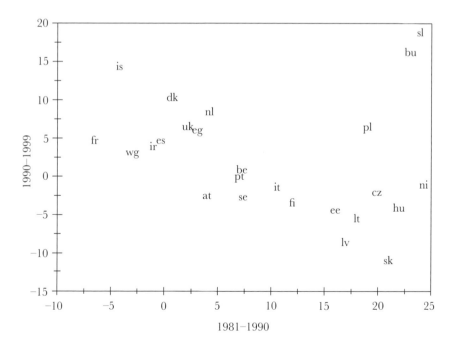

Figure 2.7   Shifts in interpersonal trust between 1981 and 1990, and between 1990 and 1999

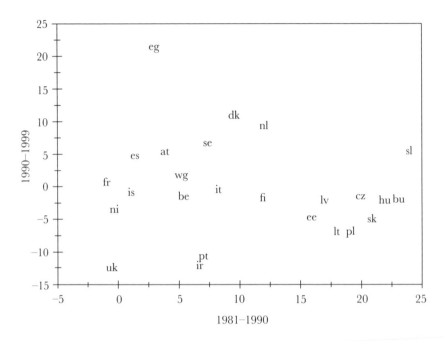

confined to Eastern European countries. In Western Europe, it hardly occurred on the mainland, but interpersonal trust has declined in English speaking countries: Great Britain and Ireland, and also in Portugal. In the Scandinavian countries and the Netherlands, inter-personal trust has recently increased.

Institutional trust is not uniformly declining in Europe. The more general pattern is that institutional trust is rather stable or increasing. This is, however, not the case in Ireland and Northern Ireland. Also in many East-Central European countries, confidence levels declined, particularly in Hungary, Bulgaria, the Czech Republic, and Poland. In Slovakia institutional trust increased and this is the more remark-able because Czech people trust their institutions to a lesser degree in 1999 than in 1990. Remarkably is also that the three Baltic States show differential trends: institutional trust declined in Estonia and Lithuania, but increased in Latvia. In Portugal, an increase in insti-tutional trust took place while interpersonal trust declined.

It seems as if not only Giddens's and Beck's Grand Theory of

Figure 2.8   Shifts in confidence in institutions between 1981 and 1990, and between 1990 and 1999

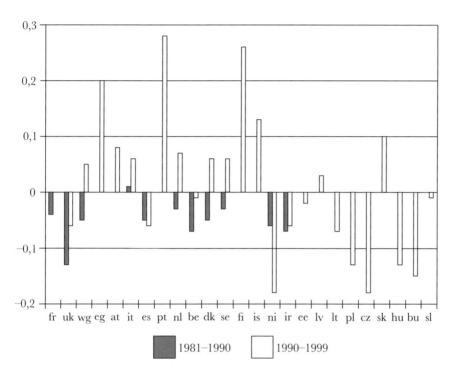

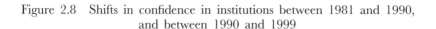

reflexive modernization needs to be revised; this is true for Ingleharts theory of post-modernization as well. The trajectory of change does not shift authority away from religion and the state to the individual as suggested by him (Inglehart, 1997: 74). The expected growing rejection of authority does not seem to have occurred. On the contrary, people appear to trust state and religious institutions to an increasing degree.

Not only because the shift in confidence in institutions is not as predicted by Inglehart, but also because post-materialism is not increasing in Europe, Inglehart's theory needs revision. His theory of post-materalism is corroborated when one confines the analyses to the period between 1990 and 1999 and focuses on Austria, Italy, Sweden, the Czech Republic and Slovenia. If one focuses on other European countries, post-materialism seems to be on the decline in the majority of them. In the Netherlands, which turned out to be one of the most post-materialistic countries in Europe in 1990, post-materialism seems to be diminishing. The same is true as well for France. In Spain, Belgium and Ireland, the increase in post-materialism during the eighties has been stopped. These societies have not become more post-materialistic during the last decade. As noted before, Inglehart's theory of a value change from materialism towards post-materialism cannot be corroborated.

There is another argument about why it seems necessary to reflect on the theory of value change from materialism towards post-materialism. In most of the countries studied, neither the post-materialist group nor the materialist group form a majority, and even if both groups are combined they are not majorities in the various countries. The group of people with a mixed answer pattern, combining both materialist and post-materialist preferences, is much larger than the group of pure materialists and pure post-materialists together. In 1999, in Denmark and Sweden, more than 70% of the respondents are in this mixed group.

Figure 2.9   Shifts in postmaterialism between 1981 and 1990, and between 1990 and 1999

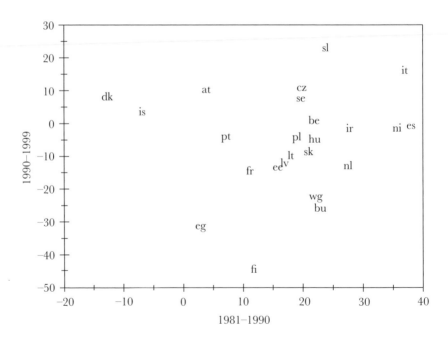

Figure 2.10   Percentages of respondents with mixed preferences in 1981, 1990 and 1999

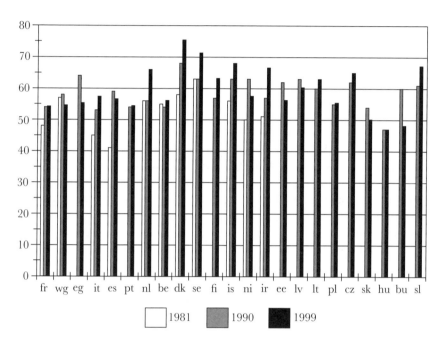

Only in Hungary and Bulgaria the size of the mixed group is less than 50%. In 14 from the 23 countries, the size of the mixed group grew during the nineties and the mixed group also increased in most of the countries during the eighties. Therefore, the value change from materialist to post-materialist is not so much due to the fact that an increasing number of people prefer post-materialist options rather than materialist preferences, but more because a declining number of people prefer the materialist ones and increasingly select both, materialist and post-materialist options.

8   *Conclusion*

The EVS project was designed to measure values in Europe and to picture the diversity and similarities in value patterns. One of the main aims was to investigate whether modernization processes and its underlying pattern of structural and cultural changes would lead to

value changes in the predicted direction among the populations of
Europe. The empirical evidence is, however, not very convincing and
quite often inconsistent with the ideas of economic and technological
determinism.

The results of the analyses of the EVS data reveal notable differences,
but also some interesting and unexpected similarities in values and
changes of these values. They demonstrate that modernization theory
is far too general not only to explain the varieties and similarities in
values, but also the dynamics of change in the various value domains
in the different countries.

However, modernization theorists were not silent after the empirical
critique. They reformulated and adapted the theory taking into account
the findings of empirical research. A new step forward was set when
Grand Theorists such as Beck and Giddens proposed a new theory
of reflexive modernization. According to them, contemporary post-
industrial society cannot any longer be described in terms of simple
modernity, emphasizing (economic) certainties and control over life,
but should be described in terms of reflexive modernity. People in
such societies are confronted with high levels of risk and must cope
with much 'manufactured' uncertainty.

This paper offers a preliminary test of the idea that modernization has entered a new stage, that of reflexive modernity. This stage
has been described, among others by Beck, in terms of the risks and
turbulence people cope with, without having recourse to traditional
ties and commitments. We theoretically reconstructed a number of
conjectures and expectations from Giddens' and Beck's Grand Theory.
We derived predictions from them and empirically tested these predictions using survey data from the European Values Study.

Most of the expectations we derived from Beck's and Giddens's
Grand theory were not corroborated, or at best were only partially
corroborated. This theory appears to be too broad, and too general.
Is presupposes too much necessity, and too little contingency. It does
not take into account nation specific ways of development. Each
country seems to have followed not only a more or less general path
towards modernity, but also its own specific trajectory of change.
There is as much diversity as previously, and what populations have
in common is often difficult to understand and interpret. Why are
the French closer to Russians and Hungarians than to other Europeans?
That Austrian, West German, and Italian orientations are alike may

be understood from history, but why are these orientations so similar to the orientations found in Ireland, Bulgaria, Ukraine, Luxembourg and Belgium? What do East-Germans, Spaniards, Northern Irish, Belorusians, and Icelandic people have in common that explains why they resemble each other in terms of levels of trust, levels of control and post-materialism? Such patterns are hard to understand and interpret, and it seems as if these patterns are not really as strongly related to economic development, as Ronald Inglehart, among others, would like us to believe. The only cluster of countries, which seems to make sense is the group of Nordic countries. However, The Netherlands also belongs to this Nordic pattern, while Iceland deviates from it.

Inglehart's theory of value change could not be confirmed. Post-materialism is not on the rise in most of the countries investigated here. The pattern emerging from our analysis is a much more confusing one. Indeed, materialist goals are less preferred, but this does not imply an increase of post-materialist preferences. The mixed group, that is the group of people who prefer one of the materialist and one of the post-materialist goals, is growing in almost all countries. This is not as predicted in Inglehart's influential theory on value change.

Giddens and Beck have argued that the traditional models for conducting life were replaced by models based on welfare state regulations. However, the analyses do not unequivocally support this idea of differences between countries based on different welfare state regimes. Other country characteristics may be important; the question is which ones are relevant. What is clear from the analyses is that the new theoretical ideas on modernization, post-modernization or reflexive modernity do not deal with these country specific characteristics and historic roots, which appear to be the most important attributes of understanding country differences in value orientations. Describing cross-national and over time continuities and varieties in value orientations is one thing, explaining and interpreting them theoretically is quite something else. What is clear from our analyses is that nation-specific features should not be neglected in international comparative research on values. Religious, linguistic, economic, political, geographical and other factors will play an important role. The values of people in a country reflect the entire cultural heritage of their country.

References

Arts, W., P. Hermkens & P. van Wijck 1995. Anomie, distributive justice and dissatisfaction with material well-being in Eastern Europe: a comparative study. *International Journal of Comparative Sociology* 36: 1–16.

—— 1999. Modernisation theory, income evaluation, and the transition in Eastern Europe. *International Journal of Comparative Sociology* 40: 61–78.

Bailey, J. 1992. Social Europe: Unity and diversity—An introduction. Pp. 1–14 in J. Bailey (ed.), *Social Europe*. London: Longman.

Beck, U. 1992. *Risk Society: Towards a New Modernity*. London: Sage.

—— 1999. *World Risk Society*. Cambridge: Polity Press.

—— 2000. *What is Globalization?* Cambridge: Polity Press.

——, A. Giddens & S. Lash 1994. *Reflexive Modernization: Politics, tradition and aesthetics in the modern social order*. Cambridge: Polity Press.

De Moor, R. 1994. Epilogue. Pp. 229–232 in P. Ester, L. Halman & R. de Moor (eds.), *The Individualizing Society. Value Change in Europe and North America*. Tilburg: Tilburg University Press.

Dingwall, R. 1999. "Risk society": The cult of theory and the Millennium? *Social Policy & Administration* 33: 474–491.

Ester, P., L. Halman & R. de Moor (eds.) 1994. *The Individualizing Society. Value Change in Europe and North America*. Tilburg: Tilburg University Press.

Giddens, A. 1990. *The Consequences of Modernity*. Cambridge: Polity Press.

—— 1991. *Modernity and Self-Identity: Self and Society in the Late Modern Age*. Cambridge: Polity Press.

—— 1994. *Beyond Left and Right*. Cambridge: Polity Press.

—— 1998. *The Third Way*. Cambridge: Polity Press.

—— 2000. *The Third Way and its Critics*. Cambridge: Polity Press.

Goldthorpe, J. 2001. Globalisation and Social Class. *Mannheimer Vorträge*, 9.

Halman, L. 2001. *The European Values Study: A Third Wave*. Tilburg: EVS, WORC, Tilburg University.

Hechter, M. 1992. Should Values Be Written Out of the Social Scientist's Lexicon? *Sociological Theory* 10: 214–230.

—— 1993. Values research in the social and behavioral sciences. Pp. 1–28 in M. Hechter, L. Nadel & R. Michod (eds.), *The Origin of Values*, New York: Aldine De Gruyter.

——, J. Ranger-Moore, G. Jasso & C. Horne 1999. Do values matter? An analysis of advance directives for medical treatment. *European Sociological Review* 15: 405–430.

Inglehart, R. 1977. *The Silent Revolution: Changing Values and Political Styles in Advanced Industrial Society*. Princeton, NJ: Princeton University Press.

—— 1990. *Culture Shift in Advanced Industrial Society*. Princeton, NJ: Princeton University Press.

—— 1997. *Modernization and Postmodernization: Cultural, Economic, and Political Change in 43 Societies*. Princeton, NJ: Princeton University Press.

—— & W. Baker 2000. Modernization, cultural change, and the persistence of traditional values. *American Sociological Review* 65: 19–51.

Inkeles, A. 1960. Industrial man: The relations of status to experience, perception, and value. *American Journal of Sociology* 66: 1–31.

Koralewicz, J. (ed.) 1999. *The European Value System*. Warsaw: Institute of Political Studies.

Mills, M. 2000. *The Transformation of Partnership. Canada, the Netherlands, and the Russian Federation in the Age of Modernity*. Amsterdam: Thela Thesis Population Studies.

Müller, K. 1992. 'Modernising' Eastern Europe. Theoretical problems and political dilemmas. *Archives Européennes de Sociologie* 33: 109–150.

Münch, R. 2002. Die "Zweite Moderne": Realität oder Fiktion? Kritische Fragen an die Theorie der "reflexiven" Modernisierung. *Kölner Zeitschrift für Soziologie und Sozialpsychologie* 54: 417–443.

Polanyi, K. [1944] 1957. *The Great Transformation. The Political and Economic Origins of our Time.* Boston: Beacon Press.

Streeck, W. & P.C. Smitter 1981. Community, market, state—and associations? *European Sociological Review* 1: 119–138.

Svallfors, S. 1995. Preface. Pp. 7–9 in S. Svallfors (ed.), *In the Eye of the Beholder.* Stockholm: The Bank of Sweden Tercentenary Foundation.

Wallerstein, E. 1979. *The Capitalist World-Economy.* New York: Cambridge University Press.

PART ONE

CIVIL SOCIETY/CITIZENSHIP

CHAPTER THREE

THE LINK BETWEEN SUBJECTIVE WELL-BEING AND OBJECTIVE CONDITIONS IN EUROPEAN SOCIETIES

Tony Fahey & Emer Smyth

1 *Introduction*

It might seem self-evident that one way to measure people's well-being is to ask them, and surveys that do just that are common. These surveys deal with one or more dimensions of people's subjective assessment of their circumstances: how satisfied people are either with life in general or with one or more of its many dimensions (work, family, health, financial circumstances, etc.), how happy they are, how secure and loved they feel, and so on (for overviews see Veenhoven 2002; Frey & Stutzer, 2002; Ryan & Deci 2001; Hagerty et al., 2001; Diener et al., 1999; Allardt, 1993; Campbell et al., 1976; see also the bibliography and databases in the World Database of Happiness at www.eur.nl/fsw/research/happiness).

Yet the measures which have been produced by this body of work have had difficulty gaining acceptance in the social sciences as valid or useful measures of human welfare. This is so largely so because many social scientists are dubious about the consistency and reliability of people's subjective assessments of their own situation in life. Those data are often regarded as liable to 'inauthentic self-reports' from respondents in survey interviews (Hagerty et al., 2001: 8) or as reflections of respondents' aspirations rather than their real circumstances in life (Vogel, 2002). The implication often drawn is that to ask people how they feel is likely to produce answers of uncertain meaning rather than reliable indicators of their true welfare.

Three specific features of these measures have been pointed to as justification for this position. First, countries with relevant time-series suggest that average national levels of subjective well-being are largely invariant over time. For example, in the United States over the period 1946 to 1990 and in Japan over the period 1958 to 1992, the trend lines in life satisfaction levels remained entirely flat (Diener et al., 1999: 288, Frey & Stutzer, 2002: 413). Second, relativities between countries seem to be more or less fixed. Among current EU countries, for example, Denmark and the Netherlands have consistently shown the highest life satisfaction scores over the past three decades, while France and Italy have consistently shown the lowest (Inglehart & Klingemann, 2002). These country relativities have been so difficult to explain in objective terms that cultural explanations (relating to linguistic variations, differences in aspirations, or normative differences in how far complaint is tolerated) have come to the fore. Thirdly, individual level variance in life satisfaction within countries seems to be at most only weakly connected with variance in objective conditions. Individual-level factors such as income and educational level seem to have either zero or only marginal impact on individual happiness or life satisfaction, and even though certain other factors (especially unemployment and marital status) do show consistent, statistically significant correlations (Oswald, 1997; Diener et al., 1999), all such factors together normally typically succeed in explaining less than five percent of the individual-level variance (Inglehart & Klingermann, 2000). This is consistent with the view in psychology that personality and genetic factors are more important than social circumstances as influences on individual subjective well-being (Diener et al., 1999: 279).

These patterns, then, suggest that some of the more widely used indicators of subjective well-being are unresponsive to variations in objective social conditions, and so have limited social-scientific interest. Those indicators may tap into personality and cultural differences and so may have a valid role in psychology or cultural studies. They might also have a value in specific domains of life, especially mental and physical health where subjective states have a direct and important bearing. But they would seem to have less interest for disciplines concerned with variations in broader aspects of human welfare across time, place, and socio-economic condition, that is, for economics, social policy, and much of political science and sociology.

However, certain aspects of the research findings in this field should give us pause before accepting this conclusion. One is that much of the existing research has been concentrated within a small number of highly developed societies (with research on the United States especially prominent). When the focus is extended to include poorer countries, a striking regularity emerges: national levels of subjective well-being are strongly and positively related to level of economic development—the populations of rich countries are happier and more satisfied with life than the populations of poor countries (Ryan & Deci, 2000; Inglehart & Klingemann, 2000). This regularity restores a certain credibility to measures of subjective well-being in that it establishes at least one strong axis of interconnection between life satisfaction and material conditions. While it has been well established by previous research, we would contend that its full significance for welfare measurement has not been drawn out, and this is a neglect we wish to address here.

A second feature of existing research is that cross-country comparisons have focused on *levels* of subjective well-being, as measured by national means on subjective well-being scales or percentages scoring above or below certain happiness or satisfaction thresholds. They have paid little attention to the *distribution* of subjective well-being, that is, to differences in the degree of inequality in subjective well-being across countries (for a rare exception, see Veenhoven, 2000). This, as we shall argue, is an important oversight since cross-country differences in the variances of subjective well-being are as great and as revealing as differences in the means, and in particular point to important hypotheses about the nature and subjective impact of social inequalities. A third limiting feature is that detailed analysis of individual level correlates of subjective well-being has focused on countries where the variance in subjective well-being is narrow and where the scope for influence from socio-economic conditions is thereby restricted. Less attention has been paid to situations where the variance in subjective well-being is much wider and there is an *a priori* case for expecting stronger linkages between such variance and the socio-economic context.

The purpose of the present paper is to develop analysis which goes beyond these limitations, that is, which includes poorer as well as richer countries, which examines the country-level differences in the distribution as well as the level of subjective well-being, and which focuses on individual-level correlates of subjective well-being in societies with high variance compared to those with low variance on relevant indicators. It contends, first, that an approach which addresses these aspects identifies stronger relationships between subjective well-being and objective conditions than has been previously recognized, both at the country level and the individual level, and second, that these linkages point to suggestive and potentially important insights about human welfare and how its should be conceptualized and measured in research on social inequality. Data limitations mean that these insights can be proposed only tentatively here (as is outlined further below). Nevertheless, enough is possible on the basis of the present data to establish the interest of our contention and to point to the need for further investigation along similar lines.

2   Data

The primary data source for the paper is the 1999–2000 European Values Study. These data are supplemented in the present paper by country-level indicators on economic conditions drawn from various sources (the World Bank, the United Nations and Eurostat's Euro-barometer surveys). These sources together give rise to a two-level data set used in the present analysis, one consisting of country-level data relating to the 33 societies included in the 1999–2000 EVS (these data are set out Table 3.1), and the other of individual-level data on the 39,799 individuals contained in the EVS samples within those countries.

An important feature of the 1999–2000 EVS data is their inclusion of much of central and eastern Europe as well as western Europe. The data therefore provide coverage of societies at widely different levels of economic development: GDP per capita in 1997 in the poorest of these societies (the Ukraine) was just over $2,000, which was only one-tenth of the level found in the more developed countries of the EU. While none of the countries in this data-set would be counted among the poorest in the world, they nevertheless meet our present requirement that analysis of subjective well-being should extend beyond rich countries.

The measurement of global subjective well-being in the EVS utilized two indicators—questions which asked respondents how happy they are and how satisfied they are with life as a whole. These questions are normally regarded as tapping two different dimensions of sub-jective well-being. Happiness has to do primarily with mood or affect (how one *feels*), while satisfaction has to do primarily with cognitive evaluations (what one *thinks* about the adequacy of one's situation) (Diener et al., 1999: 279; Ryan & Deci, 2001). The present paper focuses on the life satisfaction indicator from this source. This is so

Table 3.1   Life satisfaction and related indicators in 33 European societies

	(1) EVS sample size	(2) Life satisfaction		(3) GDP per capital PPS 1997	(4) Gini Index	(5) Ann. av. GDP growth 1990–99	(6) % 'very difficult to get by' on income
		Mean	Std deviation				
Denmark (DK)	1023	8.24	1.82	23690	24.7	2.8	1.0
Malta (MT)	1002	8.21	1.62	13180			6.0
Rep Ireland (IE)	1012	8.20	1.83	20710	35.9	7.9	3.3
Iceland (IS)	968	8.05	1.59	22497			
Austria (AT)	1400	8.03	1.92	22070	23.1	2	2.4
Nth Ireland (NI)	1000	8.00	1.75	20730	36.1	2.2	3.9
Finland (FI)	1038	7.87	1.65	22150	25.6	2.5	3.7
Netherlands (NL)	1003	7.85	1.34	21110	32.6	2.7	2.8
Luxembourg (LU)	1211	7.81	1.87	30863			2.2
W Germany (WG)	1037	7.64	1.74	22030	30	1.5	1.9
Sweden (SE)	1014	7.64	1.86	19790	25	1.5	2.1
Belgium (BE)	1912	7.43	2.13	22750	25	1.7	4.2
Gt Britain (GB)	994	7.40	1.94	20730	36.1	2.2	5.4
Slovenia (SL)	1006	7.23	2.15	11800	26.8	2.4	5.0
E Germany (EG)	999	7.18	2.13	15000			2.9
Italy (IT)	2000	7.17	2.11	20290	27.3	1.2	3.1
Spain (ES)	1200	7.09	2.01	15930	32.5	2.2	3.5
Czech Rep (CZ)	1908	7.06	1.97	10510	25.4	0.9	10.0
Portugal (PT)	1000	7.04	1.96	14270	35.6	3.1	12.5
France (FR)	1615	7.01	1.99	22030	32.7	1.7	5.3
Croatia (HR)	1003	6.68	2.3	4895	26.8	−0.4	
Greece (GR)	1143	6.67	2.19	12769	32.7	1.9	10.2
Poland (PL)	1095	6.20	2.53	6520	32.9	4.7	21.0
Slovakia (SK)	1327	6.03	2.22	7910	26.8	1.9	17.0
Estonia (EE)	1005	5.93	2.18	5240	35.4	−1.3	21.0
Hungary (HU)	1000	5.80	2.42	7200	30.8	1	22.0
Bulgaria (BG)	1000	5.50	2.65	4010	28.3	−2.7	62.0
Latvia (LV)	1013	5.27	2.39	3940	32.4	−4.8	28.0
Romania (RO)	1146	5.23	2.77	4310	28.2	−1.2	36.0
Lithuania (LT)	1018	5.20	2.66	4220	32.4	−3.9	21.0
Belarus (BY)	1000	4.81	2.21	4850	21.7	−4.3	
Russia (RU)	2500	4.65	2.57	4370	48.7	−6.1	
Ukraine (UA)	1207	4.56	2.59	2190	32.5	−10.8	

Note: Countries ordered by mean life satisfaction score.

Sources: 1–2: 1999–2000 EVS data files; 3: UNDP 1999; 4–5: World Bank 2001; 6: Eurobarometer 65.1 and Candidate Country Eurobarometer 2002 micro-data files.

partly because of limitations of space but also for data reasons. The EVS surveys utilize a more refined scaling of life satisfaction than of happiness, the former based on a ten-point scale, where the latter is based on a four-point scale. The 10-point satisfaction scale is more effective in capturing variance both within and between countries than the four-point happiness scale, and given the focus here on variance in subjective well-being, this is an important consideration.

The EVS data have certain drawbacks in the present context which result from the purpose for which they were gathered. The EVS is primarily concerned with attitudes and values and gathers only limited information on the objective situation of respondents (for example, in regard to health status, housing, working conditions, etc). It is therefore less than ideal as a source for analyzing the relationship between objective conditions and objective well-being. Nevertheless, it does contain a certain number of key relevant variables, and these, taken together with the range of societies it covers (not to speak of the lack of better alternatives), justifies its use here. We will return to the limitations in the 'objective' variables below when examining individual-level correlates of life satisfaction in the EVS societies.

3 Country differences in levels of satisfaction

We look first at a number of striking regularities revealed by the country-level data in Table 3.1. One of these is that the wide differences in the mean level of life satisfaction across European societies are closely linked to their level of economic development as measured by GDP per capita, a pattern consistent with previous findings mentioned earlier. Broadly speaking, EU countries have higher satisfaction levels than do central and eastern European countries, while within the EU, northern countries (such as Netherlands, Ireland and the Scandinavian countries) have higher satisfaction levels than southern countries (such as Greece, Spain, Portugal, Italy and France). A certain number of countries in central and eastern Europe (Slovenia, East Germany, the Czech Republic, and Croatia) overlap with the southern EU countries, but most fall well below that level, that is, having means on the life satisfaction scale below 6.5 and in three cases (Belarus, Russia, and the Ukraine), below 5.

Figure 3.1 shows the close correlation between these country-level differences in mean life satisfaction and GDP per capita. A curvilinear regression of GDP per capita on country-level mean life satisfaction for the 33 European societies accounts for 84.5 per cent of the variance in the latter indicator. If one were to focus narrowly on the group of EU countries which cluster closely together in Figure 3.1, Ireland and Denmark would appear to be anomalously high on life satisfaction, Italy and France would appear to be anomalously low, and the overall link with GDP would seem to be weak. These within-EU patterns are in keeping with the apparent disjunction between economic conditions and level of life satisfaction which emerges from analyses focused on rich societies (Inglehart, 1990). However, viewed within the larger picture presented by Figure 3.1, which includes

Figure 3.1   Mean life satisfaction and GDP per capita in 33 European societies

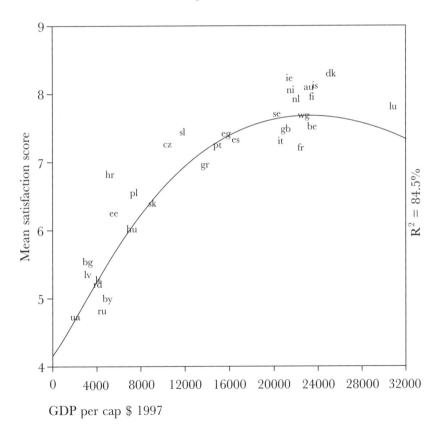

GDP per cap $ 1997

countries with levels of economic development well below that of the EU countries, these anomalies seem less significant and seem hardly to be anomalies at all. In this perspective, the richer countries cluster closely together both on GDP and life satisfaction, while across all the 33 societies, it is the consistency and closeness of the association between GDP per capita and life satisfaction which stand out.

It would also appear from additional data in Table 3.1 that perceptions of economic hardship provide a link between GDP and life satisfaction. The data on perceived economic hardship used here are drawn from Eurobarometer surveys on the EU Members States and Candidate Countries, 28 of which are common to the EVS data-set (Eurobarometer 65.1 and Candidate Country Eurobarometer 2002 micro-date files). Taking as the key indicator the percentages across countries who report 'great difficulty' in getting by on their incomes, we get a close fit ($R^2 = 86.4\%$) between perceived economic hardship and mean life satisfaction (Figure 3.2). Separate analysis not shown here also indicates that perceived economic hardship is closely predicted by GDP per capita ($R^2 = 81.5\%$), so that at the country level there would appear to be close inter-connections between objectively poor economic conditions, the perception of economic hardship, and level of life satisfaction.

Given that almost half the societies we are looking at in the EVS data are former communist societies which have made a sudden, and in some cases traumatic, transition to capitalism since 1989, it is possible that it is the trend towards improvement or disimprovement in economic circumstances over recent years, rather than the current level of economic development, which influences life satisfaction. A crude test of this possibility can be applied by examining the impact of recent economic performance on country-level mean life satisfaction, using annual average GDP growth rate over the transition period (1990–1999) as a relevant indicator. This indicator on its own correlates less well with mean life satisfaction ($R^2 = 66\%$) than does GDP per capita ($R^2 = 86.4\%$) but if the two indicators are combined together in a regression model, they produce a 90 per cent fit to mean life satisfaction level (Table 2). The regression coefficients for both independent variables are quite strong, though GDP per capita (with a standardised coefficient of 0.66) has a stronger influence than the growth rate (coefficient of 0.372).

In sum, therefore, societal means of life satisfaction in Europe are strongly tied to societal economic performance levels, as indicated primarily by comparative levels of economic output per capita and

Figure 3.2   Perceived economic hardship and mean life satisfaction in 28 European societies

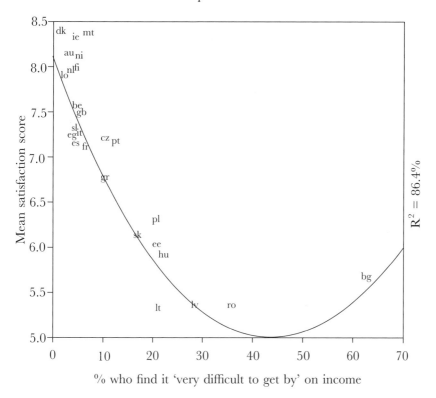

Table 3.2   Regression of GDP per capita and annual average GDP growth 1990–1999 on mean life satisfaction scores for 33 European societies

	OLS regression coefficients (*dependent variable = mean life satisfaction*)		
	Unstandardized	*Standardized*	*Significance*
Constant	5.34		
GDP per capita 1997	9.27e−5	0.660	0.000
Annual average GDP growth 1990–1999	0.116	0.372	0.000
R^2	90%		

secondarily by recent economic growth rates. It is possible that these economic effects on mean life satisfaction may hide further complexities, since the economic indicators are themselves correlated with other factors. It is notable, for example, that the EU countries with the lowest life satisfaction—Greece, Spain and Portugal—have the most recent historical experience of non-democratic government, while within central and eastern Europe, the countries which were under communist rule since 1918 generally have lower life satisfaction than those which were brought into the Soviet sphere after 1945. Thus the GDP effect on life satisfaction may be compounded with institutional and historical effects in the political sphere which are beyond the scope of the present paper to examine (for further comments along these lines, see Inglehart & Klingemann, 2000). However, the point to note here is that, looking across this range of societies, at least some aspects of their objective situation—whether it be economic or political—have a strong bearing on aggregate life satisfaction. At this level, therefore, what one sees is not the kind of disjunction between subjective well-being and socio-economic context which has previously drawn attention as much as an exceptional closeness between the two.

4 Levels of variance in life-satisfaction

A third important pattern emerging from the data in Table 3.1 is the wide diversity in levels of variance in life satisfaction across countries. This pattern is indicated by the standard deviations in life satisfaction, which range from 1.34 in the case of the smallest (for the Netherlands) to almost double that, 2.59, for the largest (for the Ukraine). The intriguing aspect of this pattern is that, as the scatterplot in Figure 3.3 reveals, the standard deviation in life satisfaction across the 33 societies varies closely and inversely with mean level of life-satisfaction—the lower the mean, the larger the standard deviation ($R^2 = 77\%$).

Table 3.3 gives examples of full frequencies for the life satisfaction variable for three sample societies to show what these differences amount to in detail. Denmark, which has a high mean and low variance, has a modal score on the life-satisfaction scale of 10 (that is, the highest point on the scale), and almost 77 per cent score 8 or higher. In Greece, an intermediate country, the modal life satisfaction score is 8, 41 per cent score 8 or above but 27 per cent score 5 or

Figure 3.3   Mean life satisfaction and standard deviation in life
satisfaction in 33 European societies

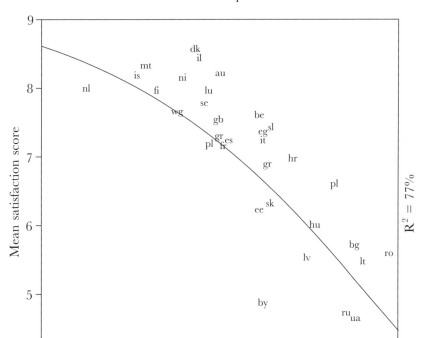

below. In Belarus, a country with a low mean, the modal score is 5,
only 14 per cent score 8 or above, while 30 per cent score 3 or below.
Thus there is little overlap in satisfaction scores between the two
countries at the extremes in this table (Denmark and Belarus): only
a small minority at the top of the scale in Belarus match the satisfaction
levels of the vast majority of Danes, while the vast majority of Bela-
rusians are less satisfied than all but the most dissatisfied of Danes.

An immediate possibility that comes to mind when trying to account
for the wider variance in life satisfaction among the poorer populations
is that those societies might have wider internal inequalities in social
conditions, for example, in incomes and living standards. Figure 3.4
tests for this possibility by examining the relationship between the
level of income inequality as measured by the Gini Index and the
standard deviation of life satisfaction across countries. The Gini Index,

Table 3.3   Levels and variance in life satisfaction within countries:
the examples of Denmark, Greece, and Belarus

	Denmark	Greece	Belarus
		%	
1 dissatisfied	1.0	2.9	7.0
2	0.3	2.3	8.6
3	1.8	4.5	14.7
4	1.2	7.8	14.0
5	3.7	9.4	22.3
6	5.9	12.3	9.2
7	14.5	19.2	10.5
8	22.3	20.9	8.4
9	18.1	14.2	3.4
10 satisfied	30.9	6.4	2.0
Totals	100	100	100
Mean	8.24	6.67	4.81
Std deviation	1.82	2.19	2.21

Source: EVS 1999–2000

where a score of 100 indicates complete income inequality and 0 indicates complete income equality, is available for different years in the 1990s for 29 of the 33 societies in our data set (compiled from national sources by the World Bank 2001). The scatterplot for these 29 societies in Figure 3.4 produces a non-significant slope and shows that there is no significant relationship between income inequality and inequality in life satisfaction at country level. Further analysis not shown here, which examined the relationship between educational inequality, as measured in the EVS data by the standard deviation in the age completed education, and level of inequality in life satisfaction similarly showed an absence of any link between the two. Furthermore, neither income inequality nor educational inequality was significantly related to the mean level of life satisfaction across country.

These correlations at the societal level would point to the hypothesis that the effect of social inequality on life satisfaction could differ between rich and poor societies. In rich European societies (some of which are quite inegalitarian), life satisfaction levels are so high on average and there are so few people with low life satisfaction that social inequality must have only limited negative impact on life satisfaction—there is too much disjunction between the two axes of inequality for it to be likely that they are linked to each other. In poor

Figure 3.4 Income inequality (Gini Index) and variance in life satisfaction in 29 European societies

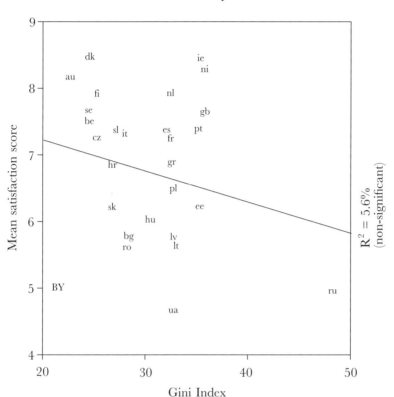

European societies (which in general are no more inegalitarian than their rich counterparts), the lower levels and wider within-country spread in life satisfaction are more in keeping with their patterns of social inequality and give rise to the possibility that social inequalities have a stronger impact in those societies. We now turn to individual-level data within the 33 societies to establish if these inferences are supported by differences within as well as between countries.

5 *From aggregate to individual-level patterns*

As we examine individual-level variance in subjective well-being, the background question is whether and by how much people's personal situations affect their life satisfaction. The context for this question is the body of research which has found that linkages between people's objective conditions and their life satisfaction are weak and which has given rise to doubts about the social-scientific interest of indicators of subjective well-being in consequence. The concern about that research which we have raised here is its focus on rich countries where variance in life satisfaction is narrow and where the scope for socio-economic effects on life satisfaction is thereby limited. The possibility we now wish to explore is whether such socio-economic effects might be stronger in poorer societies where individual-level variance in life satisfaction is wider. If such a possibility is confirmed, the insensitivity of individual-level indicators of subjective well-being to personal objective circumstances in rich countries would have quite different implications than those that have hitherto been drawn. Rather than casting doubt on the interest or usefulness of subjective indicators, it could suggest a substantively important hypothesis that rich societies, irrespective of their degree of internal inequality, provide high and uniform support for well-being in a way that poorer societies do not.

In trying to explore these issues, we run up against the data constraints mentioned earlier, that is, the limited coverage in the EVS of relevant individual-level indicators. EVS data provide no coverage of many key objective dimensions of welfare (e.g., health status, housing, employment conditions, neighborhood conditions and so on) nor do they include certain subjective variables, such as perception of economic hardship, which might mediate between socio-economic context and life satisfaction. Household income is included but is coded on a ten-point ordinal scale based on income categories which differ by society and are not recorded in the data. This closes off the possibility of adjusting household incomes for household size and of comparing absolute levels of household income across societies, both of which would be important requirements for a full investigation of our concerns here. Nevertheless, in spite of the crudeness of the income variable in the EVS data, we include it in our analysis since no better option is available. A certain number of other relevant variables are also available and are included here. They are: gender, marital status, age, employment status, educational attainment, and social class. As mentioned earlier, two of these variables have been consistently found to affect life satisfaction—marital status (the married having higher life satisfaction than other marital status categories) and employment status (the unemployed having lower life satisfaction than other categories). Of the remaining four, educational attainment is particularly important for present purposes as it may provide a more stable measure than occupational group or income in the context of rapid social change. Previous studies suggest that educational attainment is *not* strongly or consistently related to life satisfaction and so we will be particularly interested to establish here if that relationship comes to the surface and strengthens as we move beyond rich countries (i.e., those with low variance in life satisfaction) to the poorer countries where variance in life satisfaction is greater.

As a first step in the analysis we employ a multi-level approach that looks at country-level and individual-level variance in life satisfaction simultaneously. Within this approach, we present three models based on a total of 39,547 individuals within 33 countries (Table 3.4). The base model in this table (see Model 1) indicates that a variance of 1.270 in life satisfaction arises at the country level and 4.563 at the individual level—that is, 22 per cent of the variance in life satisfaction is attributable to the country level, while the balance of 78 per cent is attributable to the individual level.

Model 2 explores the impact of a range of individual factors, including employment status, marital status, gender, age, age at leaving education, social class and income, on life satisfaction. As previous research would lead us to expect, the unemployment and marital status effects are stronger than any others indicated in the table. The unemployed on average score almost one point lower on the 10-point life satisfaction scale than those who are not unemployed. Marital status is the only other variable which comes close to an effect of this size: the widowed and divorced score over 0.5 of a point lower than the married, while the single score just under 0.4 of a point lower than the married. Contrary to some previous studies, social class and income are found to play a significant role in shaping life satisfaction levels. Employers and professional workers report the highest levels of life satisfaction while the lowest levels are found among semi/unskilled manual workers and those working in the agricultural sector. Even controlling for social class, those in the highest income group are found to score 1.2 points higher than those in the very lowest income group.

In contrast, other variables play a modest or no role in determining life satisfaction levels. Gender has little effect: males have somewhat lower life satisfaction scores than females, although the difference is not statistically significant. Older people have somewhat lower levels of life satisfaction, though the effect is relatively modest in size. Those

Table 3.4 Multi-level models of the effects on life satisfaction

	Model 1	Model 2	Model 3
Intercept	6.808	6.171	5.314
Individual factors			
Male		−0.039	−0.040
Unemployed		−0.887*	−0.886*
Marital status:			
Widowed		−0.568*	−0.568*
Divorced		−0.552*	−0.551*
Single		−0.365*	−0.366*
(Ref: married)			
Age (centred on mean)		−0.010*	−0.010*
Age squared		0.001*	0.001*
Missing information on age		−0.055	−0.053
Age at leaving education		0.010*	0.010*
Missing information on education		−0.203*	−0.205*
Social class:			
Employer		0.406*	0.405*
Professional		0.357*	0.357*
Intermediate non-manual		0.264*	0.263*
Lower non-manual		0.212*	0.211*
Skilled manual/supervisor		0.196*	0.195*
Agricultural		−0.014	−0.017
Missing information		0.108*	0.107*
(Ref.: semi/unskilled manual)			
Income		0.124*	0.123*
Missing information on income		0.596*	0.597*
Country-level factors:			
GDP1			0.416
GDP2			1.367*
GDP3			1.423*
(Ref: lowest GDP)			
Gini coefficient (centred on mean)			−0.026*
Growth in GDP			0.120*
Country-level variance	1.270*	1.097*	0.132*
Individual-level variance	4.563*	4.269*	4.269*
% variance explained:			
Country level	−	6.4	89.6
Individual level	−	15.8	15.8
Log likelihood	170653	169818	169748

with higher levels of education have higher levels of life satisfaction, although some of the effect of education is mediated through social class and income. Significantly lower levels of satisfaction are found among those who did not record their age at leaving education; this may reflect the under-reporting of lower levels of education.

Overall, however, the explanatory power of all these variables taken together is relatively limited. Sixteen per cent of individual-level variation in life satisfaction is explained by gender, unemployment, marital status, age, education, social class and income. Interestingly, six per cent of the country-level variation is explained by these factors; that is, six per cent of country-level variation is, in fact, due to the population composition within countries (for example, differences in the proportion of unemployed and/or highly educated individuals).

In the case of Model 3, the focus expands to include the impact of factors at a higher level (in this case, the country). For the purpose of this model, three variables were included: GDP per capita, recent growth in GDP and the extent of income equality (measured by the Gini coefficient). Trial-and-error indicated that per capita GDP fitted best into the model if treated as a four-way categorical variable rather than a continuous variable. In the model, the reference category (GDP1) is made up of the bottom quartile of countries in GDP per capita terms. As expected from earlier analysis, level of GDP is found to be significantly associated with levels of life satisfaction; all else being equal, those in higher GDP countries tend to have higher satisfaction scores, although there is some plateauing in the effect for the highest GDP groups. Over and above the effect of level of GDP, satisfaction levels are found to respond positively to growth in GDP. Finally, controlling for GDP, those living in less equal societies tend to report lower average levels of satisfaction. The three country-level variables—per capita GDP, growth in GDP and level of income inequality—account for almost all (90 per cent) of the variance between countries in levels of life satisfaction.

The results on individual-level correlates of life satisfaction presented in Table 3.4 broadly conform to the findings of previous research outlined earlier. Marital status and unemployment have the strongest influence, many other individual-level factors have at best only modest impact, and the combined variance explained is modest, at 16 per cent. However, contrary to previous research, life satisfaction is found to be significantly related to social class and income level. The difference between the findings may be due to the inclusion of poorer countries in the pooled data set. This can be confirmed by examining whether the effect of individual factors varies across countries, in particular whether the impact increases as we move from countries with low levels of GDP and variance in life satisfaction to those with higher GDP levels and higher variance among individuals.

The results in Table 3.5 indicate that the effects of four variables— unemployment, marital status, age at leaving education and income— vary significantly across countries. Furthermore, the covariance terms indicate that the effects of income and education are not as strong in countries with higher average levels of life satisfaction. However, in the case of marital status, the opposite is the case; being single has a less negative effect in countries with higher average satisfaction levels. This pattern is explored further below. Interestingly, the effect of social class does not vary across countries in the same way as income and education. This may be related to the nature of the measure used which is categorical rather than linear in nature.

To illustrate further the different levels of impact of socio-economic conditions on life satisfaction, Figure 3.5 depicts the relationship between age at leaving education and life satisfaction, controlling for all other factors including GDP, for four cases which represent the different patterns found in the data set: the Ukraine and Hungary, where the education effect is very strong, and Iceland and Belgium where it is non-existent.

Table 3.5   Country-level variance in the explanatory variables

Country-level variance:	
Intercept	0.380*
Slope of unemployed	0.168*
Slope of widowed	0.086*
Slope of single	0.113*
Covariance intercept-single	−0.085*
Slope of age at leaving education	0.0004*
Covariance intercept-education	−0.006*
Slope of income	0.010*
Covariance intercept-income	−0.041*

Note: This model controls for gender, unemployment, marital status, age, age at leaving education, social class, income, GDP per capita, GDP growth and the Gini coefficient. The coefficients for these factors are similar to those reported in Table 7.4 above.

Figure 3.5   Predicted slope of age at leaving education for selected countries

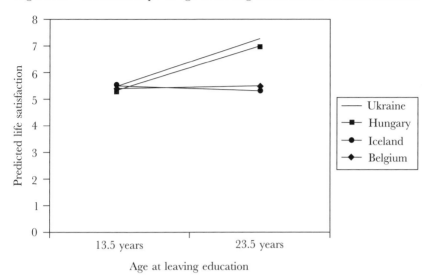

Age at leaving education

Note: This controls for a number of factors, including GDP level of the country.

A similar pattern was found when the relationship between income and predicted life satisfaction was plotted for different countries within the dataset (Figure 3.6). Life satisfaction was found to be sharply differentiated by income in the Ukraine and Belarus, for example. In contrast, in Western European countries such as Sweden and Ireland, life satisfaction levels were only modestly influenced by income level.

Further analysis was conducted to explore whether the differing effects of unemployment, marital status, education and income were related to the GDP level of the country. Table 3.6 presents the predicted coefficients for these variables by GDP level of the country.[1] Education and income are found to have much weaker effects in the two highest GDP groups of countries than in the two lowest. In contrast, the negative effects of unemployment and being single are more evident in higher GDP countries. The effect of being widowed does not vary systematically by GDP level and is likely to be

---

[1] These were calculated by including interaction terms between the relevant variables and GDP levels.

Figure 3.6   Predicted slope of income level for selected countries

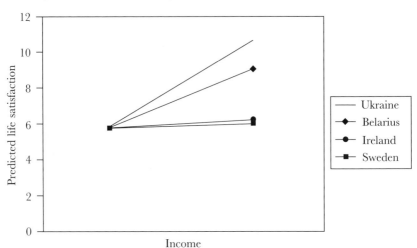

Table 3.6   Effects of selected variables on life satisfaction by
GDP level of country

	GDP group 1 (lowest)	GDP group 2	GDP group 3	GDP group 4 (highest)
Education	0.033	0.028	0.006	0
Income	0.188	0.145	0.089	0.090
Unemployed	−0.670	−0.780	−1.172	−1.062
Single	0.098	−0.305	−0.484	−0.649
Widowed	−0.436	−0.626	0.425	−0.455

related to a broader set of cultural factors within societies. Even controlling for variation in the effects of these background factors across
countries, the highest variance (5.63) among individuals within a society is found in the least wealthy countries with the lowest variance
(4.49) found in the wealthiest countries (analysis not shown here).

6 *Discussion*

The empirical findings in the present paper can be summarized in three points. First, societal levels of life satisfaction in Europe vary almost in lock-step with economic conditions, as measured primarily by GDP per capita and secondarily by recent economic growth performance—the poorer and economically more sluggish the society the lower the level life satisfaction. Secondly, the lower the level of life satisfaction in a society, the wider the inequalities in life satisfaction. Thirdly, the impact of key within-country socio-economic inequalities on life satisfaction (especially in regard to income and educational attainment) is slight in high satisfaction countries (partly because variance in life satisfaction in those countries is so narrow) but it increases steadily as we move across countries with lower overall levels and wider variance in life satisfaction.

These findings relate only to Europe and may not apply to other global regions. They relate only to life satisfaction and say nothing about other dimensions of subjective well-being, such as those relating to affect rather than cognitive evaluation. Thus, they should be regarded as tentative and as in need of much wider investigation. Nevertheless, the empirical patterns which have emerged are strong and striking enough to warrant attention. First, they argue against the view that indicators of subjective well-being are unresponsive to variations in objective conditions and are of limited social-scientific interest in consequence. They suggest, rather, that at the societal level such indicators are highly sensitive to objective socio-economic conditions and at the individual level, such sensitivity becomes clearly evident only in poorer societies where variance in life satisfaction is wide.

Secondly, the strong impact of a society's position in the international league table of economic performance on individual life satisfaction raise important questions about how social inequality (and related issues such as poverty and relative deprivation) should be conceptualized and measured. Existing sociological and social policy research focuses overwhelmingly on the nation-state as the relevant frame of reference for such analysis: social inequality and related issues are examined as properties of *societies* (societies usually being identified in nation-state terms) and are thought to be comparable across societies irrespective of their level of development. The evidence examined here would suggest that as far as subjective impacts on individuals are concerned, cross-national relativities in income (and possibly in other objective dimensions of welfare) are just as important as, and possibly even more important than, national relativities. In judging the adequacy of their personal situations, Europeans seem to have an uncanny grasp of where their societies stand in the international (or at least European) hierarchy of economic development and to take that standing into account in arriving at subjective evaluations of their personal circumstances. That international standing may even be more important to their subjective wellbeing than their household's position in the national hierarchy of advantage and disadvantage. One way of interpreting this aspect of our findings is to say that absolute household conditions (measured in a uniform way on a single standard scale across all societies, as in the case of absolute income stated in purchasing power parities) matters more than relative household income (measured by reference to widely different national means or medians) as an influence on subjective well-being. However, this interpretation would be inconsistent with the well-established time trends in life satisfaction referred to earlier: these show that life satisfaction has been unresponsive to the large increases in absolute incomes enjoyed by the majority of households in developed societies in recent decades. We would propose a related but slightly different interpretation: national populations report high satisfaction levels if the society they live in is highly prosperous by the international standards of the day, irrespective of what that means in absolute income terms. Thus the focus on cross-national relativities in incomes and related material conditions which we would point to here.

Such a cross-national frame of reference may help explain why the impact of within-country social inequalities on life satisfaction differs according to whether countries are rich or poor, that is, according to whether they are high satisfaction or low satisfaction societies. This differential impact may arise because the poor in rich societies are somehow conscious that their living standards are reasonably high compared to the general run of people in poorer countries. A somewhat different possibility is that public goods in rich societies from which the less well-off may gain considerable benefit—the shops, the streets, transport services, schools, hospitals, even the air people breathe—may be of higher quality and have a more equalizing impact on household welfare than is captured in measures based on household-level resources. The converse might be true in poorer societies—even the rich in poor societies may suffer a loss in welfare on account of the low standard of public goods or poor quality of the public sphere in their societies.

7   *Conclusion*

However the present empirical findings may be explained and inter-preted, we would conclude by identifying some of the challenges they pose for the analysis of social inequality and related issues, with ref-erence especially to Europe. They suggest that subjective indicators of welfare may be more robust and more revealing for this purpose than has previously been recognized and may have insights to offer for social inequality research that objective indicators have failed to uncover. The most important such insight may be that relativities *between* countries matter for social inequality as subjectively perceived and experienced by individuals. They may even matter more than the relativities *within* countries which have pre-occupied researchers to date and which have provided the dominant framework for social inequal-ity research. To extend and explore this possibility further, it would be well worth investigating whether the often-observed lack of cor-relation between objective measures of poverty and subjective poverty perceptions (see e.g., Gallie & Paugam, 2002: 10–11) arises because the wrong objective poverty measure is used—namely, one based on household incomes relative to national standards rather than on a combination of household incomes and access to public goods mea-sured relative to a single international standard.

As far as life satisfaction is concerned, the apparently international basis on which survey respondents assess their life satisfaction may help explain not only the different average levels of subjective well-being across countries but also the differing degrees to which within-country inequalities in objective conditions filter through into corresponding inequalities in subjective well-being among individuals. The key pos-sibility here is that low incomes and related disadvantage causes much less damage to subjective well-being in the rich parts of Europe than in the poor parts of Europe—perhaps because what we call 'low' incomes in rich parts of Europe are not really low by the standards of the poor parts of Europe. In any event, these facts alone would justify greater attention to pan-European patterns of inequality (or even to a cross-national approach which extends beyond Europe) in addition to (or perhaps instead of) the present focus on inequality as a property to be measured at the level of each national society.

References

Allardt, E. 1993. Having, loving, being: An alternative to the Swedish model of welfare research. Pp. 88–94 in M. Nussbaum & A. Sen (eds.), *The Quality of Life*. Oxford: Oxford University Press.

Campbell, A., P.E. Converse & W.L. Rodgers 1976. *The Quality of American Life: Perceptions, Evaluations and Satisfactions*. New York: Russell Sage Foundation.

Diener, E., E.M. Suh, R.E. Lucas & H.L. Smith 1999. Subjective well-being: three decades of progress. *Psychological Bulletin* 125 (2): 276–302.

Frey, B.S. & A. Stutzer 2002. What can economists learn from happiness research? *Journal of Economic Literature* 40: 402–435.

Gallie, D. & S. Paugam 2002. *Social Precarity and Social Integration. Report for the European Commission based on Eurobarometer 56.1*. Brussels: Directorate-General Employment.

Hagerty, M.R., R.A. Cummins, A.L. Ferriss, K. Land, A.C. Michalos, M. Peterson, A. Sharpe, M.J. Sirgy & J. Vogel 2001. Quality of life indices for national policy: Review and agenda for research. *Social Indicators Research* 55: 1–96.

Halman, L. 2001. *The European Values Study: A Third Wave. Source Book of the 1999/2000 European Values Study Surveys*. Tilburg: Tilburg University.

Inglehart, R. 1990. *Culture Shift in Advanced Industrial Society*. Princeton: Princeton University Press.

—— & H.D. Klingemann 2000. Genes, culture, democracy, and happiness. Pp. 165–182 in E. Diener & E.M. Suh (eds.), *Subjective Well-Being Across Cultures*. Cambridge, MA: MIT Press.

OECD 1999. *Social Indicators: A Proposed Framework and Structure*. Paris: Organisation for Economic Cooperation and Development.

Oswald, A. 1997. Happiness and economic performance. *Economic Journal* 107: 1815–1831.

Ryan, M.R. & A.L. Deci 2001. On happiness and human potentials: a review of research on hedonic and eudaimonic well-being. *Annural Review of Psychology* 52: 141–66.

UNDP 1999. *Human Development Report 1999*. New York: Oxford University Press for the United Nations Development Programme.

Veenhoven, R. 1995. The cross-national pattern of happiness. Test of predictions implied in three theories of happiness. *Social Indicators Research* 34: 33–68.

—— 2000. Well-being in the Welfare State: level not higher, distribution not more equitable. *Journal of Comparative Policy Research* 2 (1): 91–125.

—— 2002. Why social policy needs subjective indicators. *Social Indicators Research* 58 (1–3): 47–87.

Vogel, J. 2002. Strategies and traditions in Swedish social reporting: A 30-year experience. *Social Indicators Research* 58: 89–113.

World Bank 2001. *World Development Report 2000/2001*. New York: Oxford University Press.

CHAPTER FOUR

SOCIAL CAPITAL AND LIFE SATISFACTION

Helmut K. Anheier, Sally Stares & Paola Grenier

1 *Introduction*

Recent work on the decline of social capital, the rise of individualism, and increased social isolation in the United States—aptly captured in Putnam's title 'Bowling Alone' (2000)—raises the question of whether similar patterns of disengagement and loss of generalized trust can be found in European countries (Offe, 2002; Hall, 2002; Rothstein, 2002) and elsewhere (see Cox, 2002; Inoguchi, 2000). It also arouses interest in what the effects of changing levels of social capital might be on people's subjective life satisfaction. At the individual level, if variations in social capital (trust, social ties, sense of community, etc.) make a difference, they should be expected to have a significant and systematic impact on central outcome measures such as overall life satisfaction and other quality of life indicators. By extension, this relationship may be expected to hold cross-nationally. The main purpose of this chapter is to explore these aspects in the context of two competing theoretical approaches.

Like social capital, the concept of life satisfaction has received increased interest by social scientists (Veenhoven, 1997; 1996; Lane, 2000; Layard, 2003) and policymakers alike (see UK: Donovan, Halpern & Sargeant, 2002). Life satisfaction turns out to be a rather complex construct: it seems less related to basic socio-demographic categories such as gender and age (Diener et al., 1999: 276–302). Its relation to contingent socio-demographics like income and education appears mixed (Easterlin, 2001; Diener et al., 1999): while in many countries, higher income groups tend to report higher satisfaction levels than lower income groups, the results for education are different and show no apparent systematic and significant relationship. Added to this, for the US, research has found that behavioural factors such as participation in community life, socializing with friends, and having a supportive social environment are associated with greater life satisfaction (Layard, 2003), whereas the socially more isolated and those reporting disruptive life events such as divorce or ill health report lower levels of life satisfaction (Diener et al., 1999).

At the aggregate level, a positive relationship has been reported between per-capita income and life satisfaction, with countries with higher per-capita income reporting, on average, higher rates of life satisfaction (Diener & Suh, 2000). For example, countries like Denmark, the Netherlands, Britain and the United States show higher levels of life satisfaction than Russia, Ukraine, South Africa, Argentina or Georgia. However, this positive relationship is not linear; rather, increased national income appears to be associated with diminishing marginal returns with regard to subjective well-being (Helliwell, 2001). And over time, aggregate levels of self-reported happiness and life-satisfaction have remained comparatively stable in the West, despite rising aggregate income (Layard, 2003). In addition there are some notable exceptions, with some poorer countries reporting similar and, at times, higher levels of aggregate life satisfaction than many middle- and high-income countries (Peck & Douthat, 2003). Many attempts to account for this country-level pattern seem to vacillate between explanations at individual and group levels, rendering themselves vulnerable to the trap of the ecological fallacy. Intervening variables and complex functional relationships have been suggested to explain patterns in aggregate levels of subjective well-being, some of which evoke certain elements of social capital. Our investigation of such explanatory frames is conducted at the individual level, as a starting point, though we recognise that in future analyses, our models would be usefully extended by testing aggregate-level effects in conjunction with individual-level factors.

Thus, we ask if the individual with more social capital is consequently also more satisfied with his life. From a cross-national perspective, we would expect this relationship to hold in a variety of country-specific cultural and political contexts. For this purpose, we will conduct a cross-national analysis to explore the generalizability of the relationship, if any, between social capital and life satisfaction. This implies two critical research questions: first, is social capital a credible predictor of people's life satisfaction across a broad range of countries that differ in culture, politics, religion, and economic development; and, second, if so, how is it related to other putative correlates of what Veenhoven (1996) terms the 'ultimate outcome measure,' i.e., life satisfaction?

2 *Competing models*

Research has examined social capital as a resource from two per-spectives: as an individual resource, and as an emerging, structural phenomenon. The individual resource perspective suggests that ties of trust and social cohesion are beneficial to members and groups alike (Coleman, 1988). Coleman argues that 'connectivity and trust' among members of a given group or society more generally, increase characteristics associated with cohesive groups: lower delinquency, more collective action, and better enforcement of norms and values. Putnam (1993, 2000) applied this kind of thinking to economic devel-opment and social inclusion, and linked it to the realm of civil society.

It led to what could be called a Neo-Tocquevillian perspective of a 'strong and vibrant civil society characterised by a social infrastructure of dense networks of face-to-face relationships that cross-cut existing social cleavages such as race, ethnicity, class, sexual orientation, and gender that will underpin strong and responsive democratic govern-ment' (Edwards, Foley & Diani, 2001: 17). Norms of reciprocity, cit-izenship, and trust are embodied in networks of civic associations. The essence of the Neo-Tocquevillian approach is: civil society cre-ates social capital, which is good for both economy and society.

By contrast, Burt (1992) has argued that the absence rather than the presence of ties among individuals accounts for the true worth of social capital. The value of social capital is in its unequal distribution, such that some people in a society have more than others. The un-even distribution of social capital, measured as the number and reach of social ties, creates 'structural holes' between unconnected indi-viduals. These gaps in social ties allow the *tertius gaudens*, i.e. the per-son who benefits, to identify the 'structural hole' and to make the connection among otherwise disconnected individual actors. This 'gap-filling' social capital becomes the bridging material of modern society. Thus, for Burt (1992) social capital matters most and is most valuable in social systems with many weak ties (Granovetter, 1973).

In structural analysis, social capital is a scarce and valued resource, and basically a private good, and not the quasi-public good with many positive externalities in Coleman's and Putnam's thinking. However, while Burt (1992, 2000; see also Padgett & Ansell, 1993; Podolny & Baron, 1997) examines the structural effect of variations in the stock of social capital in specific networks, Bourdieu takes a different, though complimentary route and thereby lays the foundation for an alternative to the Coleman/Putnam model. He links the unequal dispersion of social capital to other forms of inequalities in modern society. In other words, the distribution of social capital does not exist in isolation of the larger society: the network configurations that create structural holes and opportunities for social entrepreneurs endowed with scarce social capital exist in a broader economic and cultural context.

Indeed, Bourdieu (1986; 1984) operates with a much broader concept of capital. It is broader than the monetary notion of capital in economics; and also broader than the concept of social capital in Coleman's and Burt's sense. In Bourdieu's thinking, capital becomes a generalized 'resource' that can assume monetary and non-monetary as well as tangible and intangibles forms. Bourdieu (1986: 243) distinguishes between three major types of capital:[1]

- *economic capital* refers to monetary income as well as other financial resources and assets, and finds its institutional expression in property rights; clearly, people differ in the extent to which they earn income from gainful employment, assets, subsidies and other sources.
- *cultural capital* exists in various forms; it includes long-standing dispositions and habits acquired in the socialization process, formal educational qualifications and training, and the accumulation of valued cultural objects like paintings or other artefacts signalling levels of refinement and status attainment.
- *social capital* is the sum of actual and potential resources that can be mobilized through membership in social networks of individual actors and organizations; as in Burt's network structures, people differ in the size and span of their social networks and memberships.

For Bourdieu, no strict causal relationships exist among the different types of capital, and it seems best to think in terms of co-variations rather than causality. The types of capital differ in liquidity, convertibility, and loss potential like attrition and inflation. Economic capital is the most liquid, and most readily convertible form to be exchanged for social and cultural capital. By comparison, the con-

---

[1] Bourdieu's usage and definition of the various forms of capital is sometimes somewhat cursory (see Anheier et al., 1995), but Bourdieu (1986) offers the most systematic treatment.

vertibility of social capital into economic capital is costlier and more contingent; social capital is less liquid, "stickier," and subject to attrition. The conversion of social to economic capital is similar to investment, as when people join exclusive clubs and prestigious boards (Glaeser, Laibson & Sacerdote 2003). While it is more difficult to convert social into cultural capital, the transformation of cultural into social capital is easier: high educational attainment provides access to a broad range of social opportunities.

The differences in the liquidity, convertibility, and loss potential of forms of capital all entail different scenarios for actors in social fields. High volumes of economic capital, yet lower volumes of cultural and social capital, characterize some positions. *Nouveau riches*, for example, are typically well-endowed with economic capital relative to a paucity of cultural capital. Others will rank high in terms of cultural capital, yet somewhat lower in other forms. International business consultants rely on high degrees of social capital, relative to cultural and economic capital, and intellectuals typically accumulate higher amounts of cultural and social capital than economic assets. In any of these cases, we would expect positive, perhaps even mutually reinforcing relationships among the three forms of capital, with subsequent effects on life satisfaction.

For the purposes of this study it is suggested here that a useful way to distinguish the two approaches outlined above, and in order to develop competing hypotheses, social capital in the Coleman/Putnam approach is understood as closely related to social cohesion and a 'sense of community', whereas the Burt/Bourdieu approach to social capital sees it is part of a wider system of social inequality and linked to stratification and status competition. These are interpretations of the theories outlined which then set a community/social cohesion model of social capital derived from Coleman/Putnam against a status competition model derived from Burt/Bourdieu.

Curiously, despite the great interest Putnam's work in particular has found among social scientists and policymakers, most research puts emphasis on social capital as the dependent variable, as the phenomenon whose patterns and variations need explanation. Some like Durlauf (2002) have lamented the potential tautological nature of the Neo-Tocquevillian thesis that equates social capital with social cohesion and functioning communities. Economists look at the medium to long term economic payoff of social capital, and relate it to general personal investment patterns. Indeed, they suggest that social

capital accumulation patterns are consistent with the standard economic model in terms of income and earning potentials (Glaeser,
Laibson & Sacerdote, 2002). This finding supports Bourdieu's notion
of significant co-variations among different forms of capital as a general measure of social status. What, then, could be a truly dependent variable associated with social capital?

We argue that notions of quality of life, general well-being or life
satisfaction would be an appropriate dependent variable to test the
impact of social capital cross-nationally. The reasoning being that
variations in social capital would be expected to have a significant
and systematic impact on how people feel about their lives and their
overall degree of happiness or fulfilment. Life satisfaction, as a subjective and open measure of individual well-being, overlaps with similar notions of quality of life, happiness and individual welfare (Peck
& Douthat, 2003). It does not form part of the constructs outlined
above, and may therefore be considered sufficiently theoretically distinct to serve as a comparative yardstick for the effects of differences
in social capital. In testing these patterns, we are not testing for the
significance of social capital as compared with other well-documented
predictors of life satisfaction, such as subjective health, mental health
or marital status, but rather adopting a strictly confirmatory approach
to test the predicted relationships in the two proposed models.

Thus, this paper explores the relationship between social capital
and life satisfaction with the help of competing hypotheses, following Bourdieu's thinking in developing one hypothesis, and Putnam's
approach for the other. Specifically, we develop

1. A *status competition* model based on notions of structural social inequality, and arguing that there are strong links between social, cultural and economic capitals jointly affect life satisfaction. This is
   referred to as Bourdieu's model, and as shown in Figure 4.1, we
   would expect significant and positive effects on life satisfaction from
   each form of capital (indicated by single-headed arrows) and positive co-variations among them (double-headed arrows).
2. A *social cohesion* model, which argues that there is a strong link
   between social capital, trust and community that jointly affect life
   satisfaction. This is referred to as Putnam's *social cohesion* model,
   and according to Figure 4.2, we would expect a direct relationship between social capital and life satisfaction, with an inter-
   linking positive relationship with sense of community.

Figure 4.1   Bourdieu's status competition model

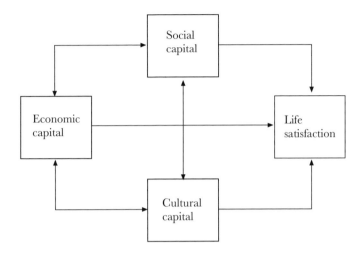

Figure 4.2   Putman's social cohesion model

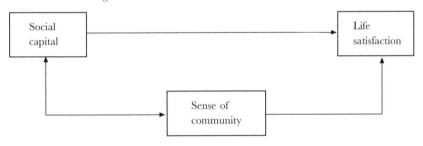

3   *Methodology and data*

We used the 1999/2000 wave of the European Value Study (Halman, 2001) as the empirical base for testing the two models. This third wave of the study was conducted using similar questions and methodologies, and the combined number of 36,908 observations from 32 countries provides a rich data set for hypothesis testing and exploration (see Appendix B for questions used).[2]

---

[2] Since West and East Germany, Great Britain and Northern Ireland were sur-

The dependent variable, *Life Satisfaction*, was measured with the help of a single question: 'All things considered, how satisfied are you with your life as a whole these days?' Respondents are asked to rank their answer on a 10-step ordinal scale from 1 = dissatisfied to 10 = satisfied. This question has been used repeatedly in cross-national surveys, and tested for validity and reliability (Veenhoven, 1997; 1999; Lane, 2000: 339–343). In the EVS survey, it is a widely-answered question. Trends in life satisfaction have been found to be similar to those for happiness, and rankings of countries on these two measures are identical (Layard, 2003).[3]

For testing the Bourdieu model, we used two social capital indicators: sociability and affiliation or membership in voluntary associations. Sociability was measured at the ordinal level and reports the frequency with which respondents see friends. Membership counts the number of reported affiliations in different kinds of voluntary organizations and groups. *Cultural capital* was measured in terms of education, i.e., the age at which formal education was completed. Finally, *economic capital* is also a single indicator construct, reporting income based on a multi-step ranking, and treated as a continuous variable in these analyses.[4]

---

veyed separately, and adequate sample sizes were achieved in each case, we kept these regions separate for the purposes of analysis. The Bourdieu model was therefore tested on 34 samples (including the US, using US World Values Survey data), while the Putnam model was tested on 33 samples (excluding the US due to the absence of any suitable indicators of community in the US survey). Following the imputation of missing values for income, cases with missing values on any of the variables used in either of the two models were deleted list-wise for analyses.

[3] We use life satisfaction rather than happiness due to higher levels of missing data on the happiness item in EVS.

[4] Finding variables to adequately represent economic and cultural capitals was a difficult exercise. For cultural capital we chose age at which formal education was completed, rather than educational qualification level, for the sake of measurement consistency between countries. For economic capital, income was the only feasible variable to use (assessments of socio-economic group, for example, were not available for many countries, and asset questions were not covered by the survey). The income variable was missing at varying rates—between 2% and 49% across the samples. To avoid losing cases, we imputed values for the missing data using multiple linear regression with predictor variables including all those contained in the Bourdieu model, plus age and gender (since variables such as socio-economic status, and those relating to occupation, varied in their presence between countries, for the sake of consistency these were not included). Clearly income is a problematic variable, and we do not deny that the amount of missing data could well affect the results we present later in the chapter. Similarly, age at which education is completed is a very crude measure of education, and even more so of the broader concept 'cultural capital'. Many thanks to Dr. Jouni Kuha for his comments on imputation and other technical aspects of the analysis.

For the Putnam model, we used three indicators for social capital: those included in the Bourdieu model, plus a measure of generalised trust. The social trust variable is based on the question, 'Generally speaking, would you say that most people can be trusted or that you can't be too careful in dealing with people?' This item is measured dichotomously.[5] In addition, we included a construct, *sense of community*, with two indicators. The first, 'caring', is measured by the question, 'To what extent do you feel concerned about the living conditions of people in your neighbourhood?' on a five step scale from 'not at all' to 'very much.' The second indicator, "helping," is measured by the question, "Would you be prepared to actually do something to improve the conditions of people in your neighbourhood/community?" with answers ranging from 'absolutely not' to 'absolutely yes'.[6]

We tested each hypothesis in over thirty countries, using the latent structural models as illustrated in Figure 4.3a and b.

The models were estimated using Lisrel 8.52 (Jöreskog & Sörbom, 2002), since many of the variables were categorical.[7] We considered it reasonable that the phenomena captured by means of categorical measurements could themselves be considered to be continuous. For instance, although trust is measured with a binary item, it seems logical to think of trust itself as a continuum, with the break between the two response options representing a cut-off criterion for that continuous variable. For each sample and each model we therefore employed the Prelis programme to take information on the distribution of responses across categories to calculate a matrix of correlations between these putative continuous underlying variables (polychoric correlations between categorical items and polyserial correlations between pairs of categorical and continuous items), and a weight

---

[5] In terms of coding, 'trust' is represented by 1 and 'distrust' by 0, so that in the analyses, positive trust coefficients indicate a positive association between trust and the construct to which it is attached (social capital).

[6] The codings on these two 'sense of community' variables have been reversed for the purposes of analysis so that higher numbers represent higher levels of care/concern.

[7] Lisrel takes any variable with more than fifteen categories to be continuous; therefore 'age at which education completed' was considered continuous; also income (which was treated as continuous for the purposes of imputation) and sum of affiliations with voluntary organisations (this was specified as continuous for all countries, for consistency, although the range of this variable did not stretch to sixteen in some samples). All other variables were specified as ordinal.

Figure 4.3a   Bourdieu's status competition model

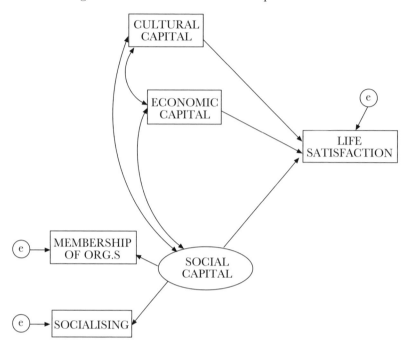

matrix of asymptotic covariances. Weighted least squares estimation was then used to obtain parameter estimates.[8]

Figure 4.3 shows the general specification of the models. In general we imposed only those constraints necessary for purposes of identification. Scaling of the latent variables was achieved by fixing their variances to 1, and the exogenous (observed predictor) variables in the Bourdieu model, i.e. economic and cultural capital, were specified by fixing their error variances to zero.[9]

---

[8] Since so many of the variables were categorical and the assumption of normality could not be met, it was decided that WLS was a more appropriate method of estimation than Maximum Likelihood. Given the relatively large sample sizes (823 for the smallest and 2266 for the largest) and the simplicity of the models tested, it was felt that WLS was theoretically the most appropriate method to use. Tests of underlying bivariate normality in Prelis revealed few serious deviations.

[9] With the Putnam model, it was sometimes necessary to fix the error variance of 'HELPING'. Where this was necessary, we adopted the value 0.41 (rather than

Figure 4.3b   Putnam's social cohesion model

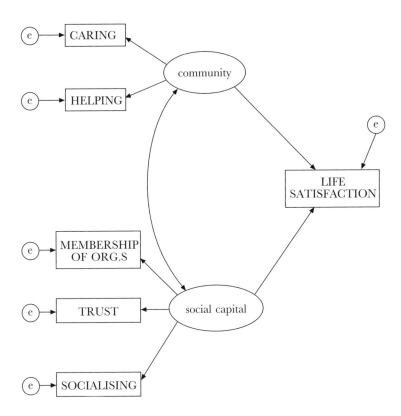

4   *Results and discussion*

The Bourdieu model hypothesizes strong links between social, cultural and economic capital, which jointly affect life satisfaction—as a construct of social inequality. By contrast, according to the Putnam model, we should expect a positive covariation between social capital and community. Both jointly affect life satisfaction—as a construct of social cohesion.

---

the somewhat common solution of zero), which was the mean of the error variances in the samples where all estimates were obtained without any difficulties; since the dispersion of error variances was quite small among the non-problematic samples, this seemed to be a reasonable solution. Similarly with the Bourdieu model, the error variance of 'SOCIALISING' was fixed to 0.84 in a few samples.

The results are presented in summarised form in Tables 4.1 and 4.2;[10] details of specific parameter estimates are given in Tables 1a and 1b of Appendix A. The results appear at first sight rather inconclusive. Although in terms of statistical model fit, as assessed by RMSEA, both models fit adequately well for most countries, Table 4.2 reveals that in no country are the expected patterns of significant positive correlations obtained for both models. Looking first to the Putnam model, it is only in West Germany that social capital and sense of community are significantly and positively related to life satisfaction and to each other. A larger group of countries shows a significant and positive relationship only between social capital and life satisfaction, but not between the latter and community. Two other countries show the opposite, whereby community spirit is related to life satisfaction, but social capital is not. Finally, in a number of countries the model proved a little problematic.[11]

While these findings may initially cast some doubts over the generalisability of the basic Coleman/Putnam approach, we do find, however, that Bourdieu's status competition model in predicting life satisfaction fares by no means better. In fact, in none of the countries did we find a positive relationship between all three forms of capital and life satisfaction. Instead, there are three frequent scenarios: in 11 samples, social capital is positively correlated with life satisfaction, but neither economic nor cultural capital is significantly related to the dependent construct. In nine samples, social capital and economic capital both reveal significant, positive relationships with life satisfaction (in one of these, cultural capital is negatively associated with life satisfaction). In eight cases all constructs seem unrelated to life satisfaction. As Table 4.2 indicates, in four samples, only economic capital has a significant positive association with life satisfaction.

---

[10] The traditional chi-square is given but alongside this, Steiger's (1990) Root Mean Square Error of Approximation (RMSEA). The chi-square statistic tests the null hypothesis that the data fit the model perfectly; this we consider to be an unreasonably strict test, so we present RMSEA as an alternative, measure of close fit. According to Brown and Cudeck (1993), an RMSEA of 0.05 or less represents a good fit, and a value of 0.08 or less an adequate fit. Table 1 also gives the coefficient of determination for our dependent variable, life satisfaction—a measure of how much of the variation in life satisfaction is explained in each sample by our model.

[11] The Putnam model is problematic for the Belarus sample; estimates are presented but should be viewed with caution. Similarly, for the Bourdieu model the Luxembourg sample was sensitive to small adjustments, and it was necessary to fix the error variance of SOCIALISING to 0.76 in order to obtain parameter estimates.

Table 4.1 Summary statistics of structural equation model

Country	n	Putnam chi-sq	d.f.*	p	RMSEA	R-sq for LIFESAT	Bourdieu chi-sq	d.f.*	p	RMSEA	R-sq for LIFESAT
Austria	1392	13.56	8	0.09	0.02	0.08	0.32	2	0.85	0.00	0.05
Belarus	848	25.33	7	0.00	0.06	0.91	3.29	2	0.19	0.03	0.25
Belgium	1697	7.38	7	0.39	0.01	0.08	0.74	2	0.69	0.00	0.11
Bulgaria	833	15.79	8	0.05	0.03	0.11	1.40	2	0.50	0.00	0.26
Croatia	920	18.24	8	0.02	0.04	0.02	0.03	2	0.98	0.00	0.03
Czech Republic	1742	45.37	8	0.00	0.05	0.11	2.09	2	0.35	0.01	0.08
Denmark	928	19.51	8	0.01	0.04	0.05	4.22	2	0.12	0.04	0.09
East Germany	938	33.20	8	0.00	0.06	0.21	8.97	2	0.01	0.06	0.07
Estonia	913	29.81	8	0.00	0.06	0.20	2.65	2	0.27	0.02	0.18
Finland	965	17.67	8	0.02	0.04	0.20	13.02	3	0.00	0.06	0.28
France	1515	10.08	8	0.26	0.01	0.05	11.39	2	0.00	0.06	0.08
Great Britain	823	9.47	8	0.30	0.02	0.04	2.95	2	0.23	0.02	0.03
Greece	932	5.63	7	0.58	0.00	0.10	2.25	3	0.52	0.00	0.24
Hungary	949	13.01	7	0.07	0.03	0.17	0.61	2	0.74	0.00	0.33
Iceland	899	16.65	8	0.03	0.04	0.02	8.72	3	0.03	0.05	0.06
Ireland	914	8.42	8	0.39	0.01	0.05	1.25	2	0.53	0.00	0.02
Italy	1861	27.15	8	0.00	0.04	0.03	0.17	2	0.92	0.00	0.03
Latvia	879	9.02	8	0.34	0.01	0.10	0.58	2	0.75	0.00	0.13
Lithuania	834	18.34	8	0.02	0.04	0.10	3.17	2	0.20	0.03	0.17
Luxembourg	1026	12.52	8	0.13	0.02	0.05	2.23	3	0.53	0.00	0.06
Malta	916	19.41	8	0.01	0.04	0.02	1.36	2	0.51	0.00	0.02
Netherlands	988	15.03	7	0.04	0.03	0.05	2.15	2	0.34	0.01	0.14
Northern Ireland	911	24.29	8	0.00	0.05	0.13	2.45	2	0.29	0.02	0.07
Poland	1018	12.85	8	0.12	0.02	0.20	1.37	2	0.50	0.00	0.20
Portugal	865	46.89	7	0.00	0.08	0.12	2.84	2	0.24	0.02	0.21
Romania	926	9.25	8	0.32	0.01	0.29	4.64	2	0.10	0.04	0.42
Russia	2266	43.21	8	0.00	0.04	0.38	4.33	2	0.11	0.02	0.52
Slovakia	1259	16.11	7	0.02	0.03	0.15	1.94	2	0.38	0.00	0.23
Slovenia	960	11.80	8	0.16	0.02	0.20	2.04	2	0.36	0.01	0.17
Spain	995	18.51	8	0.02	0.04	0.02	1.09	2	0.58	0.00	0.05
Sweden	910	10.85	7	0.15	0.03	0.04	5.23	2	0.07	0.04	0.27
Ukraine	1008	48.61	8	0.00	0.07	0.40	1.76	2	0.42	0.00	0.21
United States	1115	NA	NA	NA	NA	NA	0.70	2	0.70	0.00	0.25
West Germany	963	12.25	7	0.09	0.03	0.11	5.39	2	0.07	0.04	0.08

* where d.f. = 8, error variance of HELP was fixed to 0.41; where d.f. = 3, error variance of SOCIALISING was fixed to 0.84

In the Coleman/Putnam model, social capital turns out to be positively correlated with both life satisfaction and community. This is by far the most frequent outcome, and applies to 25 of the samples included in the analysis. This suggests that social capital is directly related to life satisfaction, whereas community tends not to be. Sense of community, therefore, is not the covarying factor that helps to explain life satisfaction as hypothesized in Putnam's model above (Figure 4.1).

Social Capital as the main covariate of life satisfaction is also the primary result that emerges from examining Bourdieu's status competition model. The fact that in 25 of the 34 samples included in the analysis, social capital loads positively on life satisfaction, provides convincing testimony of its explanatory power.

We cannot make any direct statistical comparisons of the two models, since neither is nested within the other. Given that the two hypotheses we have tested here may be considered as having fallen in conceptual terms at the first fence, it would not be appropriate to proceed to formal comparisons of the two models within countries, or of each model between countries. Our comparisons are therefore limited to level of substantive interpretation.

Table 4.3 shows the relationships among the country-based results for the Putnam and Bourdieu models combined. We see that none of the countries included fits both models, which should be no surprise given the poor substantive fits of each (Table 4.2). Equally, though, in only one country is there a complete lack of substantive fit in either model. More frequent are substantive combinations that involve mixed results, i.e., where some parts of the model fit in one model but not in the other. Twenty-three of the samples included in Table 4.3 show some fit in both, and eight countries only for the Putnam model but not in the case of Bourdieu's status competition approach. However, almost exclusively, the mixed results are a function of social capital having a positive and significant relationship on life satisfaction, whether conceived of as containing a 'trust' element or not. Thus, while social capital by itself emerges as a significant and consistent explanatory factor in predicting life satisfaction, we can reach no such conclusion for any other construct in either model. In essence, neither of the two models examined seems wholly supported by the evidence presented here.

Table 4.2   Conceptual summary of test results for substantive fit

Legend:
+   according to theoretical expectations
−   opposite to theoretical expectations
blank   indicates inconclusive, non-significant results.
SC =   social capital
C =   community
EC =   economic capital
CC =   cultural capital
LS =   life satisfaction

	Putnam			Bourdieu					
	SC-LS	C-LS	SC-C	CC-LS	EC-LS	SC-LS	CC-EC	CC-SC	EC-SC
Austria		+	+			+		+	+
Belarus		+	+		+	+			+
Belgium	+		+			+		+	+
Bulgaria	+		+	+		+			+
Croatia	+		+					+	+
Czech Rep.	+		+			+		+	+
Denmark	+	+			+	+		+	
East Germany	+	+	+	−	+	+		+	+
Estonia	+		+						+
Finland	+		+		+	+		+	−
France	+		+		+			+	
Great Britain	+		+		+				+
Greece	+		+			+		+	+
Hungary	+		+					+	+
Iceland	+		+		+				
Ireland		+	+					+	+
Italy	+		+					+	+
Latvia	+		+		+	+			+
Lithuania	+							+	+
Luxembourg	+		+			+		+	
Malta	+		+					+	+
Netherlands	+		+			+		+	
Northern Ireland	+		+		+	+		+	+
Poland	+		+		+	+		+	+
Portugal	+		+			+		+	+
Romania	+	−						+	+
Russia	+		+			+		+	+
Slovakia	+		+		+	+			
Slovenia	+					+		+	+
Spain			+		+			+	+
Sweden	+		+						+
Ukraine	+		+		+				+
United States						+			+
West Germany	+	+	+			+		+	+

Table 4.3   Theoretical comparison of test results

THEORETICAL COMPARISON		BOURDIEU	
	Fit	Mixed	No Fit
	Fit	West Germany	East Germany
PUTNAM Mixed		Austria, Belarus, Belgium, Bulgaria, Czech Republic, Denmark, Finland, France, Great Britain, Greece, Iceland, Latvia, Luxembourg, Netherlands, Northern Ireland, Poland, Portugal, Russia, Slovakia, Slovenia, Spain, Ukraine	Croatia, Estonia, Hungary, Ireland, Italy, Lithuania, Malta, Sweden
No fit			Romania[12]

One or two points are worth mentioning with regard to the measurement parts of the models (documented in Appendix A). The squared multiple correlation coefficients for life satisfaction are typically quite small. Whilst this is standard for the types of models under consideration, it does illustrate the important fact that the models depict only one of many structural relationships between measures of well-being and other features of social life. We do not aim to produce a comprehensive account of theoretical expectations related to life satisfaction—our aim is strictly to test two specific theoretical structures—nevertheless, it must be noted that there is much more to be explained than we can have covered in this paper, and further analyses of the effects of various individual- and group-level factors would be valuable.

---

[12] The theoretical analysis puts Romania into a unique position as having no link between social capital and life satisfaction. This apparent exception could be attributed to the destruction of a sense of community under the communist regime coupled with high levels of mistrust between neighbours during that time. Since the early 1990s and the transition period, geographical mobility has been low and communities and neighbourhoods have not been recreated. We are grateful to our Romanian colleagues working on the EVS, Bogdan Voicu and Malina Voicu, for providing us with some insight into these experiences in Romania.

Similar coefficients for the observed endogenous indicators in each model vary a great deal in magnitude. Such coefficients are often taken as proxies for measurements of reliability. Had we found closer theoretical fit we would have proceeded to test whether the measurement parts of the models were invariant across countries. From a cursory inspection of the R-square coefficients we can speculate that we would find a great deal of variation. This is interesting because it implies that the survey items do not function identically across countries in terms of their relationships with the constructs investigated here. At the same time questions on life satisfaction and happiness have been found to function in similar ways across countries, though that does not deny a national culture effect (Layard, 2003).

5 *Conclusion*

The purpose of this paper was to examine two hypotheses. According to the first, social capital is linked to a sense of community, leading to greater life satisfaction. The greater the overall amount of social capital, and the greater the sense of community, the greater life satisfaction will be. The second hypothesis stated that social capital covaries with economic and cultural capital to create advantages for some people in society, which then impacts on individual life satisfaction. The greater the overall amounts of capital, the greater life satisfaction will be.

The analyses did not support the hypotheses and the models they represent; neither the community image of one, nor the competitive spirit of the other. Instead, the results pointed to a much simpler, and perhaps therefore even more forceful pattern: in understanding life satisfaction social capital as a construct of sociability and participation seems to matter first and foremost, rendering other forms of capital and community aspects virtually irrelevant. In fact, economic capital and cultural capital were not found to be significantly related to life satisfaction in many countries; and similarly, a sense of community was also found not to be a consistent predictor of life satisfaction. What accounts for life satisfaction is neither the community emphasis of Neo-Toquevillian approaches, nor the broader notion of *homo oeconomicus* of Bourdieu's status competition model. Essentially, the results demonstrate a direct link between life satisfaction and 'social connectivity'.

Given that neither of the theoretical models examined here adequately accounted for life satisfaction, but social capital by itself did, it is necessary to consider alternative theoretical approaches. One way of accounting for this would be that people are fundamentally social in nature, and that therefore the construct of social capital is simply a proxy for socialising, which has been consistently found to be related to life satisfaction and happiness (Donovan, Halpern & Sargeant, 2002; Diener et al., 1999). However, this does not capture the full meaning of social capital, which includes notions of civic participation and in Putnam's formulation, trustworthiness, or generalized trust. This leads us to the idea of the reality of the 'happy participating citizen', compared with the myth of the 'happy productive worker' of the social relations school in organizational theory (Iaffaldano & Muchinsky, 1985). In effect there are intrinsic motivations for people to participate in society, and from a policy perspective, providing opportunities, mechanisms and the space within which to take part in society, to become a member or a volunteer may be more important than creating economic incentives.

At the same time we know that life satisfaction is a complex construct with varying relationships with job security and unemployment (Diener & Suh, 2000), levels of economic inequality within a country (Alesina et al., 2001; Lane, 2000), subjective health and mental health, the broader political country context and the nature of freedom, and marital status and kinship (Veenhoven, 1997). The relative power of social capital as a predictor of life satisfaction is likely to be contingent on a number of these factors, as well as directly and indirectly impacting on them. There are also likely to be effects of national culture, as suggested in this research by the fact that survey questions seem to be understood differently in different countries.

Yet even when taking these measurement aspects into account, the persistent finding of a strong relationship between social capital and life satisfaction in the great majority of the countries examined suggests a clear sociological pattern: life satisfaction is positively related to 'social connectivity'.

References

Alesina, A., R. Di Tella & R. MacCulloch 2001. Inequality and happiness: Are Europeans and Americans different? *NBER Working Paper No. w8198*, Issued in April

Anheier, H.K., J. Gerhards & F.P. Romo 1995. Forms of capital and social structure in cultural fields: Examining Bourdieu's social topography. *American Journal of Sociology* 100 (4): 859–903.

Bourdieu, P. 1986. Forms of capital. Pp. 241–258 in J.G. Richardson (ed.), *Handbook of Theory and Research for the Sociology of Education*. New York: Greenwood.

—— 1984. *Distinction: A Social Critique of the Judgement of Taste*. London: Routledge.

Bowles, S. & H. Gintis 2002. Social capital and community governance. *Economic Journal*. 112 (483): 419.

Browne, M.W. & R. Cudeck 1993. Alternative ways of assessing model fit. Pp. 136–162 in K.A. Bollen & J.S. Long (eds.), *Testing Structural Equation Models*. Newbury Park, CA: Sage.

Burt, R.S. 1992. *Structural Holes*. Cambridge, MA: Harvard University Press.

—— 2000. The network structure of social capital. Pp. 345–423 in R.I. Sutton & B.M. Staw (eds.), *Research in Organizational Behavior*. Greenwich, CT: JAI Press.

Coleman, J.S. 1988. Social capital in the creation of human capital. *American Journal of Sociology* 94: 95–120.

—— 1990. *Foundations of Social Theory*. Cambridge, MA: Harvard University Press.

Cox, E. 2002. Australia: making the lucky country. Pp. 333–358 in R. Putnam (ed.), *Democracies in Flux. The Evolution of Social Capital in Contemporary Society*. New York: Oxford University Press.

Diener, E. & E.M. Suh (eds.) 2000. *Culture and Subjective Well-Being*. Cambridge, MA: MIT Press

——, E.M. Suh, R.E. Lucas & H.L. Smith 1999. Subjective well being: Three decades of progress. *Psychological Bulletin*. 125 (2): 276–302.

Donovan, N. & D. Halpern with R. Sargeant 2002. *Life satisfaction: the state of knowledge and implications for government*. London UK: Strategy Unit, Cabinet Office.

Durlauf, S. 2002. On the empirics of social capital. *Economic Journal*. 112 (483): 459.

Easterlin, R.A. 2001. Income and happiness: toward a unified theory. *The Economic Journal* 111 (473): 465.

Edwards, B., M.W. Foley & M. Diani 2001. *Beyond Tocqueville: Civil Society and the Social Capital Debate in Comparative Perspective*. Hanover: University Press of New England.

Glaeser, E., D. Laibson & B. Sacerdote 2002. The economic approach to social capital. *Economic Journal*. 112 (483): 437.

Granovetter, M. 1973. The strength of weak ties. *American Journal of Sociology* 78: 1360–80.

Hall, P. 2002. Great Britain: the role of government and the distribution of social capital. Pp. 21–58 in R. Putnam (ed.), *Democracies in Flux. The Evolution of Social Capital in Contemporary Society*. New York: Oxford University Press.

Halman, L. 2001. *The European Values Study: A Third Wave. Source Book of the 1999/2000 European Values Study Surveys*. Tilburg: EVS, WORC, Tilburg University.

Helliwell, J. 2001. How's Life? Combining individual and national variables to explain subjective well-being. *NBER Working Paper 9065*. US: National Bureau of Economic Research, Inc.

Iaffaldano, M.T. & P.M. Muchinsky 1985. Job satisfaction and job performance: A meta-analysis. *Psychological Bulletin* 97 (2): 251–273.

Inoguchi, T. 2002. Broadening the basis of social capital in Japan. Pp. 359–392 in R. Putnam (ed.), *Democracies in Flux. The Evolution of Social Capital in Contemporary Society*. New York: Oxford University Press.

Jöreskog, K. & D. Sörbom 2002. *LISREL 8.52 Student Edition*. Chicago: Scientific Software International, Inc.

Lane, R.E. 2000. *The Loss of Happiness in Market Economies*. New Haven and London: Yale University Press.

Layard, R. 2003 Happiness: has social science a clue. *Lionel Robbins Memorial Lectures* Lecture 1 (of 3) delivered on 3 March 2003, at the London School of Economics. Available at: http://cep.lse.ac.uk.

Offe, C. & S. Fuchs 2002. A decline of social capital? The German case. Pp. 189–244 in R. Putnam (ed.), *Democracies in Flux. The Evolution of Social Capital in Contemporary Society*. New York: Oxford University Press.

Padgett, J.F. & C.K. Ansell 1993. Robust action and the rise of the Medici, 1400–1434. *American Journal of Sociology* 98:1259–1319.

Peck, D. & R. Douthat 2003. Does money buy happiness? *The Atlantic Monthly*; Boston; Jan/Feb.

Podolny, J.M. & J.N. Baron 1997. Resources and relationships: social networks and mobility in the workplace. *American Sociological Review* 62: 673–693.

Putnam, R.D. 1993. *Making Democracy Work: Civil Traditions in Modern Italy*. Princeton: Princeton University Press.

—— 2000. *Bowling Alone*. New York: Simon and Schuster.

Rothstein, B. 2002. Sweden: social capital in a social democratic state. Pp. 289–332 in R. Putnam (ed.), *Democracies in Flux. The Evolution of Social Capital in Contemporary Society*. New York: Oxford University Press.

Steiger, J.H. 1990. Structural model evaluation and modification: An interval estimation approach. *Multivariate Behavioral Research* 25: 173–180.

Veenhoven, R. 1996. A comprehensive measure of quality of life in nations. *Social Indicators Research* 39: 1–58.

—— 1997. Quality of Life in individualistic society. *Social Indicators Research* 48: 157–186.

Appendices

Appendix A

Table 4.1a Testing Putnam's cohesion model (* *indicates significance at the 5% level*)

| | structural model | | correlation | measurement model | | | | | reliabilities | | | | |
| | standardised loadings | | standardised loadings | standardised loadings | | | | | | | | | |
	social capital -> life satisfaction	community -> life satisfaction	social capital <> community	social capital -> MEMBERSHIPS	social capital -> TRUST	social capital -> SOCIAL-ISING	community -> CARING	community -> HELPING	R-sq for MEMBERSHIPS	R-sq for TRUST	R-sq for SOCIAL-ISING	R-Sq for CARING	R-sq for HELPING
Austria	0.02	0.27*	0.48*	0.51*	0.41*	0.21*	0.53*	0.77*	0.26	0.17	0.04	0.28	0.60
Belarus	1.23	-0.64	0.64*	0.15*	0.24*	0.25*	0.35*	0.96*	0.02	0.06	0.06	0.13	0.92
Belgium	0.24*	0.08	0.51*	0.50*	0.49*	0.32*	0.74*	0.75*	0.25	0.24	0.10	0.55	0.56
Bulgaria	0.35*	-0.07	0.25*	0.19*	0.62*	0.43*	0.84*	0.77*	0.04	0.39	0.19	0.71	0.59
Croatia	0.12*	0.03	0.25*	0.62*	0.33*	0.36*	0.46*	0.77*	0.39	0.11	0.13	0.21	0.59
Czechia	0.34*	-0.03	0.39*	0.39*	0.34*	0.25*	0.41*	0.77*	0.15	0.12	0.06	0.17	0.59
Denmark	0.23*	0.01	0.25*	0.60*	0.48*	0.33*	0.41*	0.77*	0.36	0.23	0.11	0.17	0.59
East Germany	0.36*	0.18*	0.36*	0.58*	0.30*	0.43*	0.93*	0.77*	0.34	0.09	0.19	0.86	0.59
Estonia	0.47*	-0.08	0.39*	0.33*	0.39*	0.20*	0.65*	0.77*	0.14	0.16	0.04	0.43	0.60
Finland	0.49*	-0.12	0.43*	0.33*	0.51*	0.07	0.55*	0.77*	0.11	0.26	0.01	0.30	0.60
France	0.25*	-0.10	0.50*	0.37*	0.57*	0.24*	0.86*	0.76*	0.14	0.32	0.06	0.64	0.58
Great Britain	0.19*	0.00	0.28*	0.26*	0.69*	0.24*	0.63*	0.77*	0.07	0.48	0.06	0.40	0.59
Greece	0.33*	-0.05	0.40*	0.38*	0.47*	0.20*	0.73*	0.80*	0.14	0.22	0.04	0.53	0.64
Hungary	0.39*	0.08	0.27*	0.37*	0.44*	0.31*	0.62*	0.73*	0.13	0.20	0.09	0.39	0.54
Iceland	0.15*	0.01	0.27*	0.47*	0.34*	0.01	0.64*	0.77*	0.22	0.12	0.00	0.41	0.59

Table 4.1a (cont.)

| | structural model | | | | measurement model | | | | | | | | |
| | standardised loadings | | correlation | standardised loadings | | | | | reliabilities | | | | |
	social capital -> life satisfaction	community -> life satisfaction	social capital <-> community	social capital -> MEMBERSHIPS	social capital -> TRUST	social capital -> SOCIALISING	community -> CARING	community -> HELPING	R-sq for MEMBERSHIPS	R-sq for TRUST	R-sq for SOCIALISING	R-Sq for CARING	R-sq for HELPING
Ireland	0.11	0.16*	0.43*	0.33*	0.46*	0.28*	0.55*	0.77*	0.11	0.21	0.08	0.30	0.59
Italy	0.17*	0.03	0.31*	0.47*	0.54*	0.34*	0.68*	0.77*	0.22	0.29	0.11	0.46	0.60
Latvia	0.33*	-0.09	0.21*	0.40*	0.31*	0.30*	0.57*	0.77*	0.16	0.10	0.09	0.32	0.59
Lithuania	0.32*	-0.08	0.09	0.19*	0.58*	0.26*	0.56*	0.77*	0.04	0.34	0.07	0.32	0.59
Luxembourg	0.23*	-0.01	0.37*	0.24*	0.63*	0.25*	0.78*	0.77*	0.06	0.39	0.06	0.61	0.59
Malta	0.15*	-0.02	0.34*	0.46*	0.39*	0.36*	0.65*	0.77*	0.20	0.15	0.13	0.43	0.59
Netherlands	0.16*	0.10	0.37*	0.49*	0.42*	0.24*	0.79*	0.67*	0.24	0.17	0.06	0.62	0.45
Northern Ireland	0.39*	-0.07	0.49*	0.35*	0.26*	0.26*	0.60*	0.77*	0.12	0.07	0.07	0.36	0.59
Poland	0.45*	-0.05	0.23*	0.34*	0.28*	0.42*	0.62*	0.77*	0.11	0.08	0.18	0.38	0.59
Portugal	0.38*	-0.07	0.47*	0.35*	0.47*	0.36*	0.73*	0.76*	0.12	0.22	0.13	0.53	0.58
Romania	0.54*	-0.18*	0.14	0.07	0.23*	0.35*	0.78*	0.77*	0.00	0.05	0.12	0.60	0.59
Russia	0.62*	-0.07	0.13*	0.22*	0.23*	0.38*	0.70*	0.77*	0.05	0.05	0.15	0.49	0.59
Slovakia	0.41*	-0.08	0.40*	0.39*	0.46*	0.25*	0.79*	0.84*	0.15	0.21	0.06	0.63	0.71
Slovenia	0.46*	-0.05	0.16	0.23*	0.55*	0.34*	0.51*	0.77*	0.05	0.30	0.12	0.26	0.59
Spain	0.08	0.08	0.35*	0.37*	0.21*	0.40*	0.67*	0.77*	0.14	0.04	0.16	0.45	0.60
Sweden	0.15*	0.09	0.28*	0.60*	0.44*	0.10*	0.68*	0.77*	0.36	0.20	0.01	0.46	0.59
Ukraine	0.65*	-0.14	0.33*	0.11*	0.31*	0.15*	0.64*	0.77*	0.01	0.10	0.02	0.41	0.60
West Germany	0.23*	0.14*	0.47*	0.47*	0.32*	0.59*	0.74*	0.82*	0.22	0.10	0.35	0.55	0.67

Table 4.1b Testing Bourdieu's status competition model

Country	structural model						measurement model			
	standardised loadings			correlations			standardised loadings		reliability of social capital items	
	cultural capital -> life satisfaction	economic capital -> life satisfaction	social capital -> life satisfaction	cultural capital <-> economic capital	cultural capital <-> social capital	economic capital <-> social capital	social capital -> MEMBER- SHIPS	social capital -> SOCIALISING	R-sq for MEMBER- SHIPS	R-sq for SOCIALISING
Austria	-0.08	-0.03	0.25*	0.33	0.42*	0.55*	0.38*	0.29*	0.14	0.09
Belarus	0.07	0.18*	0.40*	0.12	0.03	0.31*	0.17*	0.40*	0.03	0.16
Belgium	-0.27	0.15	0.37*	0.28	0.63*	0.20*	0.49*	0.33*	0.24	0.11
Bulgaria	0.14*	0.00	0.47*	0.17	0.14	0.56*	0.22*	0.37*	0.05	0.14
Croatia	0.03	0.07	0.14	0.22	0.38*	0.29*	0.44*	0.51*	0.19	0.26
Czechia	0.04	0.06	0.25*	0.22	0.18*	0.39*	0.36*	0.33*	0.13	0.11
Denmark	-0.14	0.16*	0.28*	0.13	0.26*	-0.05	0.50*	0.38*	0.25	0.14
East Germany	-0.11*	0.11*	0.22*	0.25	0.28*	0.31*	0.84*	0.32*	0.71	0.10
Estonia	0.14	0.01	0.40	0.13	-0.03	0.56*	0.37*	0.27*	0.14	0.07
Finland	0.09	0.52*	0.60*	-0.19	0.13*	-0.56*	0.14*	0.38*	0.02	0.15
France	-0.21	0.20*	0.33	0.19	0.65*	-0.09	0.29*	0.36*	0.09	0.13
Great Britain	-0.04	0.18*	-0.04	0.27	0.25	0.35*	0.41*	0.17*	0.17	0.03
Greece	-0.33	-0.01	0.62*	0.30	0.64*	0.30*	0.20*	0.39*	0.04	0.15
Hungary	-0.12	0.14	0.54	0.14	0.42*	0.49*	0.23*	0.35*	0.05	0.12
Iceland	-0.01	0.16*	-0.19	0.13	-0.12	-0.05	-0.01*	-0.40	0.00	0.16
Ireland	-0.06	0.02	0.16	0.43	0.59*	0.45*	0.47*	0.18*	0.22	0.03
Italy	-0.14	0.07	0.19	0.45	0.65*	0.44*	0.39*	0.43*	0.15	0.19

Table 4.1b (cont.)

| | structural model | | | | | | measurement model | | | |
| | standardised loadings | | | | correlations | | standardised loadings | | reliability of social capital items | |
Country	cultural capital -> life satisfaction	economic capital -> life satisfaction	social capital -> life satisfaction	cultural capital <-> economic capital	cultural capital <-> social capital	economic capital <-> social capital	social capital -> MEMBER-SHIPS	social capital -> SOCIALISING	R-sq for MEMBER-SHIPS	R-sq for SOCIALISING
Latvia	0.03	0.15*	0.28*	0.14	0.11	0.29*	0.36*	0.35*	0.13	0.15
Lithuania	-0.07	0.10	0.39	0.35	0.49*	0.35*	0.42*	0.15	0.18	0.02
Luxembourg	-0.15	0.13	0.25*	0.42	0.41*	0.06	0.12*	0.49*	0.01	0.24
Malta	-0.06	0.05	0.14	0.48	0.50*	0.32*	0.38*	0.44*	0.14	0.19
Netherlands	-0.17	0.19	0.38*	0.18	0.47*	-0.01	0.31*	0.31*	0.09	0.09
Northern Ireland	-0.12	0.16*	0.22*	0.35	0.41*	0.20*	0.36*	0.32*	0.13	0.10
Poland	-0.01	0.18*	0.38*	0.29	0.33*	0.21*	0.26*	0.49*	0.07	0.24
Portugal	-0.03	0.02	0.46*	0.49	0.47*	0.51*	0.20*	0.52*	0.04	0.27
Romania	-0.28	-0.51	1.04	0.33	0.56*	0.72*	0.12*	0.32*	0.01	0.10
Russia	-0.11	-0.01	0.76*	0.16	0.37*	0.37*	0.18*	0.35*	0.03	0.12
Slovakia	0.03	0.19*	0.43*	0.32	0.10	0.00	0.23*	0.38*	0.05	0.14
Slovenia	-0.11	0.11	0.40*	0.39	0.37*	0.27*	0.16*	0.50*	0.03	0.25
Spain	-0.05	0.10*	0.19	0.27	0.61*	0.33*	0.35*	0.42*	0.12	0.17
Sweden	-0.09	0.47	0.64	-0.21	0.20	-0.61*	0.19*	0.29*	0.03	0.09
Ukraine	0.03	0.29*	0.27	0.07	0.00	0.34*	0.33*	0.37*	0.11	0.14
United States	0.07	0.04	0.48*	-0.03	-0.03	0.29*	0.38*	0.32*	0.15	0.10
West Germany	-0.03	0.04	0.27*	0.31	0.25*	0.32*	0.54*	0.52*	0.30	0.27

Appendix B

Questions from European value survey used for social capital analysis

LIFE SATISFACTION

All things considered, how satisfied are you with your life as a whole these days? Please use this card to help with your answer.

1	2	3	4	5	6	7	8	9	10	Dk	Na
Dissatisfied								Satisfied		−1	−2

TRUST
Generally speaking, would you say that most people can be trusted or that you can't be too careful in dealing with people?

A	Most people can be trusted	1
B	Can't be too careful	2
	Don't know	−1
	No answer	−2

SOCIABILITY

I'm going to ask how often you do certain things. Giving an answer from this card please tell me how often you do each. *(Interviewer: Code 'Not applicable' when respondent is not involved in the activity at all)*

		Every week	Once or twice a month	A few times a year	Not at all	Dk	Na	Nap
A	Spend time with friends	1	2	3	4	−1	−2	−3

MEMBERSHIP

Please look carefully at the following list of voluntary organisations and activities and say . . .

a) which, if any, do you belong to? (Code all mentioned under (a) as '1')
b) which, if any, are you currently doing unpaid voluntary work for? (Code all mentioned under (b) as '1')

		mentioned	not	mentioned	not
A	Social welfare services for elderly, handicapped or deprived people	1	0	1	0
B	Religious or church organisations	1	0	1	0
C	Education, arts, music or cultural activities	1	0	1	0
D	Trade unions	1	0	1	0
E	Political parties or groups	1	0	1	0

F	Local community action on issues like poverty, employment, housing, racial equality	1	0	1	0
G	Third world development or human rights	1	0	1	0
H	Conservation, the environment, ecology, animal rights	1	0	1	0
I	Professional associations	1	0	1	0
J	Youth work (e.g. scouts, guides, youth clubs etc.)	1	0	1	0
K	Sports or recreation	1	0	1	0
L	Women's groups	1	0	1	0
M	Peace movement	1	0	1	0
N	Voluntary organisations concerned with health	1	0	1	0
O	Other groups	1	0	1	0
	None	1	0	1	0
	Don't know	-1	0	-1	0
	No answer	-2	0	-2	0

CULTURAL CAPITAL—EDUCATION

At what age did you (or will you) complete your full time education, either at school or at an institution of higher education? Please exclude apprenticeships. (*Interviewer instruction: If respondent is still at school, ask: at what age do you expect you will have completed your education?*) (Write in age). . . .

(BELOW IS THE BRITISH QUESTION, WHICH WAS SLIGHTLY DIFFERENTLY WORDED THAN IN OTHER EVS COUNTRIES)

What age were you when your education finished?
(Write in age) . . . . years old

ECONOMIC CAPITAL—HOUSEHOLD INCOME

SHOW INCOME CARD II

Here is a scale of incomes and we would like to know in what group your household is, counting all wages, salaries, pensions and other incomes that come in. Just give the number of the group your household falls into, after taxes and other deductions.

1	2	3	4	5	6	7	8	9	10	−1	−2
										Dk	Na

CARE AND COMMUNITY

SHOW CARD DD

To what extent do you feel concerned about the living conditions of: . . . . . .

	Very much	Much	To a certain extent	Not so much	Not at all	DK	Na
People in your neighbourhood	1	2	3	4	5	−1	−2

Would you be prepared to actually do something to improve the conditions of: ......

	Abso-lutely yes	Yes	Maybe yes/ maybe no	No	Abso-lutely no	DK	Na
People in your neighbourhood/ community	1	2	3	4	5	−1	−2

CHAPTER FIVE

VOLUNTARY ORGANIZATIONS AND THE DEVELOPMENT OF CIVIL SOCIETY[1]

Jerzy Bartkowski & Aleksandra Jasińska-Kania

1 *Introduction*

One of the most important aspects of the systemic transformations taking place in the countries of Central and Eastern Europe is the emergence of civil society. In political debates concentrating on these political transformations, the concept of civil society has been seen in terms of a social order based on a multiplicity of organizations and voluntary co-operation that work independent of the state. After all, the centralized state is an order imposed from above and based on coercion (often described in the case of communist states, as totalitarian or authoritarian by critics). These debates make reference to modern Western European concepts of civil society that—in keeping with Hegelian tradition—were formulated in opposition to the State. Within the framework of the concept of civil society, there are three distinct, if interrelated, dimensions.

The first dimension involves civil society's economic foundations. These have to be separate from the realm of politics, built up in opposition to the centralized system of state socialism, and developed on the basis of a free market economy as a 'network of relationships among individuals, who pursue their own private interests but have to come to an understanding and co-operate with one another' (Szacki, 1995: 141).

The second dimension 'refers to a public space between household and state, aside from the market, in which citizens may associate for

---

[1] This analysis was carried out at the ZA-EUROLAB at the Zentralarchiv für Empirische Sozialforschung (ZA), Cologne. The ZA is a large scale facility supported by the Access to Research Infrastructure action of the Improving Human Potential Programme of the European Union.

the prosecution of particular interests within a framework of law guaranteed by the state. The sociological variant of civil society affirms the self-organization of society, rejects the state-dependency of citizens and treats civil society as an entity in its own right which is irreducible to economic structure.' (Bryant & Mokrzycki 1995: 24).

The third dimension involves aspects of civic morality and cultural identity. It rests on the premise that 'the precondition for the existence of civil society is a normative consensus of its members. (. . .) It concerns both the central moral values on which civil society is based and the rules of behavior of its members (. . .) It is this normative consensus that ties together the members of civil society and makes them a moral community and a distinct entity that can act as a whole.' (Rau, 1991: 6).

Critical analyses of the political transformation processes taking place in Central and Eastern Europe, particularly in Poland, have drawn attention to the limitations of the programs for the construction of civil society, because they have concentrated only on certain dimensions. They have, in the process, underestimated the role of the state in its formation; left the economy out altogether, or underestimated the conflicts of interest and other cleavages that divide the moral and cultural unity of the nation (see Szacki, 1995: 104–109). These limitations have undoubtedly contributed to the limited success or failure of many of the political reform projects tried in East-Central Europe.

In the present chapter, we concentrate mainly on the second dimension—defined by Bryant and Mokrzycki (1995) as the sociological dimension of civil society: citizens' voluntary affiliation with and active participation in social associations. We also will attempt to verify hypotheses about the interdependence of voluntary social activity and the growth of a free market economy, the democratic state as an institution, and civic morality. These relationships are analyzed both at the level of macro-social comparisons between different countries and regions of Europe and at the micro-social level of pre-conditions for the existence of specific values, attitudes, and behavior patterns that stimulate voluntary activities of individuals.

2   *Theoretical premises and research hypotheses*

The literature of sociology and political science often distinguishes between two theoretical approaches to social functions and the results of citizens associating in voluntary organizations (see Dekker & Van den Broek, 1996).

The first approach follows the analysis of Alexis de Tocqueville (1835–1840; 1990) on the relationship between the activeness of social associations and the development of democracy in America. Just as widespread participation of citizens in the decision making process and proper articulation and representation of different interests are thought to be important elements of democracy, citizens' involvement in the activities of voluntary organizations are an integral part of the process that leads to the formation of democratic political bodies. In addition, involvement in voluntary organizations stimulates the continued growth of democracy by leading to citizens' increased interest in politics, shaping political competence and communication skills; increasing the ability to understand and accept different points of view, trust in others and the ability to work together; and improving organizational efficiency.

The second approach, elaborated by Robert Putnam (1993), is that participation in voluntary organizations increases social capital (made up of a network of relationships, of trust, and of mutual reciprocity norms facilitating the co-ordination of common tasks and furthering their effectiveness). The erosion of this capital creates a threat to civil life and to local communities. This—according to Putnam (1995)—took place in the nineties in the United States and was reflected in Americans' decreased involvement in voluntary organizations. Moreover, Francis Fukuyama (1995) has emphasized the impact this social capital has, in the form of trust and relationship networks, on economic growth and the overall prosperity level of various countries.

In connection with these two approaches, Paul Dekker and Andries van den Broek (1996) have conducted a secondary analysis that compares data on participation in voluntary associations in five countries (the United States, Great Britain, Germany, Italy, and Mexico) from the research in *The Civic Culture* (Almond & Verba, 1963) and in the *World Values Surveys* of 1990. They sought the answers to two questions: 1) to what degree does voluntary activity further the development of democracy?; and 2) does it mitigate or perpetuate inequality in the distribution of social capital and political inequalities? In their conclusions, they affirmed the expected inter-dependence between affiliation with voluntary organizations and political competence, interest in and discussion of politics, political involvement (particularly participation in protests), and trust in other people. At the same time, they found that participation in voluntary associations neither reduces nor increases the inequalities of participation in a country's political life. These result from social-demographic differences of age, gender, education, and social and economic status. Involvement in voluntary social activity was not connected with any political orientation. Thus, it did not lead to the representation of any particular political attitudes.

The questions concerning membership and activeness in voluntary organizations included in the third wave of the European Values Study (EVS) have allowed us to conduct comparative analyses with a much wider number of cases. This, to significant degree, confirms the theses of Dekker and van den Broek. Furthermore, we extended our research hypotheses by placing less emphasis on the consequences and functions of participation in voluntary associations than on the antecedents, motivations, and conditions of citizens' self-organization.

The use and expansion of social capital, set in motion by the activity of civic organizations, requires that a country has already accumulated some basic resources: the material infrastructure created in the process of a country's economic and civilizational development; an institutional base for the functioning of a democratic state, citizens' rights, their historical experiences, and patterns of behavior preserved in the collective memory and transmitted by tradition. Citizens join voluntary associations and work on their behalf not only because they are motivated by their personal needs, interests, and values but, also because they are encouraged and stimulated by cultural traditions and patterns of behavior in their countries and geographic regions. Also, they do this because they find there are opportunities for civic engagement provided by the state of the economy and political institutions in their societies. These opportunities and the resources for the development of social capital in the form of associational membership are unevenly distributed in various regions of Europe. Turbulent twentieth century history with two world wars, followed by the division of the continent into separate economic, political, and ideological systems, has deepened the contrasts in the level of socio-economic development and political freedom between Western and Eastern Europe, and to some degree, between northern and southern parts of Europe. The European integration in the West and the systemic transformation in the East have been aimed at eliminating or at least diminishing these inequalities and contrasts.

On the basis of the above premises, we hypothesized that citizens' participation in voluntary organizations (membership and activity) would be determined by various types of factors:

I. Macro-structural determinants: that is, indicators of citizens' participation in voluntary organizations will be higher in countries or geographic and cultural regions characterized by 1) a higher level of socio-economic and human development (HDI); 2) a higher degree of civil liberty and political freedom, coming from long traditions and stability of democratic government and, in post-communist Central and Eastern Europe, the advancement and success of economic reforms and the democratization process; 3) a degree of economic freedom 'defined as the absence of government coercion or constrain on the production, distribution, or consumption of goods and services beyond the extent necessary for citizens to protect and maintain liberty itself'.[2]

II. Micro-social determinants including 1) socio-demographic variables such as education and gender, and 2) individuals' values, attitudes, and beliefs, such as a) interest in politics, and readiness to participate in protest actions; b) greater support for and confidence in democratic institutions; c) a deeper acceptance of the norms of civic morality and the conviction that they are observed by the majority of citizens; d) a higher degree of trust in others; and e) a greater feeling of control over one's own life.

In order to verify these hypotheses we developed a multivariate model of regression analysis aimed at predicting the overall membership in voluntary organizations and individuals' active work in them in European countries. Also we have applied this model to explain the specific characteristics of volunteering in four East-Central European countries (the Czech Republic, Slovakia, Hungary, and Poland). In addition, using analysis of variances, we have explored whether there are significant differences in indicators of membership and activity in voluntary organizations as well as in the pre-conditions of civic engagement between European countries belonging to specific geographic and cultural regions, described in the next section of the chapter.

---

[2] www.heritage.org/index/2002/chap5.html Retrieved 12.02.2002.

3   Data and measurement

The 1999 EVS data (Halman, 2001)[3] are used to operationalize the independent variables: *membership* and *activity* in voluntary organizations, as well as their micro-social and individual determinants.

Measurement of *membership* in voluntary organizations was based on the question of whether one belongs to any type of organizations presented on the list.[4] It is constructed as a dichotomized 0–1 scale where 0 means a respondent did not belong to any organization and 1 a person was a member of at least one association. *Activity* was also measured on a 0–1 scale: 0 indicated a respondent did not report unpaid voluntary work for any association and 1 a person reported doing unpaid work for at least one of organization.

Micro-structural determinants of voluntary membership and activity included two variables: *gender* and *education*. Research in many countries has shown that women and people with a lower level of education are less involved in organizations. Differences in participation between men and women generally correspond to differences in traditional role patterns, which despite modernization are still traceable (Van Deth & Kreuter, 1998). Education, measured by the age at which a respondent completed education, enhances voluntary participation by increasing citizens' social resources (time, contacts) and specific skills (cognitive, verbal).

The individual values and attitudes included in the model embrace 12 variables that—according to Putnam's theory and previous research (Dekker & Van den Broek, 1996; Norris 2000)—correlate with voluntary participation. Two variables are used to explore the relationship between political engagement and involvement in voluntary associations: *Interest in politics*, measured by an index constructed from answers to three questions ('How important is politics in your life?'; 'How often do you discuss political matters with your friends?'; 'How often do you follow politics in the news?'). The index varies from 0 (lack of interest) to 100 (highest interest); and *readiness to protest*, a reversed count of responses to questions of what one 'would never

---

[3] The data set comprises data from 29 countries; Iceland, Luxemburg, and Malta were not included because of their specific combination of high indicators of voluntary participation and a small size of population.

[4] Women and Youth organisations were not counted in order to avoid the impact of differences in demographic structure of countries population.

do' (signing a petition, joining in boycotts, attending lawful demonstration, joining unofficial strikes, occupying buildings). In this, 0 means 'would never do', 5—might join all 5 protest actions. Feeling of *control over one's own life* and freedom of choice are measured on a scale from 1 (low) to 10 (high). They are expected to be related to self-assertiveness, competence, and efficacy, which facilitate engagement in voluntary actions.

According to Putnam, cultural and socio-psychological dimensions of social capital include norms of trust, confidence, and cooperation, as well as networks of social interaction. These dimensions are measured by the following variables: *Trust in people*, gauged by responses to 'most people can be trusted' or 'can't be too careful, in dealing with people' (reversed scale where 1 = no trust, 2 = trust). *Confidence in the church* and *confidence in trade unions* (scale reversed so that 1 = none at all, and 4 = great deal) were selected, on the basis of correlation analysis, as measures of confidence in institutions related to specific spheres of voluntary activity. *Spending time with colleagues* (scale reversed so that 1 = not at all, and 4 = every week) is an indicator of maintaining informal linkages.

Support for *Eliminating inequalities* in income as an important feature of a 'just' society (scale reversed so that 1 = not at all, 5 = very important) is considered to be a possible goal of voluntary participation. The *Civic morality* index is created by summing the score on four items (claiming state benefits to which one is not entitled, cheating on taxes, accepting a bribe, and paying cash for services to avoid taxation). The respondents were asked to assess on a ten point scale if these actions can be justified (scale was reversed so that 1 = always, and 10 = never). The index range is from 4 (most permissive) to 40 (most restrictive). *Perception of civic morality* is measured by a sum of scores on how people perceive the behavior of their compatriots for three of the above items.[5] The index range is from 3 (perception of a low morality) to 12 (perception of a strong civic morality). It is expected that stronger acceptance of civic morality norms as well as the perception that other citizens respect them should enhance voluntary activity. Also, citizens' perceptions that *human rights are respected* in their country should facilitate voluntary participation (scale was reversed so that 1 = no respect, 4 = a lot of respect). Higher *ratings*

---

[5] 'Accepting bribes' is excluded since it was dropped in the questionnaire in many countries.

of the government (on a scale from 1 = very bad to 10 = very good) were expected to encourage involvement in voluntary associations.

Macro-structural determinants of membership and activity in voluntary organizations included three component measures:

Human Development Index (HDI)—standardized average of: GDP, life span and population with higher education. The scale of 0 to 1 = maximum was used.[6]

The *Civil Liberties Rating (CL)* of the countries by Freedom House was also used. The scale reversed so that 1 is a minimum of political rights, and 7 is the maximum.[7]

The *Index of Economic Freedom (IEF)* used is a ranking of 161 countries based on an analysis of institutional factors such as trade policy, the fiscal burden of the government, monetary policy, governmental intervention in the economy, capital flows and foreign investment, banking and finance, wages and prices, property rights, regulation, and black market activity. The scale is reversed so a higher value means greater economic freedom.[8]

These measures were included in the models explaining citizens' associational membership and activity by attributing to each respondent his/her country's score on these three indexes. We assumed that these variables characterized an individuals' social environment, facilitating or hindering their volunteering. The model, thus, included both objective and subjective determinants of individual activity and embraced the institutional framework.

The same measures were used in models explaining organizational membership and activity at the cross-national level where the dependent variables were the percentages of members and activists in organizations in each country. The independent variables were the HDI, CL, and IEF scores, as well as the mean of micro-social and individual variables for each country.

In addition, the correlations of the HDL, CL, and IEF measures with membership and activity in voluntary associations were used to explore whether differences in the distribution of social capital and other indicators of civil society exist not only between nations but also between clusters of countries belonging to various regions of Europe. While we are fully aware of the arbitrariness of the various typologies for the regions of Europe (Heunks, 1996; Diez Medrano,

---

[6] www/undp.org/hdro/98hdi.htm Retrieved 6.02.2002.
[7] www.freedomhouse.org/research/freeworld/2001 Retrieved 09.02.2002.
[8] www.worldaudit.org/economicfreedom.htm Retrieved 12.02.2002.

1996), we have used the following typology. In Western Europe, or the EU member countries, three regions are distinguished: EW-North-Scandinavia (the Netherlands, Sweden, Denmark, and Finland), EW-Central (Great Britain, Northern Ireland, the Republic of Ireland, Western and Eastern Germany, Austria, France, and Belgium), and EW-South (Italy, Spain, Portugal, and Greece). In post-communist Eastern Europe, we distinguish: EE-Baltic republics (Estonia, Latvia, and Lithuania), EE-Visegrad (the Czech Republic, Slovakia, Hungary, and Poland), EE-South (Slovenia, Croatia, Bulgaria, and Romania), and EE-former Soviet republics now belonging to CIS (Russia, Ukraine, and Belarus). The countries are divided into regional groups on the basis of their geographic and cultural background, and also on the most important differences in historical, economic, and political developments (see Juchler, 1999).

4   *National and regional differences in membership and activity in voluntary organizations*

The differences in the percentages of respondents reporting membership in any type of voluntary association and unpaid activity in at least one of them, between European countries belonging to different cultural and geographic regions are illustrated in Figure 5.1.

Independently of the reasons for the success or failure of the organizational bases of civil society in the various countries, voluntary participation in associations is linked with socio-economic development, and also the institutional and cultural traditions in various regions of Europe. From a geographical and cultural point of view, the indicators for volunteer activity are characterized by a tendency to decline along two axes: one running from West to East and one running from North to South.

The indicators of socio-economic and political development of various regions of Europe reflect a similar pattern. Figure 5.2 presents the correlations of voluntary membership and activity with indicators of human development (HDI) in the seven regions of Europe. Correlations of membership and activity in voluntary associations with indicators of economic freedom (IEF) and civil liberties (CL) are similar though lower.

In the northern part of Western Europe, Scandinavian countries and The Netherlands have led the way in the development of civil society based on broad participation in voluntary associations. They

Figure 5.1 Membership and activity in voluntary organizations in 29
European countries

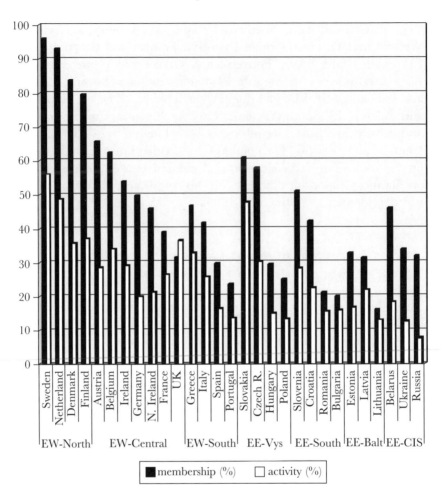

are characterized by Europe's highest indicators of affiliation and
activity in all types of voluntary associations. These indicators increased
in the last two decades of the twentieth century. The most active are
the Swedes and the Dutch (over 90% belong to voluntary organizations)
and the Danes and Finns, 80% of whom report associational membership. At the forefront is membership in organizations promoting
the realization of citizens' individual and collective interests. These
are vocational associations; sport or recreation associations; organizations acting for education, culture, environmental protection; and,

Figure 5.2 Correlations of membership and activity with socioeconomic
development in seven regions of Europe

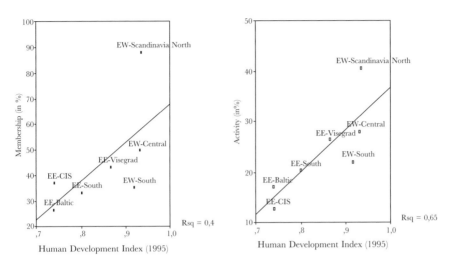

Human Development Index (1995)

in spite of the significant secularization of these countries, religious organizations (these result from the particular links between church and state and of the tax system in these countries). Such affiliation is also influenced by their higher socio-economic level and prosperity (HDI, IEF); the stability of their democratic institutions; their safeguarding of political, economic, and civic rights (CL); their recognition of the values and norms of civic political culture and morality; their acceptance of democracy, and their citizens' trust in each other.

In the center of Western Europe, the European Union member states—France, Belgium, Germany, Austria, Great Britain, Northern Ireland, and the Republic of Ireland—have a somewhat lower and more differentiated level of voluntary membership and activity. In Belgium, Austria, West Germany, and Ireland, 50–60% of citizens report associational membership. In France and Great Britain, members in voluntary organization are less numerous (over 30%) but relatively more respondents report unpaid activity. The United Kingdom is unique in that it is the only country where activity is higher than organizational membership. This is particularly true in such areas as welfare, environmental protection, youth work, peace movements, and health care. The center of Western Europe, while marked by considerable cultural differences, is characterized by a high degree of socio-economic development (HDI, IEF) and citizens' rights (CL); the long traditions of the democratic institutions; low levels of corruption; the recognition of democracy as the best form of government; the feeling of control over one's own life; and a comparatively high degree of tolerance. The indicators of voluntary participation in organizations are, though, more varied, and reflect various trends and fluctuations.

A different type of political culture and pattern of social activeness has characterized the southern countries of Western Europe: Italy, Spain, Portugal, and Greece. The causes of the lower level of social activity in these countries, in comparison to other EU countries in the eighties, seem to be their semi-peripheral location and lower level of socio-economic development (HDI); economic freedom (IEF); and civil liberties (CL). In addition, there was an impact of their particular experience of a long period of autocratic rule, which in Spain, Portugal, and Greece, was only ended in the seventies (Diez Medrano, 1996). This experience left a low degree of confidence in state institutions, a low level of political interest, a reluctance to engage in protest actions, weaker support for democracy, stronger dependence on family ties (described as 'amoral familialism'—Banfield, 1958), lower trust in others, and a weaker feeling of control over one's life. The changes in the last decade would seem to indicate an erosion of these traits of southern European political culture. Membership in the EU has not only hastened economic growth but also the tempo of their democratization and the growth of their citizens' activeness. Associational membership and activity in Greece and Italy are higher than in some nations of central Western Europe. However, in Spain, and especially in Portugal, volunteering remains much lower.

In the post-communist countries of East-Central Europe, particularly in the so-called Visegrad group[9]—Poland, Hungary, the Czech Republic, and Slovakia—the indicators of voluntary social work are also varied and reflect the different paths and tempo of systemic

---

[9] The Visegrad Four is an unofficial name given to the four Central European post communist countries: the Czech Republic, the Republic of Hungary, the Republic of Poland, and the Slovak Republic. The name of this group was chosen during a meeting of the presidents of these countries in the north Hungarian city of Visegrad on 15 February 1991. At this meeting the leaders signed a declaration on a close co-operation of these countries on their way to European integration. 'In 1335 the Castle of Visegrad, then the seat of the Kings of Hungary, was the scene of the royal summit of the Kings of Poland, Bohemia and Hungary. They agreed to cooperate closely in the field of politics and commerce, inspiring their late successors to launch a successful Central European initiative' (www.visegrad.org/group.php Retrieved 14.02.2002).

change (Juchler, 1999). These four countries stand out for having divested themselves of the communist system comparatively early, for introducing economic and political reforms at the quickest rate, and for being first to be accepted as candidates for EU membership. The level of socioeconomic development in this region is midway (HDI = .86) between that of the countries of Western Europe (HDI over .91) and the republics of the former USSR (HDI = .73). However, the degree of economic freedom and civil liberties is much closer to that of the central part of Western Europe. The historical experience of these countries encompasses various traditions of governance. These governments were mostly deficient and transitory, but their legacy nevertheless includes a relatively high degree of acceptance for democracy among the population. Furthermore, in the period of state socialism, attempts were made in Poland, Hungary, and in Czechoslovakia to utilize in democratic opposition organizations (trade unions, cultural and professional associations) initially created as 'transmission belts' to carry communist party decisions to the masses.

The differences between the countries of this region are significant. In the Czech Republic and Slovakia, indicators of affiliation and activeness are high and are growing to equal those of the more advanced nations in the central part of Western Europe. A particular gain has been seen in sports or recreation activities, cultural and religious organizations, and social welfare services. Although membership in trade unions has significantly decreased, these are still amongst the strongest organizations in this region. In Poland and in Hungary in 1990, the indicators of voluntary participation were higher than in the southern part of Western Europe. During the following ten years, indicators fell to the same levels as now exist in the countries of the former Soviet Union. In Poland, this decline in participation affects all types of organizations. A more detailed analysis and explanation of volunteering in this group of countries and particularly in Poland will be presented in the later part of the chapter.

The three Baltic nations—Estonia, Latvia, and Lithuania—are considered separately from the countries of the former USSR because 1) they were independent states before World War II and 2) their radical rejection of the communist system resulted in regaining independence. Involved in this are collective memories of their cultural ties with the western world resulting in their aspirations to join the EU. These nations were characterized, at the beginning of the transformation process, by the mass mobilization of citizens into legal protest actions aimed at gaining independence, by a higher level of participation in elections than that of many countries of Eastern Europe, by the rapid growth of non-governmental organizations (Smith-Sivertsen, 2000), and by a comparatively high ranking on the civil liberties and economic freedom scales. Their level of socio-economic development (HDI = .73) is relatively low and the indicators of membership (particularly in Lithuania) are lower than in other parts of Europe; but, the level of activity is still somewhat higher than in Russia, Ukraine, and Belarus.

The ex-Soviet republics—Russia, Ukraine, and Belarus—now belonging to the CIS have encountered the greatest obstacles on the development of civil society. Along with having the lowest levels of economic freedom, civil liberties, and socio-economic development in Europe, they have the lowest levels of voluntary activity, though the indicators of formal organizational membership here are relatively higher than in some other parts of Eastern Europe. In the former USSR, membership in organizations such as trade unions or youth organizations was, in many cases, obligatory. Most of the associations officially declared 'voluntary' were, in reality, state-controlled bureaucratic institutions. The breakdown of state socialism resulted in a drastic fall in membership and in minimal organizational activity. In Russia in 1990, before the collapse of the USSR, over 70% of the population reported membership in some organizations. In 1999, only 30% belonged to organizations. In all ex-Soviet republics, there has been a significant fall in the membership in trade unions, to which half the population belonged back in 1990. After 10 years these are still the strongest organizations in these states; but, in Russia and in Ukraine, the percentage of union members amounts to only slightly over 20% of the population. It is only in Belarus (where the legacy of the former system remains the strongest) that the percentage reaches nearly 40%. After the liquidation of the Communist Party, membership in political parties or organizations has drastically declined overall. These statistics suggest that the transformation of institutional structures at once and from above results in a destabilization and anomie, as well as a weaker than average civil society.

The southern part of Eastern Europe includes four nations—Slovenia, Croatia, Bulgaria, and Romania—in which breaking with the communist system triggered various kinds of national and ethnic conflicts and different modes and speeds of economic and political reform. The most successful systemic reforms were in Slovenia.

These are linked with its relatively high level of socio-economic development (HDI = .88), degree of economic freedom and civil liberty as well as with exceptionally high indicators of voluntary membership and activity when compared to other countries in the region. Croatia, despite having a common past with Slovenia as a part of the former Yugoslav Federation, has the lowest score of HDI (.75) in the region and a low ranking on economic freedoms and civil liberties. Nevertheless, the percentage of members and particularly activists in voluntary organizations in Croatia is closer to that of Slovenia than of Romania and Bulgaria where the other indicators of civil society are similar to Croatia's. In Romania and Bulgaria, associational membership was already fairly low at the beginning of the 90s and has fallen after ten years to the lowest level in Europe: only slightly over 20% of the country's inhabitants, though the proportion of activists is somewhat higher that in ex-Soviet republics.

In order to answer the question whether the above typology of European regions is justified not only on the basis of geographical proximity, historical, cultural and institutional similarities between nations, but that it is also supported by statistical analysis, measures of variation within regions and between regions were applied. Results of One-Way ANOVA: Post Hoc Multiple Comparisons (using Scheffe's criterion for significance of differences between groups) of voluntary membership and activity in seven regions are significant at $p<.001$.

Membership means for groups show that each of three regions (Western Europe—North, Western Europe—South, and Eastern Europe—Baltic) is significantly different from all other regions in their indicators of organizational membership. There are no significant differences in voluntary membership between Eastern Europe—South and Eastern Europe—former Soviet republics, or between Eastern Europe—Center and Western Europe—Center, although each of these regions differs significantly from five other regions.

The mean for activity show a greater overlapping between regions. However, Western Europe—North on one side and the Eastern European—ex-Soviet republics on the other differ significantly in the levels of voluntary activity from all the other regions of Europe. Eastern Europe—South (high levels of activity in Slovenia and Croatia, lower in Romania and Bulgaria) and Baltic nations (higher levels of activity in Latvia and lower in Lithuania) do not differ significantly: variation in the activity between these two regions is smaller than the variation within them. The same is true for Western Europe—

South (with high levels of activity in Greece and lower in Portugal) and Western Europe—Center (high levels of activity in Great Britain and Belgium, lower in Germany), as well as for Western Europe—Center and Eastern Europe—Center (activity in Slovakia and the Czech Republic is higher than in most Central-Western European nations, and in Poland it is as low as in Eastern Germany). However, variations in activity within these four regions is smaller than the variation between them and each of the five other regions. At the same time, the Center of Western Europe differs significantly only from four other regions: Western Europe—North and Eastern Europe—South, Baltic, and ex-Soviet republics (CIS).

Thus, the clustering of the European countries in seven regions has been to a large degree (though not completely), supported by the analysis of the variances. This indicates that, in most cases, prediction of voluntary membership and activity based on regional means significantly reduces errors in prediction. It confirms Pippa Norris' conclusions, based on the analysis of the mid-1990s World Values Study data from 47 nations, that 'social capital is not randomly distributed across the globe, instead it produces fairly predictable patterns, and ones that appear to be closely tied to patterns of socio-economic and democratic development' (Norris, 2000: 12). 'The overall distribution suggests that longstanding historical and cultural traditions function to imprint distinctive patterns on clusters of nations, despite some outliers' (Ibid.: 11).

5   Structural and individual factors affecting participation in voluntary organizations

In order to explore why citizens are willing to join voluntary associations and to engage in unpaid work on their behalf, a regression analysis was conducted on the pooled data from 29 European countries weighted for structure of population. It was then repeated on the pooled data from four Central-Eastern European nations, as well as separately on the national sample data in each country: the Czech Republic, Slovakia, Hungary, and Poland.

Predictors of membership in voluntary organizations are shown on Table 5.1.

The findings confirm our hypothesis that macro-structural and institutional variables are among the significant predictors of affiliation

Table 5.1   Predictors of membership in voluntary organizations
(beta coefficients of regression analysis with dependent variable:
membership in voluntary organizations)

Membership	Europe (country level)[a]	Europe (individual level) [b]	Visegrad countries[c]	Czech Rep.[d]	Slovakia[d]	Hungary[d]	Poland[d]
Human Development Index	.565**	.204***	.296***	n.a.	n.a	n.a.	n.a.
Civil Liberty	.384*	.051***	n.a.	n.a	n.a.	n.a.	n.a.
Economic Freedom	.388*	−.043**	n.a.	n.a	n.a.	n.a.	n.a.
Education	.354	.124***	.086***	.070**	.068*	.123**	.150***
Gender	−.224	−.024***	−.067***	−.106***	−.099**	.001	−.045
Political interest	.352	.113***	.081***	.058*	.110**	.095**	.087*
Political protest	.534**	.046***	.043**	.045	.020	.016	.071*
Control over life	.485**	.014*	.012	.016	.013	.053	−.003
Trust in people	.757***	.085***	.056***	.054*	.094**	.060	.048
Confidence, church	−.346	.030***	.079***	.039	.094**	.125***	.029
Confidence, trade unions	.543**	.073***	.082***	.092***	.070*	.102**	.064
Spend time with colleagues	.208	.093***	.096***	.153***	.076*	.040	.076*
Eliminating inequalities	−.642***	−.065***	−.011	−.030	.028	−.037	−.006
Civic morality	−.041	.006	.034*	.030	.058	.054	−.008
Perceived civic morality	.176	.007	−.020	−.016	−.014	−.055	.015
Respected human rights	.695***	.043***	.012	.018	.017	.012	−.014
Rating government	.495**	.002	.008	−.043	.032	−.017	.000
R. square	n.a.	.147	.160	.080	.085	.077	.068
Adj. R. square	n.a.	.147	.157	.072	.072	.062	.053
Degrees of freedom	28	26712	4611	1695	1033	855	926
Significance	n.a.	.000	.000	.000	.000	.000	.000

n.a. not applicable
significant at * p < .05; ** p < .01; *** p < .001

[a] standardized coefficients (beta) of one-variable regression analysis explaining level of individuals' membership in voluntary associations using the countries' means as predictors.
[b] standardized coefficients (beta) of multiple linear regression analysis explaining individuals' membership in voluntary associations in the pooled data of the surveyed 29 European countries.
[c] beta coefficients of multiple linear regression analysis explaining individuals' membership in voluntary associations in the pooled data of four countries of the Visegrad group.
[d] beta coefficients of multiple linear regression analysis explaining individuals' membership in voluntary associations for each of the four countries of the region.

with voluntary associations. Two of these—the indicators of socio-economic development (HDI) and of civil liberties (CL)—have a positive influence on individuals' affiliation with organizations. The index of economic freedom (IEF) has the opposite effect: a more regulated economy induces individuals to join organizations and the entirely unfettered action of market forces does not encourage it. However, at a national level, the correlation between the score of economic freedom and membership in associations is positive: the percentages of members in voluntary organizations are higher in countries with a higher degree of economic freedom. This could be the result of high correlations between the indexes of human development, civil liberties, and economic freedom cross-nationally.[10]

As expected, such socio-demographic variables as education and gender have a significant influence (though the effects are not very strong): a higher level of education inclines a person to join organizations and men more often belong than women do.

The results confirm the hypotheses that political engagement (interest in politics, readiness to participate in protest action, and the feeling of control over one's own life) stimulates people to join organizations. Also, in accordance with Putnam's theory and other research on social capital, trust in people, confidence in trade unions and in churches, and the maintenance of social networks by spending time with colleagues, are significant predictors of membership in associations. The perception that human rights are respected in one's own country encourages citizens to join associations.

Contrary to our hypothesis, people who favor the narrowing of the income gap and eliminating economic inequalities less often join voluntary organizations than do others; members and activists do not equate social justice with equality of income. Also, the hypothesized positive effect of acceptance of civic morality norms and the perception that the majority of other citizens observe these norms on propensity of individuals to belong to organizations is not supported by the regression analysis. Furthermore, contrary to our predictions, individuals' evaluation of the current system of government has no impact on their organizational affiliation.

---

[10] The Pearson correlations between the three indexes are following:

	CL	IEF
HDI	.559**	.700**
CL		.830**

** $p < .01$

At a cross-national level, however, there is a significant interdependence between the rating of the governmental system and associational membership: countries where the system of government is positively evaluated have higher percentages of citizens in voluntary organizations. There are some other differences in variables explaining membership in organizations at the individual and at the cross-national level. Variables such as interest in politics, confidence in the churches, and spending time with colleagues, quite significantly, more frequently characterize individuals who join voluntary organizations. But, countries with a higher percentage of members in voluntary organizations do not differ from those with lower affiliation on these characteristics. That is, variables such as interest in politics, confidence in the Church, and spending a lot of time with colleagues characterize only individuals but not the cultural patterns of nations that are richer in social capital.

Predictors of individuals' voluntary activity (see Table 5.2) are very similar to predictors of their membership in associations, though the percentage of variation explained by the model is lower in the case of activity (7.8) than in the case of membership (14.7). The number of citizens belonging to organizations in a given country is, to a large degree, determined by structural and institutional variables. Active work on behalf of an organization is more individualized and depends more on personal motives, interests, and values.

The Human Development Index still appears to be the best predictor of activity. Slightly less significant is the indicator of political freedom (Civil Liberty). The first difference between predictors of membership and activity is that the working of the free market (Economic Freedom), although it does not encourage individuals to join organizations, stimulates those who already belong to a greater activity. The second difference is that support for civic morality appears as a significant (though rather small) predictor of a person's engagement in voluntary work (but not in organizational membership). Socio-demographic variables—education and gender—have the same effect on activity as on organizational membership: people with a higher level of education more often engage in voluntary work than the less educated and men more often become activists than women.

The model of a 'voluntary activist' in Europe includes the following features that do not appear in 'non-activists': 1) more importance attached to politics; often discussing politics with colleagues, and following politics in the news; 2) readiness to be involved in protest

Table 5.2   Predictors of activity in voluntary organizations (beta coefficients of regression analysis with dependent variable: activity in voluntary organizations)

Activity	Europe (country level)[a]	Europe (individual level [b]	Visegrad countries[c]	Czech Rep.[d]	Slovakia [d]	Hungary [d]	Poland [d]
Human Development Index	.613**	.118***	.255***	n.a.	n.a.	n.a.	n.a.
Civil Liberty	.457*	.028*	n.a.	n.a.	n.a.	n.a.	n.a.
Economic Freedom	.522**	.046**	n.a.	n.a.	n.a.	n.a.	n.a.
Education	.364	.104***	.082***	.079**	.062	.104**	.059
Gender	−.338	−.026***	−.065***	−.072**	−.109**	.010	−.049
Political interest	.188	.091***	.069***	.075**	.047	.103**	.097**
Political protest	.670***	.050***	.053**	.070**	.023	.043	.045
Control over life	.507**	.026***	.029*	.039	.057	.025	.032
Trust in people	.561**	.050***	.027	.004	.050	.075*	.043
Confidence, church	−.339	.080***	.150***	.044	.162***	.079*	.068
Confidence, trade unions	−.350	.012*	.055***	.061*	.020	.049	.001
Spend time with colleagues	.251	.076***	.073***	.076**	.097**	.034	.075*
Eliminating inequalities	−.405*	−.016**	.003	−.053*	.023	−.051	.035
Civic morality	−.109	.012*	.001	.004	.081**	−.010	.012
Perceived civic morality	.098	.001	−.038*	−.040	−.068*	-.007	.021
Respected human rights	.641***	.017*	.002	.015	−.034	.014	.006
Rating government	.446*	.011	−.005	−.002	.071*	−.011	−.045
R. square	n.a.	.085	.119	.061	.085	.059	.043
Adj. R. square	n.a.	.084	.116	.053	.072	.043	.028
Degrees of freedom	28	26772	4613	1695	1033	848	926
Significance	n.a.	.000	.000	.000	.000	.000	.000

n.a. not applicable
significant at * $p < .05$; ** $p < .01$; *** $p < .001$

[a] Standardized coefficients (beta) of one-variable regression analysis explaining level of individuals' activity in voluntary associations using the countries' means as predictors.
[b] Standardized coefficients(beta) of multiple linear regression analysis explaining individuals' activity in voluntary associations in the pooled data of the surveyed 29 European countries.
[c] Beta coefficients of multiple linear regression analysis explaining individuals' activity in voluntary associations in the pooled data of four countries of the Visegrad group.
[d] Beta coefficients of multiple linear regression analysis explaining individuals' activity in voluntary associations for each of the four countries of the region.

actions; 3) the feeling of having more freedom of choice and control over one's own life; 4) greater trust in people; 5) higher confidence in institutions in which the voluntary work is being performed (church organizations, and trade unions); 6) more time spent with colleagues; 7) unwillingness to eliminate inequalities in income between citizens; 8) stronger support for norms of civic morality; 9) and the perception that human rights are respected in one's own country. These features increase the potential for citizens to mobilize resources through a social network and to contribute to the accumulation of social capital in their societies. Contrary to expectations, there is no significant difference between activists and nonactivists in their perception of their compatriots as having a strong civic morality. The difference between activists and nonactivists in their evaluations of the current government is not significant, though the interrelationship between a positive rating of the system of governance and voluntary activity is signifcantly stronger at the national level.

Predictors for a level of voluntary activity in European nations (the mean for a country) are the same as predictors for associational membership.

In accordance with our hypotheses, social capital measured by associational membership and voluntary activity is higher in countries characterized by 1) a higher level of socio-economic development (HDI); 2) a higher degree of civil liberty (CL); and 3) economic freedom (IEF); 4) a greater readiness for involvement in protest actions; 5) a stronger feeling that people have freedom of choice and control over their own life; 6) a higher interpersonal trust; 7) a higher confidence in trade unions; 8) less widespread conviction that eliminating inequalities of income is an important feature of a just society; 9) perception that human rights are respected there; and 10) a more positive rating of the current system of governing.

The above characteristics describe European nations that are rich in social capital, where the network of social capital is embedded in a system of economy, politics and culture. However, the hypothesis that the accumulation of social capital is higher in countries characterized by a stronger civic morality and a higher perception that citizens respect norms of civic morality in their behavior is not supported by our findings. This corresponds with the results of Listhaug's analysis that show no impact of activism in voluntary organizations on civic morality in all group of countries distinguished in his research: stable democracies, new democracies, and transitional regimes. Also he finds that there is no straightforward correspondence between strength of civil morality and the type of country (see Listhaug and Ringdal chapter in this volume).

6   *Sources of social capital in Central-Eastern Europe*

In the Visegrad group of four countries, there are fewer significant predictors of individuals' membership and activity in voluntary organizations. Differences in Human Development Index scores between these four countries have a significant impact on their citizens' willingness to join organizations and to engage in voluntary activities. There is no significant difference between these countries in their placement on the civil liberties scale. In pooled data for the whole group, as well as in separate national samples for each country— the Czech Republic, Slovakia, Hungary, and Poland, only the level of education and political interest have a positive effect on membership in all cases. Gender is significant both for membership and activity in the pooled group, as well as in the Czech Republic and Slovakia, but irrelevant in Hungary and Poland.

In the pooled group of four countries, values and attitudes that predict membership include: an interest in politics, a readiness to be involved in protest action, trust in people, confidence in the Church, confidence in trade unions, and spending a large amount of time with colleagues. In comparison with predictors of associational membership in the pooled European sample, in the Visegrad group, the following have no impact on citizens' propensity to join associations: the feeling of control over one's own life, the unwillingness to eliminate inequalities, and the perception that human rights are respected in these countries.

Almost the same variables appear as predictors of activity in voluntary organizations in the pooled group (with exceptions of the feeling of control over one's life that has a positive impact on activity). When compared to the overall European predictors of individuals' voluntary activity, the significance of the rejection of economic egalitarianism, of support for civic morality norms, and of the perception that human rights are respected disappears in the pooled Visegrad group. These result can lead to the conclusion that some essential sources of social capital are not equally significant or utilized equally in this region.

The four countries differ from each other not only in indicators of membership and activity in voluntary organizations but also in their predictors.

In Slovakia, where percentages of members and activists are among the highest in Europe, people who are more likely to be members of organizations, in addition to being male and slightly better educated, are more interested in politics; more trusting of others; have more confidence in the Church and in trade unions; and spend more time with their colleagues. There is no significant impact of education on Slovaks' engagement in voluntary activity; but, the effect of gender is quite strong. Slovak activists have much confidence in the Church. They spend much time with their colleagues. They support civic morality norms but perceive their compatriots as often violating them. And, they positively evaluate the current system of government. Activists, however, do not have more trust in people than non-activists.

The percentage of members in voluntary organizations in the Czech Republic is not much lower than in Slovakia and the predictors of membership are very similar. The exception comes with confidence in the Church. It is high in Slovakia due to its religious Catholic population and the highest membership in religious associations in Eastern Europe. But it has no effect in the Czech Republic, which is one of the most highly secularized nations. Here again, membership is determined by gender and education, political interest, trust in people, confidence in trade unions, and spending time with colleagues. In addition to the above characteristics (with the exception of trust in people that does not influence activity), activism in the Czech Republic is affected by a readiness to participate in protest actions, and an unwillingness to eliminate income inequalities.

In Hungary, which has much lower indicators of organizational membership and activity than the Czech and the Slovak republics, there are also fewer significant predictors. Members are more likely to have a higher level of education, to attach more importance to politics, and to have more confidence in the Church and in trade unions than are those who do not belong to organizations. Activists are better educated, interested in politics, and express confidence in trade unions (but confidence in the Church has no significant effect). In addition, and contrary to the Czech, Slovak, and Polish activists, they are also more likely to trust other people.

In Poland, percentages of members and activists in voluntary associations are the lowest in the region. Education has the strongest effect on organizational membership. But it is irrelevant for involvement in voluntary activity. Members, as well as activists, attach much importance to politics and spend a lot of time with their colleagues. Readiness to be involved in protest actions inclines Poles to join organizations, but this has no impact on engagement in voluntary work.

The differences between the four nations could result, first of all, from the process of the systemic transformation. The 'Velvet Revolution' in Czechoslovakia took place relatively quietly, and was not accompanied by large upheavals or crises. The Czech Republic has the highest level of socio-economic development (per capital GDP and HDI) in this region of Europe. Researchers emphasized that, in the Czech context, local democratization has played an important role in the transformation processes. As a result, 'new channels of participation were created, and new motives were emerging. The new democratic local councils, local political parties, new grassroot organizations and interest groups, and new local media provided new opportunities' (Illner, 1998: 75–76).

In Slovakia, after its separation from the Czech Republic and its creation of an independent state, the process of democratization was delayed. But it was precisely the grass roots development of non-governmental citizens' organizations that in large measure led to the downfall of Meciar's government and the acceleration of Slovakia's democratization process. 'Development of the non-governmental sector continued, above all, the tradition of self-help, which was always present in Slovak political culture. Authoritarian tendencies from the side of the power caused the consolidation of this sector standing in defense of its existence as well as of the interests of particular social groups' (Fialova, 1999: 112). The authoritarian government's attempt 'to establish greater legislative control over the fledgling independent sector (. . .) failed in part because it was treating it as a hierarchical structure rather than a more organic movement' (Ondrusek & Labath, 1997). An interpretation of the paradoxical finding that the perception of violation of civic morality by the majority of population has the significant impact of motivating Slovak activists to do voluntary work might be sought in an analysis of the specific situation of political conflicts in Slovakia.

In Hungary and in Poland, the transformation program was based on a 'shock therapy' strategy. This, in spite of early disturbances at the beginning of the nineties, fairly quickly brought the expected results in economic development. Later, however, as a corollary effect, various crisis phenomena appeared: the rapid growth of unemployment, the destabilization of governments and rapid acceleration of unprepared institutional reforms introduced from above by the government (particularly in Poland), and a fall in the economic growth rate. This has been accompanied by a growth in dissatisfaction with the functioning of democracy and with the ruling elite.

In Hungary, after the number of civil, nonprofit organizations more than tripled between 1989 and 1992, 'the direct influence and undisguised control of political parties and official authorities in the civil sector' as well as 'the anti-civil society attitude of the new elite contributed significantly to its paralysis.' Besides, 'In the everyday activities of newly established NGOs and other civil organizations, competition overcame cooperation' (Miszlivetz & Jensen, 1998: 88–89).

The essential role played by 'Solidarity', both as trade union and as social movement, and by the Catholic Church in dismantling the communist regime in Poland was possible because of their powerful organizational structures and massive membership, along with their moral and ideological appeal. They contributed to uniting protest actions and opposition against the communist system. After the fall of state socialism, these hierarchical, centralized, and increasingly politicized organizational structures revealed a growing inadequacy in stimulating the development of civil society 'that is increasing the importance and role of individual actors operating chiefly at the local level' (Rychard, 1998: 31). However, one specific legacy of Solidarity's role is visible in that protest actions remain the most characteristic and popular form of political participation in Poland.

The low indicators of participation and activeness of Poles in voluntary organizations, after the beginning of Poland's democratic transformations, did not meet the expectations of those who participated in the 'Solidarity' movement. They are explained above all by Poland's cultural tradition of strong family ties. That is, Poland can be counted among the most family oriented societies and, simultaneously, those with a low degree of confidence in outside organizations—'a low trust familistic society' in Fukuyama's terminology. It can also be explained by structural societal differences between the ruling elites, workers, and peasants. These have left strong resentments and have a destructive effect upon the structures of a civil society (Szawiel, 2001). In spite of the reality of these characteristics of Polish society, they do not explain the causes of the large decline in the past decade of social participation and activeness in voluntary organizations as well as of interpersonal trust and confidence in institutions. To find an explanation, it would be necessary to consider carefully changes in citizens' confidence in institutions and organizations. This is formed—as Mishler and Rose (2001) indicate—not so much by the effect of cultural traditions as by an appraisal of the effects of these institutions' and organizations' functioning. The political life in Poland during 1990–1999 and the effects of the political transformations on the life of an average citizen have not stimulated a positive appraisal. As a result, large resources of social capital have been wasted.

7   *Conclusion*

The formation of a civil society is determined by a complex combination of interrelated processes of economic development, the establishment of democratic institutions and political freedoms, the creation of a normative consensus on the moral principles regulating social co-existence, and participation and co-operation within the framework of public and state institutions. A crucial part in the development of civil society is played by social capital—a set of voluntary associations, consisting of social networks and related values and norms, that facilitate cooperation and have an effect on community productivity and well-being (Coleman, 1988; Putnam, 1998). According to the theory of social capital, engagement in associational networks is related to such values, attitudes, and behavioral patterns as political involvement, confidence in institutions, trust in people, support of civic morality norms, the creation and maintenance of a wide range of social ties, concern for others (not only those closest to one), and the feeling of control over one's life. All of these qualities stimulate citizens' self-organization and their engaging in voluntary social activity. Voluntary participation in associations has, in turn, a feedback effect, leading to the internalization of these attitudes, to economic growth and to the preservation of democracy.

The task of our analysis was to verify some hypotheses derived from a theoretical framework that rests on the concepts of 'civil society' and 'social capital'.

Our comparative analyses of voluntary membership and activity in social organizations in various regions of Europe support Putnam's thesis that social capital is strongly related to indicators of socio-economic development (HDI) and to institutional indicators of democcratization (CL). Contrary to Norris' findings from the mid-1990s World Value Surveys that 'it is only social trust that is significantly related to socioeconomic development and at the same time there is little evidence that these developmental indicators related systematically to the propensity to belong to voluntary organizations and associational activism' (Norris, 2000: 12), the 1999 EVS data gave evidence of the latter relationship that operates both on the individual and on the national level.

The Index of Economic Freedom has a positive effect on organizational membership at the national level but a negative effect at the individual level. It has a positive impact on voluntary activity at both levels. The free play of market forces does not stimulate citizens to join organizations, although it does not dissuade those who already belong from being active. This result corresponds with Dietrich and Marilyn Rueschemeyers' and Bjorn Wittrock's conclusions: 'The freedom of choice associated with the market economy is often seen as closely akin to political freedom and democracy. Both, it is claimed, reinforce each other. Yet the relationship appears in reality to be much more complex' (1998: 270). As they point out: 'While democratization in Eastern Europe opens up new possibilities and meaningful targets of social and political participation, marketization tends to undercut collective organization, at least in the short run' (Ibid.: 281). Their analysis of the most successful cases of voluntary participation in the welfare states of Northwestern Europe leads to the conclusion that 'opposite of the neoliberal tenet that popular participation and state action are inversely related, (. . .) comprehensive welfare state policies seem to protect, rather than destroy, the conditions underlying vigorous social and political participation' (Ibid.: 276, 281).

Our main hypothesis about interdependence of voluntary associational membership and activity on the one hand and socioeconomic development, democratization, the growth of free market forces, and endorsement of civic morality on the other received only partial support in our analyses. We did not find acceptance of civic morality norms among predictors of membership in voluntary organizations neither at the cross-national nor at the individual level. Civic morality appears as a predictor of individuals' activity in an overall European sample and in some countries where activity is particularly high, as in Slovakia.

The interpretation of this missing relationship between organizational membership and civic morality can be linked with debates about the positive and negative function of associations that could be used for different purposes, as financial capital can be used for producing bread or guns. 'It is difficult to differentiate between positive and negative examples provided by real, quasi, and pseudo NGOs. Jocular acronyms give a first impression of these variations among organizations that call themselves NGOs and civil society organizations. There are quasi NGOs (QUANGOs), donor-driven ones (DONGOs), money-making organizations (MONGOs), Mafia-led NGOs (MANGOs), and simply fake 'nongovernmental' organizations (FANGOs)'. (Miszlevetz & Jensen, 1998: 93). These differences cannot be explored on the basis of the EVS data, but finding the missing relationship with civic morality indicates a need for such exploration.

Cross nationally, our analysis reveals a number of significant inter-related structural and cultural factors, including a higher level of human development, civil liberty, economic freedom, propensity to participate in political protest, widespread feeling of a freedom of choice and control over life, trust in other people, confidence in trade unions, rejection of the belief that social justice entails economic equality, perception that human rights are respected, and the positive rating of the system of governance. These factors characterize the political culture of the European nations that are rich in social capital and develop a strong civil society.

The results confirm the hypotheses about structural conditions and personal interests and values that stimulate and motivate voluntary activities of individuals. Citizens join voluntary organizations and work on their behalf because 1) they find opportunities for civic engagement provided by the level of socio-economic development and civil liberty in their countries, 2) they are stimulated by their cognitive skills (level of education) and gender-role patterns, and 3) they are motivated by their interest in politics, involvement in public affairs, unwillingness to eliminate economic inequalities, and support for civic morality. They are also encouraged to participate in voluntary activities by their trust in people, confidence in institutions related to specific spheres of their activity, maintaining informal linkages with colleagues, the feeling of competence and control over own life, and the perception that human rights are respected in their country. These factors increase the potential for citizens to mobilize resources through a social network and to contribute to accumulation of social capital in their societies.

The 1999 EVS data reveal dramatic differences in the level of associational membership and voluntary activity between European nations in different regions with distinctive patterns of historical, institutional, and cultural traditions. Further analyses exploring the causes for the various changes that have occurred in certain countries and regions of Europe in the last decade, including detailed case studies of the nations that were successful in expanding their social capital as well as the nations that have wasted or lost it, are necessary to establish which factors contribute to diminishing the inequalities and contrasts in the distribution of social capital across countries.

References

Almond, G.A. & S. Verba 1963. *The Civic Culture. Political Attitudes and Democracy in Five Nations.* Princeton: Princeton University Press.

Banfield, E.C. 1958. *The Moral Basis of the Backward Society*, New York: The Free Press.

Bryant, C.G.A. 1995. Transformation and continuity in contemporary Britain. Pp. 277–292 in C.G.A. Bryant & E. Mokrzycki (eds.), *Democracy, Civil Society and Pluralism in Comparative perspective: Poland, Great Britain and the Netherlands.* Warsaw: IFiS Publishers.

—— & E. Mokrzycki 1995. Introduction: Democracies in context. Pp. 9–33 in C.G.A. Bryant & E. Mokrzycki (eds.), *Democracy, Civil Society and Pluralism in Comparative perspective: Poland, Great Britain and the Netherlands.* Warsaw: IFiS Publishers.

Dekker, P. & A. van den Broek 1996. Volunteering and politics: Involvement in voluntary associations from a 'Civic Culture' perspective. Pp. 125–151 in L. Halman & N. Nevitte (eds.), *Political Values Change in Western Democracies. Integration, Values, Identification, and Participation.* Tilburg: Tilburg University Press.

De Tocqueville, A. [1835–1840] 1990. *Democracy in America*, New York: Random House.

Diez Medrano, J. 1996. Does Western Europe stop at the Pyrenees? Pp. 103–122 in L. Halman & N. Nevitte (eds.), *Political Values Change in Western Democracies: Integration, Values, Identification, and Participation.* Tilburg: Tilburg University Press.

Fialova, Z. 1999. *Political Culture as the Main Factor Influencing the Development of Civil Society in Post-communist Slovakia.* PhD Dissertation. Warsaw: IPS PAS.

Fukuyama, F. 1995. *Trust. The Social Virtues and the Creation of Prosperity*, New York: The Free Press.

Halman, L. 2001. *The European Values Study: A Third Wave. Source book of the 1999/2000 European Values Surveys.* Tilburg: EVS, WORC, Tilburg University.

Heunks, F. 1996. Patterns of social and political integration. Pp. 15–31 in L. Halman & N. Nevitte (eds.), *Political Values Change in Western Democracies. Integration, Values, Identification, and Participation.* Tilburg: Tilburg University Press.

Illner, M. 1998. Local democratization in the Czech Republic after 1989. Pp. 51–82 in D. Rueschemeyer, M. Rueschemeyer & B. Wittrock (eds.), *Participation and Democracy East and West: Comparisons and Interpretations.* Armonk, NY: M.E. Sharpe.

Juchler, J. 1999. The transition in Eastern Europe: Economic and political changes in a comparative perspective. Pp. 151–169 in A. Jasińska-Kania, M. Kohn & K. Słomczyński (eds.), *Power and Social Structure.* Warszawa: Wydawnictwo Uniwersytetu Warszawskiego.

Mischler, W. & R. Rose 2001. What are the origins of political trust? Testing institutional and cultural theories in Post-Communist societies. *Comparative Political Studies* 34 (1): 30–62.

Miszlivetz, F. & J. Jensen 1998. An emerging paradox: Civil society from above?. Pp. 83–98 in D. Rueschemeyer, M. Rueschemeyer & B. Wittrock (eds.), *Participation and Democracy East and West: Comparisons and Interpretations*. Armonk, NY: M.E. Sharpe.

Norris, P. 2000. *Making Democracies Work: Social Capital and Civic Engagement in 47 Societies*. Paper for the European Science Foundation EURESCO Conference on Social Capital: Interdisciplinary Perspectives at the University od Exeter, 15–20 September.

Ondrusek, D. & V. Labath 1997. Conflicts in transforming society and the non-governmental Sector: The Slovak example. *The Annals of the American Academy of Political and Social Sciences* 552: 40–51.

Putnam, R.D. 1993. *Making Democracy Work: Civic Traditions in Modern Italy*. Princeton: Princeton University Press.

—— 1995. Bowling alone: America's declining social capital. *Journal of Democracy* 6/1: 65–78.

Rau, Z. (Ed.) 1991. *The Re-emergence of Civil Society in Eastern Europe and the Soviet Union*. Boulder CO: Westview Press.

Rueschemeyer, D., M. Rueschemeyer & B. Wittrock 1998. Conclusion: Contrasting patterns of participation and democracy. Pp. 266–284 in D. Rue-schemeyer, M. Rueschemeyer & B. Wittrock (eds.), *Participation and Democracy East and West: Comparisons and Interpretations*. Armonk, NY: M.E. Sharpe.

Rychard, A. 1998. Institutions and actors in a new democracy: The vanishing legacy of communist and solidarity types of participation in Poland. Pp. 26–50 in: D. Rueschemeyer, M. Rueschemeyer & B. Wittrock (eds.), *Participation and Democracy East and West: Comparisons and Interpretations*. Armonk, NY: M.E. Sharpe.

Smith-Siversten, H. 2000. Civil society and the Baltic States: Participation and NGOs. Pp. 222–242 in F. Aarebrot & T. Knutsen (eds.), *Politics and Citizenship on the Eastern Baltic Seaboard*. Kristansand: Hoyskoleforlaget AS—Nordic Academic Press.

Szacki, J. 1995. *Liberalism after Communism*. Budapest, London, New York: CEU Press.

Szawiel, T. 2001. *Uwarunkowania demokracji w Polsce postkomunistycznej: społeczeństwo obywatelskie, podziały ideowe, struktura społeczna* (Conditions for Democracy in Post-communist Poland: Civil Society, Ideological Cleavages, and Social Structure). PhD Dissertation. Warszawa: IS UW.

Van Deth, J.W. & F. Kreuter 1998. Membership of voluntary associations. Pp. 135–155 in Jan W. van Deth (ed.), *Comparative Politics. The Problem of Equivalence*. London: Routledge.

CHAPTER SIX

SOCIAL VALUES, PREJUDICE AND SOLIDARITY IN THE EUROPEAN UNION

JORGE VALA, MARCUS LIMA & DINIZ LOPES

1 *Introduction*

According to the UNO forecasts, the EU will have to receive 1.3 million immigrants each year, the equivalent to 32,5 million immigrants in the next 25 years, if it wants to maintain its economic growth and its welfare system. Even if the forecasts of international agencies regarding labour requirements are excessive, the number of new immigrants that Europe will take in should necessarily remain high. Will Europeans be open to take in these new immigrants and to help them integrate into the European society?

A number of findings lead us to believe that, nowadays, open prejudice is perceived as anti-normative in Europe.[1] In fact, the end of the Second World War and the unveiling of the horrors of a racist state, the Human Rights Declaration (1948), the UNESCO Declaration on Race (1951), social movements of various kinds in Europe, the civil rights movement of the African-Americans and the African liberation movements set in motion a process which gradually made racial discrimination illegal and racial beliefs anti-normative. But although racism became anti-normative, negative beliefs in relation to immigrants and towards people seen as belonging to different races or cultures still persist. According to the Eurobarometer n° 47.1 (Ben Brika, Lemaine & Jackson, 1997; Deschamps & Lemaine, 2001), and a survey carried out by the European Monitoring Centre on Racism and Xenophobia (Thalhammer, Zucha, Enzenhofer, Salfinger &

---

[1] According to EVS results intolerance against people of 'another race' or against immigrants was, in 1990, respectively: 10% and 13%. In 1999 these figures were similar: 10% in the case of people of 'other race' and 11% in the case of immigrants. For a detailed analysis, see Halman (1994)

Ogris, 2001), 48% of Europeans in 1997 and 52% in 2000 consider that people of 'other races, cultures or religions', 'take illegitimate advantage of the social welfare system'; 64 % in 1997 and 58% in 2000 believe that such people 'are more often involved in crime than the average person'; 46% in 1997 and 52% in 2000, consider that 'in schools where there are too many children from these minority groups, the quality of education suffers'. Open prejudice, manifest racism and xenophobia are therefore a problem that still persists in Europe today. According to these results, the behaviour of immigrants and of minority groups is perceived as being different from the behaviour of the majority. It is seen as a problem, it creates concerns, and it is viewed as transgression and as an abuse.

Prejudice gains new meaning at a time when Europe needs more immigrants, when there is a growing pressure of non-European citizens trying to enter European countries, and when European borders remain closed. How many Europeans are aware that since 1997 an estimated 6,000 people have died trying to get into Europe? This problem is particularly salient in some EU countries like Spain, Italy, and Portugal, traditionally countries of emigration rather than immigration. How do the Spanish react to the deaths of immigrants occurring on the beaches of southern Spain? And how do the Italians react to immigrants' death on the beaches of the Adriatic? What do the Portuguese think of the 150,000 immigrants from Eastern Europe who entered Portugal over the last two years, in the wake of those who came from Africa? And what do Italians have to say about the fact that 14,000 of the 56,000 people arrested in Italian prisons are immigrants?

The social sciences in general and social psychology in particular have been giving in recent years a great deal of attention to the new expressions of prejudice. These are based not so much on the notion of race and racial inferiority, but on the idea of culture and on the hierarchy of cultures. These new forms of expressing prejudice have been labelled subtle racism in Europe (see Pettigrew & Meertens, 1995) and symbolic or modern racism in the USA (see McConahay, 1986).[2]

---

[2] Despite their small differences, we will use the words open, blatant, traditional or old-fashioned prejudice as equivalents. All these terms refer a prejudice or a racist attitude rooted in the idea of race and racial hierarchies. We also use the words modern, symbolic, subtle or covert prejudice as equivalents. For the conceptual differences between these concepts see Brown (1995).

Moreover, and in order to understand why racism and discrimination persist in societies that are formally anti-racist, several models in social psychology have also studied the indirect or unintentional forms of racism, and even its unconscious or automatic expression (for a review, see Dovidio, Kawakami, Johson, Johnson & Howard, 1997). But the attention given to these new forms of racism and xenophobia has had the indirect effect of making people forget that overt racism persists and, at the same time, that there are also egalitarian and non-differentialist positions or, in other words, that racism is not inevitable.

In this chapter we will look at overt prejudice, specifically to the dimension of overt prejudice and racism that associates minorities, people perceived as culturally different, and immigrants with economic threat. We will also look at attitudes of solidarity towards these people. In the first part, we will compare these positive and negative orientations towards minority groups in countries that represent two different traditions in relation to migrations. We will look at Germany, Belgium and France as examples of countries with traditionally net immigration. We will then look at Spain, Portugal and Italy as examples of European countries that moved from being countries of net emigration to being new host countries for immigrants.

In the second part of this chapter, we will analyse positional variables and social values underlying prejudice and solidarity. In fact, while measures of prejudice in the European Values Study (EVS) questionnaire are few (Halman, 2001), this survey is a valuable source in terms of data on social values. It is therefore an excellent database for studying the predictors of prejudice, in particular those related to egalitarian and meritocracy values.

2   Overt prejudice and solidarity in countries with a tradition of emigration and of immigration

Three kinds of beliefs underlie traditional overt prejudice and are frequently identified in several studies in this domain (e.g., Pederson & Walker, 1997; Pettigrew & Meertens, 1995). One belief supposes the existence of superior and inferior human races. Another supports the idea that people perceived as belonging to other races or cultures represent an economic threat. A third belief sustains that these people are also a threat to the personal security of citizens of the host society.

Although the 1999 EVS questionnaire does not contain specific questions on these set of racial beliefs, it includes two measures of general overt prejudice: a classic measure of social distance (the rejection of members of a group on account of the perception of this group as racially, culturally or religiously different); and a measure of the perception of immigrants as an economic threat.

As referred, we will look at the answers to these questions obtained in the two groups of countries discussed above—Germany, Belgium, France and Spain, Portugal, and Italy. Our hypothesis is that the different experience of these countries with migrations will result in different attitudes towards immigrants. Specifically, a tradition of emigration, observed in countries like Spain, Portugal, and Italy, may generate more tolerance and greater solidarity towards immigrants. The social memory of the experience of emigration and the great number of people with direct or indirect experience of emigration can generate a sense of identification with immigrants and consequently positive attitudes towards them. However, these same countries are not used to dealing with immigrants and their adaptation problems, and are also economically less developed and less stable. Consequently, they can develop anxiety and fear towards immigrants coming from non-European countries and can see them as an economic threat.

Could it be that countries where there is highest orientation towards discrimination are also those where there is lowest solidarity? This question derives from the assumption according to which prejudiced attitudes may be conceptualised as ambivalent. This means that a target of a prejudiced attitude may also be the target of solidary behaviour. Katz and Hass (1988) show how prejudiced attitudes are complex, consisting of a mixture of feelings of friendliness and rejection. Moreover, some psychological models suggest that the motivational factors underlying a positive evaluation of a given stimulus may differ from those underlying a negative evaluation of that stimulus (Cacioppo, Gardner & Berntson, 1997). Consequently, our hypothesis is that countries that discriminate less are not necessarily those that manifest higher solidarity.

2.1   Method

The first question under study is, thus, a classic measure of social distance or general prejudice. The groups included in this question on the EVS belong to three different categories:[3] stigmatised people (e.g. people who are mentally disturbed, people with a criminal past), political categories (right and left-wing extremists), and categories of racialised or ethnicised people. This latter category, which is the one we will analyse in this chapter, is constituted by 'people of a different race', 'immigrants or foreign workers', 'Muslims', 'Jews' and 'Gypsies'.

The second question we analysed measuring overt prejudice concerns the perception of immigrants as an economic threat. Specifically, this measure assesses subjects' orientation towards job discrimination of immigrants.[4]

Concerning attitudes of social solidarity towards immigrants, we analysed two EVS items. One item measures the orientation towards hosting immigrants from non-EU countries,[5] i.e., the solidarity towards immigrants at the level of immigration policies. The other item measures personal orientation towards supporting the improvement of immigrants' living conditions.[6]

2.2 Results

Table 6.1 shows that the countries studied in this chapter are significantly different according to the number of rejected racialised or ethnicised groups.[7] Indeed, the highest number of rejected groups was found in Italy, followed by Belgium. Former Western Germany[8] is the country with the lowest levels of rejection of immigrants or racialised groups. Portugal and Spain are in an intermediate position.[9] Note

---

[3] The question was as follows: 'On this list are various groups of people. Could you please sort out any that you would not like to have as neighbours?' Respondents could choose more than one group.

[4] This measure asked subjects: 'Do you agree or disagree with the following statement—when the jobs are scarce, employers should give priority to . . . (nationality) . . . people over immigrants'. Agree (3), Neither agree nor disagree (2), disagree (1).

[5] The question was the following: 'How about people from less developed countries coming here to work. Which one of the following measures do you think the government should do?' 1—Anyone can come who wants to; 2—Come when jobs are available; 3—Strict limits on the number of foreigners; 4—Prohibit people coming here.

[6] 'Would you be prepared to actually do something to improve the conditions of immigrants in your country?' 5—absolutely yes, 1—absolutely no.

[7] The number of rejected groups could vary between none (0) and 5.

[8] Given that we obtained significant differences between the two German samples, and according to our hypothesis, we only took into account the responses from former West Germany.

[9] In all of these countries, the most rejected group is the gypsies (percentage of

that the mean of rejected groups in all European countries is different from zero.[10] At country level, the mean of rejected groups is also different from zero.[11]

Concerning attitudes towards job discrimination, Italy, Portugal and Spain,[12] countries with an emigration tradition, agree more with the idea that when jobs are scarce, employers should give priority to natives. German, Belgium and French people show more agreement with immigrants' rights of non-job discrimination (Table 6.2).

Note that despite the differences in the responses to both questions analysed above, they are moderately correlated at the EU level ($r = .25$, $p < .000$). Furthermore, and although the differences between countries concerning job discrimination and group rejection are statistically significant, their associated effect sizes are small, meaning that differences between countries are not strong.

Table 6.1   Rejection of racialised or ethnicised groups—EVS 1999

	M	SD
Former West Germany	0,52[a]	0,89
France	0,83[bc]	1,21
Spain	0,68[ab]	1,25
Portugal	0,67[ab]	0,98
Belgium	0,94[c]	1,42
Italy	1,12[d]	1,34

Number of rejected groups ranging from 0 to 5. $F (5, 9390) = 61,425$, $p < .000$; Eta Squared = .03; means with different subscripts are statistically different.

rejection between 32% and 56%). In all of the countries, excepting Portugal, the second most rejected group is the Muslims (20% to 11% of rejections). In Portugal, the Jews are the second most rejected group (11%). Note that 'Jew' in Portugal, in everyday language, also means a person that harms other people (for instance, a mischievous child is a 'boy rabbi'). Note also that in Portugal Arabs and Muslims are not designated as 'muslims', as in the questionnaire, but as 'Moorish'. Perhaps for these reasons, and also for historical factors linked to social memory, Jews and not Muslims are, in Portugal, the second most rejected group. The category 'people of other races' is more rejected in Belgium (14%) and in Italy (16%) but less in Germany (5%). These results refer to blatant prejudice and therefore indicate the strength of the anti-blatant racism norm in these countries.

[10] EU: $M = 0.79$, $SD = 1.26$; $t (19600) = 87.175$, $p < 0.000$
[11] Former West Germany: $t (1651) = 23.87$, $p < 0.000$; France: $t (1614) = 27.42$, $p < 0.000$; Spain: $t (1199) = 18,766$, $p < 0.000$; Portugal: $t (999) = 21.55$, $p < 0.000$; Belgium: $t (1911) = 29.18$, $p < 0.000$; Italy: $t (1999) = 38.15$, $p < 0.000$.
[12] Percentage of agreement with job discrimination: France—54%; Germany—59%; Belgium—51%; Portugal—63%; Spain- 65%; Italy—61%.

Table 6.2   Job discrimination—EVS 1999

	M	SD
Former West Germany	2,22^c	0,92
France	2,18^{ca}	0,93
Spain	2,45^b	0,80
Portugal	2,41^b	0,83
Belgium	2,07^a	0,97
Italy	2,41^b	0,80

Scale: agree (3), disagree (1).; F (5, 9133) = 48,349, p<.000; Eta Squared = .03.

As shown in Table 6.3, orientation towards active personal solidarity in order to improve immigrants' living conditions is higher in Spain and in Italy, countries that are traditionally emigrant countries.[13]

Concerning solidarity at the level of immigration policies (Table 6.4), the countries showing less solidarity are former West Germany, France and Belgium. Portugal and Spain show more solidarity. In fact, they are the less restrictive countries concerning immigration policies, with Italy occupying an intermediate position.[14] Thus, the expression of solidarity is higher in the traditionally emigrant countries. However, as previously shown, these countries are also those that express more orientation towards discrimination at the job level (Table 6.2).[15] Analysing the European countries as a whole, we found a positive correlation between the two items measuring social solidarity ($r = .34$, $p < .000$).

In order to compare discrimination and solidarity attitudes in the analysed countries, and in order to test our hypothesis concerning specific patterns of attitudes in traditionally immigrant host countries and traditionally emigrant countries, a cluster analysis was carried out (Figure 6.1). This cluster analysis was based on the four questions we analysed, and shows that Belgium, France and Germany are closer to each other than to the other three countries. Despite Italy's particular position, this country is closer to Spain and Portugal than to the other countries.

---

[13] Percentage of people answering yes (to solidarity): France: 23%; Germany: 24%; Belgium: 31%; Portugal: 21%; Spain: 36%; Italy: 46%.

[14] Percentage of people approving strict limits or prohibition of immigration: France: 61%; Germany: 63%; Belgium: 60%; Portugal: 27%; Spain: 24%; Italy: 43%.

[15] Values for these variables at the EU level: personal solidarity—M = 3.06, SD = 0.97; solidarity at the level of immigration policies—M = 2.48, SD = 0.73.

Table 6.3   Personal solidarity—EVS 1999

	M	SD
Former West Germany	2,98[a]	0,87
France	2,75[b]	1,15
Spain	3,29[c]	0,76
Portugal	2,96[a]	0,93
Belgium	2,95[a]	1,14
Italy	3,39[c]	0,81

Scale: 'Absolutely yes' (5) to 'absolutely no' (1). F (5,9196) = 99,976, p < .000; Eta Squared =.05;

Table 6.4   Attitudes towards Immigration policies—EVS 1999

	M	SD
Former West Germany	2,64[a]	0,66
France	2,66[a]	0,74
Spain	2,08[b]	0,71
Portugal	2,19[b]	0,69
Belgium	2,60[a]	0,74
Italy	2,38[c]	0,72

Scale: 'Anyone can come who wants to' (1) to 'prohibit people coming here' (4). F (5, 9004) = 153,384, p < .000; Eta Squared = .08.

In general, these results show that the experience of emigration and immigration shapes different patterns of attitudes. People from Belgium, France and Germany, traditionally immigrant countries, show less solidarity but more egalitarianism concerning job rights. On the contrary, Portugal, Italy and Spain, traditionally emigrant countries, show greater solidarity but more job discrimination. Thus, we can suppose that this feeling of solidarity is framed within the memories of emigration and that job discrimination attitudes are anchored in the perception of economic threat.

3   Predictors of prejudice in EU countries: the role of values of egalitarianism and meritocratic individualism

The previous section showed that different migration experiences can be related with different attitudes towards immigrants and minorities. Using a wide range of variables, we will now look to a more systematic analysis of the social and psychological factors underlying prejudice.

Figure 6.1   Blatant prejudice and attitudes towards solidarity

Hierarchical cluster analysis:
Dendrogram using average linkage (between groups)

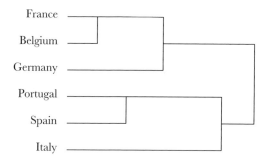

These variables were chosen according to their theoretical relevance, their association with prejudice measures in previous studies, and their independent association with at least one of our dependent variables.[16] They were classified into the following groups: positional variables; psychological individual differences; individual differences concerning orientations towards the political system; political identity; national identity; social and political values; and egalitarian values vs. meritocratic individualism.[17] Below we present a brief review of research on prejudice and discrimination that justifies the inclusion of these variables in this study, even though their effects are often controversial.

Positional variables. Age, schooling and income were the variables included on this group. *Age* has been associated to prejudice, both as a life-cycle indicator and as an indicator of generation effect, even though several studies do not show clear effects of this variable. Some researches carried out in the USA (see McConahay & Hough, 1976)

---

[16] For each independent variable, and before their inclusion in the regression analyses, correlational or variance analyses were performed in order to verify if their association with, at least, one of the dependent variables was statistically significant. These analyses were performed at the EU level.

[17] Excepting egalitarian and meritocratic values, the remaining variables are relatively common in correlational studies on prejudice. Some of this kind of studies showed (e.g., Pettigrew & Meertens, 1995) that interpersonal contact and relative intergroup deprivation are important predictors of prejudice. Unfortunately these variables were not included in the EVS. Moreover, experimental studies also showed the role of basic cognitive processes in the activation of prejudice (for a review see Fiske, 1998). Similarly, this kind of variables was not considered in the EVS.

and in Europe (see Pettigrew, & Meertens, 1995) show that the older a person is, the more likely the exhibit of racial attitudes. But in the study of Pettigrew and Meertens the effect sizes of age are not homogeneous across samples. For example, in Britain, and contrary to the European pattern, the greater the age the lesser the probability of prejudice. Moreover, in Portugal a study on racism towards Blacks (Vala et al., 1999) found that age had no effect on the expression of prejudice; and Pedersen and Walker (1997), in a study on prejudice towards the aborigines, also found no significant association between age and prejudice.

Regarding *educational level*, many studies show an association between this variable and prejudice (for a review, see Wagner & Zick, 1995). But in some other studies, this variable is not relevant (Pedersen & Walker, 1997), or its relevance is only demonstrated in predicting the traditional forms of racism (Vala et al., 1999). From an empirical point of view, the mediators of the effects of educational level haven't received that much attention. However, it does seem plausible that low levels of education should be associated with lower cognitive flexibility and complexity, which would make those with lower schooling levels more likely to accept the ideological simplicity of traditional racism (Tetlock, 1985). Consequently, the effect of this variable is unlikely to be noticed in cases of subtle racism, which is a more complex form of expressing prejudice. Such a hypothesis was verified in a study of Vala and colleagues (1999). Nevertheless, it should be noted that when high levels of schooling are associated with political conservatism, this combination might encourage approval of open forms of racism.

The third variable in this group is *income*. Income may be conceived as an indicator of objective deprivation and economic frustration. If one follows the argument underlying frustration-aggression theory hypothesis, as it was first formulated by Dollard, Doob, Miller, Mowrer and Sears (1939), economic frustration may, in certain circumstances, lead to aggression against members of minority groups. In fact, these authors analyse racism as an aggression by one economically deprived group against another group judged as responsible for their economical deprivation. This aggression is not aimed at the target which triggers deprivation (for example, the economic system or the ruling classes) but rather at a target which is perceived as responsible for that deprivation (for example, Blacks or immigrants). That target is usually a vulnerable group. This hypothesis came to be known as the scapegoat hypothesis (Hovland & Sears, 1940).

In sum and according to the studies described above, a correlation between age and open prejudice is not probable, but we should expect that the lower the educational level or the income the greater the open or blatant prejudice.

Psychological individual differences. At this level of analysis we looked at two variables included in the EVS questionnaire: life (in)satisfaction and interpersonal trust. *Life(in)satisfaction* may be interpreted as a measure of frustration and, like income, may be associated with discrimination, as we explained above. Concerning *interpersonal trust*, it is a dimension of authoritarian personality in the theory of Adorno, Frenkel-Brunswick, Levinson and Sanford (1950) and, consequently, a factor that may be associated to prejudice, as predicted by this theory.

Individual differences regarding the political system. Recently, attitudes towards immigrants began to be viewed as part of a more widespread negative reaction to the political system, and also as derived from a feeling of insecurity brought about by the perception that political institutions are not effective in protecting citizens. In this chapter, these attitudes are evaluated through measures of *confidence in political institutions* and *satisfaction with democracy* that are dimensions of political efficacy, a factor that has been linked to prejudice. In particular, Pettigrew (1999), in a study on the predictors of racism in Europe, shows an association between the feeling of political efficacy and prejudice. In other words, his results present evidence that the less a person feels able to influence the political system, the less the trust in political system, and the less the perception that this system reflects the interests of citizens, the greater the prejudice. In this study we revisit this hypothesis.

Political identity. Since the research on prejudice by Adorno et al. (1950), and more recently by Altemeyer (1994), political identity, or individual positioning in the *left wing/right wing* political spectrum, has usually been taken into account as a variable in studies on racism and xenophobia. Moreover, the simple observation of the political arena also shows that it is on the extreme right wing that we find positions that most clearly reject immigration and that are openly racist. In fact, in European countries, official policy regarding minorities and immigrants has varied systematically according to the ideological (left/right) orientation of political parties, with those on the left generally adopting more open policies towards immigration. This seems to be reflected in the positions of individuals who state they are more to the left or more to the right of the political spectrum.

Indeed Pettigrew and Meertens' study (1995) shows that political positioning is a good predictor of racism. However, left political parties have in recent times argued in favour of the so-called realistic (restrictive) immigration policies. This new position can contribute to change the traditional relationship between political identity and racism or xenophobic prejudice, as empirically found by Pederson and Walker (1997) in Australia, and by Vala and colleagues (1999) in Portugal. In the present study, however, once the measure of prejudice used is a measure of blatant prejudice we should expect that the more the identification with the right-wing political spectrum the more likely are the prejudiced attitudes.

National identity. We propose the hypothesis that the more prominent a national identity (measured in terms of national pride) is, the greater the orientation towards racism and xenophobia. In fact, national identity is usually experienced as an exclusive and not an inclusive identity. For example, despite the fact that the association between national identity and prejudice is not among the strongest associations found by Pettigrew and Meertens (1995), and even though there are some differences between European samples concerning this association, these authors do find an association between national identity and prejudice.

Nevertheless, the study by Pedersen and Walker (1997) carried out in Australia found an association between national identity and modern racism towards aborigines, but not between national identity and traditional racism. At the same time, it should be noted that Inglehart (1995), in a study covering 43 countries, found a clear association between national identity and conservatism, but not between national identity and ethnocentrism.

Other results, reported by Duckitt and Mphuthing (1998), suggest that the concept of national identity is a multi-dimensional concept, and that we should distinguish between 'patriotism' (a strong emotional attachment to one's country) and 'nationalism' (a strong orientation towards competitiveness in international comparisons). According to their results, it is only nationalism that correlates with ethnocentrism. Also in the United Kingdom, Dowds and Young (1997) showed that only exclusive nationalism was positively correlated with xenophobia.[18]

---

[18] According to a new interpretation (Mummendey, 1995) of the Tajfel's Social Identity Theory (Tajfel & Turner, 1979), ingroup identification may trigger ingroup

Despite these conceptual specifications, we can assume that national identity is more often associated with exclusive beliefs, and that, consequently, the more the national pride the more probable the exhibition of prejudice.

Social and political values. We considered three dimensions of social and political values: *moral conservatism, political conservatism* and *materialistic/post-materialistic* orientations. The distinction between moral and political conservatism derives from the hypothesis that, at least as far as prejudice is concerned, these two aspects of conservatism may produce different results. For instance results reported by Vala et al. (1999) show a clear association between moral conservatism and racism, but not between political conservatism and racism. This result may be just a reflection of the specific ideological context in Portugal, or it may be an indicator of change in attitudes identified by Adorno and colleagues in the fifties. In relation to post-materialistic/materialistic values, the study by Inglehart (1997) shows that the more the adhesion to materialistic values the more the orientation towards discrimination, even though the measures used in his data tap overt prejudice. In summary, we should expect a positive correlation between moral conservatism and prejudice, and a negative correlation between this attitude and the support of post-materialistic values.

Values of egalitarianism and meritocratic individualism. The variables mentioned above have been analysed in numerous studies on prejudice and racism. However, little attention has been given to the role played by *egalitarian* values and *meritocratic individualism* in generating and legitimising prejudice and racist beliefs.

In European culture there is a profound ambivalence between the egalitarian values on which modernity is based and the values of competition and meritocratic individualism on which economic success is supposed to be based. According to our hypothesis, the former generate solidarity and anti-racism, and the latter generate a hierarchisation of human groups and an orientation towards competition and discrimination. Some studies support this hypothesis. For instance, in a transnational research project Doise, Clémence, and Spini (1999) found a positive association between the values of universalism and

favouritism but not outgroup derogation (for instance, prejudice or racism). In this line, the hypothesis of Duckitt and Mphuthing (1998) suggest that national identification triggers outgroup derogation only if accompanied by orientations towards competition.

egalitarianism and the belief in Human Rights. Schwartz (1996), in a recent review on the study of human values, describes various studies which show that the values of universalism and benevolence (for example, equality, social justice and intellectual openness) are associated with openness to inter-group contact. These same studies show that values of power and achievement, which are close to the pattern generally designated as meritocratic individualism (for example, orientation towards power, social recognition and ambition), are predictors of competitive strategies in inter-group relationships. In Portugal, a representative correlational study (Vala et al., 1999) shows that the belief in meritocratic justice, as opposed to the norm of egalitarianism, is a significant predictor of subtle racism. Katz and Hass (1988) put forward the idea that a tension between values of egalitarianism and meritocratic individualism is the foundation of ambivalent attitudes towards Blacks. Moreover this hypothesis takes up the approach to the analysis of racism in the USA proposed in the middle of the last century by Myrdal (1944) in a work entitled 'An American Dilemma'. In this work, Myrdal analyses racism in the context of the conflict between a belief in humanist egalitarianism and the pressure of personal interests. But, as Schwartz (1996) demonstrates, the conflict between the values of universalism and the values of meritocracy and power is not a conflict that is specific to the USA, and may therefore be relevant in explaining racism in other social and cultural contexts.

In agreement with this line of thought, we expect that the more the orientation to meritocratic values and the lesser the orientation to egalitarian values the more likely is the prejudice. In order to test this hypothesis the following variables were used as measures of egalitarian and meritocratic individualistic values: freedom vs. equality, non orientation vs. orientation towards secondary victimization (i.e., considering poor people as personally responsible for their current situation); non orientation vs. orientation towards competition, positive vs. negative attitudes to welfare rights as citizenship rights; and orientation vs. non orientation towards social and community participation.

3.1 Method

In order to analyse the contribution of the referred variables (see Appendix) to predict prejudice and solidarity towards immigrants and people perceived as racially or culturally different, regression analyses were performed.[19] In a first step data was analysed at the level of the EU as a whole, at the level of Portugal as an example of a traditionally emigrant country, and at the level of Belgium as an example of a traditionally host country for immigration.

In a second step, and in order to clarify the effects of egalitarianism and meritocratic individualism *per se* in the activation of prejudice and solidarity, we carried out specific procedures: in the first regression equation we only entered positional variables; in the second we added variables concerning psychological individual differences, and so on. Finally, in the seventh regression equation, all predictor variables were included. Thus, to test against the hypothesis of the importance of egalitarian/meritocratic values in the explanation of prejudice, these last variables were only included in the last regression equation. As these variables were the last ones to enter, their increase of the explained variance is a robust test of their predictive power. These analyses covered all the six selected countries and the EU as a whole.

3.2 *Results*

Considering the first set of results, at the level of EU as a whole (Table 6.5) we can observe that age, interpersonal trust, political identity, materialistic values and secondary victimisation are among the most important predictors of discrimination. These results are in line with most results obtained in the literature on prejudice. Note, moreover, that three of the five egalitarianism indicators are negatively associated with discrimination. Thus, people that don't make secondary victimisation, that defend welfare rights as basic rights, and that declare to be involved in community associations are the ones that express less discrimination against immigrants or minorities.

In Belgium, the pattern of predictors is similar to that of the EU. Moreover also in this case three indicators of egalitarian values are associated to discrimination. Thus, lower levels of discrimination are associated with people that value equality over freedom, that do not

---

[19] Prejudice was measured through a new variable that joins the two indicators of open prejudice presented in the previous part of this paper. Solidarity was also measured through a new variable that integrates the two items of solidarity used.

make secondary victimisation and that are driven toward participation in their community. In Portugal, the number of predictors is more reduced and the explained variance is lower. However, one of the measures of egalitarian values is amongst the best predictors of prejudice. Moreover, note that income is negatively associated with income in Portugal, and in Belgium is not associated to it. It's probable that in Portugal, but not in Belgium, immigrants are seen as an economic threat to the less privileged people.

Concerning social solidarity towards minorities and immigrants, the pattern of predictors in the EU is slightly different from the pattern of predictors of discrimination (Table 6.6). Nevertheless, concerning the indicators of egalitarian values, we can see that, again, they are amongst the best predictors. Thus, a higher manifestation of sol-

Table 6.5   Predictors of blatant prejudice—EVS 1999
Regression analysis

	Discrimination		
	EU	Portugal	Belgium
Positional variables			
Age	.11***	–	.14***
Income	−.04***	−.14**	–
Educational level	−.02*	–	−.12***
Psychological individual differences			
Life satisfaction	−.04***	–	–
Interpersonal trust	−.13***	−.11*	−.11***
Evaluation of political system			
Satisfaction with democracy	−.06***	−.10*	–
Trust in political institutions	−.07***	–	−.06*
Political identity (left/right)	.12***	–	.16***
National identity	.08***	–	–
Socio-political values			
Political conservatism	.07***	–	.11***
Moral conservatism	.07***	–	.07**
Mat./Post-mat. Values.	−.10***	–	−.14***
Egalitarian vs Meritocratic values			
Freedom/equality	–	–	−.08**
Secondary victimization	.10***	–	.11***
Competition	–	–	–
Pro welfare rights	−.05***	−.10*	–
Social and community participation	−.08***	–	−.06*
Adjusted R^2	.19	.07	.24

Note: Values are standardised beta (***p < .000, **p < .01, *p < .05).

Table 6.6   Predictors of solidarity towards immigrants—EVS 1999
Regression analysis

	Solidarity		
	EU	Portugal	Belgium
Positional variables			
Age	–	–	–
Income	–.02*	–	–
Educational level	.14***	–	.12***
Psychological individual differences			
Life satisfaction	.03*	–	–
Interpersonal trust	.11***	.12**	.12***
Evaluation of political system			
Satisfaction with democracy	.05***	–	–
Trust in political institutions	.05*	–	.11***
Political identity (left/right)	–.13***	–	–.18***
National identity	–	–	–
Socio-political values			
Political conservatism	–.09***	–	–.13***
Moral conservatism	–.05***	–	–
Mat./Post-mat. Values.	.10***	–	.09***
Egalitarian vs Meritocratic values			
Freedom/equality	.06***	.11*	–
Secondary victimization	–.09***	–	–.06*
Competition	–	–	–
Pro welfare rights	.04***	.10*	.07**
Social and community participation	.08***	.11*	.12***
Adjusted R^2	.16	.05	.24

Note: Values are standardised beta (***p < .000, **p < .01, *p < .05).

idarity is associated with people that value equality, that do not make secondary victimisation, that defend welfare rights, and that participate in their community.

The pattern of predictors in the Belgium sample is very similar to the European pattern. In the Portuguese sample, there is a clear and stronger association between egalitarian/meritocratic values and attitudes towards solidarity than between these values and the orientation towards discrimination.[20]

---

[20] Since the correlations between the two measures of solidarity as well as of the measures of discrimination were moderate (0.25 and 0.35 respectively), we performed regression analysis for each one of these measures. The results are very similar across the 12 regression analyses performed.

The previous analysis presented some evidence supporting egalitarianism and meritocratic individualism as predictors of solidarity and prejudice. Nevertheless, until now only indirect evidence supported the role of these values in the prediction of prejudice. Consequently, as referred above, we carried out specific procedures in order to clarify the effects of egalitarianism and meritocratic individualism *per se*.

In the case of regressions concerning prejudiced discrimination, the results presented in Table 6.7 show that the most important variables are positional variables, although the remaining groups of variables contribute more than 50% of the explained variance of discrimination. This result shows that the explanations of blatant prejudice based solely on positional variables are clearly insufficient. Furthermore, in all regression analyses, except for Spain, a significant increase of the explained variance occurs when egalitarian/meritocratic values are introduced. The impact of egalitarian/meritocratic values on prejudice seems to be more important at the level of EU, Germany and Belgium, than at the level of Portugal, France, Italy and Spain. This result was not expected in our hypotheses and deserves to be better explored.

In the case of solidarity (Table 6.8), results show that positional variables are less important predictors of solidarity than of blatant prejudice. Results also show a stronger increment of the explained variance when egalitarian/meritocratic values are introduced in the regression models than in the case of blatant prejudice.

4   *Conclusions*

In this chapter we analysed prejudice in the EU towards immigrants or people perceived as belonging to other races, cultures or religions. In the first part of this study, we studied two groups of countries with different traditions regarding to migration. A cluster analysis showed that in countries traditionally receptors of immigrants (former Western Germany, Belgium and France) beliefs were organised differently from countries with an emigration tradition (Portugal, Spain, Italy). These two groups of countries show ambivalent attitudes towards immigrants, but structure their ambivalent attitudes in different ways. Countries with an immigration tradition make less open job discrimination but show less solidarity towards immigrants.

Table 6.7   Predictors of blatant prejudice
Regression analysis (Cumulative Explained Variance)

	EU	Portugal	Belgium	West Germany	France	Italy	Spain
				Discrimination			
Positional variables	6%***	3%***	9%***	8%***	11%***	8%***	6%***
Psychological individual differences	10%***	4%**	12%***	10%***	13%***	12%***	7%**
Evaluation of political system	11%***	5%	12%	10%	13%	12%	7%
Political identity (left/right)	13%***	5%	17%***	12%***	17%***	15%***	9%**
National identity	14%***	5%	18%	12%	18%***	15%	9%
Socio-political values	17%***	6%	21%***	14%***	23%***	17%***	12%**
Egalitarian vs Meritocratic values	19%***	7%*	24%***	18%***	24%***	18%***	12%

Notes: Values are cumulative percentages of explained variance. In the first equation only positional variables were computed. In the following equations variables presented in the previous equations were added. In the final equation all categories of variables are present. Significance of the R^2 change: *** p < .001, ** p < .01, * p < .05

Table 6.8   Predictors of solidarity
Regression analysis (Cumulative Explained Variance)

	EU	Portugal	Belgium	West Germany	France	Italy	Spain
				Solidarity			
Positional variables	5%***	0%	7%***	2%***	7%***	3%***	4%***
Psychological individual differences	8%***	3%**	12%***	4%**	13%***	8%***	6%**
Evaluation of political system	9%***	3%	14%***	4%	13%	9%**	6%
Political identity (left/right)	11%***	3%	19%***	6%***	19%***	13%***	8%***
National identity	11%	3%	19%	6%	20%***	13%	8%
Socio-political values	14%**	3%	23%***	10%***	26%***	16%***	14%***
Egalitarian vs Meritocratic values	16%**	5%**	24%***	15%***	28%***	18%***	16%**

Notes: Values are cumulative percentages of explained variance. In the first equation only positional variables were computed. In the following equations variables presented in the previous equations were added. In the final equation all categories of variables are present. Significance of the R^2 change: *** p < .001, ** p < .01, * p < .05.

Emigrant countries show more solidarity at the level of personal action and concerning immigration policies, but manifest more job discrimination. Despite the statistically significant differences found between countries, the associated effect sizes are small, i.e., the correlations between type of country and the measures of prejudice or solidarity are relatively low. This result indicates that differences between countries are effective, but less important than normally expected.

A second aim of this paper was to analyse the predictors of prejudice, specifically the association between social values and the orientation towards discrimination. This analysis was performed in two stages. In the first stage, we analysed different predictors of prejudice and solidarity together. The results evidenced the importance of positional variables as predictors of this kind of attitudes. But results also show the relevance of socio-political values and, specifically, the importance of egalitarian/meritocratic values on the explanation of the roots of prejudice and of solidarity. Moreover, all hypotheses we put received support except those concerning age and political conservatism. Contrary to our hypothesis and some previous studies, age is the main positional predictor of prejudice. This result should be clarified in order to disentangle if it is a generation effect or a life cycle effect. Also important are the results showing that moral and political conservatism still as predictors of blatant prejudice. Perhaps this will not be the case for new indirect forms of prejudice.

Note also that the explained variance by the variables included in the models is low, particularly in Spain, Italy and Portugal. This result was also found in other similar studies, specifically in the study of the European Monitoring Centre on Racism and Xenophobia (Thalhammer et al., 2001). In this study, none of these three countries presented explained variance values equal or higher than 15%, against values between 15% and 21% in the remaining European countries. We can therefore hypothesise that in Spain, Portugal, and Italy attitudes towards immigrants are only beginning to structure, given that only recently immigrants began being seen as a problem in these countries. Also, the explained variance in the remaining countries (Belgium, former West Germany, and France) is not high but still higher than the one obtained in the European study of Thalhammer and colleagues. The reason why, in our study, the explained variance is not high may be due to the fact that in the EVS database we do not have any data concerning two of the more important predictors of prejudice in the European context: interpersonal contact with immigrants or people belonging to minority groups; and relative intergroup deprivation (Pettigrew & Meertens, 1995).

In a second stage of the analysis of the predictors of prejudice and solidarity, we analysed the specific role played by egalitarian vs. meritocratic individualistic values. The results show that these values significantly contribute to the explained variance of those attitudes. In fact, in the EU as a whole but also in emigrant countries as well as in immigrant countries, prejudice and negative attitudes towards solidarity to immigrants are associated to a higher value placed on freedom than on equality; to a blaming of the poor for their own situation (secondary victimisation); to the non valuing of social and welfare rights as citizenship rights; and the non orientation for social and community participation. This result is relatively new in the literature on prejudice and supports the importance of those values for the understanding of the roots of prejudice. This result should be integrated in the framework of larger typologies of values, such as the one proposed by Schwartz (1996). This articulation can provide an understanding of prejudice in the broader directions of values change.

This study shows that it is still important to analyse open and blatant expressions of prejudice, racism, and xenophobia. However, this is only a small part of this phenomenon. From the time of the seminal work of Allport (1954) to the present prejudice changed its expressions. In order to understand prejudice in formally anti-racist societies, it is important to study its new expressions, such as the ethnicisation of minorities or cultural racism. Cultural racism is a new implicit social theory according to which tradition generates a cultural essence and that some cultural essences are superior to others (Vala, Lopes, Lima & Brito, 2002). This implicit theory, or social representation, sustains, for instance, the set of beliefs that Pettigrew and Mertens (1995) call 'subtle racism', as well as the beliefs that organise modern or symbolic racism (McConahay, 1986). The new prejudiced attitudes also manifest themselves through other diffuse ways like outgroup infra-humanisation at the emotional level (Leyens, Paladino, Rodriguez-Torres, Vaes, Demoulin, Rodriguez-Perez, & Gaunt, 2000) or outgroup naturalisation at the level of their attributes (Moscovici & Pérez, 1997, 1999; Lima & Vala, 2001). The articulation between these indirect expressions of prejudice and social values, namely egalitarian and meritocratic values, haven't received sufficient attention from mainstream research on prejudice, racism, and xenophobia. This articulation can be developed in future researches, namely in the context of the EVS project.

References

Adorno, T.W., E. Frenkel-Brunswick, D. Levinson & R.N. Sandford 1950. *The Authoritarian Personality.* New York: Harper & Row.
Allport, G. 1954. *The Nature of Prejudice.* Reading: Addison-Wesley.
Altmeyer, B. 1994. Reducing prejudice in right-wing authoritarians. In M. Zanna & J. Olson (eds.), *The Psychology of Prejudiec,* Ontario symposium (vol. VII). Hillsdale: lawrence Erlbaum.
Ben Brika, J., G. Lemaine & J. Jackson 1997. *Racism and Xenophobia in Europe.* Brussels: European Commission.
Brown, R. 1995. *Prejudice: Its Social Psychology.* Oxford: Blackwell.
Cacioppo, J., W. Gardner & G. Berntson 1997. Beyond bipolar conceptualizations and mesures: The case of attitudes and evaluative space. *Personality and Social Pschology Review* 1: 3–25.
Deschamps, J.C. & J.M. Lemaine 2001. Racisme flagrant et racisme masqué en Europe. Analyses secondaires de l'Eurobaromètre 47.1. Unpublished manuscript. Lausanne: Université de Lausanne.
Doise, W., D. Spini & A. Clémence 1999. Human rights studied as social representations in cross-national context. *European Journal of Social Psychology* 29:1–29.
Dollard, J., L. Doob, N. Miller, O. Mowrer & R. Sears 1939. *Frustration and Aggression.* New Haven: Yale University Press.
Dowds, L. & K. Young 1997. National identity. In R. Jowell, J. Curtice, A. Park, L. Brook & K. Thomson (eds.), *British Social Attitudes: The 13th Report.* Dartmouth: Social and Community Planning Research.
Dovidio, J., K. Kawakami, C. Johson, B. Johnson & A. Howard 1997. On the nature of prejudice: Automatic and controlled process. *Journal of Experimental Social Psychology* 33: 510–540.
Duckitt, J. & T. Mphuting 1998. Group identification and intergroup attitudes: A longitudinal analysis in South Africa. *Journal of Personality and Social Psychology* 74: 80–85.
Fiske, S. 1998. Stereotyping, prejudice, and discrimination. Pp. 357–414 in D.T. Gilbert, S. Fiske & G. Lindsey (eds.), *The Handbook of Social Psychology.* Boston: The MacGraw-Hill.
Gaertner, S. & J. McLaughlin 1983. Racial stereotypes: Associations and ascriptions of positive and negative characteristics. *Social Psychology Quarterly* 46 : 23–30.
Halman, L. 2001. *The European Values Study: A Third Wave.* Tilburg : WORC, EVS, Tilburg University.
—— 1994. Variations in tolerance levels in Europe. Evidence from the Eurobarameters and European Values Study. *European Journal on Criminal Policy and Research* 2/3: 15–38.
Hovland, C. & R. Sears 1940. Minor studies in aggression. *Journal of Pschology* 9: 301–310.
Inglehart, R. 1997. *Modernization and Postmodernization. Cultural, Economic and Political Change in 43 Societies.* Princeton: Princeton University Press.

Kats, I. & R.G. Hass 1988. Racial ambivalence and American value conflict: Correlational and priming studies of dual cognitive structures. *Journal of Personality and Social Psychology* 55: 893–905.

Lima, M. & J. Vala, J. (in press). Individualismo meritocrático, diferenciação cultural e racismo. *Análise Social*, 37: 181–207.

Leyens, J.P., P. Paladino, R. Rodriguez-Torres, J. Vaes, S. Demoulin, A. Rodriguez-Perez & R. Gaunt 2000. The emotional side of prejudice: The attribution of secondary emotions to ingroups and outgroups. *Personality and Social Psychology Review* 2: 186–197.

McConahay, J.B. 1986. Modern racism, ambivalence, and the modern racism scale. Pp. 91–125 in J.F. Dovidio & S.L. Gaertner (eds.), *Prejudice, Discrimination, and Racism*. New York: Academic Press.

Moscovici, S. & J.A. Pérez 1999. A extraordinária resistência das minorias à pressão das maiorias: O caso dos ciganos. In J. Vala (eds.), *Novos racismos: Perspectivas comparativas*. Oeiras: Celta.

Mummenday, A. 1995. Positive distinctiveness and social discrimination: an old couple living in divorce. *European Journal of Social Psychology* 25: 657–670

Myrdal, G. 1944. *An American Dilemma. The Negro Problem and Modern Democracy*. New York: Harper & Brothers.

Pedersen, A. & I. Walker 1997. Prejudice against Australian Aborigines: Old fashioned and modern forms. *European Journal of Social Psychology* 27: 561–587.

Pettigrew, T.F. & R.W. Meertens 1995. Subtle and blatant prejudice in Western Europe. *European Journal of Social Psychology* 25: 57–75.

Pettigrew, T.F. 1999. Sistematização dos preditores do racismo. In J. Vala (Coord.), *Novos racismos: Perspectivas comparativas*. Oeiras: Celta.

Schwartz, S.H. 1996. Value priorities and behaviour: Applying a theory of integrated value systems. Pp. 1–24 in C. Seligman, J.M. Olson & M.P. Zanna (eds.), *The Psychology of Values: The Ontario Symposium* (Vol. 8). Mahwah: LEA Pub.

Tajfel, H. & J. Turner 1979. An integrative theory of social conflict. In W.G. Austin & S. Worchel (eds.), *The Social Pshychology of Intergroup Relations*. Montery: Brooks/Cole.

Tetlok, P.E. 1985. Integrative complexity and political reasoning. In S. Krauss & A.M. Perlhoff (eds.), *Mass Media and Political Thought*. Beverly-Hills, CA: Sage.

Thalhammer, E., V. Zucha, E. Enzenhofer, B. Salfinger & G. Ogris 2001. *Attitudes Towards Minority Groups in the European Union*. Vienna: European Monitoring Centre on Racism and Xenophobia.

Vala, J., R. Brito & D. Lopes 1999. *Expressões dos racismos em Portugal: Perspectivas psicossociológicas*. Lisboa: Imprensa de Ciências Sociais.

———, D. Lopes, M. Lima & R. Brito 2002. Cultural differences and hetero-ethnicisation in Portugal: The perceptions of white and black people. *Portuguese Journal of Social Sciences*, 1(2): 111–128.

Wagner, U. & A. Zick 1995. The relation of formal education to ethnic prejudice: Its reliability, validity and explanation. *European Journal of Social Psychology* 46: 137–143.

Walker, I. & T. Pettigrew 1984. Relative deprivation theory: An overview and conceptual critique. *British Journal of Social Psychology* 23: 301–310.

Appendix

Independent variables used in regression analyses

Positional variables

Age: v292—Can you tell me your year of birth, please 19. . . .
Income: v320—Here is a scale of incomes and we would like to know in what group
your household is, counting all wages, salaries, pensions and other incomes that
come in. Just give the letter of the group your household falls into, after taxes and
other deductions. Scale: (1) Lowest to (10) Highest.
Educational Level: v304—What is the highest level you have reached in your education? Scale: (1) Lowest to (8) Highest.

Psychological individual differences
Life satisfaction: v68—All things considered, how satisfied are you with your life as
a whole these days? Scale: (1) Dissatisfied to (10) Satisfied
Interpersonal trust: v66—Generally speaking, would you say that most people can be
trusted or that you can't be too careful in dealing with people? Options: (2) Most
people can be trusted, (1) Can't be too careful

Evaluation of political system
Satisfaction with democracy: v213—On the whole are you very satisfied, rather satisfied,
not very satisfied or not at all satisfied with the way democracy is developing in
our country? Scale: (4) Very satisfied to (1) Not at all satisfied.
Trust in political institutions: Please look at this card and tell me, for each item listed,
how much confidence you have in them, is it a great deal, quite a lot, not very
much or none at all? v202—The education system; v205—The police; v206—
Parliament; v211—Health care system; v212—The justice system. Scale: (4) A great
deal to (1) None at all (Index: 1 to 4).

Political identity
v185—In political matters, people talk of 'the left' and the 'the right'. How would
you place your views on this scale, generally speaking? Scale: (1) Left to (10) Right

National identity
v255—How proud are you to be a [country]citizen? Scale: (4) Very proud to (1)
Not at all proud

Socio-political values
Political conservatism—An index composed by the three following indicators. A) I'm
going to describe various types of political systems and ask what you think about
each as a way of governing this country. For each one, would you say it is a very
good, fairly good, fairly bad or very bad way of governing this country? v216—
Having a strong leader who does not have to bother with parliament and elections
(Scale: (4) Very good to (1) Very bad). B) I'm going to read off some things that
people sometimes say about a democratic political system. Could you please tell me
if you agree strongly, agree, disagree or disagree strongly, after I read each of them?
v220—Democracy may have problems but it's better than any other form of government; v223—Democracies aren't good at maintaining order (Scale: (1) Agree
strongly to (4) Disagree strongly). Index: 1—low conservatism, 4—high conservatism.

Moral conservatism: Here is a list of qualities which children can be encouraged to learn at home. Which, if any, do you consider to be especially important? v174—Obedience. Scale: (1) Important to (0) Not mentioned

Materialism/Post-materialism: v190/v191—There is a lot of talk these days about what the aims of this country should be for the next ten years. On this card are listed some of the goals which different people would give top priority. If you had to choose, which of the things on this card would you say is most important? And which would be the next most important? Options: Maintaining order in the nation; Giving people more say in important government decisions; Fighting rising prices; Protecting freedom of speech. Recoding: (1) Materialists; (2) Mixed; (3) Post materialists.

Egalitarian vs meritocratic values

Competition: v188—Now I'd like you to tell me your views on various issues. How would you place your views on this scale? Scale: (10) Competition is good. It stimulates people to work hard and develop new ideas. To (1) Competition is harmful it brings out the worst in people.

Freedom and equality: v184—Which of these two statements comes closest to your own opinion? Options: (1) Agree with statement A: I find that both freedom and equality are important. But if I were to choose one or the other, I would consider personal freedom more important, that is, everyone can live in freedom and develop without hindrance. (2) Agree with statement B: Certainly both freedom and equality are important. But if I were to choose one or the other, I would consider equality more important, that is, that nobody is underprivileged and that social class differences are not so strong.

Welfare rights: v187—Now I'd like you to tell me your views on various issues. How would you place your views on this scale? Scale: (1) People who are unemployed should have to take any job available or lose their unemployment benefits. To—(10) People who are unemployed should have the right to refuse a job they do not want.

Secondary victimization: v69/v70—Why are there people in this country who live in need? Here are four possible reasons. Which *one* reason do you consider to be most important? And which reason do you consider to be the second most important? Options: (1) Because they are unlucky; (2) Because of laziness and lack of willpower; (3) Because of injustice in our society; (4) It's an inevitable part of modern progress; (5) None of these. Recoding: (1) Don't make secondary victimization; (2) Make some secondary victimization; (3) Make a lot of secondary victimization.

Social and community: v12/v26—Look carefully at the following list of voluntary organisations and activities and say: which if one you belong to/which if any are you currently doing unpaid voluntary work for? Scale: 0 (none) to 15 (involvement with all organisations).

PART TWO

FAMILY AND WORK

CHAPTER SEVEN

FAMILIES AND VALUES IN EUROPE

James Georgas, Kostas Mylonas, Aikaterini Gari &
Penny Panagiotopoulou

1 *Introduction*

Demographic statistics can provide a snapshot of the status of current European family. The proportion of persons living in households by type of household for the 15 member states of the European Union in 1995 were measured by the Eurostat-European Community House-hold Panel (cited in Fotakis, 2000). The average of households with two adults and one or more dependent children, a nuclear family structure, is 36% in the 15 EU countries, with the lowest Austria (30%) and Germany (33%) and the highest Denmark and France (43%). The average of households with three or more adults with dependent children, which can be a brother or sister of one of the parents or a non-family member living with them, is 12% in the 15 EU countries, with the lowest the Netherlands (6%) and Denmark (7%) and the highest Spain (24%) and Ireland (23%). The single-parent with depen-dent children family has an average of 3% with the lowest Spain (1%) and the highest the UK (6%). Fotakis concluded that the most conventional family patterns and household forms are found in south-ern Europe. Four or more person households account for over 40% of the total number in southern Europe, primarily due to the high proportions of younger people aged 16–30 living with their parents (up to two thirds in Italy). The average of three-generation house-holds, which corresponds to an extended family type with at least one grandparent, one parent and one child, is 10.8% in Europe, with Greece (21.7%) and Portugal (18.9%) having the highest percent while Finland (1.3%) and Sweden (1.3%) had the lowest. Greece and Portugal also have lowest percent of single parent families and cou-ples without children. On the other hand, the Nordic member states have the highest percent of single parent families and one-person households and the lowest percent of three-generation households.

Another demographic statistic is the increasing divorce rate. According to Fotakis (2000) marriage rate has decreased and the divorce rate has increased in almost all EU nations between 1970–74 and 1988. The highest crude marriage rate in 1998 was in Portugal and Denmark with nearly 7 per 1000 population and lowest in Sweden with less than 4 per 1000. Divorce rate has also increased between 1970–74 and 1998; the divorce rate in Denmark and Sweden has remained unchanged, and the lowest increase in divorce rate has been in Greece and Ireland. The highest crude divorce rate in 1998 was found in the UK and Finland with nearly 3 per 1000 of the population, and the lowest in Ireland, Greece and Spain with less than 1 per 1000.

On the other hand life expectancy in Europe is increasing, estimated at 80.8 years for females and 74.5 years for males (Fotakis, 2000). The implications for the family are the increased presence of grandparents in the lives and potential care of grandchildren in the future. However, fertility is decreasing, estimated at 1.45 children/woman, the lowest, together with Japan, in the world.

The demographic statistics provide a picture of a variety of family types in today's Europe. They also suggest differences in types of families in northern Europe and southern Europe. Three-generation families are more prevalent in the south and one-parent families more prevalent in the north. However, the same is not the case with nuclear families. Indeed, one would not have predicted that Austria and Germany have the lowest percent of nuclear families in Europe, lower than Greece and other countries with higher percents of extended family systems. This is a fact of some importance in the issue of the 'autonomy' of the nuclear family, and in the issue of the importance of family networks; residence, frequency of contact and communication.

The decline of the family, the crisis of the family, the breakdown of the family, the rise of individualism, are phrases which reflect one school of thought during the past few decades. The increased divorce rate, the increase in unmarried one-parent families, the increase in remarriage and families with step-parents and step-brothers and sisters, the decrease in the birth rate, the increase in single-parent households, the gradual replacement of marriage by consensual union, same-sex couples, certainly provide support to the arguments of the breakdown of the family (Cuyvers, 2000). Over thirty years ago Laing

(1971) argued that the family is doomed, and the wrong setting to raise children.

An opposite school of thought questions whether these changes reflect a 'disintegration' of the family. As Aerts (1993) has argued, children continue to be born and raised by adults in a household. Also, the increase in divorce rates are a consequence of changes in the economic and social role of women since the 1950s. Thus, divorce represents the opportunity of women or men to leave an unsatisfactory marriage in which in the past, when the sanctity of the family was the social norm, the 'integrity' of the family often led to pathological relations between the mother and father in some families. Skolnick (1993) believes that rising divorce rates do not reflect a flight from marriage so much as rising expectations for satisfaction in marriage.

Aerts (1993) emphasizes that the major institutional change in USA and Europe is the rupture between marriage and family formation in the sense that marriage is no longer a socially sanctioned prerequisite of child-bearing. Men no longer have either the institutional or legal power to control the lives of spouses and mothers. Changes in the roles of women have altered profoundly the dynamics within the family. Women, because of their entry into the labor market, can control the number of births through contraception and abortion, can freely choose their spouses, and can leave an unsatisfactory relationship with the husband. Aerts concludes that although the idea of family remains valued, it is pragmatically accepted under compromised forms at the cultural and individual levels. However, Aerts pessimistically concludes that although family ties may develop between the child and father, grandparents, uncles, aunts, etc., it cannot be assumed any longer, considering the high divorce level, that significant, long lasting ties of this kind will develop, except with the mother, and be sustained for a period long enough to make a significant impact on the child's socialization.

On the other hand, Muncie and Sapsford (1995) argue that it was rare in 1900 for a young child to reach adulthood with grandparents still surviving, but because of increased life expectancy today, even great-grandparents are not uncommon in a family. They also argue that the twentieth-century family is a strengthened version of its predecessors, and that the modern family offers opportunities for greater closeness and intimacy than was possible in pre-industrial

societies. Cuyvers (2000) comes to the conclusion that in the Netherlands, the 'breakdown of family/commitment' has no empirical basis.

Thus, there are conflicting viewpoints about the status of today's
family in Europe centering around whether it is in crisis and disin-
tegrating, or whether these changes in family types are at a phenom-
enological level with the bonds between family members and the
importance of the kin continuing to be maintained. In addition, most
of this research has taken place in the countries of northern Europe,
in which the nuclear family system has been in place for more
decades than in southern Europe.

Another conclusion regarding the evaluation of the status of the
family in today's Europe is that demographic statistics are necessary
in providing information about the family and its changes, but provide 'surface' information, difficult to interpret without data about
attitudes, values, and interactions between family members. In addition there is a paradoxical confusion between the notions of 'household' and 'family', as employed in demographic studies. Household
refers to counting the number of persons in a house; and it does not
provide much more information than counting the number of items
in a supermarket basket. There is a distinction between a 'house'
and a 'home'. Who lives in a house does not necessarily constitute
a person's social representation of 'home', which has a value-laden
connotation referring to one's 'family'. Perhaps this can explain why
in an era where there are so many types of families, which people
consider to be the consequence of the 'disintegration' of the family,
95.7% of respondents in EU countries believe that the family is the
most important thing in their lives (Eurobarometer no. 39.0/1993).
That is, perhaps two adults, married or not, and a child live in a
house, but each one's social representation of his/her 'family' most
likely includes a mosaic of parents, brothers and sisters, grandparents, uncles, aunts and cousins on both sides, together with different
degrees of emotional attachments with each one, different types of
bonds, memories, etc. All of this leads to a suspicion that it is not
so important 'who lives in the box,' but what are the types of relationships and ties with the constellation of different family members
in the person's conception of his/her 'family.'

Changes in family types should also be reflected in changes in
family values. This does not imply a causal relationship, and indeed
most likely reflects a more complex relationship which includes the
perception of societal changes. Studies of values related to family

structure and function in Greece (Georgas, 1989, 1999; Georgas, Bafiti, Papademou & Mylonas, 2004) indicated three dimensions of family values: *hierarchical roles of father and mother, responsibilities of parents toward children*, and *responsibilities of children toward family and relatives*. Results indicated that adolescents and young people in Greece do not reject all the values of the traditional extended family, but only those associated with the traditional hierarchical roles of father and mother, son and daughter, male and female. These are roles related to father having the economic and social power, the strict obedience of children, of the dutiful and acquiescent mother, etc., roles consistent with the agricultural extended family in many cultures. Safilios-Rothschild (1967) found that in Athenian nuclear families, with fathers employed in the professions, the father's social power was diminished in relation to mother's. The findings suggested that father's power within the family had lessened and mother's had increased, a finding which has also been widely observed in Europe and the US with the nuclear family (Aerts, 1993). On the other hand young people in Greece agreed with values of the traditional extended family in regard to the importance of maintaining ties with kin, of respect for grandparents, of offering help to parents, of obligations towards the family, etc. In a recent study of attitudes of EU 12–year-olds (Eurobarometer, 1993) in response to the question, 'If in the future working people should care more for their elderly parents,' Greek children had the highest level of agreement (80%) as compared to less than 40% in Belgium. Thus, there is evidence that many values of the traditional Greek extended family are still functional within the present family unit.

The purpose of this chapter is to analyze relationships between cultural variables, demographic variables, and family values and attitudes in European countries, based on information from 33 countries.

The European Value Study family data are analyzed at two levels: the individual-level (scores of individuals), and the country-level (relationships of the country-means with demographic and social indices).

Based on the literature, one hypothesis of this study is that family values and attitudes differ in different cultural regions in Europe. Instead of employing a country by country analysis of the means of values, we will search for clusters of European countries which share common cultural patterns of family values and attitudes. It is hypothesized that there will be vestiges of traditional values such as religion or close family interactions in southern European culture with a history of extended family systems. Another hypothesis is that Northern European countries, with a history of nuclear family systems would have more independent values and less related to religious values than those with close family relationships.

Also we would hypothesize that, at the individual-level, older people would have more traditional values than younger; that males would have more traditional values and females; that highly educated and high-income respondents would have less traditional values than respondents with lower levels of education and low income; that married respondents would have more traditional values than unmarried, that respondents with stable relationships would not differ from those with un-stable relationships and that Catholics and Christian Orthodox would have more traditional values than Protestant sects.

Unfortunately, because of methodological problems, it will not be possible to identify the type of family structure of the individuals in the study. Thus, it will not be possible to analyze the statistical relationships between family type and values.

2 Analyses

This section presents the results in terms of three types of analyses. 1) The first part will determine the 'overall' dimensions of family value types or construct equivalence across the 33 European countries of the EVS. This is done by an exploratory factor analysis of the items based on the total sample of 39,799 respondents across all countries (Poortinga, 1989; Van de Vijver & Leung, 1997, Van de Vijver & Poortinga, 2000). This will be referred to as the factor analysis of *universals*, that is, dimensions of family attitudes and values common to the 33 European countries. 2) The second analysis will attempt to determine construct equivalence within *clusters of countries*. That is, it is likely that, although there may be some 'universal' patterns of family attitudes and values in these 33 countries, it is also likely that there are different cultural clusters in Europe, with characteristic patterns of family attitudes and values. 3) The third section will analyze relationships between the underlying family value and attitude dimensions and demographic dimensions.

The data analyses were carried out on 51 items of family values and attitudes (Table 7.1) from the 33 European countries of the EVS Study. The measurement scales for the 51 items were not the same: some were at the ordinal level with two levels or three levels, and some were at the ordinal level with four to eleven levels of measurement. Thus, some variables had to be recoded in order to be comparable in meaning with other measures and in order to avoid data at the nominal level. For example, categories 'approve' 'disapprove' and 'don't mind' were recoded so that the data could be regarded as measured on an ordinal scale. In addition, the direction of some of the variables was changed so that all had the same psychological meaning.

Because the items were at different levels of measurement, Spearman Rho coefficients were more appropriate in the factor analyses of the data, rather than Pearson r coefficients. Employing Spearman Rho rather than Pearson r in factor analysis where there are problems with the metric scale has been supported by Thurstone (1947), Tabachnick & Fidell (1989), Kline (1993), Guilford (1956), Graziano & Raulin (1989). Thus, Spearman Rho coefficients for the 51 questions for all 39,799 participants (weighted data) from the 33 countries in the sample were calculated and inserted into a square matrix for further exploration of the 'overall' factor structure.

2.1 *Exploratory factor analysis of respondents in 33 European countries*

The 'overall' exploratory factor analysis was based on the pooled data-set of 39,799 subjects across the 33 countries. Principal component analysis and varimax rotations resulted in seven factors (using the Kaiser-Guttman and the Scree test criteria) explaining 37.9% of the total variance (Table 7.2). Loadings greater than |.40| were interpreted. Factor 1 was named *Religiosity and Family life*. Factor 2 was named *Companionship in marriage*, and appeared to be consistent with the relationship between husband and wife or partners, in which they actively share problems and interests, spend time together, have a happy sexual relationship, and have an atmosphere of equality. Factor 3, was named *Abortion, divorce and adultery*. Factor 4 was named *Children, family life, and marriage*; this factor is most likely related to a traditional nuclear family structure. Factor 5 was named *Family Security* and associated with housing and income prerequisites and mutual trust in the family. Factor 6 was named *Importance of living conditions of family and the elderly*. Factor 7 was named *Working wife and mother* and refers to working mother relationships with her children, fathers looking after children and income provision from both husband and wife.

Table 7.1   Family value variables in the analysis

	Measures*	Measurement scale
1b	Importance of family in life	1 very important 2 quite important 3 not important 4 not important at all
1c	Importance of friends and acquaintances in life	1 very important 2 quite important 3 not important 4 not important at all
1f	Importance of religion in life	1 very important 2 quite important 3 not important 4 not important at all
6a	How often do you spend time with friends?	1 every week 2 once-twice a month 3 few times a year 4 not at all
6c	How often do you spend time in church?	1 every week 2 once-twice a month 3 few times a year 4 not at all
8	Can people be trusted?	1 most people can be trusted 2 One cannot be too careful
9	Freedom of choice and control over life	1 not at al 2 . . . .9 10 a great deal
10	Are you satisfied with life?	1 I am dissatisfied 2 . . . .9 10 I am satisfied
41	Both parents are needed for a child to grow up happily in a family	1 Tend to agree 2 Tend to disagree
42	A woman has to have children to be fulfilled	1 She needs children 2 It is not necessary
43	Marriage is outdated	1 Disagree 2 Agree
44	If a woman wants to have children as a single parent, without having a stable reationship or being married, do you approve?	1 Disapprove 2 Depends 3 Approve
45b	Marriage or long-term relationship is necessary to be happy	1 Agree strongly 2 Agree 3 Neither-nor 4 Disagree 5 Strongly disagree
47	Love and respect for one's parents	1 One must always love them, regardless of their faults 2 Parents have to earn their children's respect
48	Parental responsiblities	1 Should do their best for children 2 Neither-nor 3 Should not sacrifice their well-being
50a	Approve of abortion if woman not married?	1 Approve 2 Disapprove
50b	Approve of abortion if the married couple does not want more children?	1 Approve 2 Disapprove
57f	Is it a good thing to give more emphasis on family life in the future?	1 Good thing 2 Don't mind 3 Bad thing
65f	Is adultery justified?	1 Never 2 . . . .9 10 Always
65i	Is abortion justified?	1 Never 2 . . . .9 10 Always
65j	Is divorce justified?	1 Never 2 . . . .9 10 Always
79a	To what extent are you concerned with the living conditions of your immediate family?	1 Very much 2 Much 3 To a certain extent 4 Not so much 5 Not at all
80a	To what extent are you concerned with the living conditions of your elderly people?	1 Very much 2 Much 3 To a certain extent 4 Not so much 5 Not at all

Code	Question	Answer options
81a	Are you prepared to actually do something to improve family living conditions?	1 Absolutely Yes 2 Yes 3 Maybe yes, maybe no 4 No 5 Absolutely no
81c	Are you prepared to actually do something to help the elderly?	1 Absolutely Yes 2 Yes 3 Maybe yes, maybe no 4 No 5 Absolutely no
40a	Faithfulness	1 Very important 2 Rather important 3 Not important for a successful marriage
40b	Adequate income	1 Very important 2 Rather important 3 Not important for a successful marriage
40c	Same social background	1 Very important 2 Rather important 3 Not important for a successful marriage
40d	Mutual respect and appreciation	1 Very important 2 Rather important 3 Not important for a successful marriage
40e	Shared religious beliefs	1 Very important 2 Rather important 3 Not important for a successful marriage
40f	Good housing	1 Very important 2 Rather important 3 Not important for a successful marriage
40g	Agreement in politics	1 Very important 2 Rather important 3 Not important for a successful marriage
40h	Understanding and tolerance	1 Very important 2 Rather important 3 Not important for a successful marriage
40i	Living away from in-laws	1 Very important 2 Rather important 3 Not important for a successful marriage
40j	Happy sexual relationships	1 Very important 2 Rather important 3 Not important for a successful marriage
40k	Sharing household chores	1 Very important 2 Rather important 3 Not important for a successful marriage
40l	Children	1 Very important 2 Rather important 3 Not important for a successful marriage
40m	Discussing marriage problems	1 Very important 2 Rather important 3 Not important for a successful marriage
40n	Spending time together	1 Very important 2 Rather important 3 Not important for a successful marriage
40o	Talking on mutual interests	1 Very important 2 Rather important 3 Not important for a successful marriage
46a	A working mother can establish warm relationship with her children	1 Strongly disagree 2 Disagree 3 Agree 4 Strongly agree
46b	Children suffer if their mother works	1 Strongly agree 2 Agree 3 Disagree 4 Strongly disagree
46c	Most women want a home and children	1 Strongly agree 2 Agree 3 Disagree 4 Strongly disagree
46d	Being a housewife is just as fulfilling as working for pay	1 Strongly agree 2 Agree 3 Disagree 4 Strongly disagree
46e	A job is the best way for a woman to be independent	1 Strongly disagree 2 Disagree 3 Agree 4 Strongly agree
46f	Both husband and wife should contribute to household income	1 Strongly disagree 2 Disagree 3 Agree 4 Strongly agree
46g	Fathers are well suited to look after children	1 Strongly disagree 2 Disagree 3 Agree 4 Strongly agree
46h	Men are less able in handling emotions	1 Strongly agree 2 Agree 3 Disagree 4 Strongly disagree
25	How often do you attend religious services?	1 More than once a week 2 Once/week 3 Once/month 4 Once/year 5 Less often 6 Never
28	Are you a religious person	1 Yes 2 Not religious 3 Convinced atheist
29b	Is church giving adequate answers to problems of family life?	1 Yes 2 No

* The codes in the first column are the ones used in the EVS sourcebook (Halman, 2001).

Table 7.2   Factor analysis outcomes for all 33 countries

Factors	1	2	3	4	5	6	7
% of variance explained	12.21	7.39	5.62	3.55	3.39	2.98	2.77
Attend religious services	**.79**	.04	.22	.03	−.02	.07	.09
Importance of religion	**.78**	.07	.21	.05	.03	.10	.03
Are you a religious person	**.74**	.02	.09	.03	.03	.04	.05
Spend time in church	**.69**	.00	.21	.05	−.09	.04	.05
Church and family life	**.60**	−.01	.11	.15	.02	.04	-.04
Shared religious beliefs	**.48**	.11	.17	.09	.08	.02	.03
Discussing problems	.02	**.73**	.00	−.08	−.04	.06	-.02
Talking about mutual interests	.09	**.70**	.05	.10	.08	.11	-.03
Spending time together	.08	**.66**	.10	.13	.15	.09	-.04
Understanding & tolerance in marriage	−.01	**.60**	−.02	−.03	−.11	.01	.02
Mutual respect and appreciation	.02	**.56**	−.01	−.05	−.13	−.02	-.01
Happy sexual relationship	−.09	**.51**	−.06	.00	.30	−.02	.02
Sharing household chores	.02	**.51**	.00	−.05	.23	.07	-.22
Abortion justified?	.23	−.02	**.81**	.13	.10	.03	.03
Approval of abortion if not wanting more children	−.24	−.05	**−.79**	.07	.05	−.02	−.10
Approval of abortion if woman not married	−.22	−.03	**−.79**	.01	.03	.00	−.07
Is divorce justified?	.18	−.04	**.63**	.24	.14	.03	−.01
Marriage or long-term relationship is necessary for one to be happy	.07	.07	.06	**.67**	.06	.06	−.08
Woman needs to have children to be fulfilled	.07	−.07	.01	**.64**	.09	.01	−.01
Both parents needed in a family	.04	−.02	.10	**.62**	.03	−.03	.17
Adequate income	.00	.08	.00	.12	**.71**	.01	.01
Good housing	.00	.21	.00	.13	**.62**	.01	−.06
Can people be trusted?	−.01	.00	−.14	−.09	**−.40**	−.01	−.13
Concerned with elderly	.17	.09	.06	.05	.00	**.70**	−.04
Help elderly	.15	.19	.02	−.06	−.11	**.69**	−.03
Prepared to do something to improve conditions of family	−.05	.03	.00	.03	.02	**.64**	.03
Concerned with living conditions of immediate family	.00	−.05	.05	.09	.19	**.54**	.01
Working mother & children can have warm relationships	.05	.00	.12	.15	−.01	.01	**.69**
Fathers looking after children are well suited for doing so	.10	−.13	.01	.03	.07	−.02	**.65**
Income should come from both husband and wife	.00	−.12	.04	−.30	−.08	−.05	**.56**

For Table 7.2, all questions with a loading of |.39| or less (not participating in any of the factors) are not reported; total variance explained = 37.9%

2.2   Factor equivalence across all countries

That seven factors were obtained from the exploratory factor analysis of the 39,799 respondents does not necessarily imply that each of the 33 countries has identical factor structures. The methodology of testing for construct equivalence across countries (Poortinga, 1989;

van de Vijver & Leung 1997; van de Vijver & Poortinga, 2000) requires comparisons of the factor structure of each country with the overall factor structure of the pooled data-set in order to determine the factorial agreement of the factorial structure of each country with the overall factor solution. Tucker's Phi is employed as the coefficient of agreement with the criterion for agreement .90 or greater.

Exploratory factor analyses of each country with varimax rotations resulted in seven factors per country, and factor loadings for each factor for each country were rotated and then compared to the overall factor structure.

Separately, for each of the seven overall factors, Tucker coefficients with each of the 33 countries factors resulted into 100% factor equivalence for the first overall factor *Religiosity and family life* in the 33 countries. The second overall factor *Companionship in marriage* reached only 48% of equivalence (16 countries with Tucker Phi coefficients greater than .90) and the third overall factor *Abortion, divorce and adultery* reached 81% of equivalence across countries. Only 6% of countries had Tucker Phi coefficients greater than .90 on *Children, family life marriage* and 3% on *Family security*. *Importance of living conditions*, the sixth overall factor showed 36% of Tucker Phi agreement, but the seventh overall factor, *Working wife and mother* showed 0% agreement.

Thus, the Tucker Phi coefficients indicated that not all country factors were identical or similar to the 'overall' factor structure. A ratio of the observed factor equivalence to the expected overall factor equivalence for the total of the seven factors was only 39% (factor equivalence was observed for 92 Tucker coefficients for the seven factor structures elicited for each country in comparison to the overall seven factor structure, with the expected 100% factor equivalence being $7 \times 33 = 231$ coefficients of agreement higher than .90).

Each of the seven factors of the 33 countries were then tested for factor equivalence on a one-to-one basis (between all pairs of countries). The loadings of each factor for all pairs of countries were compared with Tucker Phi as the factorial coefficient of agreement $(33 \times 32 \div 2 = 528)$ x 7 factors $= 3,696$ Tucker Phi coefficients. Only 881 coefficients (24%) were equal or greater than .90. Thus, although factor equivalence was high for the first 3 factors, it was relatively low for the comparisons of all seven factors.

2.3   *Clusters of countries with similar value structures*

The process of attaining factor equivalence across countries is dependent on selection of the items loading on these common factors, so that the degree of equivalence is above Tucker Phi .90. Factor equivalence is often attained by deleting 'discrepant' items—items not found in the factor structure in all the countries (Van de Vijver & Poortinga, 2000). In some cases, countries which do not have an equivalent factor structure with other cultures are also deleted.

A basic hypothesis of this study is that in addition to some common European patterns of family attitudes and values, other family attitudes and values may be characteristic of different cultural clusters of countries in Europe. Thus, instead of attempting to eliminate 'discrepant' items or countries in order to determine those items, which are universal across European countries, another procedure was followed. This method could identify common or 'universal' items in each factor and also items specific to the factor structure of each country cluster. In this procedure, we first employed cluster analysis of values and attitudes and at a second stage, factor analyzed the values and attitudes for each country cluster (Georgas & Mylonas, in press). The standardized transformations of the 51 item means were inserted into a 51 items by 33 countries matrix and cluster analyzed in an attempt to form homogeneous country sets, that is, to determine clusters of countries with similar patterns of family attitudes and values. Four clusters of countries were obtained:

1. Austria, Belgium, Czech Republic, France, West Germany, East Germany, Luxembourg, Slovenia, Spain, and the United Kingdom. This cluster is composed primarily of Western European Countries, seven members of the European Union, with two exceptions, the Czech Republic and Slovenia (n = 12,861).
2. Belarus, Bulgaria, Estonia, Hungary, Latvia, Lithuania, Romania, Russia, Slovakia, and Ukraine. This cluster is clearly composed of Eastern European and Socialist countries associated with the former Soviet Union (n = 11,527).
3. Croatia, Greece, Ireland, Northern Ireland, Italy, Poland, and Portugal. This cluster is also composed primarily of Western European countries, five members of the EU, with exceptions Croatia and Poland (n = 8,358).
4. Denmark, Finland, Iceland, the Netherlands, and Sweden. Except for the Netherlands, this cluster is composed of Scandinavian countries (n = 5,560).

The next step was to factor analyze of the data separately for each cluster of countries. For all matrices, Spearman Rho coefficients were computed and factor analyzed.

A summary of items loading on factors of the four country clusters is presented in Table 7.3. Inspection of the items loading on factors of each country cluster reveals common or universal items across the four country clusters and also items specific to each cluster. For example, Factor 2 *Companionship in marriage* has four common items across the four country clusters. However, cluster 1 (Austria–UK) has one additional item *Family security*. Cluster 2 (Belarus–Ukraine) has four additional items. Cluster 3 (Croatia–Portugal) has the same items as cluster 1, the addition of *Faithfulness in marriage*. Cluster 4 (Denmark–Sweden) is similar to cluster 1, except for one item.

The items of the exploratory overall factor structure for the entire sample are also presented for comparison purposes. Factor equivalence between clusters (and also with the overall factor structure) was tested by comparison of all pairs of countries for each factor with Tucker Phi coefficients. Table 7.4 presents the factors of the entire sample, and the factors from each cluster, together with the percent of explained variance for each factor. Factor equivalence between the overall factors and the cluster factors was highest with clusters 1 (Austria . . . UK), 2 (Belarus . . . Ukraine), and 3 (Croatia . . . Portugal), indicating that the factor structure for these three clusters may essentially determine most of the variance of a 'universal' structure of family values and attitudes for the European countries.

Comparisons of factor equivalence between the country clusters also revealed the number of identical and similar factors. Cluster 1 (Austria . . . UK) and 3 (Croatia . . . Portugal) exhibited the most similar factor structures (four identical and two similar factors). Clusters 1 (Austria . . . UK) and 4 (Denmark . . . Sweden) had three identical and two similar factors. Clusters 2 (Belarus . . . Ukraine) and 3 (Croatia . . . Portugal) were rather similar with four identical and one similar factors. Clusters 1 (Austria . . . UK) and 2 (Belarus . . . Ukraine) had three identical and one similar factors and clusters 3 (Croatia . . . Portugal) and 4 (Denmark . . . Sweden) had two identical and two similar factors. The lowest similarity was between the 2nd (Belarus . . . Ukraine) and the 4th cluster (Denmark . . . Sweden) with two identical and two similar factors.

One can conclude at this point that universality or factor equivalence of family values and attitudes was found for four factors across the 33 European countries. On the other hand, each country cluster

Table 7.3   Items participating in the Overall and Cluster factor structures

	Items	Overall	Cluster 1	Cluster 2	Cluster 3	Cluster 4
1F	importance of religion	A	A	A	A	A
6C	Spend time in church	A	A	A	A	A
25	Attend religious services	A	A	A	A	A
29B	Church and family life	A	A	A	A	A
28	Are you a religious person?	A	A	A		A
40E	Shared religious beliefs	A	A	U2	Ee	
40K	Sharing household chores	B	B	B	B	Bb
40M	Discussing problems	B	B	B	B	Bb
40N	Spending time together	B	B	B	B	Bb
40O	Talking about mutual interests	B	B	B	B	Bb
40J	Happy sexual relationship	B	E	B	B	Bb
40D	Mutual respect and appreciation	B		B	B	
40H	Understanding & tolerance in marriage	B		B	B	
40L	Children are part of a successful marriage			B	B	U4a
40A	Faithfulness in marriage				B	U4b
65I	Is abortion justified?	C	C	C	C	C
65J	Is divorce justified?	C	C	C	C	C
50A	Approval of abortion if woman not married	C	C	C	C	C
50B	Approval of abortion if not wanting more children	C	C	C	C	C
65F	Is adultery justified?		C	C		U4b
45B	Marriage or long-term relationship is necessary for one to be happy	D	D	Dd	D	Dd
41	Both parents needed in a family	D	D	Dd	D	Dd
42	Woman needs to have children to be fulfilled	D	D	Dd	D	Dd
44	Woman single parent without relationship			Dd		Dd
48	Love and respect for one's parents			Dd		
40B	Adequate income	E	E		Ee	U4a
40F	Good housing	E	E		Ee	U4a
8	Can people be trusted?	E				
40C	Same social background			U2	Ee	
40G	Agreement on politics			U2	Ee	
80A	Concerned with eldery	F		FU2–OVR		
81A	Prepared to do something to improve conditions of immediate family	F		FU2–OVR		
81C	Help eldery	F		FU2–OVR		
79A	Concerned with living conditions of immediate family	F				U4a
46A	Working mother & children can have warm relationship	G	G		Gg	G
46F	Income should come from both husband and wife	G	G		Gg	G
46G	Fathers looking after children are well suited for doing so	G	G		Gg	G
46E	Job gives women independence		G		Gg	G

Table 7.3 (*cont.*)

	Items	Overall	Cluster 1	Cluster 2	Cluster 3	Cluster 4
46B	Children suffer with working mother			H	HU2U3	
46C	Women want home and children			H	HU2U3	
46D	Housewife is just as fulfilling as working for pay			H	HU2U3	
1B	Importance of family in life		U1			U4b
57F	In future, more emphasis on family life		U1			U4b
43	Marriage is outdated		U1			

Key: ('U' stands for factors unique in one cluster structure, OVR stands for Overall factor):

A	Religiosity and Family life
B	Companionship in marriage
C	Abortion, divorce & adultery
D	Children, family life, and marriage
E	Family security
G	Working wife and mother
FU2–ovr	Importance of living conditions of family and the elderly (cluster 2 & overall)
HU2U3	Woman's role as a housewife (clusters 2 & 3)
U1	Importance of marriage and family life (cluster 1 only)
U2	Same social, political and religious background (cluster 2 only)
U4a	Adequate income, good housing and children (cluster 4 only)
U4b	Importance or keeping the family together (cluster 4 only)

had some factors specific to each cluster, or shared by one other cluster. This provides further support for the existence of different cultural clusters of family values and attitudes in these European nations.

2.4   *Mean composite scores of factors and clusters*

The overall factor structure and the cluster factors provide information regarding the content—the dimensions of family values and attitudes. The next step was to compare the means of country clusters on similar factors. This would provide information regarding the degree of acceptance or rejection of the values and attitudes by the country clusters. Because, as discussed above, the EVS questions have different metric scales, it was necessary to employ a common metric scale in order to compare means of the different dimensions of family values and attitudes for the different clusters. This was done by employing composite scores, that is, each item on a factor for each country cluster was transformed to T-scores (Mean = 50, Standard

Deviation = 10). Composite scores were computed as the mean T-scores of the items for each factor for each cluster and for the overall factor structure. Mean T-scores across cultures were compared with a series of one-way analyses of variance, for each equivalent factor (Table 7.4). Because the number of respondents in each cluster is very large, mean differences between the clusters for each factor were highly significant. Thus, the magnitude of the significance of the mean differences between the clusters on a factor are reported in terms of effect size, η^2.

Religiosity and family life. Values and attitudes relating to the importance of religion and family life, attending church, shared religious beliefs were found to be universal constructs in all four country clusters (Figure 7.1). The analysis of variance indicated significant differences between clusters. Cluster 3 (Croatia . . . Portugal) had the highest composite mean 53.97, followed by 51.45 for the former Eastern European countries of Cluster 2 (Belarus . . . Ukraine). The primarily Western European countries of Cluster 1 (Austria . . . UK) and the primarily Scandinavian countries of Cluster 4 (Denmark . . . Sweden) had approximately the same means, 48.91 and 48.74 respectively, with the lowest values for the importance of religiosity. The effect size of $\eta^2 = .08$ indicates relatively low to medium degree of variance explained.

Companionship in marriage. This factor was also found in the four country clusters, indicating it is a universal construct in the European countries. It concerns communication, sharing of household chores, mutual respect, happy sexual relationship, which may be consistent with the relationship between husband and wife, with or without children, and between unmarried partners. However, the effect size of $\eta^2 = .01$ indicates no important differences, or very little variation between the European countries on these attitudes and values.

Abortion and divorce. A factor regarding whether divorce is justified, and the justification or approval of abortion if the woman is not married or if more children are not wanted was also found in the four clusters of countries. Disapproval with mean 52.62 (high scores indicate disapproval; the directions of the scores are reversed for this factor) was found in Cluster 3 (Croatia . . . Portugal), followed by slight approval 49.65 in the former Eastern European countries of Cluster 2 (Belarus . . . Ukraine) and 48.97 in the countries of Cluster 1 (Austria . . . UK). The highest level of approval was found in the primarily Scandinavian countries of Cluster 4 (Denmark . . . Sweden)

Table 7.4 Factors-percent of variance explained, for the general factor structure and for each country cluster and analysis of variance measures of association

General Factor	Cluster 1	Cluster 2	Cluster 3	Cluster 4	η^2
A. (1) Religiosity and family life (12.2%) Mean T-score = 51.03	A. (1) (11.6%) Mean T-score = 48.91	A. (2) (7.8%) Mean T-score = 51.45	A. (2) (7.8%) Mean T-score = 53.97	A. (2) (6.6%) Mean T-score = 48.74	.08 >50: Important
B. (2) Companionship in marriage (7.4%) Mean T-score = 50.14	B. (3) (4.7%) Mean T-score = 50.19	B. (1) (11.2%) Mean T-score = 49.04	B. (1) (12.0%) Mean T-score = 50.92	Bb*. (5) (3.6%) Mean T-score = 50.22	.01 >50: Important
C. (3) Abortion, divorce, adultery (5.6%) Mean T-score = 49.92	C. (2) (7.1%) Mean T-score = 48.97	C. (3) (4.2%) Mean T-score= 49.65	C. (3) (5.7%) Mean T-score = 52.62	C. (1) (10.8%) Mean T-score = 45.85	.07 >50: Disapproval
D. (4) Children, family life, and marriage (3.5%) Mean T-score = 51.05	D. (4) (3.7%) Mean T-score = 49.24	Dd**. (5) (3.5%) Mean T-score = 51.78	D. (5) (3.6%) Mean T-score = 49.75	Dd**. (6) (3.2%) Mean T-score = 45.17	09 >50: Important
E. (5) Family security (3.4%) Mean T-score = 51.01	E. (5) (3.4%) Mean T-score = 49.62		Ee***. (4) (3.7%) Mean T-score = 50.65		.01 >50: Important
FU2–OVR. (6) Importance of living conditions of family and the elderly (3.0%) Mean T-score = 50.03		FU2–OVR. (4) (3.7%) Mean T-score = 48.31			No comparison
G. (7) Working wife and mother (2.8%) Mean T-score = 49.85	G. (6) (3.1%) Mean T-score = 49.90		Gg****. (6) (3.1%) Mean T-score = 50.81	G. (4) (3.9%) Mean T-score = 49.56	.01 >50: Important
		U2U3. (7) Woman's role as a housewife (2.9%) Mean T-score = 51.91	U2U3. (7) Woman's role as a housewife (2.9%) Mean T-score = 49.56		.03 >50: Approval

Table 7.4 (cont.)

General Factor	Cluster 1	Cluster 2	Cluster 3	Cluster 4	η²
	U1. (7) Importance of marriage and family life (3.0%) Mean T-score = 49.66				No comparison
					>50: Important
		U2. (6) Same social, political and religious background (3.0%) Mean T-score = 49.55			No comparison
					>50: Important
				U4a. (3) Adequate income, good housing and children (4.7%) Mean T-score = 49.16	No comparison
					>50: Important
				U4b. (7) Importance or keeping the family together (2.9%) Mean T-score = 50.36	No comparison
					>50: Important

The order of each factor in each factor solution is denoted in the parenthesis, followed by the percent of variance explained by the factor. 'U' stands for presence of a factor 'uniquely' for one cluster of countries.

Variance accounted for (rightmost column) refers to comparisons among similar or identical factors clusters of countries, excluding the overall factor structure, which is, however, reported as a point of reference.

* This factor (Bb) was similar and not identical to the 'Companionship in marriage' factor present in all other clusters of countries and in the overall structure.

** This factor (Dd) was similar and not identical to the overall and the cluster 1 and 3 'Children, family life, and marriage' factors.

*** This factor (Ee) was similar and not identical to the overall and the cluster 1 'Family security' factor.

**** This factor (Gg) was similar and not identical to the overall and the cluster 1 and 4 'Working wife and other' factors.

Figure 7.1   Factor composite T-scores for the four clusters of countries; two identical (Religiosity and family life, Abortion-Divorce-Adultery) and two similar factors

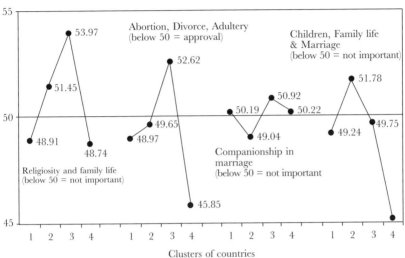

Clusters of countries

with mean = 45.85. The effect size of η^2 = .07 indicates a relatively low to medium degree of variance explained.

Children, family life, and marriage. Marriage or long-term relationship is necessary for one to be happy, a woman needs to have children to be fulfilled, and both parents needed in a family, values related to the traditional nuclear family system, were common factors found in the four clusters of countries. The highest mean 51.78 was in Cluster 2 (Belarus . . . Ukraine). Cluster 3 (Croatia . . . Portugal) and Cluster 1 (Austria . . . UK) had values 49.75 and 49.24 respectively, slightly below the mean, while Cluster 4 (Denmark . . . Sweden) with mean = 45.17 disapproved most of the values of related to this family system. The effect size of η^2 = .09 again indicates a relatively low to medium degree of variance explained.

Working wife and mother. These attitudes emerged in three of the four clusters (1, 2 and 3), but the effect size of η^2 = .01 indicates that the percent of variation explained is too small to conclude that the mean differences are significant.

Comparisons of the other factors shared by only two clusters also did not result in important mean differences. The remainder of the factors are specific for each cultural cluster.

One conclusion that can be drawn from the comparisons of the mean scores between the cultural clusters on the above factors was that even when mean differences were found, they were 'relatively' small and not indicative of extreme differences in these family values and attitudes in European countries.

2.5   *Demographic correlates*

This stage of analysis explored the relationships between the family values factors and demographic variables at the individual level. The factor indices employed for this stage of analysis were the 'overall' structure composite factor scores and the composite factor scores for each of the four clusters of countries.

Employing the scores for the overall factor structure could be a problem since the analysis indicated four clusters of countries with some identical, some similar and some unique factors across the four clusters of countries. However, for comparability reasons and in order to combine the similar (although not identical across countries) factor patterns into a single interpretative framework, this factor structure was also used together with the cluster of countries factor structures.[1]

The demographic variables employed were: a) gender, b) age, c) having a stable relationship or not, d) level of education, e) household income, f) marital status and g) religious denomination. All comparisons were at the individual-level. Some other demographic measures that could be employed at this stage, e.g., if the respondents were married to their partners, were highly unbalanced in regard to the number of respondents in each cell and were not pursued further; other sparsely distributed measures were not pursued further, as well. For some of the above demographic measures, Pearson correlation coefficients were computed and for others analysis of variance was applied. In Table 7.5, the results for the measures of association (r^2 or η^2) are summarized. A general finding was that the measures of association between the demographic variables and the factor indices were not very large.

---

[1] If we tested for this combined-universal factor structure through a confirmatory factor analysis model, universalism would not be supported across all 33 countries but this was not the main target at this point; concurrent description of even similar patters across these countries was of more interest.

Table 7.5   Measures of association for all factor indices* with age, education level, household income, gender, marital status, stable relationship and religious denomination

	Age	Education level	Income	Gender	Marital status	Stable relationship	Religious denomination
Overall factors	r^2	r^2	r^2	η^2	η^2	η^2	η^2
Religiosity and family life (high=important)	.06	.02	.01	.03	.04	.00	.05
Companionship in marriage (high=important)	.00	.00	.00	.00	.00	.00	.00
Abortion, divorce & adultery (high=disapproval)	.01	.00	.00	.00	.01	.00	.02
Children, family life, and marriage (high=important)	.04	.01	.02	.00	.05	.00	**.09**
Family security (high=important)	.01	.00	.00	.00	.00	.00	.01
Living conditions of family and elderly (high=important)	.01	.00	.00	.00	.02	.01	.01
Working wife and mother (high=disapproval)	.01	.00	.00	.01	.00	.00	.01
Cluster 1 factors							
Religiosity and family life (high=important)	.06	.02	.01	.02	.04	.00	.02
Abortion, divorce & adultery (high=disapproval)	.05	.07	.02	.00	.05	.00	.01
Companionship in marriage (high=important)	.00	.00	.00	.00	.00	.00	.01
Children, family life, and marriage (high=important)	.06	.03	.02	.00	.06	.01	.02
Family security (high=important)	.00	.01	.00	.00	.00	.00	.00
Working wife and mother (high=disapproval)	.01	.01	.00	.01	.01	.00	.01
Importance of marriage and family life (high=important)	.02	.00	.00	.01	.08	.04	.00
Cluster 2 factors							
Companionship in marriage (high=important)	.00	.00	.00	.01	.00	.00	.00
Religiosity and family life (high=important)	.05	.05	.02	.05	.03	.00	.03
Abortion, divorce & adultery (high=disapproval)	.05	.06	.03	.00	.03	.00	.03
Living conditions of family and elderly (high=important)	.00	.00	.01	.00	.02	.01	.01
Children, family life, and marriage (high=important)	.07	.04	.01	.00	.06	.01	.02
Same social, political, religious background (high=important)	.03	.01	.01	.00	.01	.00	.01
Woman's role as a housewife (high=approval)	.02	.01	.01	.00	.01	.00	.00
Cluster 3 factors							
Companionship in marriage (high=important)	.00	.00	.00	.00	.00	.00	.02

Table 7.5   (*cont.*)

	Age	Education level	Income	Gender	Marital status	Stable relationship	Religious denomination
Religiosity and family life (high=important)	.07	.02	.03	.03	.05	.01	.04
Abortion & divorce (high=disapproval)	.07	.04	.01	.00	.05	.00	.07
Family security and same background (high=important)	.05	.01	.02	.00	.02	.00	.02
Children, family life, and marriage (high=important)	.02	.00	.01	.00	.03	.02	**.09**
Working wife and mother (high=disapproval)	.02	.01	.00	.01	.01	.00	.02
Woman's role as a housewife (high=approval)	.05	.03	.05	.01	.04	.01	.02
Cluster 4 factors							
Abortion and divorce (high=disapproval)	.03	.06	.01	.00	.03	.00	.07
Religiosity and family life (high=important)	.07	.01	.01	.02	.06	.00	.08
Adequate income, good housing, and children (high=important)	.05	.01	.00	.00	.07	.00	**.10**
Working wife and mother (high=disapproval)	.00	.00	.00	.03	.01	.00	**.13**
Companionship in marriage (high=important)	.00	.00	.00	.00	.00	.00	.01
Children, family life, and marriage (high=important)	.05	.02	.00	.03	.04	.00	.02
Keping the family together (high=important)	.00	.02	.00	.01	.07	.02	.02

* The order of factors for each cluster reflects the decreasing amount of percent of variance explained for that factor. All underlined r^2 indices denote inversely related variables.

The highest percent of variance explained was between *Age* and *Religiosity* and *family life*. The $r^2 = .06$ between the overall factor structure and age is relatively low to medium. Approximately the same explained variance was found in each of the country clusters. Thus, older respondents tend to have higher religious values than younger respondents do.

A second association was found between *Age* and *Abortion and divorce* in Clusters 1, 2 and 3, with $r^2 = .05$, $r^2 = .05$, $r^2 = .07$ respectively. The explained variances were again relatively low to medium, with older respondents tending to reject abortion, divorce and adultery.

Similar associations were found with *Children family life and marriage* in Clusters 1, 2, and 4 with older respondents more in favor of these values.

Similar associations were also found with *Family security and same background* in Cluster 3 and *Adequate income* in Cluster 4.

The overall conclusions are that older and younger respondents differed in their adherence to these values.

No associations between *education* and the overall factors were found. However, the percent of variance explained between *Education* and *Abortion and divorce* was again relatively low to medium in all Clusters, ranging from $r^2 = .04$ in cluster 3 to $r^2 = .07$ in cluster 1, indicating a tendency that the more highly educated approve of these values.

The only other associations were found in Cluster 2 between education and *Religiosity and family life* ($r^2 = .05$) and *Children, family life, and marriage*, indicating that the more highly educated disapprove of these values.

It is of interest that analysis of variance indicated no mean differences in level of income for the family values factors, with the exception of *Woman's role as a housewife* in Cluster 3, which might be a chance relationship.

Another surprising finding, in light of the current arguments regarding women's roles is that no gender differences were found in any of the factors, except for *Religiosity and Family life* in Cluster 2 ($\eta^2 = .05$).

The effect sizes between *married* and *unmarried* respondents and the overall factors *Religiosity and family life* ($\eta^2 = .04$) and *Children, family life, and marriage* ($\eta^2 = .05$), with higher values for married respondents. Low to medium effect sizes for *Religiosity and family life* were also found in Cluster 1 ($\eta^2 = .04$), Cluster 3 ($\eta^2 = .05$) and Cluster 4 ($\eta^2 = .06$). Effect sizes for *Children, family life, and marriage* were also found in Cluster 1 ($\eta^2 = .06$), Cluster 2 ($\eta^2 = .06$) and Cluster 4 ($\eta^2 = .04$). A related factor, *Keeping the family together* in Cluster 4 had an effect size of $\eta^2 = .07$, together with *Importance of marriage and family life* ($\eta^2 = .08$) in Cluster 1. *Abortion, divorce and adultery* was disapproved by married respondents in Cluster 1 ($\eta^2 = .05$) and Cluster 3 ($\eta^2 = .06$).

No significant differences were found for the variable, except for *Importance of marriage and family life* in Cluster 1 ($\eta^2 = .04$).

For *Religious denominations*, one-way analyses of variance were carried out for each of the overall factors, and for each of the Cluster factors. The religious denominations employed were: Roman Catholics, Protestants, Free Church/Non-conformists/Evangelists, Christian Orthodox, Muslims, and 'non-affiliated'. The numbers of Hindu, or Muslims was not sufficient in some categories. For the overall factor

Children, family life, and marriage Protestants and Evangelists have lower means (47.22 and 47.14, respectively) than Muslims (54.23) and Christian Orthodox (54.19) who stated that Children, family life, and marriage are very important. The mean for Roman Catholics (49.98) indicated neither approval or disapproval. The effect size ($\eta^2 = .09$) is a low medium effect. No other significant differences were found.

Similar results were found for Cluster 3 countries (Croatia . . . Portugal), but because this cluster contained no Muslims, they will not be discussed. One more finding concerning the effect of religious denomination was found in cluster 4 (Denmark . . . Sweden). Three denominations of the respondents were reported in these countries: Roman Catholics, Protestants and Free Church/non-conformist/evangelical. In the factor *Adequate income, good housing, and children*, the means of Protestants (44.4) indicated low approval, while Roman Catholics (49.3) and Evangelists (48.7) were more in favor. The same pattern was found for *Working wife and mother* (47.9, 52.5 and 53.5, for Protestants, Roman Catholics, and Evangelists, respectively). The effect sizes for these findings are $\eta^2 = .10$ and $\eta^2 = .13$ respectively, which are the highest among the demographic variables.

Overall, the effects of religious denominations across all European countries on these family values appear to be restricted to a traditional scheme of the nuclear family, with values of Protestants and Evangelists on the disapproval side, Catholics and Jews in the center, and Christian Orthodox and Muslims on the approval side. One would have expected more differentiated attitudes and values shaped by religious denominations on other factors such as, *Abortion and divorce* and perhaps other variables.

The family values and attitudes as well as their correlations with demographic variables were analyzed at the individual level. A second type of analysis is at the country-level, that is, based on the means of variables for each country and has been termed ecological level analysis (Hofstede, 1980, 2001). The method employs statistical data, e.g., means, percents, of nations, often based on economic, political, population indices from statistical yearbooks, encyclopaedias and atlases. In Georgas and Berry (1995) it was demonstrated that nations could be grouped into clusters based on ecosocial indices. In Georgas, Van de Vijver and Berry (2004) these aggregate scores on ecosocial indices of nations were analyzed in terms of their relationships with the mean scores of nations on psychological variables.

The country-level ecological and social indices employed are: a measure of economic level called affluence, educational variables, population measures, number of births, population growth, etc. Northern Ireland was excluded, since they are incorporated into the UK indices and no separate indices are reported. Also, West Germany and East Germany data were combined, since ecological indices are available for Germany as a single country.

For the multiple regression analyses (Table 7.6), Births are in numbers per 1,000 and Population growth is in percentages. For the Number of births and the Population growth indices, some effects would appear to be present, although because of the low number of countries with published indices, they were not statistically significant. The *Population growth* index was inversely related to three of the 7 overall factors; *Abortion, divorce, and adultery* were disapproved when the population growth index was low, whereas *Family security and Children, family life, and marriage* value-factors were considered important. *Companionship in marriage* and *Family security* were also considered more important when the number of births per thousand inhabitants is higher.

The *Affluence* index was developed by Georgas and Berry (1995) for employing several indices in order to derive a single and more stable measure of economic status of countries. For our analysis we used seven indices, based on more recent social indices than those employed in the 1995 study: (1) Gross National Index (per capita, in $US); (2) Purchasing Power (per capita); (3) Commercial Energy

Table 7.6   Multiple regression models (measures of association and standardized regression coefficients) of 31 country-level scores with the universal factors as dependent variables on ecocultural indices: Number of Births/1000, Percent of population growth

Ecocultural predictors: Number of Births per 1000 & Percent of population Growth	R^2	NB	PGr
Religiosity and family life (high=important)	.03	.26	−.16
Companionship in marriage (high=important)	.20	.37	.10
Abortion & divorce (high=disapproval)	.31	−.03	−.54
Children, family life, and marriage (high=important)	.34	−.28	−.34
Family security (high=important)	.23	.41	−.72
Living conditions of family and elderly (high=important)	.07	.27	−.02
Working wife and mother (high=disapproval)	.13	.29	.09

The underlined standardized regression coefficients are statistically significant at the .05 level.

Use (in million tonne oil equivalent); (4) Commercial Energy Use (per capita, in Kg of oil equivalent); (5) Electricity Power Consumption (per capita, in KWh); (6) Percentage of labor force employed in Agriculture; and (7) Percentage of labor force employed in Industry.[2] All indices were derived from statistical information databanks such as the United Nations Organization and the World Bank Organization. In all, seven indices per country were inserted into a rectangular 32 countries by 7 factors matrix; however, Northern Ireland data were not available since none was reported in the databanks, thus the final matrix to be analyzed was a 31 countries by 7 indices rectangular matrix.

The statistical method applied was simple exploratory factor analysis for these 7 measures. The extraction method was principal component analysis and no rotation was performed since only one dimension was expected in the data. The outcomes (accounting for approximately 70% of the variance) resulted in regression factor scores where the lower the factor score, the less the affluence index for this country. The patterns of standardized regression coefficients, along with their respective R^2 indices are presented in Table 7.7. Country-level Affluence was negatively correlated with *Religiosity and family life* ($\beta = -.52$). Abortion and divorce was highly negatively correlated with Affluence ($\beta = -.79$); because high scores are scored as 'disapproval' on this variable, they are reversed in the table so that the correct interpretation of the direction of correlations is 'high affluent countries tend to approve of abortion and divorce, while low affluent disapprove.'

---

[2] Percentage of labor force employed in services was not a part of this multivariate analysis, since it would create statistical discrepancies, due to its complementary nature to the 6th and 7th financial indices. For the 3rd index (Commercial Energy Use in million tons oil equivalent), a special procedure had to be carried out, since it was the only index directly related to the area of each country and also to its actual population size (one would expect that countries with fewer people would overall consume less energy in million tons oil equivalent). The rest of the indices were not susceptible to this issue, since they were either expressed as percentages of labor force or were per capita measures. For the Commercial Energy Use in million tons oil equivalent measure though, some form of weighting had to be applied. Thus, we also retrieved the actual population indices for each of these 31 countries and we computed a weight coefficient for each country as if its population was equal to the largest participating population (in our data, Russian Federation). For example, Iceland has approx. 523 times less population than the Russian federation. To remedy for such incompatibilities, the weight coefficients were used to compute the new commercial energy use in million tons oil equivalent index per country; this index, along with the rest of the financial indices was employed in the analysis.

Table 7.7   Percent of respondents declaring Roman Catholic (RC), Protest-
ant/Anglicans (PA), Christian Orthodox (CO), Evangelical/Free Church
(Ev), Islam (M), Unaffiliated, atheistic, not declared (Unaf)

	RC	PA	CO	Ev	M	Unaf
Austria	85	6	0	0	0	0
Belarus	0	0	80	0	0	20
Belgium	75	1	1	0	4	10
Croatia	76.5	0.4	11.2	0	1.2	0
Czech Republic	4.5	1	3	0	0	64
Denmark	0	0	0	85	2	9
Estonia	0	0	38	58	0	0
Finland	0	0	1	89	0	9
France	90	2	0	0	1	6
Germany	37	45	0	0	0	18
Greece	0	0	98	0	1.3	0
Hungary	67.5	20	0	5	0	7.5
Iceland	0	3	0	96	0	1
Ireland	93	5	0	0	0	1
Italy	98	0	0	0	2	0
Latvia	27	16	19	34	1	0
Lithuania	26	46	0	0	0	12
Luxembourg	97	2	0	0	0	0
Malta	98	2	0	0	0	0
Netherlands	34	25	0	0	3	38
Poland	95	2.5	2.5	0	0	0
Portugal	97	1	0	0	0	0
Romania	6	6	86	0	0	2
Russian Federation	0	0	60	0	0	31
Slovak Republic	64.7	8.4	4.1	6.2	0	9.7
Slovenia	95	1	2.5	0	1	0
Spain	99	0	0	0	0	0
Sweden	1,5	0	0	94	0	0
Ukraine	15	0	70	0	0	0
United Kingdom	10	57	0	0	0	28
Bulgaria	0.7	0.5	85	0	13	0

Also note that because three of the four items of this factor refer to
abortion, interpretation of its meaning should be weighted toward
abortion and not divorce. *Children, family life and marriage* was negatively correlated with country level of affluence ($\beta = -.73$). Affluence
was not significantly related to the other factors, *Companionship in marriage, Family security, Living conditions of family and elderly, Working wife
and mother.*

The percent of adherents per country to religious denominations
(Roman Catholic, Protestants/Anglicans, Christian Orthodox, Free
Church/Evangelical, Muslim, and Unaffiliated) are presented in Table
7.7. Measures of association with the overall factor means were calculated with weighted least squares regression models to compensate

for the very low percentages for specific religious denominations in some countries. Weights were calculated in such a way that, for the countries with some religious denomination missing, the sum of these weights was equal to one. In Table 7.8, the measures of association of the Religion ecocultural variable with the ten overall factors and the respective standardized regression coefficients are presented. As can be seen, for the Roman Catholic countries a β of .48 indicates that the living conditions of family and the elderly are considered important. The same relationship was found for the Protestant/Anglican countries (β =.39). However, working wife and mother was disapproved for the Protestant/Anglican countries (β =.35). For the Christian Orthodox countries abortion and divorce were disapproved (β =.42), together with working wife and mother (β =.35), but children, family life and marriage were considered important (β =.46). The more the unaffiliated with a religion in a country the less important the 'Religiosity and family life' factor was considered (β = −.41). No rela-

Table 7.8 Measures of association and standardized regression coefficients: simple regression models with the 10 universal factors as dependent variables; affluence and religious denomination ecocultural indices

	Affluence		R.Cath.		Protest.		C.Orth.		Evang.		Muslim		Unaf.	
Overall family value factors	r^2	β	r^2	β	r^2	β	r^2	β	r^2	β	r^2	β	r^2	β
Religiosity and family life (high=important)	.28	**−.52**	.05	.21	.03	.17	.05	.23	.01	−.11	.01	−.07	.17	**−.41**
Companionship in marriage (high=important)	.08	.28	.04	.19	.02	.14	.06	−.24	.01	−.11	.01	.10	.02	−.13
Abortion & divorce* (high=disapproval)	.62	**−.79**	.02	.13	.02	.13	.18	**.42**	.00	.01	.00	.03	.00	.01
Children, family life, and marriage (high=important)	.53	**−.73**	.00	−.01	.01	−.07	.21	**.46**	.01	−.08	.01	.07	.06	−.25
Family security (high=important)	.10	−.31	.00	.01	.01	−.11	.04	.19	.01	−.12	.11	−.33	.03	.16
Living conditions of family and elderly (high=important)	.00	−.00	.23	**.48**	.16	**.39**	.06	−.25	.02	−.14	.01	.04	.08	−.29
Working wife and mother* (high=disapproval)	.00	.00	.04	.21	.12	**.35**	.16	**−.41**	.11	−.33	.01	−.08	.01	−.09

Religious Denomination Ecocultural Index (column group heading)

* Reversed variables

tionships were found with Evangelists and Muslims. It is likely that this was due to the low percentages of these religious denominations in the countries involved in the analysis.

3   Discussion

The primary purpose of the analysis was to attempt to delineate clusters of countries with similar patterns and with similar positions of agreement or disagreement on these family values and attitudes. Thus, the family values and attitudes in the EVS study were not analyzed for each country separately at the individual level.

The first major finding in this study is that there are common family value and attitude constructs shared by all the European countries as well as specific family value and attitude constructs characteristic of one or two European clusters of countries. The second major finding was that country clusters sometimes had distinctly different positions on some family values and attitudes, but did not differ on others.

The four 'universal' or common family values and constructs across the European countries were *Religiosity and family life*, *Companionship in marriage*, *Abortion and divorce*, and *Children, family life and marriage*. *Working wife and mother* was found in three of the four country clusters.

The country groupings were determined by cluster analyzing the items by the 33 countries. Four country clusters, with similar patterns of family values and attitudes were found. Cluster 1 was composed primarily of Western European countries, seven members of the European Union. Cluster 2 was composed of Eastern European, countries associated with the former Soviet Union. Cluster 3 was also composed primarily of other Western European countries and members of the EU along with Croatia and Poland. Cluster 4 was composed primarily of the Scandinavian countries together with the Netherlands.

3.1   *Family values and attitudes, demographic variables, and country clusters*

3.1.1   *Religiosity and family life*
Family values and attitudes relating to religion and family life: *attending religious services, importance of religion, are you a religious person, spending time in church, church and family life,* and *shared religious beliefs* were found in

all four country clusters. The highest level of approval of these religious values was in the countries of Cluster 3 (Croatia . . . Portugal), followed by the former Eastern European countries of Cluster 2 (Belarus . . . Ukraine). The primarily Western European countries of Cluster 1 (Austria . . . UK) and the primarily Scandinavian countries of Cluster 4 (Denmark . . . Sweden) slightly disapproved of the importance of these religious values and attitudes. However, the composite T-scores indicate that the differences between these clusters of countries are relative and not extreme.

The demographic variables of the individuals in the study indicate, as it might be predicted, that older respondents tend to approve of religious values more than younger ones. Education was not related to religious values across all European countries, except for the Eastern European countries of Cluster 2 (Belarus . . . Ukraine), where there was a positive association between education and religious values. The same patterns were observed in relation to Gender, with again, only a small positive association in the countries of Cluster 2. A small effect was found between marital status and religion across all countries, with married respondents having higher levels of approval than unmarried respondents. Income and Stable relationships were not related to religious values.

At the country level, the higher the economic index—the level of affluence—of a country the lower the values related to Religiosity and family life.

3.1.2 *Companionship in marriage*

Values and attitudes on this dimension were: *discussing problems, talking about mutual interests, spending time together, understanding and tolerance in marriage, mutual respect and appreciation, happy sexual relationship* and *sharing household chores.* These behaviors were all in regard to questions about '. . . things which make for a successful marriage.' These behaviors may be consistent with the relationship between husband and wife, with or without children, or between unmarried partners. They have less to do with the structure of the family, nuclear or extended, than with communication and interaction among couples. This dimension was a universal construct in the European countries. It is important to note that no differences between the European countries were found, suggesting that these elements of communication and interaction were not controversial and that although there may be individual differences regarding their importance, they are equally valued in all European cultures.

The same picture emerges in regard to their relationships with demographic variables. No significant relationships with this dimension were found.

3.1.3 *Abortion and divorce*

This dimension was also universal in the European countries. Three items concerned abortion; *if abortion is justified, approval of abortion if the woman is not married, approval if more children are not wanted*, and one item inquired if *divorce is justified*. The highest approval on these attitudes and values was found in the primarily Scandinavian countries of Cluster 4 (Denmark ... Sweden), which might be expected since demographic statistics indicated (Fotakis, 2000) they have the highest percents of single parent families and one-person households in the EU, and the lowest percent of three-generation households. Lower levels of approval of Abortion and divorce were found in the Western European countries of Cluster 1 (Austria ... UK), followed by the former Eastern European countries of Cluster 2 (Belarus ... Ukraine). The primarily EU countries in Cluster 3 (Croatia ... Portugal) disapproved of Abortion and divorce. However, as with the Religion and family life dimension, the differences are relative between these country clusters.

Some relationships with demographic variables were found. Older and married respondents tended to reject *Abortion and divorce* more than younger and unmarried ones. More highly educated respondents tended to approve more than those with lower education. However, neither income nor gender nor whether or not the respondent had a stable relationship differentiated between attitudes and values toward Abortion and divorce. Also, no differences were found between the different religions regarding attitudes toward abortions.

Abortion and divorce was positively correlated with the level of country Affluence; high affluent countries tend to approve of abortion and divorce, while low affluent countries disapprove.

3.1.4 *Children, family life, and marriage*

As suggested, attitudes and values centering around *marriage or long-term relationship is necessary for one to be happy, a woman needs to have children to be fulfilled*, and *both parents needed in a family*, appear to be related to the nuclear family system, or possible even with the extended family system. Whether this is the traditional family system composed of working father and housewife mother, or the two-generation family with working mother and father, or the three-generation household of grandparents or aunts uncles living could not be determined by the methodology of the study. Approval of these values was found in the Eastern European countries of Cluster 2 (Belarus . . . Ukraine). Cluster 3 (Croatia . . . Portugal) and Cluster 1 (Austria . . . UK) were slightly disapproving. That the Scandinavian Cluster 4 (Denmark . . . Sweden) had the strongest disapproval of these values would also be consistent with their high levels of one-parent families and the lowest number of three-generation families in the EU (Fotakis, 2000).

Older respondents and married respondents approved of these values but gender, education, level of income and stable or unstable relationships were not related to this dimension in the overall sample. Some minor effects were found in country clusters, but they do not appear to be of significant importance.

Membership in a religious denomination was related to approval or disapproval of the values associated the nuclear family. Protestants and Evangelists were on the disapproval side, Catholics and Jews in the center, and Christian Orthodox and Muslims on the approval side of this family values dimension.

3.1.5 *Working wife and mother*

Surprisingly, no large effect sizes were observed on the values of this dimension, and it appears that there are no significant differences in the three of the four clusters of countries in Europe in which this dimension appears. Again, no demographic differences were found in this factor except for the effect of religious denomination in Cluster 4 (Denmark . . . Sweden). Protestants indicated low approval, while Roman Catholics and Evangelists were slightly in favor.

3.2 *Patterns of country clusters and family value dimensions*

The differences between the country clusters on the four value dimensions are not polar differences. It would be a mistake to conclude that the four European clusters of countries differ widely in their positions on family values. The differences are more a matter of degree and rather small.

However, a comparison of the four country clusters and the four value dimensions reveals some consistent patterns of differences. The order of the country clusters, in respect of approval or disapproval of the values, is consistent across the four value dimensions. The Cluster 3 countries, Greece, Ireland, Northern Ireland, Italy, Portugal, Croatia and Poland, appear to approve most highly values associated with religiosity and family life, and to disapprove most highly values associated with abortion and divorce, and are also ranked second in their approval of values associated with the importance of children, family life and marriage. The Cluster 2 countries associated with the former Soviet Union, Belarus, Bulgaria, Estonia, Hungary, Latvia, Lithuania, Romania, Russia, Slovakia, and Ukraine, are close to the positions of the Cluster 3 countries on these values. These are values associated with the conventional European family, either the nuclear family or the three-generation family with close ties.

On the other hand, the primarily Scandinavian countries, Denmark, Finland, Iceland, and Sweden, together with the Netherlands of Cluster 4, hold opposite positions on all three dimensions. They disapprove most of the importance of values associated with religiosity and family life and conventional family life, and approve most highly abortion and divorce.

The countries of Cluster 1, Austria, Belgium, France, West Germany, East Germany, Luxembourg, Spain, United Kingdom, the Czech Republic and Slovenia are consistently third in this pattern, and closer to the position of the Scandinavian countries than the Eastern European countries.

Is there a Northern Europe versus Southern Europe divide in these family values? Perusing the countries on each factor, except for the Scandinavian countries, there does not appear to be a northern-southern European countries divide on these family values.

A possible explanation might be religion. The cluster 3 countries with conventional family values and the highest disapproval of abortion are Catholic, except for Christian Orthodox Greece. Of the ten Cluster 2 Eastern Europe countries, five are predominantly Christian Orthodox. Of the ten Cluster 1 countries, six are Roman Catholic. The four Scandinavian countries are predominantly Evangelical/Free Church.

It is important to distinguish between individual-level analyses of declared religion and the country-level discussion above. The individual-level analyses were based on the declaration of adherence to a religion by respondents across all the countries. The results there, which are not entirely inconsistent with the above discussion, reflect the positions of, e.g., all Roman Catholics across all countries. The country-level discussion refers to the predominant religion in each country, e.g., since 98% of Italians declare their Religion is Roman Catholic, Italy can be considered to be a country in which its social institutions have been shaped over the centuries by the Roman Catholic Church, as Weber (1904) has stated (see Inglehart & Baker, 2000).

It appears that the dominant religion in a European country may influence position on family values. Thus, the Catholic and Christian Orthodox countries may strongly influence conventional family values, influencing them through national institutions. On the other hand Scandinavian countries may have different positions on family values and attitudes.

The distinction also holds between individual-level analysis of affluence, that is, the level of income of the respondents and the country-level analysis of affluence, the index based on country level measures of GNP, energy production, etc. Level of income was not correlated with any of the above family value dimensions, either the overall factors or within country clusters. That is, whether an individual has a high level of income or low level, there was no relationship with their position on these family values.

However, the country's level of affluence is highly related to positions of approval of these family value dimensions. The wealthy Scandinavian countries and the Netherlands had the highest level of disapproval of conventional family values and the highest level of approval of abortion and divorce. Demographic statistics also indicate they have the highest percents of one-parent families. The poorest countries are, as expected, the former Eastern European countries, which approve of conventional family values.

It should also be noted that these poorer countries are also predominately Christian Orthodox and Roman Catholic, so that there might well be an interaction between Affluence and religion in determining approval or disapproval of these family values. These combined effects have been found in Georgas, van de Vijver and Berry (2004) and in Inglehart and Davis (2000). The explanation would be that affluent countries shape their institutions according to both religion and level of affluence. In high affluent countries, a young couple can buy or rent their own apartment because banking institutions encourage loans for young couples, laws which protect unmarried parents are active, etc.

It was highly surprising that gender was not related to these family value dimensions. One might have predicted that women would have a different position on abortion and divorce, or perhaps a more conservative position on religiosity and family life, etc. However, the results of these thousands of respondents indicate no significant differences, in the sense of a powerful effect of gender differences on these family values. Men and women essentially agree on these family values.

Another surprising finding was the relatively low relationship between level of education and these family values. A relatively small association was found in regard to abortion and divorce, in which more highly educated tend to approve. But, the correlation was very low, a suggestion of a small percent of variance explained. Education was not significantly and consistently correlated with the other family values, either with the overall factors or those within country clusters, suggesting again, that other variables play a significant role, or that this powerful social dimension, which influences many attitudes, does not strongly influence family values.

Age does correlate with these family values in the predicted directions; approval of the conventional family, disapproval of abortion and divorce, etc. However, once again, the size of the correlations were relatively low; much lower than one would have predicted if there is truly a 'gender gap' regarding family values.

4 Conclusions

This was basically a descriptive and exploratory study, searching for associations between the questions about family values and attitudes and demographic and other cultural variables. The methodology was not that of presenting independent variables and systematically testing their effects on dependent variables. As in many such exploratory studies, the questions generated by the results are perhaps more interesting and worthy of further systematic investigation than the questions initially asked.

The methodology of this study did not permit studying the relationship of these family values to family types, e.g., the nuclear family, the extended family, one-person family. This would have necessitated a different method asking specific questions about which members of the extended family live in the household, or live near the household, the amount of interactions and communication between members of the nuclear family and kin (Georgas, 1998; Georgas, et al., 2001; Georgas, et al., 2004). Nor did the methodology of this study permit studying the relationship between family roles and values. Also, it should be noted that the items employed in the EVS are a small subset of the potentially larger number of family value dimensions that could be studied. The analyses in this study are restricted to the family values and attitudes employed in the EVS. The results should be evaluated in this context. However, the results described in this study are useful in the area of the study of the family.

In closing, perhaps the general conclusion that could be drawn from this study is that while there are different positions on family values in different European countries, or more accurately, clusters of European countries, these differences are not extreme at the country level. It appears that the differences in family values between European countries are relatively moderate.

References

Adler, N. 1994. Health psychology. *Annual Review of Psychology* 45: 229–259.

Aerts, E. 1993. Bringing the institution back in. Pp. 3–41 in P.A. Cowan, D. Field, D.A. Hansen, A. Skonick & G.E. Swanson (eds.), *Family, Self, and Society*. Hillsdale, NJ: Erlbaum.

Bott, E. 1955. Urban families: conjugal roles and social networks. *Human Relations* 8: 345–384.

—— 1971. *Family and Social Network*. New York: Free Press.

Cassia, P.S. & C. Bada 1992. *The Making of the Modern Greek Family*. Cambridge: Cambridge University Press.

Cuyvers, P. 2000. You can't have it all—at least at the same time. Segmentation in the modern life course as a threat to intergenerational communication and solidarity. Pp. 30–43 in S. Trnka (ed.), *Family Issues between Gender and Generations*. Luxembourg: European Commission: Employment & Social Affairs.

Eurobarometer (no. 39.0/1993).

Fotakis, C. 2000. How social is Europe? *Family Observer* 2: 32–40.

Georgas, J. 1989. Changing family values in Greece: From collectivist to individualist. *Journal of Cross-Cultural Psychology* 20: 80–91.

—— 1999. Family as a context variable in cross-cultural psychology. Pp. 163–175 in J. Adamopoulos & Y. Kashima (eds.), *Social Psychology and Cultural Context*. Beverly Hills: Sage.

—— & J.W. Berry 1995. An ecocultural taxonomy for cross-cultural psychology. *Cross-Cultural Research* 29: 121–157.

—— & K. Mylonas (in press). Cultures are like all cultures, like some other cultures, like no other cultures. In U. Kim & K.-S. Yang (eds.), *Indigenous Psychologies*. New York: Kluwer Academic Publishers.

——, T. Bafiti, L. Papademou & K. Mylonas (2004). Families in Greece. In J.L. Roopnarine & U.P. Gielen (eds.), *Families in Global Perspective*. Boston: Allyn & Bacon.

——, J.W. Berry, F. van de Vijver, Ç. Kagitçibasi & Y.H. Poortinga (eds.), (In preparation). *Family Structure and Function Across Cultures: Psychological Variations*. Cambridge: Cambridge University Press.

——, K. Mylonas, T. Bafiti, S. Christakopoulou, Y.H. Poortinga, Ç. Kagitçibasi, S. Orung, D. Sunar, K. Kwak, B. Ataca, J.W. Berry, N. Charalambous, R. Goodwin, W.-Z. Wang, A. Angleitner, I. Stepanikova, S. Pick, M. Givaudan, I. Zhuravliova-Gionis, R. Konantambigi, M.J. Gelfand, M. Velislava, M. McBride-Chang & Y. Kodiç 2001. Functional Relationships in the nuclear and extended family: A 16 culture study. *International Journal of Psychology* 36: 289–300.

——, F.J.R. van de Vijver & J.W. Berry 2004. Ecosocial Indicators and Psychological Variables in Cross-cultural Research. *Journal of Cross-Cultural Psychology* 35: 74–96.

Graziano, A.M. & M.L. Raulin 1989. *Research Methods: A Process of Inquiry*. New York: Harper and Row Publishers, Inc.

Guilford, J.P. 1956. *Psychometric Methods*. New York: McGraw-Hill.

Halman, L. 2001. *The European Values Study: A Third Wave. Sourcebook of the 1999/2000 European Values Study Surveys*. Tilburg: EVS, WORC, Tilburg University.

Hofstede, G. 1980. *Culture's Consequences*. Beverly Hills, CA: Sage.

—— 2001. *Culture's Consequences* (2nd ed.). Thousand Oaks, CA: Sage.

Inglehart, R. & W.E. Baker 2000. Modernization, cultural change, and the persistence of traditional values. *American Sociological Review* 65: 19–51.

Kessler, R.C., R.H. Price & C.B. Wortman 1985. Social factors in psychopathology. *Annual Review of Psychology* 36: 531–72.

Kline, P. 1993. *The Handbook of Psychological Testing*. London: Routledge.

Kluckhohn, C. 1951. Values and value orientations in the theory of action. Pp. 388–433 in T. Parsons & E.A. Shilds (eds.), *Toward a General Theory of Action*. Cambridge, MA: Harvard University Press.

Kroeber, A.L. & C. Kluckhohn 1952. *Culture: A Critical Review of Concepts and Definitions 47(1)*. Cambridge, MA: Peabody Museum.

Laing, R.D. 1969. *The Divided Self*. New York: Pantheon.

Laslett, P. & R. Wall (eds.) 1972. *Household and Family in Past Time*. Cambridge: Cambridge University Press.

Levinson, D. & M.J. Malone 1980. *Toward Explaining Human Culture*. New Haven, Ct: HRAF Press.

Muncie, J. & R. Sapsford 1995. Issues in the study of 'the family'. Pp. 7–37 in J. Muncie, M. Wetherell, R. Dallos, & A. Cochrane (eds.), *Understanding the Family*. London: Sage.

Murdock, P.M. 1949. *Social Structure*. New York: Free Press.

Parsons, T. 1943. The kinship system of the contemporary United States. *American Anthropologist* 45: 22–38.

—— 1949. The social structure of the family. In R.N. Anshen (ed.), *The Family: Its Functions and Destiny*. New York: Harper.

—— 1953. *The Social System*. New York: Free Press.

—— 1965. The normal American family. Pp. 34–36 in S.M. Farber (ed.), *Man and Civilization: The Family's Search for Survival*. New York: McGraw-Hill.

Poortinga, Y.H. 1989. Equivalence of cross-cultural data: An overview of basic issues. *International Journal of Psychology* 24: 737–756.

Popenoe, D. 1988. *Disturbing the Next-Family Changes and Decline in Modern Societies*. New York: Aldine De Gruyter.

Safilios-Rothschild, K. 1967. A comparison of power structure and marital satisfaction in urban Greek and French families. *Journal of Marriage and the Family* 29: 345–349.

Segalen, M. 1986. *Historical Anthropology of the Family*. Cambridge: Cambridge University Press.

Skolnick, A. 1993. Change of heart: Family dynamics in historical perspective. Pp. 43–68 in P.A. Cowan, D. Field, D.A. Hansen, A. Skolnick & G.E. Swanson (eds.), *Family, Self, and Society*. Hillsdale, NJ: Erlbaum.

Smith, S. 1995. Family theory and multicultural family studies. Pp. 5–35 in B. Ingoldsby & S. Smith (eds.), *Families in Multicultural Perspective*. New York: The Guilford Press.

Stanton, M.E. 1995. Patterns of kinship and residence. Pp. 97–116 in B. Ingoldsby & S. Smith (eds.), *Families in Multicultural Perspective*. New York: The Guilford Press.

Tabachnick, B.G. & L.S. Fidell 1989. *Using Multivariate Statistics*. New York: Harper & Row Publishers, Inc.

Thurstone, L.L. 1947. *Multiple Factor Analysis: A development and expansion of The Vectors of Mind*. Chicago, IL: The University of Chicago Press.

Uzoka, A.F. 1979. The myth of the nuclear family. *American Psychologist* 34: 1095–1106.

Van de Vijver, F. & K. Leung 1997. *Methods and Data Analysis for Cross-cultural Research*. Thousand Oaks, CA: Sage.

—— & Y.H. Poortinga 2000. *Structural Equivalence in Multilevel Research*. Manuscript in preparation.

Weber, M. [1904] 1958. *The Protestant Ethic and Spirit of Capitalism*. New York: Charles Scribner's Sons.

CHAPTER EIGHT

PRIVATIZATION IN THE FAMILY SPHERE: LONGITUDINAL AND COMPARATIVE ANALYSES IN FOUR EUROPEAN COUNTRIES

Leen Vandecasteele & Jaak Billiet

1 Introduction

Individualization is a process of cultural change that has been flooding across Western societies since the mid-20th century. Many sociologists have studied this basic process in our changing society, a process which, in the first place, is a symptom of the diminishing impact of traditional institutions, norms and values. Church, marriage, political parties, government, etc. . . . all have become less important. The impact of belonging to traditional social categories such as a particular social class, gender, family or neighborhood is beginning to fade (Beck & Beck-Gernsheim, 1996: 24). When traditional frames of reference disappear, individuals are forced to rely on their own frames of reference. This can be seen as a shift from standardized biographies to do-it-yourself biographies (Beck & Beck-Gernsheim, 1996: 25). In every domain of life, the authority of traditional institutions is being replaced by individual autonomy. Another aspect of the individualization process is the emphasis on self-realization (Van den Elzen, 1996: 30). When physical needs and the need for security are fulfilled, as is the case in more industrialized welfare states, people's needs shift more toward the psychological necessities of recognition and self-realization. This theory of Maslow was the basis for Inglehart's materialism-postmaterialism scale (Lesthaeghe & Meekers, 1987: 141).

The individualization process is having an impact on various spheres of life. Among others, the area of family and primary relations is being hit by the process of change. Think, for example, of the growing equality between man and woman, the changing attitudes toward sexuality, and the changing attitudes toward marriage. Here we are especially interested in certain aspects of a successful marriage. With reference to aspects considered crucial for the success of a marriage, the traditional family ethos puts a strong emphasis on homogamy. It requires that partner relationships be formed within the person's own ethnic, social, religious and/or age group. In the traditional ethos, homogamy means higher marriage satisfaction (Van den Troost, 2000: 136). With individualization, quality becomes an important determinant for a successful marriage. When traditional reference points disappear, human beings focus their attention on those who are closest to them, i.e. those with whom they have emotional ties. The immediate vicinity is indispensable in helping people to find their place in the world and to maintain their physical and mental well-being (Beck-Gernsheim, 1995: 49–50). In short, quality within the relationship is becoming an emotional necessity.

In this paper, we are principally interested in a specific aspect of the individualization process, which we call the *privatization of value orientations*. Privatization refers to the declining impact of collectivities and traditional institutions on personal value orientations. To understand this evolution, we turn back to the basic principles of individualization: the declining influence of traditional institutions and the growing importance of personal autonomy and self-realization. With the growing emphasis on individual autonomy, values and norms are also becoming more and more personal. The impact of traditional institutions such as the church and of social categories such as generation and social class will gradually disappear. In a time where every aspect of life is subject to personal choice, the impact of traditional social collectivities and institutions on personal value orientations are diminishing.

The main aim of our analyses is to elaborate on the impact of social background variables on marriage success factors. First of all, theoretical arguments can be given to hypothesize that some social background variables will be predictors of what people think is important for success in marriage. So we can expect that young people, highly educated persons and persons of the higher social classes are more inclined to support quality aspects of marriage than older people, people with less education and lower class people. On the other hand we expect that, with the ongoing privatization of value orientations, these effects will diminish. With the help of longitudinal and comparative analyses of the European Values Studies datasets, we can empirically test these propositions in four west European countries. In such a test, we expect to find different European countries to be in different stages of the privatization process.

2 Research questions and hypotheses

In this paper we want to test certain hypotheses about the impact of social background variables on marriage success factors.

In the European Values Studies, a variable is included relating to what respondents think is important for success in marriage. In what follows we speak of marriage success factors. We have seen that due to the individualization process there is a growing emphasis on quality within the relationship and less emphasis on the traditional homogamy values. Within the marriage success factors, the emphasis on quality within the relationship and the diminishing homogamy norm are considered to be signs of the individualization process.

When speaking about individualization in the family sphere, we must definitely be aware that not all groups in society are equally sensitive to the new values of marriage quality and intimacy. Beck asserts that 'it is necessary, therefore, to check each group, milieu and region, to determine how far individualization processes—overt or covert—have advanced within it' (Beck & Beck-Gernsheim, 1996: 28). Most authors in the debate argue that individualization emerges first within the higher social classes and among highly educated people (Laermans, 1992: 67–69; Felling, Peeters & Scheepers, 2000: 39–40; Lesthaeghe & Surkeyn, 1988: 17). The material prerequisites that make an individual life course possible are particularly present in the higher social classes. They can afford the luxury to leave traditional paths. More highly educated people have the necessary cultural capital to live an individualized life. Their stronger skills give them more opportunities, for example, in the labour market, where they can more easily make their own way. Next to the effects of class and educational level, there is the effect of belonging to the younger generation, in the sense that young people are more inclined toward the individualized value orientations. Young people have been socialized within a society that is already characterized by modernity. In this respect there is a clear difference between the pre-war and the post-war generations. Finally, we expect that persons with a stronger church commitment will be less individualized, because of the dominance of traditional values in the churches. Concerning the effects of education level, age and church commitment,[1] we can formulate the following four hypotheses:

- H1: Education level has an effect on quality of marriage and on marriage homogamy. More highly educated people will put more emphasis on the quality aspects of marriage and will be less inclined to support the homogamy aspects.
- H2: We expect to find an age effect on the variables quality of marriage and marriage homogamy. Younger people will be more interested in the quality of marriage, and less in homogamy aspects.
- H3: The stronger the church commitment, the more a person emphasizes the homogamy aspects of marriage, and the less attention he or she pays to quality of marriage.

In a second step, we plan to empirically test the privatization hypothesis. We expect individuals to be responsible for their own values, and we expect the social collectivities to lose their impact. The effect of social variables such as generation, social class, education level, etc. will decrease as the individualization process goes on. This process can also be understood by the trendsetter and diffusion theory of Middendorp (1979: 170–171). Some social groups are trendsetters with the breakthrough of new developments. These groups are most committed to new developments. In a later stage, the trend will disperse among the other groups as well. It is time to formulate the privatization hypothesis:

- H4: The impact of social background variables on marriage success factors will decrease over time.

We may wonder whether the privatization process proceeds in the same way all over Europe. To answer this question, reference is made to the embeddedness of individualization processes in the modernization theory. Privatization and the declining impact of collectivities and traditional institutions on individual values are conceived

---

[1] It would be interesting to test the effect of social background as well, but since the SES variable is not available for all the waves of the data in Ireland and Denmark, this cannot be done.

as part of a wider modernization process that has shaped society since the end of the Middle Ages. This process consists of interrelated transformations in the field of economics (e.g., industrialism and capitalism), in the social and political field (e.g. mass education, democratization, urbanism, etc.) and in the cultural field (e.g., individualization and secularization) (Felling et al., 2000: 31). As these changes are interrelated, we can expect that value changes go hand in hand with structural changes in society. Countries characterized by a high level of structural modernization will also be characterized by a higher level of cultural modernization. Thus, privatization processes will be clearer in countries where structural modernization has already reached a higher level. Several researchers tried to classify countries according to their rate of structural modernization (Halman, 1991: 9–10). Usually several indicators are used: number of people working in farming, number of telephones, education participation, etc. Within Western Europe, there is a rough distinction between Northern and Southern countries with respect to structural modernization. Overall, northern European countries are thought to be more modern than southern European countries. Ireland is an exception since, structurally speaking, it belongs to the southern European group of countries (Halman, 1991: 8–11). In our analyses, we use data from Belgium, Denmark, Ireland and Spain. The last two countries are characterized by less structural modernization. With regard to the privatization process, we expect a difference between Belgium and Denmark, on the one hand, and Spain and Ireland, on the other. We can thus formulate the following hypothesis:

- H5: Privatization processes will be clearer in Belgium and Denmark compared to the situation in Spain and Ireland, because of the higher level of structural modernization in Belgium and Denmark.

3   Data, constructs and method

The hypotheses are tested with the surveys from the European Values Studies. The EVS project consists of an international, comparative and longitudinal study concerning values in different spheres of life. With its three cross-sectional surveys in a number of European countries, the EVS data make comparison possible among countries and over time. Surveys were taken in 1981, 1990 and 1999. For our analyses we will use the data of Belgium, Denmark, Spain and

Ireland, and we will work with the three waves. Most analyses are conducted on weighted data,[2] except for the multi-group comparisons in LISREL.[3]

In the domain of family values, we focus on the aspects of a successful marriage. In the EVS questionnaire, the following question is included:

> Here is a list of things which some people think make for a successful marriage. Please tell me, for each one, whether you think it is very important, rather important, or not very important:
> - Faithfulness;
> - An adequate income;
> - Being of the same social background;
> - Mutual respect and appreciation;
> - Shared religious beliefs
> - Good housing
> - Agreement on politics
> - Understanding and tolerance
> - Living apart from in-laws
> - Happy sexual relationship
> - Sharing household chores
> - Children
> - Tastes and interests in common (not in 1999)
> - Willingness to talk about problems arising between man and wife (only in 1999)
> - Spending as much time as possible together (only in 1999)
> - Talking a lot about common interests (only in 1999)

On theoretical grounds and on the basis of other research, we expect to find three dimensions: material aspects, homogamy and quality aspects (Van den Troost, 2000; Van den Elzen, 1998; Dobbelaere et al., 2000: 225–230).

Before testing the hypotheses, we set up a measurement model for these three expected marriage success factors. We also investigate the construct equivalence of the latent variables in the three waves and the four countries. Are we really measuring the same constructs in the twelve groups? Rensvold and Cheung (1998) define

---

[2] The weighting variable for age and gender in the individual countries is used.
[3] For the factor analyses in LISREL, we work with unweighted data. A correction for the data in Belgium in 1990 was necessary because there is an overrepresentation of some regions in the original dataset. Therefore we take a random sample of the original dataset in which we take a correct representation of the regions.

construct equivalence operationally as factorial invariance. This means that a construct is equivalent across two or more cultural groups if the loadings of a certain indicator on that construct in one group can be set equal to the corresponding loadings in the other groups. This condition applies to all indicators of the construct. The test starts with a model of complete invariance across the groups of the measurements and with complete invariance of the relationships between the concepts. We then move step by step to an acceptable model.

On the basis of factor analyses in the separate datasets we decide to test a model with three correlated factors. Of the twelve marriage success aspects apparent in the three datasets, nine items are included in the model: mutual respect and appreciation, understanding and tolerance, happy sexual relationship, sharing household chores, good housing, adequate income, same social background, shared religious beliefs and agreement on politics. Three of the other items, faithfulness, living apart from in-laws and having children, did not have strong loadings on one of the extent factors. And other items are excluded because they are not repeated in all three waves. A completely invariant model is tested for twelve groups: four countries (Belgium, Denmark, Spain and Ireland) and three waves (1981, 1990, 1999). Figure 8.1 shows the tested model.

Table 8.1 shows statistics of the successive tested models. The models are cumulative, which means that parameters that are unconstrained in a given model x will be unconstrained in the following models x + 1, x + 2 . . . as well. Model 1 accepts covariance between the residuals of 'adequate income' and 'same social background'. Model 2 accepts covariance between the residuals of 'understanding and tolerance' and 'mutual respect and appreciation'. Both sets of indicators have something in common, apart from the common latent variable.[4]

For the evaluation of the models, we use several criteria. First of all, we use the drop in the chi-square value for one degree of freedom. As long as the drop in value is substantially more than three units, one can conclude that there is an improvement. Furthermore,

---

[4] 'Adequate income' and 'same social background' both refer to an aspect of social status. 'Understanding and tolerance' and 'mutual respect and appreciation' both refer to the aspect tolerance.

Figure 8.1   Multi-group comparison for marriage success factors:
path diagram of the model

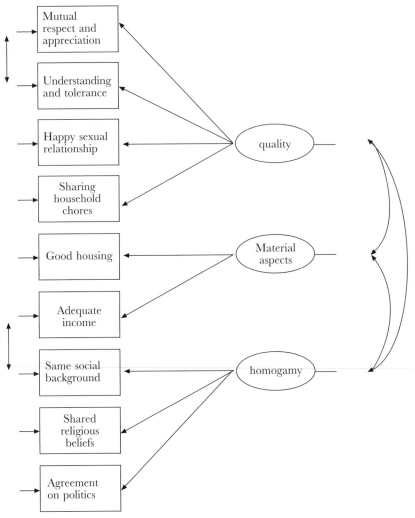

Table 8.1   Summary of the tested measurement models
(Multi-group comparisons)

Model	Chi-square	Df	RMSEA	P (close fit)	NIF
Model 0: completely constrained	3065,4	519	0,058	1	0,85
Model 1: TD (6,7) free, completely constrained	2711,99	518	0,054	1	0,87
Model 2: TD (1,2) free, completely constrained	2247,82	517	0,048	1	0,89

the p-value of close fit should be near to 1.0 and the Normed Fit indices (NFI) should be close to 1. Ideally, the root mean square error of approximation (RMSEA) should be lower than 0.05 (Bollen & Long, 1992). In the Bollen and Long model, this value is almost obtained. It is possible to decrease this value (and improve the model fit) if some error covariances are accepted, but we decided not to do so when there were no theoretically meaningful arguments for taking such a course of action. Theoretical considerations should also be taken into account in the decision about the acceptance of a model (Saris & Satorra, 1987). However, it is difficult to use this criterion for the structural relations in situations with several cultural groups, since we can never exclude non predicted differences in relationships between substantive variables across the cultural groups. Actually, in this respect we expect invariance.

The chosen model 2 shows a good fit. The RMSEA falls under 0.05 and moving from model 1 to model 2 shows a considerable decrease of chi-square for the loss of only one degree of freedom. We can conclude that it is possible to find a factor model that holds for the four countries studied and the three waves of the EVS. The standardized factor loadings can be found in the appendix.

Likert scales are constructed for further analysis. On the basis of the results, a material scale, a homogamy scale and a quality scale are constructed.

For determining the effect of social background variables, a multivariate linear regression model[5] is built for the four countries. The model estimates the effect of some social background variables on the marriage success factors. The independent variables are age, education level, church commitment, gender and legal marital status.[6] Education level, operationalized as 'age when education completed', and age are considered metric variables. Church commitment is a quasi-metric construct with scores from 1 to 6. It is based on four observed indicators: belonging to a religious denomination, attending religious services, membership in a religious organization and doing voluntary work for a religious organization. Gender and legal marital status are nominal variables.

---

[5] The Likert scales are considered to be quasi-metric variables.
[6] The variable 'legal marital status' is not present in the dataset of Ireland for 1999. Therefore we will not use that variable for the analyses of the Irish data.

We are interested in the net effect of these social variables. The variables are correlated, for example, education level is higher among the younger age groups and church commitment increases with age. So we are looking for the partial influence of each background variable.

For each marriage success scale, our aim is to find the best fitting model. The starting model consists of the five social background variables. Then, one by one, we drop those variables that have a non-significant partial sum of squares (= type 3 SS). In each step, the variable that shows the highest p-value is removed from the model. Only those variables with a type 3 SS significant at level 0.05 are included in the final model. On the basis of these regression models, we can draw conclusions about trendsetters for the more modern values.

To acquire a view of privatization processes we need a model with a period variable. In this way we can compare the effect of the main background variables over time. For each country, the three waves are now included as a categorized variable 'period' in the regression model, together with relevant social background variables.[7] The interaction term of each social background variable with period is included as well. Analysis of the VIF's[8] in our regression models shows that the introduction of interaction terms creates a high multicollinearity between the variables. To mitigate this factor, for the quasi-metric variables age, education level and church commitment, we work with variables that are centered around the mean. Once again, only significant effects are included in the final model. Non-significant interaction terms with the highest p-value, and the corresponding principal effect, are removed first.[9]

4   Results

First of all, we are interested in the effect of certain background variables on the marriage success factors. The aim is to trace trendsetters and to observe whether younger people, people who are more

---

[7] Social background variables that show no significant effect for regressions in the datasets of 1981, 1990 and 1990 (see tables 8.2, 8.3 and 8.4) are kept out of this analysis.

[8] The Variance Inflation Factors (= VIF's) indicate the impact of multicollinearity between the independent variables on the estimate.

[9] The principal effect period will be restrained in any way.

highly educated and people who are less religiously involved are indeed more inclined to value the quality aspects of marriage rather than the homogamy aspects. Furthermore we want to see whether there are differences between the countries in this respect. Tables 8.2, 8.3 and 8.4 report the regression parameters for the best fitting models.

Concerning the material marriage aspects, in Table 8.2 we find the overall effects of age, education level, church commitment and marital status. Older people are more inclined to stress the material marriage aspects. More highly educated people show less interest in the material aspects. The effects of age and education level are present in all four countries. We find some effects of church commitment in Belgium and Ireland, in the sense that people who are more committed are also more interested in the material marriage aspects. In Denmark in 1981 we find an opposite effect: church commitment is negatively related to interest in the material marriage aspects. In Belgium, Denmark and Spain, the analyses indicate that unmarried people are less materially oriented with respect to marriage success aspects. As can be seen with type 3 SS,[10] generally speaking, the effect of marital status is not very strong. It does not appear in all the waves, and in Spain it is even absent.

Concerning the homogam marriage aspects, Table 8.3 indicates an obvious effect of age and church commitment. In line with our hypothesis (H2), older people are still more inclined to homogam marriage aspects. This trend is present in all four countries and over all the waves. As can be seen with the type 3 SS, the effects are rather strong. For the effect of church commitment, it is clear that higher church commitment leads to a stronger emphasis on the homogamy aspects of marriage. This effect is also apparent in every country and every wave. It is in line with the stated hypothesis (H3). As can be seen with the type 3 SS, the effect of church commitment is high in Belgium and Spain. It is an important variable in explaining the homogam marriage orientation. Next to the effect of age and church commitment, there are indications of the effect of education level, gender and marital status. In Denmark, Ireland and Spain, the regression parameters show us that more highly educated

---

[10] The Type 3 SS measures the total effect of the considered variable. In that way we can compare how much the different social background variables contribute tot the explained variance of the model.

Table 8.2 Regression parameters for the dependent variable 'material marriage aspects' (Belgium, Denmark, Ireland, Spain, 1981–1990–1999, multiple linear regression, weighted data)

Parameter	Df	Belgium			Denmark			Ireland			Spain		
		1981 Estimate (Type 3 SS)	1990 Estimate (Type 3 SS)	1999 Estimate (Type 3 SS)	1981 Estimate (Type 3 SS)	1990 Estimate (Type 3 SS)	1999 Estimate (Type 3 SS)	1981 Estimate (Type 3 SS)	1990 Estimate (Type 3 SS)	1999 Estimate (Type 3 SS)	1981 Estimate (Type 3 SS)	1990 Estimate (Type 3 SS)	1999 Estimate (Type 3 SS)
Intercept		4,46***	5,24***	4,73***	4,13***	3,21***	3,05***	4,34***	4,96***	4,19***	4,55***	4,31***	3,95***
Age	1			0,01*** (21,63***)	0,01*** (23,29***)	0,01*** (42,86***)	0,01*** (32,04***)	0,00** (10,20**)	0,01*** (11,95***)	0,01*** (25,05***)		0,01*** (31,62***)	0,01*** (29,37***)
Education level	1		-0,07*** (91,38***)	-0,07*** (44,72***)	-0,03** (8,55**)		-0,03* (3,50*)		-0,08*** (24,31***)	-0,07*** (22,76***)	-0,04*** (31,82***)	-0,03*** (19,02***)	
Church commitment	1	0,05* (6,06*)			-0,10** (9,93**)			0,09** (10,81**)		0,10*** (16,09***)			
Marital status	2												
unmarried		-0,23**	-0,25***		-0,22**	0,08					-0,17**		
divorced		0,31	-0,21**		0,01	-0,34**					0,62**		
ref cat: married/widowed		10,97**	30,13***		8,67*	9,87**					22,26***		
R²		0,02	0,05	0,05	0,06	0,05	0,06	0,02	0,06	0,11	0,02	0,03	0,02

* p < 0,05; ** p < 0,01; *** p < 0,001

Table 8.3 Regression parameters for the dependent variable 'homogamy' (Belgium, Denmark, Ireland, Spain, 1981–1990–1999, multiple linear regression, weighted data)

Parameter	Df	Belgium			Denmark			Ireland			Spain		
		1981 Estimate (Type 3 SS)	1990 Estimate (Type 3 SS)	1999 Estimate (Type 3 SS)	1981 Estimate (Type 3 SS)	1990 Estimate (Type 3 SS)	1999 Estimate (Type 3 SS)	1981 Estimate (Type 3 SS)	1990 Estimate (Type 3 SS)	1999 Estimate (Type 3 SS)	1981 Estimate (Type 3 SS)	1990 Estimate (Type 3 SS)	1999 Estimate (Type 3 SS)
Intercept		3,68***	3,48***	3,22***	3,56***	3,03***	3,03***	3,18***	2,95***	3,09***	4,06***	3,56***	3,72***
Age	1	0,02*** (86,00***)	0,02*** (286,99***)	0,02*** (130,23***)	0,02*** (127,29***)	0,02*** (115,89***)	0,02*** (79,54***)	0,03*** (245,22***)	0,03*** (203,21***)	0,03*** (157,69***)	0,02*** (142,66***)	0,02*** (217,25***)	0,02*** (47,05***)
Education level	1				−0,04* (12,78*)	−0,04* (7,87*)		−0,06** (18,29**)		−0,04* (9,21*)			−0,06*** (28,61***)
Church commitment	1	0,30*** (231,82***)	0,23*** (384,68***)	0,28*** (358,10***)	0,21*** (37,12***)	0,19*** (27,64***)	0,15*** (17,45***)	0,28*** (113,12***)	0,22*** (57,35***)	0,18*** (55,14***)	0,21*** (217,88***)	0,23*** (283,25***)	0,27*** (140,06***)
Gender female (ref.cat. male)	1			0,14* (9,03*)	0,19* (9,66*)	0,28** (18,37**)							
Marital status unmarried	2					0,24*					0,03	−0,19*	
divorced						−0,19					1,10**	−0,50*	
ref cat: married/widowed						(13,11*)					(29,08**)	(22,55*)	
R²		0,12	0,13	0,14	0,11	0,13	0,08	0,18	0,13	0,18	0,09	0,14	0,15

* p < 0,05; ** p < 0,01; *** p < 0,001

people are less homogamy oriented. This effect is not clear in every wave. For the effect of gender, there are indications that women in Belgium and Denmark are more inclined to the homogamy aspects of marriage. The direction of the effect of marital status is not clear.

Table 8.4 shows the parameters for the quality aspects of marriage. The most important effects are again in support of our hypotheses. In Belgium and Spain, and also in Ireland in 1981, there are indications that more highly educated people are more quality-oriented. The parameters in Denmark and Ireland indicate that younger people are more interested in quality aspects. And the parameters in Spain favor the hypothesis that the more religiously committed people are less interested in the newer quality values. As for the effect of gender there are indications that women support the quality aspects more than men do.

As for the effects of the background variables, in general the findings go in the direction of the formulated hypotheses. In comparison to less highly educated people, more highly educated people put more stress on the quality aspects of marriage and are less interested in the material and homogamy aspects. Younger people are more interested in the quality of marriage, and less in the material and homogamy aspects. And those who are more committed to the church still have a more traditional view with respect to marriage success factors. The effects of gender and marital status are not clearly interpretable. There are indications that women are more homogamy oriented than men, and women are also more inclined to favor the quality aspects of marriage. Also, the effects of marital status are not going in the same direction.

One indicator of the strength of the effects found is the R^2 statistic. This is a measure of the variance explained by all of the dependent variables included. In the above tables, we can see that this statistic generally takes on a very low value, especially for regressions on the quality scale and the material marriage aspects. These findings necessitate us to be very careful when interpreting the results. The low R^2 is an indication of the small effect of social background variables. One possible explanation could be that in the period studied, the privatization processes had nearly come to and end. Before reaching this conclusion, further analyses must be carried out, because even at the end of the privatization process we expect to find a further decline in the effect of background effects over time.

Table 8.4 Regression parameters for the dependent variable 'quality aspects of marriage' (Belgium, Denmark, Ireland, Spain, 1981–1990–1999, multiple linear regression, weighted data)

Parameter	Df	Belgium			Denmark			Ireland			Spain		
		1981 Estimate (Type 3 SS)	1990 Estimate (Type 3 SS)	1999 Estimate (Type 3 SS)	1981 Estimate (Type 3 SS)	1990 Estimate (Type 3 SS)	1999 Estimate (Type 3 SS)	1981 Estimate (Type 3 SS)	1990 Estimate (Type 3 SS)	1999 Estimate (Type 3 SS)	1981 Estimate (Type 3 SS)	1990 Estimate (Type 3 SS)	1999 Estimate (Type 3 SS)
Intercept		9,54***	10,38***	10,44***	10,90***	10,81***	10,75***	10,27***	10,35***	11,02***	9,75***	9,97***	10,07***
Age	1		0,00** (14,38**)		−0,01*** (32,66***)	−0,01** (15,22**)	−0,01*** (23,93***)	−0,01** (23,50**)		−0,01* (7,29*)			
Education level	1	0,11*** (82,33***)	0,04** (21,70**)	0,03* (8,37*)				0,05** (16,29**)			0,06*** (95,41***)	0,05*** (68,77***)	0,07*** (51,16***)
Church commitment	1										−0,13*** (90,15***)		−0,09** (18,96***)
Gender female ref. cat. male	1	0,26**				0,21*	0,25**		0,30***		0,27***		0,26**
Marital status ref. cat. married/ widowed	2	16,90**			12,56*	11,23*	15,65**		22,01***		37,92***		16,91**
unmarried					−0,10								
divorced					0,42*								
R²		0,04	0,01	0,00	0,02	0,01	0,02	0,02	0,01	0,00	0,03	0,01	0,04

* p < 0,05; ** p < 0,01; *** p < 0,001

For what concerns the privatization process, we hypothesized that this process will be clearer in countries where structural modernization has reached a higher level. Accordingly, we could expect the effect of background variables to be greater in Spain and Ireland, as compared to Belgium and Denmark. As for the effects that have been discussed, our analyses show no clear differences between the countries. The effects of age, education level and church commitment on material marriage aspects reappear in the four countries under consideration. For the homogam marriage orientation it is the same, except that the education level does not play a role in Belgium. The regressions for the quality marriage aspects also show no clear distinction between Belgium and Denmark, on the one hand, and Spain and Ireland, on the other.

In the next step, our goal is to evaluate the effect of background variables over time. In line with the privatization hypothesis, we want to know whether the effect of social background variables is indeed decreasing over time in the four European countries we have studied.

The privatization hypothesis is tested in a regression model with inclusion of the interaction between the social background variables and the period variable. Considering the effect of social background variables over time enables us to handle certain questions about the effect of age/generation. From Tables 8.2, 8.3 and 8.4 we find that younger people are more interested in the quality aspects of marriage, and older people are drawn more to the homogamy and material marriage orientations. This fact may be due either to an age effect or a generation effect (Kerkhofs et al., 1992: 35; Dobbelaere et al., 2000: 222–223; Hagenaars, 1998: 211–215; Becker, 1991b; Lesthaeghe & Surkyn, 1988: 17–23). The term 'generation effect' refers to the fact that people who are born and socialized in a certain time period will have the same value orientations, which do not change over time. 'Age effect', then, refers more to the life cycle. As people get older, their value orientations change. As we have seen earlier, many authors expect a difference between pre-war and post-war generations with respect to the new values. The post-war generation has been socialized primarily within an individualizing society, so we expect this generation to have internalized the new values better than the pre-war generation. In the next regression models, we try to detect age and/or generation effects. Technically, this is done by introducing an age as well as a generation variable into the basic model. Strictly speaking, a period of 20 years is rather short for distinguishing between age and generation effects. However, the EVS data are better suited for studying shifts in value orienta-tions because they cover a longer period than most other studies. For the generation variable, we use the four-generation model of Becker,[11] who distinguishes between the 'pre-war generation' (born between 1910 and 1930), the 'silent generation' (born between 1930 and 1940), the 'protest generation' (born between 1940 and 1955) and the 'lost generation' (born after 1955) (Becker, 1991a: 25–33). As explained earlier, the non-significant effects[12] are removed step by step.

Table 8.5 gives the regression equations for Belgium. As can be seen, for the material marriage aspects, a generation effect is detected. For the homogamy marriage orientations, both an age effect and a generation effect are found. The quality aspects of marriage are only affected by age. Concerning the privatization hypothesis, there are some indications in the regression model for the quality aspects of marriage. The effects of education level and gender decrease over time. For the other marriage aspects, we find no clear indication of privatization. In the regression model for material marriage aspects, the effect of education level even increases over time.

In Denmark, there are also indications of the privatization effect. As can be seen in the table below, between 1981 and 1990 the effect of marital status on material marriage success factors disappears. In 1981, unmarried people were inclined to support the material aspects less, but by 1990 the effect had disappeared. As for the homogamy marriage aspects, between 1990 and 1999 the effect of age decreased. Between 1990 and 1999 the effect of gender also disappeared. For the other background variables, the effect is not changing over time. For the quality aspects of marriage, there are no interaction effects whatsoever according to period. The fact that older people think more traditionally is generally due to the combined effect of age and generation. Only regression for the quality aspects of marriage indi-cates a pure age effect.[13]

---

[11] A model with generation as well as age, may cause problems with respect to multicollinearity. Therefore, in the regression models where age and generation both are included, we dichotomise the generation variable (born before 1945/born after 1945). As soon as the age-variable is dropped out, we switch to the four-generation-model. Inspection of the VIF shows that this method of working is not problematic with respect to multicollinearity.

[12] For the effect of age and generation, therefore we are looking to head-effect, as well as interaction-effect. For the other background variables, only interaction-effects are point of interest.

[13] Not in the table.

Table 8.5   Regression parameters for the dependent variables 'material marriage aspects', 'homogamy' and 'quality aspects of marriage' (Belgium, multiple linear regression, weighted data)

Parameter		MATERIAL MARRIAGE ASPECTS			HOMOGAMY			QUALITY ASPECTS MARRIAGE			
	Reference period 1981		Reference period 1999		Reference period 1981		Reference period 1999		Reference period 1981		Reference period 1999	
	Cat.	Estimate	Cat.	Estimate	Cat.	Estimate	Cat.	Estimate	Cat.	Estimate	Cat.	Estimate
Intercept		4,53***		4,47***		5,03***		4,59***		10,21***		10,65***
Period	90	0,21	81	0,06	90	-0,24***	81	0,43***	90	0,19*	81	-0,44***
	99	-0,06	90	0,27***	99	-0,43***	90	0,20***	99	0,44***	90	-0,25***
Age						0,02***		0,02***		0,00		0,00
Age*Period									90	0,00	81	-0,01
									99	0,01	90	-0,01*
Generation	pre-war	0,05	pre-war	0,41***	born before '45	0,33***	born before '45	0,33***				
	silent	0,16	silent	0,27***								
	protest	-0,09	protest	0,03								
Generation*Period	90 pre-war	-0,06	81 pre-war	-0,35*								
	90 silent	0,03	81 silent	-0,11								
	90 protest	0,00	81 protest	-0,12								
	99 pre-war	0,35*	90 pre-war	-0,41***								
	99 silent	0,11	90 silent	-0,08								
	99 protest	0,12	90 protest	-0,12								
Education level		-0,01		-0,07***						0,09***		0,03*
Education level*Period	90	-0,06***	81	0,06***					90	-0,05*	81	0,06**
	99	-0,06***	90	0,00					99	-0,06**	90	0,01
Gender									female	0,26**		-0,06
Gender*Period									female 90	-0,22**	female 81	0,32**
									female 99	-0,32**	female 90	0,10
Marital status	unmarried	-0,14	unmarried	0,11								
	divorced	0,31	divorced	-0,02								
Marital status*Period	90 unmarried	-0,09	81 unmarried	-0,25*								
	90 Divorced	-0,53***	81 divorced	0,33								
unmarried	99 unmarried	0,25*	90 unmarried	-0,34***								
	99 Divorced	-0,33	90 divorced	-0,20								
R²		0,05				0,08				0,03		

* p < 0,05; ** p < 0,01; *** p < 0,001

Table 8.6 Regression parameters for the dependent variables 'material marriage aspects', 'homogamy' and 'quality aspects of marriage' (Denmark, multiple linear regression, weighted data)

Parameter	MATERIAL MARRIAGE ASPECTS				HOMOGAMY			
	Reference period 1981		Reference period 1999		Reference period 1981		Reference period 1999	
	Cat.	Estimate	Cat.	Estimate	Cat.	Estimate	Cat.	Estimate
Intercept		3,88***		3,36***		4,44***		4,19***
Period	90	−0,52***	81	0,52***	90	−0,33**	81	0,25*
	99	−0,18**	90	0,33***	99	−0,25*	90	−0,07
Age		0,01***		0,01***		0,02***		0,01**
Age*Period					90	0,00	81	0,01*
					99	−0,01*	90	0,01**
Generation	born before '45	0,23***	born before '45	0,23***	born before '45	0,21*	born before '45	0,21*
Gender					female	0,27**	female	0,04
Gender*Period					female 90	0,08	female 81	0,23
					female 99	−0,23	female 90	0,31*
Marital status	unmarried	−0,16*	unmarried	−0,01	unmarried	0,09	unmarried	−0,19
	divorced	0,02	divorced	−0,17	divorced	0,14	divorced	−0,24
Marital status*Period	unmarried 90	0,23*	unmarried 81	−0,15	unmarried 90	0,15	unmarried 81	0,28
	divorced 90	−0,37*	divorced 81	0,19	divorced 90	−0,38	divorced 81	0,38
	unmarried 99	0,15	unmarried 90	0,08	unmarried 99	−0,28	unmarried 90	0,43**
	divorced 99	−0,19	divorced 90	−0,18	divorced 99	−0,38	divorced 90	0,00
R^2		0,11				0,13		

* $p < 0,05$; ** $p < 0,01$; *** $p < 0,001$

In Ireland, we observe interactions with period only for the material marriage aspects. For the homogamy marriage aspects and the quality aspects of marriage, the effect of background variables has not been changing over time. The effects that we observed in Table 8.7 are clearly not in favour of the privatisation hypothesis. Between 1990 and 1999, the effect of age even increased. Between 1981 and 1990, the effect of education level increased as well. For the three marriage scales, there is a pure age effect.

From the regression analyses for Spain we learn that, for the material marriage aspects, there is a stable and pure age effect. For the homogamy marriage orientation, we find a combined effect of age and generation. Generally, there are not many interaction effects between period and the social background variables. With respect to marital status, in 1981 divorced people were more materially oriented and also more inclined to the homogamy marriage aspect. By 1990 these effects had changed significantly. We understand this as evidence for the privatization process. The impact of church commitment on marriage quality aspects decreased from 1981 to 1990, but then increased from 1990 to 1999.

Table 8.7   Regression parameters for the dependent variables 'material marriage aspects', 'homogamy' and 'quality aspects of marriage' (Ireland, multiple linear regression, weighted data)

| Parameter | MATERIAL MARRIAGE ASPECTS | | | |
| | reference period 1981 | | reference period 1999 | |
	Cat.	Estimate	Cat.	Estimate
Intercept		4,94***		4,65***
Period	90	−0,15**	81	0,29***
	99	−0,29***	90	0,14**
Age		0,00**		0,02***
Age*Period	90	0,00	81	−0,01***
	99	0,01***	90	−0,01**
Education level		−0,02		−0,06***
Education level*Period	90	−0,05*	81	0,04
	99	−0,04	90	−0,02
R^2		0,07		

* p < 0,05; ** p < 0,01; *** p < 0,001

Table 8.8 Regression parameters for the dependent variables 'material marriage aspects', 'homogamy' and 'quality aspects of marriage' (Spain, multiple linear regression, weighted data)

Parameter	MATERIAL MARRIAGE ASPECTS				HOMOGAMY				QUALITY ASPECTS MARRIAGE			
	reference period 1981		reference period 1999		reference period 1981		reference period 1999		reference period 1981		reference period 1999	
	Cat. / Estimate		Cat. / Estimate		Cat. / Estimate		Cat. / Estimate		Cat. / Estimate		Cat. / Estimate	
Intercept		4,40***		4,43***		5,42***		4,91***		9,75***		10,27***
Period	90	0,18***	81	−0,04	90	−0,36***	81	0,51***	90	0,45***	81	−0,51***
	99	0,04	90	0,14**	99	−0,51***	90	0,15*	99	0,51***	90	−0,06
Age								0,02***		0,02***		
Generation	born before '45					0,22**		0,22**				
Church commitment										−0,12***		−0,11***
Church commitment*Period									90	0,12***	81	−0,01
									99	0,01	90	0,11**
Marital status	unmarried	−0,28***	unmarried	−0,32***	unmarried	0,06	unmarried	−0,21				
	divorced	0,54*	divorced	0,07	divorced	0,82*	divorced	−0,17				
Marital status*Period	90 unmarried	0,00	81 unmarried	0,04	90 unmarried	−0,30**	81 unmarried	0,26				
	90 divorced	−1,02***	81 divorced	0,48	90 divorced	−1,52***	81 divorced	0,99*				
	99 unmarried	−0,04	90 unmarried	0,03	99 unmarried	−0,26	90 unmarried	−0,04				
	99 divorced	−0,48	90 divorced	−0,54*	99 divorced	−0,99*	90 divorced	−0,53				
R²		0,02				0,11				0,03		

* p < 0,05; ** p < 0,01; *** p < 0,001

5 *Discussion*

At the end of the 20th century, social background variables are still playing a role in explaining value orientations with respect to marriage success factors. The more highly educated people are, the more they support the quality aspects of marriage and the less they are interested in the material and homogamy aspects. The higher the church commitment, the more a person will be attached to homogamy and the material marriage aspects and the less they will support the quality aspects. Younger people are more adherent to the quality aspects of marriage and less to the material and homogamy marriage aspects. This fact is due either to an age effect, or else to a combined age-generation effect. Only for the material marriage aspects in Belgium, there is a pure generation effect at work. Therefore the idea that the new values are being introduced by the younger generations and that certain generations do not change their values over time cannot be confirmed by our analyses. It is better to accept the view that all generations are prone to the new value orientations, but that younger people are more susceptible. For gender and marital status, the effects are not clear. In general, the results of our analyses support the hypotheses with respect to social background variables. For the more individualized value orientations, young people, more highly educated people and more secularized people are the trendsetters. In this respect there is no clear difference between the countries.

As for the strength of these effects, we must be aware that the overall R^2 values are rather low. We already suggested above that this could be an indication of the end of the privatization processes. Now we can reject this hypothesis since, even if the privatization process were drawing to an end, a further decline in background effects should be clearly noticeable over time. A comparison over 20 years should reveal this trend. In our analyses, we cannot find convincing evidence for this evolution. In addition, the fact that most regression models come up with significant effects for the relevant social background variables is a sign of the non-negligible effect of social background variables on the marriage success factors.

Nevertheless, there are some indications of the increasing privatization of marriage values. Mainly in Denmark and Belgium, there are traces of the diminishing effect of marital status, gender, education level and age. In Ireland and Spain, there is hardly any evolution in this respect. These findings can be interpreted as support for the claim that privatization processes have further progressed in the more structurally modernized countries Belgium and Denmark. We must be very careful, however, in drawing conclusions. The effects of most social background variables are remaining stable over time in every country. Even in Belgium and Denmark, the indications of the privatization process are not really convincing. We must admit that even in the structurally more modern countries, the effects of social background variables are still larger than would be expected on the basis of the individualization literature. In the age of reflexive modernization, social collectivities have lost little of their power. Sociologists talking about a "general" phenomenon must be convinced that the new individualized value orientations are restricted to small segments of society: the highly educated, the young and those who are less religious.

References

Ashford, S. & N. Timms 1992. *What Europe Thinks. A study of Western European Values*. Hants: Dartmouth Publishing Company.

Beck, U. 1992. *Risk Society. Towards a New Modernity*. London: Sage.

—— 1995. Love or freedom. Living together, apart or at war. Pp. 11–44 in U. Beck, E. Beck-Gernsheim (eds.), *The Normal Chaos of Love*. Cambridge: Polity Press.

—— & E. Beck-Gernsheim 1996. Individualization and precarious freedoms: perspectives and controversies of a subject-oriented sociology. Pp. 23–48 in P. Heelas, S. Lash & P. Morris (eds.), *Detraditionalization*. Cambridge: Blackwell.

—— 1997. The age of side-effects: on the politicization of modernity. In U. Beck, *The Reinvention of Politics*. Cambridge: Polity Press.

—— 1998. The democratization of the family, or the unknown art of free association. Pp. 65–83 in U. Beck, *Democracy Without Enemies*. Cambridge: Polity Press.

Beck-Gernsheim, E. 1995. From love to liaison. Changing relationships in an individualized society. Pp. 45–77 in U. Beck, E. Beck-Gernsheim (eds.), *The Normal Chaos of Love*. Cambridge: Polity Press.

Becker, H.A. 1991a. Dynamics of life histories and generations research. Pp. 1–55 in H.A. Becker (ed.), *Life Histories and Generations*. Utrecht: ISOR.

—— 1991b. *Life Histories and Generations*. Utrecht: ISOR.

Bollen, K.A. & J.S. Long 1992. Tests for Structural Equation Models. *Sociological Methods and Research* 2: 123–131.

De Moor, R. (ed.) 1995. *Values in Western Society*. Tilburg: Tilburg University Press

Dobbelaere, K., M. Elchardus, J. Kerkhofs, L. Voyé, & B. Bawin-Legros 2000. *Verloren zekerheid. De Belgen en hun waarden, overtuigingen en houdingen*. Tielt: Lannoo.

——, J. Gevers & L. Halman 1999. Religion and the family. Pp. 67–81 in L. Halman & O. Riis (eds.), *Religion in Secularizing Society. The Europeans' Religion at the End of the 20th Century*. Tilburg: Tilburg University Press.

Ester, P., L. Halman & R. de Moor (eds.) 1993. *The Individualizing Society. Value Change in Europe and North America*. Tilburg: Tilburg University Press.

Felling, A., J. Peters & P. Scheepers 2000. *Individualisering in Nederland aan het einde van de twintigste eeuw. Empirisch onderzoek naar omstreden hypotheses.* Assen: Van Gorcum.

Hagenaars, J.A. 1998. De onzichtbare kleren van de generaties. *Mens en Maatschappij* 73 (2): 211–215

Halman, L. 1991. *Waarden in de westerse wereld. Een internationale exploratie van de waarden in de westerse samenleving.* Tilburg: Tilburg University Press.

——— 1996. Individualism in individualized society? Results from the European Values Surveys. *International Journal of Comparative Sociology* 12: 195–214.

———, F. Heunks, R. de Moor & H. Zanders 1987. *Traditie, secularisatie en individualisering. Een studie naar de waarden van de Nederlanders in een Europese context.* Tilburg: Tilburg University Press.

———, T. Pettersson & J. Verweij 1999. The religious factor in contemporary society. The differential impact of religion on the private and public sphere in comparative perspective. *International Journal of Comparative Sociology* 40: 141–160.

Harding, S. & D. Phillips 1986. *Contrasting Values in Western Europe. Unity, Diversity and Change.* London: The Macmillan Press Ltd.

Kerkhofs, J., K. Dobbelaere, L. Voyé & B. Bawin-Legros 1992. *De versnelde ommekeer. De waarden van Vlamingen, Walen en Brusselaars in de jaren negentig.* Tielt: Lannoo.

Laermans, R. 1992. *In de greep van De Moderne Tijd: modernisering en verzuiling. Evoluties binnen de ACW-vormingsorganisaties.* Leuven: Garant.

Lesthaeghe, R. & R. Meekers 1987. Demografische verschuivingen en de evolutie van waardenpatronen in de Europese gemeenschap. *Tijdschrift voor Sociologie* 8: 131–200.

——— & J. Surkeyn 1988. Cultural Dynamics and Economic Theories of Fertility Change. *Population and Development Review* 14: 1–45.

Middendorp, C.P. 1979. *Ontzuiling, politisering en restauratie in Nederland: progressiviteit en conservatisme in de jaren 60 en 70.* Meppel: Boom.

Rensvold, R.B. & G.W. Cheung 1998. Testing measurement models for factorial invariance: a systematic approach. *Educational and Psychological Measurement* 58: 1017–1034.

Saris, W.E., A. Satorra, & D. Sörbom 1987. The detection and correction of specification errors in structural models. Pp. 105–129 in C.C. Clogg (ed.), *Sociological Methodology.* San Francisco: Jossey Bass.

Sharma, S. 1996. *Applied Multivariate Techniques.* New York: Wiley & Sons.

Van den Elzen, A. 1996. Gezinsoriëntaties in de Westerse wereld: een benadering met latente klasse-analyse. *Tijdschrift voor sociologie* 17: 29–49.

——— 1998. Culturele ontwikkelingen rondom het Westerse gezin. *Sociale wetenschappen* 40: 47–65.

Van den Troost, A. 2000. De relationele markt anno 2000. Een exploratie van waardeoriëntaties en vormgeving. *Tijdschrift voor Sociologie* 21: 131–158.

Appendix

Standardized factor loadings for marriage success factors

	Quality aspects	Material aspects	Homogamy aspects
Mutual respect and appreciation	0.58		
Understanding and tolerance	0.57		
Happy sexual relationship	0.74		
Sharing household chores	0.57		
Good housing		0.63	
Adequate income		0.90	
Same social background			0.66
Shared religious beliefs			0.74
Agreement on politics			0.70

CHAPTER NINE

WORK AND FAMILY LIFE IN EUROPE: VALUE PATTERNS AND POLICY MAKING[1]

Mălina Voicu

1 *Introduction*

European countries differ with respect to policies for women support. The differences are not structured only on the West—East axis or depending on the degree of industrialization of societies. One can expect that countries with a high degree of industrialization promote similar policies for women support, which encourage the women participation in the labor market. Despite the existence of some commune directions traced by the Union legislation, industrialized countries from the European Union do not promote similar policies. States vary depending on the measures for promoting women participation in the labor market, on those for encouraging shared of domestic work between men and women and on the facilities offered for childcare.

The promoting of one type of policies for women support depends not only on the degree of industrialization of the economy or on the political or the welfare regime, but also on other factors like labor force, shared values, ideas that are considered to be legitimate at a social level. The concepts of values and legitimacy are strongly linked, but their semantic sphere is different. Legitimacy involves values but it includes others factors too, like self-interest or affective factors. The process of legitimating one political object is mainly based on the values shared by the collectivity. The lack of concordance between the value orientations of the population and a specific policy promoted by the government determines the failure of the policy, at least in a democratic society. On the other hand, the

[1] The article was realized with the support of EUSSIRF Program—European University Institute—Florence.

efficiency of one policy increases the people's support for this policy, increasing its legitimacy. In this context, Easton (1965) speaks about the specific support granted to one type of policy measures, which satisfy the immediate interests of individuals. The specific support differs from the diffuse support, which is based on deep factors, like values, and which provides a reservoir of social support for the political system in the long run.

In spite of the common legislative framework imposed by the European Union, states differ with the respect to adopted measures for reconciliation between paid work and family life. Each state has adopted specific measures depending on the values shared by its population and on the economic and politic context. Hantrais and Letabiler (1996) show that the social acceptability of women employment, and the men willingness to contribute to domestic work differ depending on the cultural context and on the political climate. Other authors point out that different social policy regimes reflect and generate different patterns of gender roles and of family forms (O'Connor, Orloff & Shaver, 1999). Therefore, there is interdependence between policy regimes and values shared by the population, each of them having an influence on the other. It is very hard to say which one is the dependent and which one is the independent variable, as long as between them there is a reciprocal interdependency.

The paper tries to investigate the existence of a relation between the type of policies for women support and the value orientations of the population in different European countries. Starting from the assumption that, in order to be effective, a promoted policy must be considered legitimate by the population, my hypothesis is that there is a link between the type of women support policies promoted by different countries and the type of values shared by the population regarding women's position in the society. The paper tries to show that there is a link between type of values and type of policies, without to consider one variable as dependent and the other as independent, because both of them have an influence on the variation of the other. The analysis focuses only on the reconciliation policies between work and family life, referring to those policies aimed to facilitate women access to the labor market and sharing domestic work between partners. I try to draw a map of values shared by populations form different European countries and to compare this map with that of reconciliation policies followed by the European states. I intend to bring evidences that endorsed gender policies fit the map of values related with gender equality. More, I suggest that the lack of correspondence between the two maps (gender values and policies) find its roots in the influence of other type of values, like the religious or the postmaterialist orientation.

The first part of the paper is focused on the presentation of the concept of legitimacy, stressing the relation between legitimacy and values. The second part is dedicated to a presentation of the policy models for women support in different European countries. The last section is concentrated on data analysis and on testing the proposed hypothesis.

2   Theoretical framework

'Legitimacy involves the capacity of the system to engender and maintain the belief that the existing political institutions are the most appropriate ones for the society' (Lipset, 1960: 77). The author points out that the legitimacy is evaluative, because 'groups regard a political system as legitimate or illegitimate according to the way in which its values fit with theirs'. Zamfir (1997) enounces an alternative definition of legitimacy, starting from the relation existing between the value concept and legitimacy concept. From his perspective, legitimacy refers to 'the correspondence between a form of organization, a political option, on the one hand, and the experience, values, community philosophy, on the other' (Zamfir, 1997: 75).

The analysis of the concept of legitimacy cannot be reduced only to the analysis of value options. Lillbacka (1999) indicates that values are not the only elements that influence the general orientation toward the political object. The attitude toward this political object is influenced by factors like self-interest or irrational 'affective' identification with it. The author makes the distinction between central legitimacy, based on values, and paralegitimacy, based on the other factors. Furthermore, Berger and Luckmann (1999) point out that legitimacy 'has a cognitive element, like a normative one'. One can say that value is a fundamental constituent of legitimacy, but there is no equivalence between the two concepts.

On the other hand, political regimes are based on some values and principles, which influence the politically promoted goals (Easton, 1965). Easton indicates that 'the kinds of policies pursued, would enable us to infer the nature of implicit values' (Easton, 1965: 290).

Therefore, one can deduce the values that support one political regime, starting from the policies promoted by it. But, as I have shown before, the values promoted by a regime must be concordant with those shared by the population, otherwise the regime looses its legitimacy. In order to be legitimate a regime has to establish a set of values concordant with those shared by the majority. Thereby, one can affirm that between the type of promoted policies at one moment in time and the values shared by the population there is a concordance. This correspondence is needed in order to preserve the legitimacy of the regime.[2]

Moreover, referring to the connection between gender relation and state policies, Gal and Kligman (2000) indicate that the effects are reciprocal here. The authors point out the fact that 'not only do state policies constrain gender relation, but ideas about the differences between men and women shape the ways in which states are imagined, constructed and legitimated' (Kligman, 2000: 4). Therefore, the association between the values involved in the gender relations and the policies promoted by the state for women support is not a just 'one way' relation. Each variable has an effect on the variation of the other variable.

Starting form the assumption of correspondence between the promoted policies and the values shared by the population, my hypothesis is that there is a connection between the type of policies promoted in one country for women support and the type of values shared by the population regarding woman's position in the society. That is to say that, *different types of policies, which aim to support women, promoted in different countries, are sustained by different kinds of women valorization in different societies.* I will present further the types of policies for women support promoted by some European states, in order to test my hypothesis.

Each European state has adopted the common European legislation depending on its own legislation, on its own culture and on the support given by the population to the specific policy measures. Furthermore, member states of the European Union have joined the Union having 'differentiated set of interests and expectations, in terms of its political culture and policy environment, which have influenced

---

[2] I am speaking about the democratic regimes, based on population support, not about the totalitarian ones.

the approach of gender issues at supranational level' (Hantrais, 2000: 19). Therefore, not only the Union legislation has an influence on member states and on candidate states, but also these states have a specific contribution to the policies adopted by the Union.

Many studies classify the Europeans countries depending on their reconciliation policies between paid work and family life. Esping-Anderson (1990, 1997) adds a gender dimension of his welfare states classification, showing that each type of welfare regime is characterized by a different pattern of women employment. Social-democratic countries promote the equalization of women's and men's status and have a high level of women employment, especially in the public sector; liberal countries are characterized by a moderate level of women involvement in the paid work; conservative countries have the lowest level of female participation in the labour market. Other authors show that countries from the same welfare state regime do not cluster in the same group according to their reconciliation policies and gender issues and there are many intra-cluster variation (Sainsbury, 1999a; Gornick, Meyers & Ross, 1996). Speaking about public provision of welfare, Sainsbury (1999a: 246) indicates that 'countries representing the conservative welfare regime displayed the widest range of variation'. Gornick, Meyers and Ross show that Esping-Anderson clusters failed to cohere 'with respect to policies that affect women's employment (Gornick, Meyers & Ross, 1996: 28).

Trifiletti (1999) used two criteria: whether state treats women like mothers and wives or as workers and the Esping-Anderson decommodification criteria. She identified four types of welfare regime: breadwinner welfare regime, mediterranean welfare regime, universalist welfare regime and liberal regime (Trifiletti, 1999: 54). On her turn, Sainsbury (1999b) focused on several aspects of women support policies: representation on ideal family, entitlement to social benefits, basis of entitlement, recipient of benefits, unit of benefits, unit of contribution, taxation, employment, and wage policies, sphere of care and caring work (Sainsbury, 1999b: 153). She classified countries in two categories: those which have adopted the breadwinner model and those which have opted for individual model, considering as classification criteria. O'Connor (1996) uses an OECD classification according to which there are two extremes in terms of childcare policy: at one extreme there 'are countries that adopt maximum public responsibility for childcare and have generous and well-funded leave provision' (O'Connor, 1996: 89). Nordic countries are included in this category. At the other extreme, there are countries like the United States and Great Britain, which impose maximum private responsibility for childcare, have a meager leave provision and a relatively low or inexistent wage replacement (O'Connor, 1996: 89). All others lie in between.

Lohkamp–Himmighofen and Dienel (2000) identify in Europe 6 models or ideal types of policies aimed to promote the equal opportunities between women and men through the reconciliation between paid work and family life. Even if there are some variations within each group of countries, this classification is more detailed than the others are and includes the Central and Eastern European countries. On the other hand, it is more complex and includes the other typologies. For these reasons, I have used it in my analysis. The six models identified by the authors are: the women-friendly egalitarian model, the labor market oriented demographic model, the liberal labor market orientation model, the three-phase model, the Mediterranean family-based model, the socialist East European model.

1. Scandinavian countries have implemented *the women-friendly egalitarian model*. The promoted policy is focused on promoting equality between men and women in all sectors of the social and economic life, including the equal distribution of paid work and of the household unpaid work. The policy measures aim to stimulate women participation in the labor market and to involve men in childrearing and in the household work. The concrete measures used to implement these policies are: active labour market policies for women, the introduction of paid parental leaves for both parents, the introduction of a flexible work schedule, and the establishment of public childcare facilities. An important element of this model is represented by the measures aimed to involve both parents in the domestic work and in childcare. These are trying to increase the role equality within the family. In Sweden, parents can share the parental leave between them in many ways and fathers must take at least one month of parental leave, which is not transferable to mothers (Sainsbury, 1996). The negative effect of this model resides in horizontal occupational segregation, women being employed mostly in the public sector, while men are in the private sector (Esping-Anderson, 1997). There are some variations within this cluster of countries. In Sweden, the model of dual breadwinner family is much more developed than in other European Union countries (Bergqvist & Jungar, 2000), while Norway

is providing quite poor child care services (Gornick, 1999; Gornick, Meyers & Ross, 1996).

2. *The labor market oriented demographic model* can be identified in France and Belgium. The model promotes women friendly policies, but with a different goal as compared to the first model. The goal of the first model was to promote equal opportunities for women and men, but, for the second model, the goal is to exploit the entire potential of labor force and to maintain the demographic balance. Therefore, the promoted measures aim to encourage the high participation of women in the labor market, with a quite reduced interruption needed to give birth to and rear the children. A good system of public childcare exists in both countries and it provides facilities for working women. Therefore, in France and Belgium mothers can enter and remain in full-time paid work, with a minimal interruption (Gornick, Meyers & Ross, 1996). In France, where the appearance of a child does not have a big impact on the mother's employment (Hantrains & Letablier, 1996), the involvement of mothers in the economic activity is among the highest in all European Union countries (Fagnani, 1998). The difference between this model and the Nordic one is that this one does not support the sharing of unpaid housework, because its main goal is not to promote the equal opportunities of the two sexes.

3. *The liberal labor market orientation model* is promoted by the United Kingdom and Ireland. The reconciliation between paid work and family life was not a priority on the political agenda, the state being not involved in the development of such policies. The employers assume the concern for providing for childcare, only if they are interested in using female labor force. The family must find the best arrangements for child caring, without any help from the state. In addition, there are no measures aimed to promote the sharing of the housework between partners. One can mention that in the United Kingdom fathers are not allowed to have parental leave. In this context, the British developed a model of role segregation in the family, women being considered mainly housekeepers and secondly earners. But there are some differences between the two states. Ireland has the lowest rate of women employment among the EU countries (35% in 1995) and it has the lowest level of childcare providing in the EU (Mahon, 1998: 179). In Great Britain mothers usually come back to work after an interruption for childrearing (Hantrais & Letablier,

1996). The New Labour government supports some measures intended to encourage employers to accept the flexible work schedule, but only if these measures do not involve extra costs for the employer (Bagilhole & Byrne, 2000).

4. *The three-phase model*, developed by Austria, Germany, Luxembourg and the Netherlands, favors men work involvement and the women retirement from the labor market after marriage. All these countries have developed a similar model of women employment and of the house responsibility distribution between partners, the man being usually the breadwinner of the family and the woman the house-keeper. This model was associated in the cases of Germany and the Netherlands, with a non-individualized taxation system, which encourages women to stay at home. The authors identify the existence of a pattern with three phases. The first phase is prior to the family constitution. This stage is characterized by women involvement in full time jobs. The second phase is that of family building in which women quit the labor market in order to take care of children and of the household. The third stage occurs especially with women having school-aged children and it is characterized by the gradual return to the labor market, often in part-time jobs. There are quite few public childcare facilities because it is considered that mothers provide the best care for children. These countries have introduced parental leave dedicated to mothers and provided for a long period of time, but this is paid at a low level. The policies devoted to sharing the childrearing and the domestic work are not so developed. Within this model there are some variations. One can mention that the Netherlands have the highest level of women employment in part-time jobs among the EU countries (Gornick, 1999).

5. *The Mediterranean family-based model* is adopted by Spain, Italy, Portugal and Greece. In these countries, the childcare is the family's responsibility, especially the responsibility of the extended family, without any help from the state. Furthermore, there is no question of gender roles division, women being in charge with the domestic work, while men are in charged with the paid work, outside the household. Because of the lack of law regulations, which should guarantee the preserving of the working place during the maternal leave, most women from the Mediterranean countries leave the labor market after the birth of their first child. The policies for promoting equal access to the labor market for men and women have become policy goals during '90s, under the pressure of the European Union

legislation. But for most of these countries (excepting Italy) the public providing for childcare has a very low level. In Spain, the model is also sustained by the characteristics of the economy and of the labour market, the level of unemployment being quite high (around 16%) (Valiente, 2000).

6. *The socialist East European model*, specific for ex-communist countries, has the same characteristics like the labor market oriented demographic model. In the context of full employment policy supported by the communist countries, the goal of this model was to encourage the high participation of women in the paid work. On the other hand, one of the declared goals of the communist regime was to promote equality among all the members of the society. In these circumstances, Eastern-European countries have developed policy measures aimed to encourage women employment, and have developed an extended public system of childcare facilities supported by the state. Like in the case of the demographic model, the promoted policies did not encourage the sharing of the domestic work between partners, the housekeeping remaining a task for women. In addition, the lack of household endowment with modern facilities, like home appliances, has increased the amount of time and work put into housekeeping (Brainderd, 1997; Pascal & Manning, 2000; Zamfir et al., 1999).

After 1990, the women's situation has changed in all East European countries. The social and economic changes have diminished the role of the state in welfare providing. Furthermore, the modification of the former social protection system has affected the public childcare. During the communist period, most of childcare facilities were provided by the enterprises, but after 1989 the economic decline has affected the benefits offered to working mothers. UNICEF (1999) shows that the dominant trend is to deinstitutionalize childcare for the younger children, by offering generous parental leaves. In this way, the care for younger children become less expensive for the state and the burden of childcare is transferred to the family.

The transition countries have adopted some legislative measures aimed to encourage the sharing of the domestic work between men and women, trying to improve women's situation, but men involvement in childrearing remains quite low, less then 1% of men using parental leave schemes (UNICEF, 1999: 54).

However, the women's situation and the policies for women support differ from one country to another, even if there are some similar

Table 9.1   Labor force participation rate (percentages) for women and
men in Eastern Europe (1999)

	Men	Women
Croatia*	54.6	43.2
Czech Republic	70.6	52.1
Estonia	69.6	53.0
Hungary	61.4	45.4
Latvia	67.8	50.3
Lithuania	69.2	55.7
Poland	64.5	49.6
Romania	71.4	56.3
Russian Federation	67.1	51.8
Slovakia	67.7	52.2
Slovenia	64.9	51.8
Ukraine	63.6	49.7

Data source: International Labor Organization—"World Employment Report 2001"
*1998 data

trends in the region. It is to early to identify some trends with respect
to reconciliation policies among the countries from region, due to
short period of democracy and free market economy (only 12 years
passed from 1990) and to the high economic instability, but there
are some differences among them.

   Speaking about welfare regimes in Eastern Europe, Deacon (1993),
using the similar criteria that are used by Esping-Anderson in building his classification, has identified four types of welfare regimes in
the region: liberal regimes (Hungary, Slovenia, Croatia), conservative corporatist regime (Eastern Germany), social-democrat model
(Czech Republic) and post-communist conservative corporatism
(Bulgaria, Romania, Serbia, Russia). Nielsen (1996) reanalyzed the
typology proposed by Deacon according to the political and economical evolution of the Eastern European states, and indicates that
'there is a stronger general trend towards (traditional) corporatist
regimes than foreseen by Deacon' (Nielsen, 1996: 210). However,
this typology is built using the similar criterion as Esping-Anderson
and, as I have shown before, his typology of the welfare regimes has
been strongly criticized because is not enough 'gender sensitive'.
Therefore, the typology proposed by Deacon emphasizes only the
differences among Eastern European state with respect of the welfare
providing, without to stress the aspects related to the gender relation
and the women situation.

Analyzing the public childcare provision and the women employment in different welfare regimes, Van Dijk (2001) shows that there are only minor differences with the respect of the women employment among Eastern European countries. The explanation resides in the low level of incomes in the region, which 'force' women to get in the labour market. In addition, according to the author, the 'women in the Eastern Europe are hesitant to give up their position in society' (Van Dijk, 2001: 54). In this context, the women's situation is quite similar in some countries in the region, even if the different economic situation and the different policies promoted by the new politicians are different in different ex-communist countries.

It is quite probable that candidate countries to European Union accession to promote different policy measures in order to adapt their legislation to that of European Union. Therefore, one can suppose that candidate countries have adopted some political measures aimed to encourage women involvement in the labor market and the sharing of the domestic work. Data on labor force participation for women and men (Table 9.1) do not indicates differences among candidate countries and the rest of Eastern European countries, but other studies point out some differences among Russia and Ukraine and the others countries from region. Brainerd (1997) indicates that in Russia and Ukraine women are more exposed to discrimination in the labour market and UNICEF reports that in Ukraine the number of childcare facilities was dramatically decreased after 1990.

A different situation was identified in Poland, compared to the other candidate countries. The women situation in Poland is the worst. The unemployment rate is much higher for women then for men and only 28% of pre-school children are going to the kindergarten (UNDP, 1998). The percent is among the smallest in Europe. In addition, only 25% of men agree to share the domestic work (UNDP, 1998). According to the European Union (2001), Poland did not make any progress in 2000 with respect to the adaptation of its policy to that of the Union.

With respect to the reconciliation policies, Malta is an outlier. The Maltese Islands are not only completely lacking such policies, but also they promote a very traditional family model. In Malta 'there is no recognized status of divorce or co-habitation' (Abela, 2000: 61) and the fertility rate is over the European mean, being 1.92 in Malta compared to 1.79 for the others European countries (Abela, 2001: 31). Therefore, Malta is promoting a traditional family model and according to this model, women are in charge with child rearing and with domestic work, while men are involved in paid work outside home. In Malta only fewer women reconcile the paid and the domestic work (Abela, 2000), the level of women employment and the gender gap being below the European Union Average (European Commission, 2001). Moreover, the childcare facilities are scarce and the parental leave is inadequate (European Commission, 2001).

As I have shown, my hypothesis is that there is an association between the type of promoted policies for women support in different countries and the values regarding woman position in the society shared by the population. I will focus on two basic values, shaping the space of attitudes toward women. The first one refers to gender equality within household. This includes the representation of the household role division, with special focus on the traditional childcare role of woman. I will call this dimension *household modernity*. The second dimension includes value orientations toward the equal access of women and men in the labour market. It becomes manifest through an increase acceptance of the women as an employee, through the rejection of the housekeeper—breadwinner model, through the opinion that fathers could be as efficient as women in the domestic work. I will call this dimension *equal labor*. One can expect that people from countries that have promoted woman participation at labor market and the sharing of domestic work will accept the equal access to jobs and reject the traditional role division within household. Whereas, countries in which women participation in paid work was not doubled by policies for encouragement of sharing domestic work, are likely to largely accept the traditional role of women.

3   Data and operationalisation

In order to test the hypothesis I have used the EVS 1999 data that allow comparing the value orientations of different European Countries.[3] The confirmatory data analysis validated the model. Two basic factors explain the space of gender values: gender equality within house-

---

[3] The Republic of Ireland, Northern Ireland and Austria were excluded from the analysis because they have used a different scale for all the items included in the analysis.

hold (HOUSEHOLD MODERNITY) and equal access in labour market (EQUAL LABOUR). Diagram 1 shows the structure of the two latent variables. The latent variable which indicates the gender equality within household explains the variation of variables: 'Working mother can establish just as warm and secure a relationship with her children as a mother who does not work'; 'Pre-school child is likely to suffer if his or her mother works'; 'Job is alright but what most women really want is a home and children'; 'Being a house-wife is just as fulfilling as working for pay'. The latent variable that indicate the equal access in labour market explains the variation of the following variables: 'Working mother can establish just as warm and secure a relationship with her children as a mother who does not work'; 'Having a job is the best way for a woman to be an independent person'; 'Both the husband and wife should contribute to household income'; 'In general, fathers are as well suited to look after their children as mothers'. Therefore, *equal labor* is sustained by those who agree with women and men equal participation in the labour market and in the domestic work. Those who score high on *household modernity* dimension reject the idea that mother provides the best childrearing and that the most fulfilling role for a women is that of wife and mother.

In order to verify if the structure of the model is the same for all the European countries included in the model, I have run the analysis maintaining the loadings constant (at levels that have resulted from the analysis realized for entire data set and that are presented in Figure 9.1). The coefficients for each country that was introduced in the analysis are presented in the Annex. The analysis for each country has shown that the model is valid for the population of each state.[4]

4 *Analysis*

The comparative analysis of the position of the countries depending on the means of the two latent variables indicates the existence of

---

[4] For some countries like Germany, Lithuania, Czech Republic, not all of the fitting criteria are satisfied (RMSEA has a quite big value) but if one for three fit criteria are satisfied (Delta 2IFI, CFI, RMSEA) the model fits the data (Baer, 2001). Therefore, one can consider that the model is valid also for these countries.

Figure 9.1   Factorial structure of the gender related values

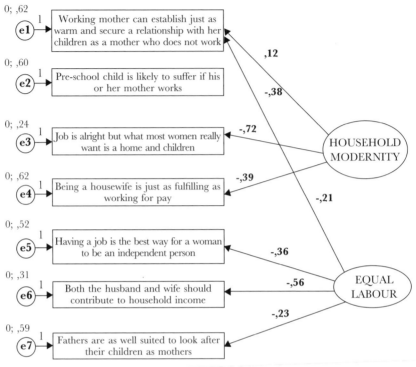

$$\chi^2 = 2174,383 \ (\nu = 19) \ p = 0.000$$
Delta 2 IFI = 0,996; RMSEA = 0,053

five clusters of countries and of one outlier. The first group of countries consists of two Nordic countries: Sweden and Denmark. The Central and Eastern European countries are split into two groups. The first one includes also France and Belgium, while the second one is composed of Russia, Ukraine, Poland, Lithuania, and Greece. The fourth group of countries clusters the Mediterranean countries, Luxembourg, Finland, and Germany. The last group contains the United Kingdom, the Netherlands, and Iceland. The outlier is represented by Malta, which has a special position, scoring low on both dimensions equal labour and household modernity.

As it is shown in Figure 9.3, the map of European countries, depending on values relating women's position in society, does not accurate fit the map reconciliation policies, but generally respects the

Figure 9.2   Distribution of countries depending on role modernity and gender equality

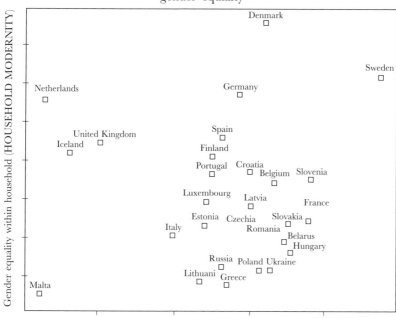

support for EQUAL access in LABOR market

main policy trends noticed in the previous section. There are several overlapping between the two maps and some differences that can be explained by the influence of other factors. I will describe each group of countries and I will try to explain the position of each country on the map.

The first group of countries includes two Scandinavia countries: Sweden and Denmark. Values shared by the populations of these countries are high modernity within household and high acceptance of the equal access in the labour market. For the Scandinavian people there are not different roles for men and women and gender equality is a wide shared value in the society. In the case of these two countries, the values shared by the population fit very well the reconciliation policies promoted by the state. As I have shown before, the women friendly egalitarian model, which was adopted by these two countries, promotes gender equality in all spheres of social and professional life, such as the sharing of domestic work. These equalitarian policies are accompanied, at the value level, by the strong

Figure 9.3   Values vs. reconciliation policies types

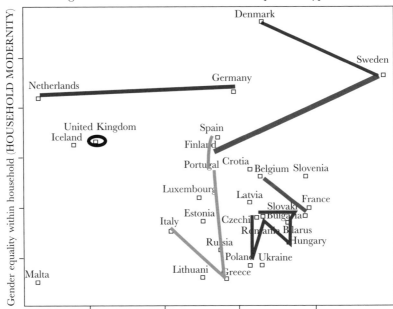

acceptance of the gender equality status and of the role similarity for men and women.

The second group, those of ex-communist states and the countries that have adopted the labor market oriented demographic model, is composed of France, Belgium and some Eastern-European countries (Croatia, Slovenia, Latvia, the Czech Republic, Slovakia, Romania, Bulgaria, Belarus, and Hungary). The values wide shared by the population of these states are strong acceptance of equal access of men and women in the labour market and high support of the traditional role of women within the household. In fact, the citizens of these countries sustain that women and men are equal in society, in the public sphere, but women have to carry on their traditional role in the family, being in charge of housekeeping and childrearing. The values orientation have theirs correspondent in the types of reconciliation policies promoted by these states.

As I have shown before, the former communist regimes have promoted a policy of gender equality. Furthermore, the support of women participation in paid work offered by the state, had sustained the idea of equal access in the labour market and of equal earnings for both partners. In this context, the wide social support of gender equality fits the type of policy developed both in the past and in present. However, the communist regimes did not promote policies aimed to encourage the sharing of the domestic work between partners. This fact determines the preserving of the traditional roles within the household, which means that women were in charged with housekeeping and with childcare. Therefore, this model assume that women are workers and mothers/wives at the same time and that they have equal access in the paid work as men, but they have to carry the burden of domestic work, too.

Similar value orientations are shared by the people of the regimes that have adopted the labor market oriented demographic model. France and Belgium have encouraged women participation in the labour market, without a strong support for sharing domestic work between partners. One can say that similar policies are associated to similar value orientations, even if the political regime was different. This second group is quite homogenous from the point of view of the endorsed policies and it sustains the hypothesis that similar policies are associated to similar value orientations.

The third group includes Russia, Ukraine, Poland, Lithuania and Greece. The group represents a mix between some ex-communist countries and a Mediterranean one. The value orientations shared by the population of these countries are maximum traditionalism within the household and moderate acceptance of equal access in the labour force. In fact, the group of ex-communist countries is split into two parts. Some of the ex-communist states are included in the second group, while other four are clustering with Greece. The population of these states shared with the other Eastern-European countries the acceptance of equal access to work, which can be explained by the measures promoted by the communist regimes, aimed to encourage equality among all members of society, including equality of men and women. From this point of view, ex-communist states shared similar value orientations. However, Russia, Ukraine, Poland and Lithuania are more disposed to support the household traditionalism than other citizens from the ex-communist European states. This difference reflects a greater inclination to traditionalism in family relation with the citizens of these four states. As Inglehart (1997: 93) showed, Poland has more traditionalist values than other ex-communist societies of the Eastern-Europe; Poland 'strongly emphasizes traditional cultural values concerning not only religion, but also politics, gender roles, sexual norms and family values' (Inglehart, 1997: 99).

It is likely that Russia and Ukraine share with Poland a quite strong orientation to traditionalist family values. A good indicator of this traditionalism could be the worsening of women's situation in these two states after 1990 compared to other Eastern-European states (Brainerd, 1997). As Brainerd points out, in Russia and Ukraine the position of women on the labour market was strongly affected by the discrimination practiced by employers. This discrimination could be interpreted as an expression of the traditionalist values.

Greece is another state included in this group. The strong Greek orientation to traditionalist religious values can be an indicator of a traditional cultural pattern, which also includes traditionalism in family relations. As Papadopulos (1998: 54) indicates, in spite of the legislative rhetoric, the Greek family remains strongly patriarchal in its structure.

The fourth group is a heterogeneous one and it includes the Mediterranean countries (excepting Greece) together with Germany, Finland, Luxembourg, and Estonia. The values shared by the populations of these countries consist of a quite high gender inequality within household and a quite low acceptance of equal access in the labour market. The countries that have promoted the Mediterranean family-based model do not sustain neither female participation in the labour market, nor gender equality. The role of caregiver is reserved exclusively to the family and to women. These countries have promoted a traditional model with respect to women's position in society.

Even if Lohkamp-Himmighofen and Dienel have included Luxembourg into the three phases model, other authors show that in Luxembourg women often leave the labour market after the formation of the family or after childbirth (Hantrais & Letablier, 1996). This indicates that, from the point of view of the women employment pattern, Luxembourg is much closer to the Mediterranean model, in which women are permanently quitting the labour market after childbirth, but it differs with the respect to the generous benefits offered to women by the state. From the values point of view, this country is clustering with those from the Mediterranean model, being oriented to traditionalism and inequality in family relations.

Germany can be included in the same group, but it scores higher on the household modernity dimension than the other countries from group. If one tries to look at Figure 9.2 considering only the household modernity dimension, can observe that some countries score higher on this: Sweden, Denmark, Iceland, Germany, the United Kingdom and the Netherlands. They have a quite high score on household modernity, even if they are clustering in different groups. According to Inglehart these countries are strongly oriented to Post-materialist values (Inglehart, 1997: 93) and in this kind of society 'there is a growing emphasis on self-realization of women, linked with a shift of emphasis from the role of mother to emphasis on careers' (Inglehart, 1997: 88). Even if these states have endorsed different reconciliation polices, the high level of affluence and of materialistic security has determined a shift to Postmaterialism in value orientations.

The last group is composed of the United Kingdom, Iceland, and the Netherlands. All of them have promoted different types of policies for women support, but their populations shared similar value orientations to respect of gender relations. Britons, Icelanders, Dutch are oriented toward the highest household modernity and toward the lowest equal access to work. In spite of their different women support policies, the Netherlands and the United Kingdom have two common elements: the lack of public childcare facilities and the lack of measures for the encouragement of sharing domestic work between partners. In the United Kingdom, women take at least one-year break when they have young children (Hantrais & Letablier, 1996), probably because of the lack of childcare facilities. Women usually return on the labour market and the rate of female labour market participation in the United Kingdom is quite high—65% in 1990 (OECD 1992; O'Connor, 1996: 79). The frequent interruption of the working life and the lack of equal opportunities measures put women in a worse position on the labour market, compared to that of men. In the Netherlands, married women with children return on the labour market but usually in part-time jobs. Even if women from the United Kingdom and the Netherlands are participating at higher level in the labour market, they do not have an equal status with men and this corresponds to the values shared by the population.

The Malta's position on the map is consistent with the policies promoted by this country. As I have shown before, Malta has adopted a very traditional family model, with a quite high fertility rate, and the reconciliation between paid employment and housework is much reduced. The analyzed data show that Maltese people are scoring very low on both dimensions of the analyses. In Malta the gender equality within household is much reduced as well as the equal access of women in the labor market.

After an analysis of the values map, one could say that Europeans are quite different with respect to the valorization of gender relations and of family life. The populations of the Nordic countries score higher on equal access to work and on household modernity than the other Europeans. Some parts of the Eastern-Europe score quite high on equal access but lower on household modernity, while other ex-communist countries (Russia Ukraine, Poland, and Lithuania) are the most traditionalistic in Europe, but they do accept moderate women equal access in the labour market. Mediterranean countries and some of the continental countries (Luxembourg) do not accept equal access to work and reject the modern role of women. The United Kingdom, Iceland, and the Netherlands are the most inequalitarian countries in Europe but they are favorable to the gender equality within household. The analysis indicates that the most Postmaterialist European countries (Germany, Sweden, Denmark, the Netherlands, United Kingdom, and Iceland—according to Inglehart) are the most favorable to the modern role of women.

5   Conclusions

The data analysis partially confirms the hypothesis of the correspondence between family and gender relation values shared by the populations of European countries and the reconciliation policies between paid work and family life adopted by the European states. As I have shown before, if one uses value orientations about gender equality within household and equal access in labour market as classification criteria, will obtain several groups of countries. These groups are partially overlapping with the six models of reconciliation policies identified by Lohkamp-Himmighofen and Dienel (2000). The best overlappings between values shared by the population and policies promoted by the state can be observed for the demographic model, for the ex-communist countries and for the equalitarian model. For the other models, there is not a very good fit between population values and the promoted policies. One can mention that many Eastern-European countries have followed similar policies to the demographic model and they display the same value orientations like

France and Belgium. Therefore, even if the political context was completely different, analogous policy measures are associated to similar value orientations.

The countries with high level of Postmaterialism represent a special case. Even if they have promoted different policy measures for reconciliation and for women support, the high level of affluence and of material security has determined a shift in value orientations form the traditionalist family values to the modern ones. Therefore, countries like Germany, the Netherlands or the United Kingdom did not encourage women involvement in the labour market using explicit measures, but their population strongly rejects the traditional role of the woman as housekeeper and mother. A good example in this respect would be like the population of the Nordic countries.

Looking at the legitimacy problems, one can say that usually reconciliation policies are mainly legitimized by the value orientations about women's role in society and gender relations. This is the case of Sweden and Denmark, of the Mediterranean countries, of Eastern-Europe and of France and Belgium. In other cases, the promoted policies are only in a limited degree sustained by the value orientations of the citizens. For these countries, the legitimacy of the reconciliation policies is acquired with the support of other kinds of value orientations or of other factors, like paralegitimacy factors. Legitimating a gender related political measure is a complex process that includes as main factor value orientations to gender relations and to women's position in society. Some other values, like political options or religious values are also involved. It is likely to be the case of the lack of overlapping between the value orientations of the population and the endorsed gender policies.

One can say that the European countries are quite different with respect to gender value orientations and with respect to reconciliation policies between family life and paid work. In spite of these differences, the analysis revealed that similar policy measures are associated to the same value orientations, even if the political regimes were completely different, and that resembling social and economical contexts determine similar value orientations despite of the promotion of different policies.

References

Abela, A. 2000. *Values of Women and Men in the Maltese Islands—a comparative European Perspective.* Valletta: Commission for the Advancement of Women, Ministry for Social Policy.

Baer, D. 2001. *Latent Variable Structural Equation Models.* ICPSR Summer Program.

Bagilhole, B. & P. Byrne 2000. From hard to soft law and from equality to reconciliation in the United Kingdom. Pp. 124–142 in L. Hantrais (ed.), *Gendered Policies in Europe. Reconciling Employment and Family Life.* London: Macmillan Press; New York: St. Martin's Press.

Berger, P. & T. Luckmann [1966] 1999. *Construirea socială a realității* [The Social Construction of the Reality]. Bucharest: Univers Publisher house.

Bergqvist, C. & A.-C. Jungar 2000. Adaptation or diffusion of Swedish gender model. In L. Hantrais (ed.) *Gendered Policies in Europe. Reconciling Employment and Family Life.* London: Macmillan Press; New York: St. Martin's Press.

Brainerd, E. 1997. Women in transition: Changes in gender wage differentials in Eastern Europe and the former Soviet Union. Luxembourg: Luxembourg Income Study. Working Paper.

Easton, D. 1965. *A System Analysis of Political Life.* New York, London, Sydney: John Wiley & Sons.

Esping-Anderson, G. 1990. *The Three Worlds of Welfare Capitalism.* Princeton, NJ: Princeton University Press.

—— 1997. After the Golden Age? Welfare state dilemmas in global economy. In G. Esping-Anderson (ed.), *Welfare State in Transition—National Adaptation in Global Economies.* London: Sage Publications

European Commission 2001. *Equal Opportunities for Women and Men in the European Union. Annual Report.* Brussles: Directorate-General for Employment and Social Affairs.

Fagnani, J. 1998. Recent changes in family policies in France. Political trade-offs and economic constraints. Pp. 58–65 in Eileen Drew, Ruth Emerek & Evelyn Mahon (eds.), *Women, Work and the Family in Europe.* London, New York: Routledge.

Gal, S. & G. Kligman 2000. *The Politics of Gender After Socialism.* Princeton NJ: Princeton University Press.

Gornick, J. 1999. *Gender Equality in the Labour Market: Women's Employment and Earnings.* Luxembourg: Luxembourg Income Study, Working Paper No. 206.

——, M. Meyers & K. Ross 1996. *Supporting the Employment form Mothers: Policy Variation Across Fourteen Welfare States.* Luxembourg: Luxembourg Income Study, Working Paper No. 139.

Hantrais, L. 2000. From equal pay to reconciliation of employment and family life. In L. Hantrais (ed.), *Gendred Policies in Europe—Reconciling Employment and Family Life.* London: Macmillan Press.

—— & M.-T. Letablier 1996. *Families and Family policies in Europe.* London, New York: Longman

Inglehart, R. 1997. *Modernization and Post-Modernization. Cultural, Economic and Political Change in 43 Societies.* Princeton NJ: Princeton University Press

Lillbacka, R. 1999. *The Legitimcy of the Political System- The Case of Finland.* Åbo: Åbo Akademi University Press.

Lipset, S. M. 1960. *Political Man—The Social Bases of Politics.* New York: Doubleday & Company.

Lohkamp-Himmighofen, M. & C. Dienel 2000. Reconciliation policies from a comparative perspective. In L. Hantrais (ed.), *Gendered Policies in Europe—Reconciling Employment and Family Life.* London: Macmillan Press.

Mahon, E. 1998. Class, mothers and equal opportunities to work. Pp. 170–181 in E. Drew, R. Emerek & E. Mahon (eds.), *Women, Work and the Family in Europe*. London, New York: Routledge.

Nielsen, K. 1996. Eastern European welfare systems in comparative perspective. Pp. 185–213 in B. Greve (ed.), *Comparative Welfare Systems: The Scandinavian Model in a Period of Change*. London: MacMillan Press.

O'Connor, J. 1996. From women in the welfare state to gendering welfare regimes. *Current Sociology* 44

——, A. Shola Orloff & S. Shaver 1999. *States, Markets, Families—Gender, Liberalism and Social Policy in Australia, Canada, Great Britain and the United States*. Cambridge: Cambridge University Press.

Papadopulos, T. 1998. Greek family policy from a comparative perspective. Pp. 47–57 in E. Drew, R. Emerek & E. Mahon (eds.), *Women, Work and the Family in Europe*. London, New York: Routledge.

Pascal, G. & N. Manning 2000. Gender and social policy: Comparing welfare states in Eastern Europe and Former Soviet Union. *Journal of European Social Policy* 10: 240–266.

Sainsbury, D. 1996. *Gender, Equality and Welfare States*. Cambridge, New York, Melbourne: Cambridge University Press

—— 1999a. Gender, policy regimes and Politics. Pp. 245–275 in Diane Sainsbury (ed.), *Gender and Welfare State Regimes*. Oxford: Oxford University Press.

—— 1999b. Women's and men's social rights: Gendering dimensions of welfare states. Pp. 150–169 in Diane Sainsbury (ed.), *Gender and Welfare State Regimes*. Oxford: Oxford University Press.

Trifiletti, R. 1999. Southern European welfare regimes and the worsening position of women. *Journal of European Social Policy* 9: 49–64.

UNDP 1998. *National Human Development Report—Poland 1998*. Warsaw: UNDP.

UNICEF 1999. *Women in Transition. Regional Monitoring Report*. Florence: UNICEF International Child Development Centre.

Valiente, C. 2000. Reconciliation policies in Spain. Pp. 143–159 in Linda Hantrais (ed.), *Gendered Policies in Europe—Reconciling Employment and Family Life*. London: Macmillan Press.

Van Dijk, L. 2001. Macro changes in public childcare provision, parental leave, and women's employment—An international comparison. Pp. 37–58 in T. van der Lippe & Liset van Dijk (eds.), *Women's Employment in a Comparative Perspective*. New York: Aldine de Gruyter.

Zamfir, C. 1997. The government legitimacy. In UNDP, *National Human Development Report—Romania 1997*. Bucharest: Expert Publisher house.

Zamfir, E. et al. 1999 Policies for women support. In C. Zamfir (ed.), *Social Policies in Romania: 1990–1998*. Bucharest: Expert Publisher house (in Romanian).

Appendix

Goodness-of-fit indexes

Country	χ^{2}*	Δ2 IFI	RMSEA
Belgium	140,356	0,995	0,058
Belarus	41,283	0,998	0,043
Bulgaria	91,186	0,995	0,062
Czech Republic	462,645	0,986	0,111
Croatia	127,644	0,993	0,076
Denmark	215,504	0,987	0,101
Estonia	81,464	0,996	0,057
France	146,810	0,994	0,065
Germany	677,030	0,979	0,130
Greece	116,438	0,994	0,067
Iceland	176,934	0,990	0,093
Italy	237,360	0,993	0,076
Latvia	132,773	0,993	0,077
Lithuania	376,456	0,978	0,136
Luxemburg	133,478	0,992	0,071
Malta	283,263	0,985	0,118
Great Britain	169,042	0,991	0,089
Netherlands	183,651	0,990	0,093
Poland	80,234	0,996	0,054
Portugal	165,947	0,991	0,088
Romania	192,020	0,988	0,089
Russia	411,816	0,989	0,091
Slovakia	120,519	0,994	0,063
Slovenia	90,604	0,995	0,061
Spain	102,212	0,995	0,060
Sweden	147,516	0,991	0,082
Ukraine	195,392	0,990	0,088
Hungary	98,731	0,994	0,065

Note: * Degrees of freedom = 19.

CHAPTER TEN

EUROPEAN WORK ORIENTATIONS AT THE END OF THE TWENTIETH CENTURY

Hans de Witte, Loek Halman & John Gelissen

1 *Introduction*

When examining values and their evolution, the domain of 'work' cannot be ignored. After all, the overwhelming majority of the population spend significant parts of their lives 'working', either in the form of a paid job, or in various forms of unpaid labour. However, few themes are as *ambivalent* as 'work'. A review of the literature reveals that the same dissension almost always returns: work is as much a blessing as a curse (see, e.g., Achterhuis, 1984; Kerkhofs, 1997). There are innumerable references to the philosopher Hannah Arendt, who once made the distinction between 'work' and 'labour' (see e.g., Drenth, 1984; Lagrou, 1997). 'Work' has a positive meaning: performing meaningful, creative activities, which allow one to develop. 'Labour' has a negative connotation: it refers to aggravating, dulling, routine work, which affects one's well-being. The 'work' or 'labour', which we all perform, contains elements from both sides.

This chapter is on *work orientations* in Europe and particularly the job aspects considered important. The literature pertaining to work orientations usually distinguishes fundamental dimensions (e.g., Centers & Bugental, 1966; MOW, 1987) that strongly correspond with Arendt's distinction between those work attributes that stimulate personal development ('work'), on the one hand, and the less pleasant attributes of a paid job ('labour'), on the other.

A so-called *intrinsic* work orientation emphasizes that the *aim* of labour is found *in the work itself*: the employee who wishes to develop him- or herself by means of his or her work. This orientation is also commonly referred to as 'expressive' work orientation. This resembles Arendt's conception of 'work'. Individuals with this orientation emphasize the importance of work, which is interesting, enabling them to utilize their capacities and proving opportunities for personal development and unfolding. They prefer work in which they 'can achieve something', and in which they can show initiative and take responsibility.

The *extrinsic* work orientation stresses work as a *means* of achieving goals that are *outside* work. Therefore, it is also referred to as the 'instrumental' work orientation. People with this orientation stress the importance of income and the securities offered by work. The exact job content is of less importance. Thus, favourable circumstances and working conditions, such as a good physical working environment, not too much stress and pressure, good working hours, and generous holidays are considered highly important. As such, this orientation aims at reducing unpleasant job characteristics ('labour' in Arendt's vision).

These two orientations can be easily linked to the broader developments within society which are usually denoted by the umbrella term, *modernization*. The modernization perspective usually describes a process of declining traditional or conventional views in favour of more 'modern', individualistic orientations (see, e.g., Ester, Halman & de Moor, 1994; Harding & Hikspoors, 1995). According to the modernization ideas, modern values strongly emphasize an individual's self-determination and his or her personal development. Applied to the domain of work orientations, this evolution implies that a strong, intrinsic (or expressive) work orientation is developing at the cost of an extrinsic (or instrumental) one. More than before, work has become a domain in which people can develop, unfold, and realize themselves. Such arguments not only make *evolution over time* understandable and interpretable, they also enable the formulation of a number of hypotheses about the *differences between countries* at a certain point in time. One of the many conclusions of previous studies, based among other things on earlier data collections in 1981 and 1990, was that Europe is far from unity when it comes to work orientations. Zanders (1994a; 1994b) concluded that this variety in work orientations remained during the eighties in Europe. This diversity 'seems to characterise Europe' (Zanders, 1994b: 312). His conclusions pertained to 12 European countries. The most recent 1999/2000 survey data enable Europeans' work orientations to be updated or upgraded and show to what extent European citizens still differ or resemble each other in these orientations. Not only is it possible to make that sort of comparison between the inhabitants of the 12 countries already included in previous waves of data collection, but comparisons can also be made with people from Central and Eastern European countries. In many ways, these countries differ from those of Western Europe. The Communist ideology imposed by the Soviet Union is only one—although a major—distinguishing feature. There are also marked differences between Eastern and Western European countries in other respects, for example, with regard to economic development, the labour situation, level of unemployment, and women's participation in the job market. The question arises as to whether this also has had repercussions for the work orientations, which may have become even more diverse in Europe.

2 Individualization and economic development as possible causes for differences in work orientation

The term 'modernization' denotes the long-term and continuous process according to which societies evolve from the traditional to the modern (Van der Loo & Van Reijen, 1990; Van Hoof & Van Ruysseveldt, 1996). The term 'modernizing' summarizes a large number of fundamental changes in economic, technological, political, social, and cultural parts of society (Van der Loo & Van Reijen, 1990; Halman, 1991). At the economic level, economic growth and an increase in prosperity constitute major trends that triggered increasing levels of professionalization and specialization, and a strong increase in levels of education of the (working) population (Ester, Halman & De Moor, 1994). These processes have been conducive to the expanding opportunities and choices of individuals. The latter is the basis for the *individualization process*: individuals have become increasingly free and able to decide for themselves, also with regard to values and convictions. They have gradually freed themselves from traditional institutions that imposed and structured people's opinions and views. However, the concept of individualization has many meanings and interpretations (Peters, 1995; Felling, Peters & Scheepers, 2000). A major attribute of individualization is called de-traditionalizing: a cultural change that limits the power of traditions and traditional institutions while personal autonomy, self-discipline, individual responsibility, and self-control gradually increase (Peters & Scheepers, 2000).

Applied to the domain of labour, it means that the intrinsic (or expressive) work orientations gradually become more important, emphasizing personal autonomy and self-development. In order to demonstrate such developments, Yankelovich and his colleagues distinguished three phases in the modernization process (Yankelovich, Zetterberg, Strümpel, Shanks et al., 1985). In each phase, a specific work orientation is emphasized. In a traditional, agrarian society, survival is a core issue. Work is regarded as a 'necessary evil', aimed at existential security. In an industrial society, material success and the accumulation of money and possessions become more important. An instrumental (or extrinsic) work orientation is of prime importance. In contemporary welfare states, work is no longer essential to provide security. High levels of prosperity and well-developed social security systems guarantee the satisfaction of basic human needs. As a result, people no longer need to focus on material needs, but are enabled to focus on the satisfaction of non-material needs, such as personal development and self-fulfilment.

In order to understand the transformations in society, Inglehart also emphasized the importance of increasing levels of security. His ideas are based on Maslow's theory of the satisfaction of basic human needs. According to Maslow, human needs are hierarchically ordered. The 'lower' or fundamental needs (physiological needs, safety and social security) are at the bottom. On top of these are the so-called 'higher' needs, such as appreciation and self-development. In Maslow's view, these higher needs only become relevant when the lower, fundamental needs have been satisfied. Inglehart builds on Maslow's ideas in his scarcity hypothesis, which states that an individual's priorities reflect his or her socio-economic circumstances: people will attach particular value to what is scarce. When the labour situation offers little safety or security (e.g., no career certainty, insufficient pay, or an unsafe working environment), people will cling to an extrinsic (or instrumental) work orientation, because these aspects are insufficiently satisfied. When the labour situation is secure—in the sense of low levels of unemployment, sufficient pay, etc.—and thus the basic needs are satisfied, people will stress intrinsic (or expressive) work orientations. The lower needs are then satisfied, and thus people do not have to be concerned about those and can focus on the realization of higher needs. Therefore, it is suggested that an increase in prosperity goes hand in hand with the reinforcement of an intrinsic work orientation. However, this also implies that an economic recession and rising levels of unemployment are likely to produce a return to material priorities. In times of insecurity and economic instability, people will be highly concerned with job and income security and thus emphasize instrumental or extrinsic work qualities. In an American study, Schor (1992) demonstrated that, in times of economic recession, the population indeed places greater value on income and job security than before.

Thus, an individual's preference or priority is co-determined by the presence of (material and immaterial) possibilities (or resources) and limitations (see, e.g., Van den Elzen, 2002). This applies to the individual level, as well as to the level of the country in which the individuals live. We will elaborate on this thesis in the next sections.

2.1 *Individual characteristics and their connection with work orientations*

In the first step, we investigated the explanatory power of six individual background characteristics (gender, age, level of education, performing paid work, being unemployed, and family income) and two value orientations (post-materialism and self-determination). We included these characteristics firstly, because we were interested in the explanatory power of each individual characteristic. Secondly, the additional benefit of introducing these individual characteristics was that they enabled us to understand and explain differences in work orientations between countries. If these individual characteristics correlate with the work orientations, the differences between countries may be due to differences in social and demographic compositions in the countries. Thus, a difference between two countries may be ascribed to the simple fact that one country's population is younger and higher educated than the population of the other country: the so-called 'composition effect' (Snijders & Bosker, 1999). In a multilevel analysis, both individual and country effects were estimated and thus enabled us not only to determine the degree to which individual characteristics affect work orientations, but also the extent to which these characteristics contribute to explaining differences between countries.

2.2 *Background characteristics*

In his theory of postmaterialism, Inglehart (1977; 1990; 1997) makes an appeal to the socialization hypothesis. This hypothesis states that individuals develop value orientations that reflect the socio-economic living conditions of the period in which they were raised and socialized. An important assumption is that this orientation remains relatively stable for the rest of their lives (the cohort effect). This implies that it can be expected that young people will display a more intrinsic (or expressive) work orientation, because they were raised and socialized in a prosperous post-war period in which the basic human needs were satisfied. Older generations were raised and socialized during a period when scarcity and insecurities played an important role. Hypothesis 1 thus reads as follows: young people are more likely to emphasize the intrinsic (or expressive) work qualities than older people. However, the research literature reveals contradictory results pertaining to this hypothesis. In the 'Meaning of working' study, it was found that older persons are somewhat more intrinsically orientated than younger ones (MOW, 1987: 240), while analyses of the survey data of previous EVS waves revealed that, as could be expected, young people appeared to exhibit the intrinsic orientation more (Zanders, 1994a). Other studies found no clear linkages between age and the intrinsic (or expressive) work orientation (Van den Elzen, 2002).

One can also expect a correlation between work orientation and *level of education*: the higher the level of education, the greater the tendency towards intrinsic work aspects (Hypothesis 2). People with lower levels of education usually have less job and income security and often perform jobs that are physically harder and more dangerous. Seen from Maslow's and Inglehart's perspective, their priority is to improve their job environment and conditions and thus they display an extrinsic work orientation. The job situation of higher educated people means that the 'lower' needs will be satisfied. Their material position is such that they can focus on 'higher' needs and, consequently, they can develop an intrinsic work orientation. This correlation has been observed in numerous studies in industrial psychology and industrial sociology done in the course of the last 50 years (for an overview see De Witte, 1990; see also: Zanders, 1994a, 1994b). A similar argument could be made with regard to whether a person works or not.[1]

We expected *unemployed* people to exhibit a less intrinsic (or expressive) work orientation (Hypothesis 3). After all, they are confronted

---

[1] It would have been preferable to introduce further distinctions in the rather vague and diffuse category of working respondents. For example, by distinguishing between career groups and/or positions, but that would have resulted in halving the number of respondents: 53% of the interviewees indicated that they were not working.

with a number of unsatisfied fundamental needs, such as job security and (adequate) income. The reverse applies to *employed* people.
They may participate in the work process, which meets their basic
need for more security and which also offers them the possibilities
of and opportunities for self-development and fulfilment (Van der
Elzen, 2002). We also expected this category to exhibit an intrinsic
(or expressive) work orientation to a greater degree (Hypothesis 4).

Because a higher family income increases choice opportunities and
reduces financial limitations, favourable conditions seem to be met
for expanding an orientation towards more self-fulfilment. Thus, the
expectation was that a higher (family) income will involve a more
intrinsic (or expressive) work orientation (Hypothesis 5).

Finally, we examined the extent to which *gender* correlates with a
specific work orientation. Here, the hypothesis is less obvious. The
conclusion that women often occupy less favourable positions within
the job market could lead to the assumption that they are less intrinsically orientated. However, the labour market position correlates to
a large extent with levels of education and (family) income. Because
these variables were controlled for in the analysis, it was unnecessary
to establish a pure gender difference. The research literature draws
contradictory conclusions pertaining to gender effects. Previous EVS
studies yielded that men are somewhat more intrinsically orientated
than women (Zanders, 1994a; Van den Elzen, 2002). The reverse,
however, was found in another international research study, 'Meaning
of working' (MOW, 1987). Therefore, we did not formulate a concrete hypothesis pertaining to differences between men and women.
We included these variables in our analysis simply for exploratory
reasons and to control all other associations for possible gender
differences.

2.3   *Value orientations*

As previously indicated, Inglehart describes the cultural shift from
materialism to post-materialism in his *post-materialism theory* (Inglehart,
1977, 1990, 1997). Based on the scarcity hypothesis, in combination
with the socialisation hypothesis, he expects value changes as a result of
the replacement of generations during the post-war prosperity period.
Older persons with their mainly materialistic orientations, emphasizing
economic growth, career certainty, and security, are gradually replaced
by younger persons with a principally post-materialistic orientation,

emphasizing the satisfaction of higher needs, such as self-development, autonomy, and emancipation. In the light of this interpretation, it seems plausible to assume an association between a post-materialistic orientation and an intrinsic (or expressive) work orientation (Hypothesis 6). After all, individual autonomy and self-development are at the core of both orientations. Moreover, post-materialism is not strictly limited to a specific domain of existence (even though the spheres of society and politics occupy central positions), whereas work orientation is obviously limited to the work domain.

A similar tendency towards autonomy and self-development, which is characteristic of a post-materialistic orientation, comes to the fore in the distinction between 'self-determination' and 'conformism', which are key notions in the work of Melvin Kohn and his collaborators (e.g., Kohn, 1977; Kohn & Schooler, 1983). Central is the association between an employee's career position and his or her value orientation. Employees in higher career positions emphasize the importance of *self-determination*. They find it preferable to rely on their own insights and judgements, and stress personal responsibility and individual autonomy. Employees in lower job positions put more emphasis on the importance of *conformism*. The standard for personal behaviour is sought in external authorities: from a person in a higher position or from the current norms and values within a company or the broader community (see also Tax, 1982). Kohn attributes this to the association between the level of education and the characteristics of the job performed (in particular, autonomy or 'occupational self-direction'). Particularly in Kohn's initial studies, values in education were at the core, but in later studies, he also paid attention to other domains of existence. Given the definition of self-determination, a correlation with an intrinsic (or expressive) work orientation (Hypothesis 7) was expected. After all, an intrinsic (or expressive) work orientation can be conceived of as the realization of the value orientation of self-determination within the work domain.

2.4 *Country characteristics and their association with work orientations*

In order to explain the differences between countries, we first of all explored the possible impact of several structural country characteristics. As argued at the individual level, economic development and the resulting increase in wealth and welfare are considered 'determining forces' for the expansion of individual choice. Therefore, it can be assumed that work orientations are linked with a country's level of prosperity. Our hypothesis was that the inhabitants of more prosperous societies would have a greater tendency towards an intrinsic (or expressive) work orientation (Hypothesis 8). Although economic development generally leads to improved living conditions and greater wealth, it does not mean that all uncertainties have been removed. For example, unemployment is outside the control of national governments. Levels of unemployment may, however, have a strong influence on work orientations. After all, a high unemployment rate in a country turns work into a scarce product: in such a country, the emphasis is (or is put) on securing jobs and the certainties they provide. In other words, the higher the level of unemployment in a country, the greater the emphasis on the extrinsic aspects and the smaller the emphasis on the intrinsic aspects of work (Hypothesis 9).

Characteristics of a *cultural* nature may also play a role in explaining the differences and similarities in work orientations between the countries. Again, numerous factors can be mentioned. However, we limited ourselves to the two value orientations, which were mentioned above. Firstly, we examined the impact of the 'level' of *post-materialism* within a country (qualified score) on the extent to which individuals in these countries exhibit an intrinsic (or expressive) work orientation. The measure of post-materialism is (co-)determined by economic development; prosperity creates an increase in post-materialistic orientations (Inglehart, 1977; 1997). It was expected that the population of a country with a post-materialistic culture would be more likely to emphasize the intrinsic work orientation (Hypothesis 10). This hypothesis implied an additional test of Hypothesis 6, in which a similar connection was assumed at an individual level. Using similar arguments, we postulated a correlation between the extent of self-determination within a given country and the degree to which that country's population favours the intrinsic work orientation (Hypothesis 11). Here, too, it was assumed that a culture characterized by self-determination results in a more intrinsic work orientation amongst its inhabitants, when compositional differences and the other contextual variables are controlled for.[2]

---

[2] Our study is not the first in which the influence of individual and contextual

3 Research design

3.1 Data and sample surveys

Our work orientations study was limited to 31 countries. Northern Ireland was excluded from the analysis, because—Northern Ireland being part of the UK—, the contextual data was not available for this country separately. The data collected in East Germany was combined with that collected in West Germany, because the contextual data available pertained to Germany as a whole. The sample survey within every country was weighed to correct for variables such as gender and age, in order to assure representativeness. All countries were weighted equally in the final analysis (each country's N was set at N = 1,000), so that the pooled data set included 31,000 respondents.

3.2 Measurements

Apart from the individual data collected in the EVS surveys, we also used data from international data bases (structural contextual data).

The *background characteristics* originate from EVS. *Age* was measured using year of birth which (bearing in mind the survey date) was translated into years of age. The average age of the respondents was 45.15 (SD = 17.23) years. To determine the *level of education*, the respondents were asked their age when they completed full-time education. On average, this was 18.14 (SD = 4.65) years of age. At the

---

characteristics on work orientations was analyzed. Van den Elzen (2002) analysed work orientations based on the 1990 EVS data collected in 15 countries by means of multi-level analysis. Furthermore, the modernization thesis was tested at an international level, including the gross national product (GNP) as an indicator of the level of prosperity. No single contextual characteristic in the multi-level analysis made a significant contribution to elucidating an intrinsic work orientation. The author suggests that, amongst other things, this is attributable to the relatively small number of countries (only 15) included in her analysis, perhaps representing too little variation in terms of modernization. In our study, we tried to overcome that problem by including more countries, particular countries from Eastern Europe, which possibly resulted in more variation as regards economic development and related aspects, as was argued in the introduction. Further, in comparison with Van den Elzen's analysis we used more recent data, and also in our analysis, the modernization thesis as well as the scarcity hypothesis was put into practice at a contextual level. Finally, this study also differs from previous ones in the number of value orientations included in the analyses, at individual as well as contextual level.

time of the interview, 53.8% of the respondents were employed in a paid job (*employed*); 7% were *unemployed*. The family *income* was determined using a 10-point scale. This variable was standardised within each country, in such a way that the income categories in the various countries could be compared. Finally, sex was also included (*gender*): 46.9% of respondents were men.

In the EVS survey, 15 job qualities were submitted to the respondents, and they were asked to indicate those aspects that were important to them personally (possible answers: 'important' and 'not important'). In Appendix 10.1, the frequencies of all separate items are displayed. A principal component analysis was performed on 13 of these aspects using Varimax rotation.[3] This yielded the expected two-dimensional structure (see also Appendix 10.1). Intrinsic work orientation was principally indicated by such qualities as being able to take initiative, having a responsible job, and being able to achieve something. Extrinsic orientation pertained particularly to good working hours, a good holiday regulation, and good pay. Items pertaining to a specific orientation were added and divided by the number of items, resulting in an index varying between '0' and '1' for each work orientation. In order to confine further analyses to one index only, extrinsic orientation was subtracted from intrinsic orientation. In this way, an index was constructed ranging from '−1' (emphasizing extrinsic qualities above intrinsic job aspects) to '+1' (emphasizing intrinsic qualities above extrinsic aspects). A positive score thus expresses that people are more intrinsically (or expressively) orientated than extrinsically (or instrumentally). This index simplified the analyses and, as far as content is concerned, was more in accordance with the theoretical points of departure of, e.g., Maslow and Inglehart. Following these authors, one may assume that preference for an intrinsic work orientation is to the cost of an extrinsic orientation because intrinsic orientation only becomes relevant after conditions have been met to satisfy lower or more fundamental needs. However, the analyses were also performed on the two work orientations separately. The results and interpretations of the separate analyses do not appear to deviate much from those of the analyses of both orientations combined.

---

[3] Two items were omitted because previous studies had shown that these did not belong to both dimensions ('pleasant people to work with'), or because they appeared to be multidimensional ('good promotion opportunities').

The operationalization of the (post-) materialistic value orientation was originally proposed by Inglehart (1977). Four long-term aims of a country were submitted to the respondents. Two of these indicated materialistic aims ('maintaining order' and 'countering price increases'), and two indicated post-materialistic aims ('having a say' and 'assuring free expression of opinions'). The respondents were asked to indicate the most important goal and the second most important goal. On the basis of their preferences, the respondents were divided into four groups: if preference was expressed for the two materialistic aims, people were considered 'pure materialist' (score '1'). If the first preference was materialistic and the second a post-materialistic aim, people were considered to belong to the mixed group of 'materialists with post-materialism as second choice' (score '2'). A post-materialistic first preference together with a materialistic second preference was the mixed pattern of the 'post-materialists with materialism as second choice' group (score '3'), and people who found two post-materialistic aims most important, were placed in the 'pure post-materialist' group (score '4'). A high score on this variable thus refers to a more post-materialistic orientation.

The 'self-determination conformism' value dimension, proposed by Kohn, was indicated largely in the original way, namely, by submitting a list of 11 educational values to respondents ('aspects which children should learn at home'). For each of the values, they had to indicate whether they found them important or not (dichotomies). A principal component analysis was performed on four items and that provided a one-dimensional structure, with 'obedience' and 'good manners' on the conformist side, and 'independence' and 'a sense of responsibility' on the side of self-determination. Factor scores were calculated, whereby positive scores reflect the orientation towards self-determination.

International characteristics or contextual data originate from two sources. *Structural* contextual data was derived from two international data bases. A country's prosperity was measured using the 'gross domestic product per capita, ppp': GDP, as suggested by Van Snippenburg (1986). This measure was derived from the 2000 Human Development Report's (UNDP, 2001) Human Development Indicators. The percentage of unemployment within a country was derived from the World Development Indicators (World Bank, 2001). Both structural contextual characteristics pertain to 1999.

The *cultural* contextual data was deduced from the EVS data by calculating each country's mean scores on the post-materialism and self-determination indexes. These aggregated scores were consequently added as an international characteristic to the data-set at aggregate level.

3.3 *Analysis*

A multi-level design was applied using the HLM 5-program (Raudenbush, Cheong & Congdon, 2001). This technique was specifically developed to examine which part of the variance in a dependent variable (in this case, a work orientation which is more intrinsic than extrinsic) is attributable to individual as opposed to international characteristics. We opted for the 'random intercept model'. In such a multi-level model, the clustered structure of the data (individuals within countries) is taken into account and the relations between countries and within countries are modelled simultaneously. In the random intercept model, countries differ with regard to the mean value of the dependent variable: the random intercept is the only random 'country effect'. As regards the individual background variables' regression coefficients in this model, it is assumed that they are 'group independent' (or 'fixed'). All coefficients in the following tables are un-standardised coefficients. These are thus not mutually comparable.

The analysis was performed in five steps. First, a zero model was calculated, i.e., a model without explanatory variables. The purpose of this model was to determine how much variance there was at an international as well as individual level. After this basis model, the hypotheses were tested in four cumulative models. The first model included only the individual background characteristics. In the second model, the two value orientations at the individual level were entered. In the third model, all individual variables were supplemented with structural contextual data. The fourth and last model comprised all preceding variables and the cultural contextual data (value orientations at an aggregated level).

A number of measures were considered for each model. Apart from the intercept and the regression coefficients, two variance components were calculated. These last two measures reproduced the estimate of the variance between countries (at an 'international level') and between individuals within the analysed countries (at an 'individual level'). In this way, the variance in work orientations was determined, while a comparison was also made of the variance between and within countries. The latter was also expressed in the intra-class correlation. This measure reproduced the proportion of variance that can be assigned to differences *between* countries. A low value indicates that there is little variety between countries. Most of the variety can be observed at an individual level ('amongst individuals'). In conclusion, we also present the proportional reductions in the estimated variance components in the random-intercept model. These may be viewed as the model's 'explained variances' (for the individual as well as the contextual level).

4   Results

4.1   Preliminary description of the differences between European countries

Before testing our hypotheses, we first needed to examine whether there was variation in the dependent variable. Because we were dealing with a difference score, the dependent variable expressed preference for a 'more intrinsic than extrinsic' work orientation. For reasons of simplicity, we refer to this measure as a 'preference for an intrinsic' work orientation. An analysis of variance with the 31 countries as independent variables and the preference for an intrinsic work orientation as dependent variable yielded that the countries do indeed differ (significantly) from one another ($F (30, 30846) = 84.95$; $P < .0001$). The non-linear association measure 'eta' amounted to .28, which indicates a moderate correlation. The averages of the various countries are displayed in Figure 10.1.

Figure 10.1 reveals that the country means for the dependent variable are far from extreme. On the intrinsic side of the scale, the maximum score is only 0.13 (Slovenia). High up on the intrinsic pole, four West European countries obtained a high score: the Netherlands, Denmark, France, and Iceland. On the extrinsic side, the score was −0.20 (Lithuania). A high extrinsic score was also found in two other East European countries: Slovakia and Belarus. The inhabitants of Spain and Great Britain also appear to be more extrinsically than intrinsically orientated as far as work is concerned. Thus, there is a clear distinction between Eastern and Western Europe.

Figure 10.1   Country mean scores on work value intrinsic minus extrinsic

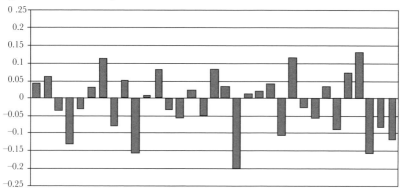

at be bg by cz de dk ee eg es fi fr gr hr hu ie is it lu lv mt ni nl pl pt ro ru se si sk ua uk

4.2   *Testing the hypotheses*

Table 10.1 contains the results of the multi-level analyses.

The test of the *zero model* was significant. As mentioned before, European countries differ in work orientations. Inspection of the variance components at the bottom of Table 10.1 indicates, however, that the variance at international level is less than that at an individual level. The work orientation is thus mainly explained by differences at an individual level, and to a much lesser extent by differences between countries, even though the variance component for the international level is statistically significant. The difference in explanatory power is also revealed in the low value of the intra-class correlation: only 7.5% of the variance deals with differences between countries; the remaining 92.5% is situated amongst individuals.

Model 1 introduced the individual respondents' *background characteristics* to the analysis, testing the first five hypotheses simultaneously. The first hypothesis proposed that younger persons would be more intrinsically oriented. This supposition was falsified by the analysis: the older respondents appeared to adhere to the more intrinsic work orientation. The coefficient has a positive sign instead of the expected negative. As was supposed in Hypothesis 2, higher levels of education do indeed go hand in hand with a more intrinsic orientation. The hypothesis regarding the state of unemployment was also confirmed (Hypothesis 3): unemployed people obtained lower scores (negative sign), which indicates a less intrinsic work orientation. Strangely

Table 10.1   Results of multilevel analyses with work orientation (intrinsic qualities minus extrinsic qualities) as dependent variable (unstandardized coefficients)

Model	0	1	2	3	4
Intercept	−.011	−.010	−.011	−.010	−.010
Background characteristics					
Sex (0 = male; 1 = female)	−.005 (n.s.)	−.004 (n.s.)	−.004 (n.s.)	−.004 (n.s.)	
Age	.001***	.001***	.001***	.001***	
Education	.012***	.010***	.010***	.010***	
(age when completed)					
Employed (dummy)	−.016***	−.020***	−.020***	−.020***	
Unemployed (dummy)	−.033**	−.035***	−.035***	−.035***	
Family income	.022***	.019***	.019***	.018***	
Attitudes (individual level)					
Postmaterialism		.029***	.029***	.029***	
Autonomy		.019***	.019***	.019***	
Structural context charateristics					
GDP in 1999			.000 (n.s.)	.000 (n.s.)	
Unemployment (in %)		−.005 (n.s.)	−.005 (n.s.)		
Cultural context characteristics					
Postmaterialism			.013 (n.s.)		
Autonomy			.018 (n.s.)		
Variance components					
Country level	.00715	.00724	.00641	.00523	.0056
Individual level	.08792	.08447	.08334	.08334	.08334
Chi-square	2146.76	2329.97	2014.48	1387.18	1394.46
df	30	30	30	28	26
p	.000	.000	.000	.000	.000
Deviance	12122.52	11005.57	10625.80	10652.42	10660.59
Intra-class correlation	.0752	.0789	.0714	.0590	.0630
Explained variances					
Individual level	0	.036	.052	.052	.052
Country level	0	.013	.104	.269	.217

*** p < .001

enough, the same applies to employed people: they also obtained lower scores (negative sign). Hypothesis 4 was thus rejected. As regards Hypothesis 5, our expectation was confirmed: a higher family income does indeed go hand in hand with a more intrinsic work orientation. Finally, no gender effect was found: men and women do not differ as regards their work orientation. We did not formulate a hypothesis in this regard.

As indicated before, analyses of work orientations were also performed separately. The results mostly confirm the results presented here. Thus, both educational level and family income exhibited a positive relation with the intrinsic work orientation and a negative relation with the extrinsic orientation. These correlations were expected. Employed people did not differ from the other respondents with regard to the intrinsic work orientation. They did, however, exhibit a stronger extrinsic (or instrumental) work orientation. This some-what qualifies the correlation found between 'employed' and a less intrinsic work orientation. This correlation is thus caused exclusively by employed persons' stronger extrinsic work orientation. Separate analyses did in fact, lead to a somewhat different conclusion with regard to the older persons' work orientation, which, according to our analysis, is more intrinsic than extrinsic. Compared with younger persons, older respondents adopted a less intrinsic attitude, and com-bined this (expected) result with a somewhat less extrinsic work ori-entation. On both separate measures, they thus obtained lower scores than younger persons. However, the largest difference pertains to extrinsic orientation. When both scores were subtracted from one another, older persons scored more intrinsically than younger respon-dents, relatively speaking. This difference seems, however, an arte-fact, caused by the combination of two separate scores.

Introducing background characteristics allowed the examination of composition effects. These effects were almost absent. The intro-duction of the six background characteristics did not alter the vari-ance at international level. The intra-class correlation even increased somewhat instead of decreasing. In other words, when composition effects were controlled for, the precision of the estimated variance of the context increased. This suggests that the introduced back-ground characteristics can explain a part of the variance within coun-tries in the dependent variable (R-square = .036). However, this explains the differences between countries to a much lesser extent (R-square = .013).

In the second model, two *value orientations* were entered into the analyses next to the background characteristics, which were already included in the previous model. Both value orientations emerged as significant predictors of the dependent variables. As expected, it was found that a more post-materialistic orientation goes hand in hand with a more intrinsic work orientation. Hypothesis 6 was thus confirmed. A stronger tendency towards self-determination was also found to accompany a more intrinsic work orientation, which implies a confirmation of Hypothesis 7. The introduction of value orientations reduced the coefficients of two background characteristics to a certain degree: the coefficients of educational level and of family income dropped slightly. This suggests that a part of the influence of these background characteristics was through the two value orientations. It is remarkable that the coefficients of a few background characteristics increased after the introduction of value orientations. To a certain degree, the introduction of value orientations thus increased the effect of age and of the 'employed' and 'unemployed' dummies.

The introduction of both value orientations showed a limited composition effect, while the variance component at an international level decreased somewhat (from .007 to .006). To a certain extent, the differences in work orientation between the different countries can thus be attributed to country differences in post-materialism and educational values. After all, the explained variance at aggregate level increased from .013 to .104. At an individual level, the explained variance of the social background characteristics and value orientations together amounted to approximately 5 per cent.

In model 3, the first series of contextual data was entered into the analysis: GDP and the percentage of unemployed people. The simultaneous introduction of both contextual characteristics, however, had no significant effect.[4] Hypotheses 8 and 9 were thus rejected: the differences in work orientation between the countries cannot be attributed to the level of prosperity or the degree of unemployment. The variance component's drop at the aggregate level suggests that the entered variables had explanatory power. However, their direct effects were not statistically significant. Compared with the zero model, the variance component for the aggregate level dropped by 26.9 per cent when these contextual variables were added to the model.

The fourth model completed the analysis by including the *cultural contextual characteristics* in addition to the preceding variables. This did not confirm the expectations either. Neither the aggregated score for post-materialism, nor that for self-determination, seemed to correlate with the work orientation. Hypotheses 10 and 11 were thus also

---

[4] This was the case when both contextual characteristics were introduced separately. In each case, a weak effect was established, which was also the expected orientation. When both variables were introduced simultaneously, they no longer exhibited a significant effect. This may be attributed to their mutual correlation ($r = -.43$ at an international level ($N = 31$; $p < .05$), whereby they possibly had too much variance in common to have any influence separately.

rejected. The various measures at the bottom of Table 1 hardly differ, which likewise indicates that the introduced variables had no explanatory power. In terms of explained variance, the power of explanation even decreased (R-square = .217).

5 Conclusions

In this study, we focused on the differences in work orientations between European countries using a multi-level analysis. The data from the third wave of the European Values Study (EVS) including 31 countries was analysed. Individual (background characteristics and value orientations) as well as country characteristics were included in these analyses. A distinction was made between two types of work orientation: an intrinsic (or expressive) one, in which work is regarded an aim in itself, and an extrinsic (or instrumental) one in which work is regarded as a means of reaching goals situated outside the work situation. The dependent variable was the extent to which people are more intrinsically than extrinsically work-orientated. In developing hypotheses, the point of departure was the idea that preference for a specific work orientation is co-determined by an individual's possibilities (or resources) and his/her limitations. In this study, two processes were described which shape the conditions and the possibilities and limitations: modernization and scarcity. The modernization thesis puts forward that a rise in prosperity increases an individual's choice possibilities. This possibly facilitates a more intrinsic work orientation, in which self-development and self-fulfilment are at the core. Likewise, Inglehart's post-materialism theory assumes that job scarcity goes hand in hand with a more extrinsic work orientation. Hypotheses were deduced from both processes regarding individual background characteristics and contextual data, supplemented by two hypotheses about the connections between an intrinsic work orientation and other value orientations.

Our first, important conclusion is that the intrinsic tendency towards work only varies to a limited extent between the countries concerned. Differences were indeed established, but these were rather modest. Greater variation exists at individual level. This finding corroborates the conclusions from studies using data from previous waves of the EVS, thus pertaining to a more limited set of countries (Van den Elzen, 2002).

Therefore, it does not come as a surprise that especially those hypotheses pertaining to the *individual* level were confirmed. The theoretical points of departure of the hypotheses at the individual level thus seem to make sense. A (more) intrinsic work orientation appears to go hand in hand with indicators for prosperity and scarcity, as assumed in the modernization thesis and the scarcity hypothesis. Thus, higher educated respondents and those with a higher family income exhibit a stronger intrinsic work orientation. This finding corroborates the results of other studies (e.g., MOW, 1987; Zanders, 1994a, b). Apart from this, we found that unemployed people exhibit a less intrinsic work orientation, as was predicted by the scarcity hypothesis.

However, two conclusions deviate from our suppositions. Working people emerge as being less intrinsically directed towards work than expected. This may result from our not including in the analyses the concrete characteristics of the jobs involved. In the research literature, it is suggested that the work orientation of employed people is strongly influenced by the characteristics of the job, e.g., the extent to which they can work autonomously (e.g., De Witte, 1990). The category of 'working persons' is thus extremely heterogeneous. Dividing this ambiguous category into a number of categories of workers in specific jobs would possibly have yielded different results. After all, it is possible that the group of extrinsically oriented workers was over-sampled in the current survey exactly because they performed jobs that require or boost such an orientation.

We also found that older people are more intrinsically orientated towards work than younger people, while the reverse was expected. This might be an artefact. The results of the separate work orientations were different and partially more in line with our hypotheses. Older persons appeared not only to be less intrinsically oriented towards work than younger people, but they were also are less extrinsically oriented towards work. Thus, they obtained lower scores than younger people for both orientations. However, the biggest differences occurred with regard to the extrinsic orientation. When both scores were subtracted from one another, older people scored more intrinsically than younger people, relatively speaking. The difference thus has a purely methodological cause, because it is the result of the combination of two distinctive scores. Nevertheless, it undermines our theoretical points of departure. The lower intrinsic work orientation of older persons is in accordance with our expectations, but the lower extrinsic orientation contradicts our hypothesis. Indeed, Inglehart's scarcity and socialisation hypothesis led us to expect a more extrinsic (or instrumental) work orientation in this age category. A possible explanation for this surprising observation may be that younger people are just starting their professional careers (Van den Elzen, 2002) and still have to earn a place in society and in the workplace, resulting in extrinsic aspects, such as good pay and job security being emphasized. As soon as they are in a more secure position, they may focus more on self-development in their jobs.

In addition to individual background characteristics, two *value orientations* were included in the analyses. Existing studies were usually confined to the analysis of these background characteristics (e.g., Zanders, 1994a; Van den Elzen, 2002) and were not especially focused on the impact of orientations. However, these value orientations also appear to correlate with an intrinsic work orientation. In line with our expectations, a post-materialistic tendency and an orientation towards self-determination (instead of conformism) were found to go hand in hand with an intrinsic work orientation. These results are in line with the theories of Inglehart (1977; 1990) and Kohn, respectively (1977; Kohn & Schooler, 1983). They also suggest that an intrinsic work orientation may be viewed as the realization of both broader and more general value orientations.

Finally, our analyses revealed that the differences *between* various European countries could be explained only to a very limited extent. At country level ('contextual level'), the various hypotheses deduced from the modernization thesis and the scarcity hypothesis were not confirmed. It appears that differences in prosperity (using gross domestic product) and the extent of unemployment at country level were not directly related to the intrinsic work orientation ('structural contextual data'). These variables did, however, explain about 17 per cent more of the variation at country level than the model in which only composition effects were included. The aggregated scores of the value orientations of post-materialism and self-determination (versus conformism) also seemed to have no direct impact ('cultural contextual data'). The differences between the countries seem to be attributable to a small extent to a difference in composition of the background characteristics of the national samples. A similar composition effect was indeed established regarding the value orientations of post-materialism and self-determination at the individual level. These composition effects explain a substantial part of the variation between countries.

The observation that differences with regard to work orientations between countries are difficult to explain using contextual data (or composition effects) is not new. In her study, Van den Elzen concluded the same (Van den Elzen, 2002). It is, however, remarkable that her results were replicated, because we included more countries in the analysis and thus, possibly, also more variation. Also, we tried to operationalize both the modernization thesis and the scarcity hypothesis at individual as well as aggregate level. Apparently, this expansion was not sufficient to explain the European differences in work orientation. Therefore, we would like to consider possible explanations to be investigated in future research.

One explanation of why contextual characteristics proved not to have much effect is the modest variation in work orientation between European countries. There appears to be more variation at an individual level than at aggregate or country level. When there is little variation, little can be explained (statistically speaking). The extent to which this provides a conclusive explanation is uncertain. The variation at an international level was perhaps small, but it was not totally absent (see Figure 10.1).

A second possible explanation pertains to the level of the analysis. The national level may be too 'high'. After all, certain countries are very large and are rather heterogeneous. Within such countries, there may be huge differences, for example, the extent to which people experience unemployment. In 2000, unemployment rates varied from around 2% in Noord Brabant and Utrecht, both regions in the Netherlands, to 31% in Seevrozapdu in Bulgaria, 27% in Calabria in Italy, and 25% in Andalusia in Spain (see Eurostat). With regard to degree of industrialisation, an important feature of modernization, significant differences may also occur between regions within countries. Italy is such a country, with substantial regional differences between Northern, Central, and Southern Italy. In future analyses, an effort can be made to collect contextual data at a 'lower'—and thereby possibly more relevant—level, and to add this to the analysis. The use of theoretical notions such as modernization as an explanatory framework should not be abandoned before similar analyses have been performed.

A last possible explanation pertains to the number of indicators used in our analyses. We included a very limited number of explanatory factors and possibly excluded the more important ones. For example, the modernization thesis could be tested bearing in mind the type of welfare state people live in. On the basis of Esping-Andersen's analysis, four types of welfare states can be distinguished, which could result in a certain differentiation in work orientations (Esping-Andersen, 1990; Arts & Gelissen, 1999). However, this is not certain, because the addition of a similar typology did not lead to other conclusions (see, e.g., Van den Elzen, 2002). Political-historical characteristics may also be more powerful explanatory factors. It can be argued that the East-West divide may explain differences in work orientations because people in Eastern Europe have been raised and socialised with different work situations and orientations than people in Western Europe.

For the time being, the conclusion is that differences do indeed exist between the countries, but that the differences are not very marked, whereas, for example, on the basis of recent political and historical developments, (large) differences between, for example, Eastern and Western European countries could have been expected. The fact that differences in economic development did not lead to differences in work orientations seems to indicate that modernization in the work domain is different from that in other spheres of life. Economic development does not seem to have led to a stronger emphasis on intrinsic orientations. In other words, in the more prosperous countries, extrinsic orientations also seem to be broadly exhibited, generally speaking. One could argue that this is not surprising, because work and the money that is earned with it not only generate more security, but also make a more luxurious life possible. The necessity of work for survival in the present welfare state may have disappeared, but that does not make the extrinsic aspects less important. Furthermore, work also has immaterial advantages. A broader social network can develop through work and, for many, the broader social network can also be an important source of satisfaction. The one (extrinsic) thus does not need to exclude the other (intrinsic). Intrinsic job aspects are still important, also for people who live in societies that offer more security.

References

Achterhuis, H. 1984. *Arbeid, een eigenaardig medicijn.* Baarn: Ambo.
Arts, W. & J. Gelissen 1999. Verzorgingsstaten in soorten. Op zoek naar ideaal- en reële typen. *Mens & Maatschappij* 74: 143–165.

Ashford, S. & N. Timms 1992. *What Europe Thinks. A Study of Western European Values.* Aldershot: Dartmouth.

Centers, R. & D. Bugental 1966. Intrinsic and extrinsic job motivations among different segments of the working population. *Journal of Applied Psychology* 50: 193–197.

De Witte, H. 1990. *Conformisme, radicalisme en machteloosheid. Een onderzoek naar de sociaal-culturele en sociaal-economisch opvattingen van arbeiders in Vlaanderen.* Leuven: HIVA-KuLeuven.

Drenth, P. 1984. Centraliteit van werken. Pp. 97–114 in A. Soudijn & R. Takens (eds.), *Psychologie en economische recessie.* Lisse: Swets en Zeitlinger.

Esping-Andersen, G. 1990. *The Three Worlds of Welfare Capitalism.* Cambridge: Polity Press.

Ester, P., L. Halman & R. de Moor (eds.) 1994. *The Individualizing Society. Value Change in Europe and North America.* Tilburg: Tilburg University Press.

Felling, A., J. Peters. & P. Scheepers 2000. *Individualisering in Nederland aan het einde van de twintigste eeuw. Empirisch onderzoek naar omstreden hypotheses.* Assen: van Gorcum.

Halman, L. 1991. *Waarden in de Westerse wereld. Een internationale exploratie van de waarden in de Westerse samenleving.* Tilburg: Tilburg University Press.

—— 2001. *The European Values Study: a Third Wave. Source book of the 1999/2000 Eurepean Values Study Surveys.* Tilburg: EVS, WORC, Tilburg University.

Harding, S. & F. Hikspoors 1995. New work values: in theory and in practice. *International Social Science Journal* 145: 441–455.

Inglehart, R. 1977. *The Silent Revolution.* Princeton: Princeton University Press.

—— 1990. *Culture Shift in Advanced Industrial Society.* Princeton: Princeton University Press.

—— 1997. *Modernization and Postmodernization.* Princeton: Princeton University Press.

Kerkhofs, J. 1997. *De Europeanen en hun waarden. Wat wij denken en voelen.* Leuven: Davidsfonds.

Kohn, M. 1977. *Class and Conformity: A Study in Values. With a Reassessement 1977,* Second edition. Chicago: The University of Chicago Press.

—— & C. Schooler 1983. *Work and Personality. An Inquiry into the Impact of Social Stratification.* New Jersey: Ablex Publishing Corporation.

Lagrou, L. 1997. De zin van arbeid en werk. Pp. 43–69 in B. Raymaekers & A. van de Putte (eds.), *Lessen voor de eenentwintigste eeuw.* Leuven: Universitaire Pers.

Maslow, A. 1954. *Motivation and Personality.* New York: Harper and Row.

MOW International Research Team 1987. *The Meaning of Working.* London: Academic Press.

Peters, J. 1995. Individualization: fiction or reality? *Sociale Wetenschappen* 38: 18–27.

—— & P. Scheepers 2000. Individualisering in Nederland: sociaal-historische context en theoretische interpretaties. Pp. 9–47 in A. Felling, J. Peters & P. Scheepers, *Individualisering in Nederland aan het einde van de twintigste eeuw. Empirisch onderzoek naar omstreden hypotheses.* Assen: van Gorcum.

Raudenbush, S.W., A.S. Bryk, Y.F. Cheong & R. Congdon, R. 2001. *HLM 5: Hierarchical Linear and Nonlinear Modelling.* Scientific Software International, 2nd edition.

Schor, J. 1992. *The Overworked American. The Unexpected Decline of Leisure.* New York: Basic books.

Snijders, T. & R. Bosker 1999. *Multilevel Analysis. An Introduction to Basic and Advanced Multilevel Modeling.* London: Sage.

Tax, B. 1982. *Waarden, mentaliteit en beroep. Een onderzoek ten behoeve van een sociaal-culturele interpretatie van sociaal-economisch milieu.* Lisse: Swets & Zeitlinger.

UNDP 2000. *Human Development Report 2000*. New York/Oxford: Oxford University Press.

Van den Elzen, A. 2002. *Zekerheid of zelfontplooiing? Een internationaal vergelijkend onderzoek naar arbeids- en gezinswaarden*. Nijmegen: Dissertation.

Van der Loo, H. & W. van Reijen 1990. *Paradoxen van modernisering. Een sociaal-wetenschappelijke benadering*. Muiderberg: Coutinho.

Van Hoof, J. & J. van Ruysseveldt (eds.) 1996. *Sociologie en de moderne samenleving. Maatschappelijke veranderingen van de industriële revolutie tot in de 21ste eeuw*. Heerlen: Open Universiteit.

Van Snippenburg, L. 1986. *Modernisering en sociaal beleid. Een landenvergelijkende studie*. Nijmegen: dissertation.

World Bank 2001. *World Development Report 2000/2001*. Oxford: Oxford University Press.

Yankelovich, D., B. Zetterberg, B. Strümpel, M. Shanks et al. 1985. *The World at Work. An International Report on Jobs, Productivity and Human Values*. New York: Octogon Books.

Zanders, H. 1994a. Changing work values. Pp. 129–153 in Ester, P., L. Halman & R. de Moor (eds.), *The Individualizing Society. Value Change in Europe and North America*. Tilburg: Tilburg University Press.

—— 1994b. Veranderende arbeidsoriëntaties in Europa 1981–1990. Pp. 292–314 in H. de Witte (ed.), *Op zoek naar de arbeidersklasse. Een verkenning van de verschillen in opvattingen en leefstijl tussen arbeiders en bedienden in Vlaanderen, Nederland en Europa*. Leuven: Acco.

Appendix

Percentages of respondents saying that presented work qualities are important (merged data)

	Percentage 'important'
Good pay	80,5
A job that is interesting	65,7
Good job security	64,8
A job that meets one's abilities	60,3
A job in which you feel you can achieve something	55,9
Good hours	50,1
Meeting people	47,9
An opportunity to use initiative	47,1
A job respected by people in general	44,6
A responsible job	42,6
A useful job for society	42,0
Not too much pressure	35,2
Generous holidays	30,3

PART THREE

RELIGION AND MORALITY

CHAPTER ELEVEN

RELIGIOUS BELIEFS AND PRACTICES IN CONTEMPORARY EUROPE

Loek Halman & Veerle Draulans

1 *Introduction*

There is much discussion about religion in contemporary Europe. According to the prevalent view, Europe is secularized and evidence is found in the levels of church attendance, which have declined dramatically in the last few decades. But do such figures tell the whole story? Do they also reveal that religious beliefs have declined? Davie characterizes the European situation in terms of 'believing without belonging', indicating that the 'marked fall-off in religious attendance (especially in the Protestant North) has not resulted, yet, in a parallel abdication of religious belief' (Davie, 2002: 5). Thus, instead of speaking of secular Europe, she regards it more appropriate and accurate to speak of unchurched Europe. There may be a discrepancy between religious practices and actual beliefs.

In this chapter, religious orientations and practices of Europeans are explored. We did not include the US in our analyses, because the trajectory of secularization in the US appears to be different from that in Europe. Indeed, secularization theory seems to offer 'a relatively plausible account of European developments, but is unable or unwilling to take seriously, much less to explain the surprising vitality and extreme pluralism of denominational forms of salvation religion in America, notwithstanding the pronounced secularization of state and society' (Casanova, 2001: 426), nor does it explain why 'most of the world is bubbling with religious passions' (Berger, 2001: 445).

Secularization, being a European phenomenon does not imply, however, that Europe is homogeneously secular. Secularization is usually seen as part of a complex modernization process. A conglomerate of diverse dynamics undermined the medieval system. The most mentioned influencing factors are the Protestant Reformation, the rise of the modern states, the growth of capitalism and the expansion of sciences. All these different dynamics stimulated the so-called process of differentiation, in which religion lost its former coordinating influence, described by Berger as the 'sacred canopy'. But sciences, modern states, and modern capitalism did not develop in a similar way all over Europe. Nor was the Reformation movement equally successful all over the continent. So, the conclusion is clear: 'As each of these carriers developed different dynamics in different places and at different times, the patterns and the outcomes of the historical process of secularization should vary accordingly' (Casanova, 1994: 24–25). Thus, describing Europe and its population as unchurched or secular does not do justice to the variety that likely exists in Europe in general but also within countries. In this regard, it is common practice to divide Europe in North-South and East-West; the North being less religious and/or less active in church activities and the South being much more religious and also more involved in church activities. These differences are regarded by many as the consequences of differences between the spirits of Protestantism in the North and Catholicism in the Southern parts of Europe (e.g., Davie 2000, Halman & de Moor, 1994).

David Martin (1978a, b) also emphasized the crucial role of the theological differences between Catholicism and Protestantism, but he added that it is necessary to take account of the degree of competition between denominations in a country to understand and clarify the degree to which secularization has proceeded in a society. In the next section, we elaborate on his secularization perspective and present our expectations about differences and similarities in religious patterns in Europe.

Not only have the specificities of the religious traditions had severe consequences for the secularization processes that developed differentially across Europe, but varieties in countries' degrees of secularization may also be attributed to a number of country-specific characteristics, and in this chapter a few of these characteristics are explored.

Even within societies, populations may vary in their degree of secularization. Secularization is likely to depend on age, levels of education and gender, but also on other personal characteristics and orientations. The effects of some such attributes of individuals will also be investigated in this chapter.

In section 2, we summarize the main aspects of the secularization process and we present our hypotheses on the micro- and macro-level attributes. The measurements and analytical design are described in section 3, and in section 4, the results of our analyses are presented. The conclusions/discussion can be found in section 5.

2 Trajectories of secularization

Although the concept of secularization has different meanings and interpretations in empirical research and in theoretical discussions, there is general agreement that secularization refers to the process in which religion gradually loses the encompassing and important role which it had in traditional society. Some attribute the gradual decline of religion to the rationalization and disenchantment of the world, while others explain the decreased significance of religious institutions, religious activities, and religious modes of thinking by reference to social differentiation and specialization as the main forces of modernization (Wilson, 1982).

In traditional societies, individual belief systems were strongly dependent on what the community believed and the churches prescribed. Social control and the religious practices of the community played a decisive role in the individual's belief system. The effect of cultural and social differentiation is that people increasingly participate in different universes of meaning, each governed by its own set of values. Within each institutional sphere, norms and values have become functional, rational, and above all autonomous. In this interpretation, secularization can be seen as 'the repercussion of these changes on the religious subsystem. It denotes a societal process in which an overarching and transcendent religious system is reduced to a subsystem of society alongside other subsystems, the overarching claims of which have a shrinking relevance' (Dobbelaere, 1995: 1; see also Dobbelaere, 2002: 166). The individual has become the main point of reference in the shaping of values, attitudes, and beliefs, and people believe in what they themselves want to believe in, and this is not necessarily what the churches tell them to believe.

Traditional dogmatic beliefs have been replaced by a more modern, personalized way of believing. Some analysts have emphasized this development and they regard the situation 'as a shift away from the traditional churches (. . .) with larger numbers of people defining and practicing their religiosity in non-traditional, individualized and institutionally loose ways' (Berger, 2001: 447). Institutional religion is assumed to have become marginalized and consequently to have lost much of its influence on people's lives. As such, it seems as if the religious decline is mainly confined to institutional decline and does not indicate a decline in religious beliefs. In many European countries, this eventuated in a situation that Davie characterized by 'believing without belonging' (Davie, 2000: 3).

In Europe, secularization 'has been an uneven process. It has affected the major Protestant Churches more strongly than the Catholic Church, and more fundamentalist brands of Protestantism least' (Therborn, 1995: 274). The explanation for this uneven process is partly found in the theological differences between Catholicism and Protestantism. The 'seeds of individualism were manifest much earlier in Protestantism. In contrast to Catholics, Protestants are personally responsible before God in religious matters, and the church has a lesser role as mediator between the believer and God. The Catholic Church, (. . .) imposes a more collective identity upon its faithful' (Jagodzinski & Dobbelaere, 1995: 81). Thus, even five centuries after the Reformation, there are obvious differences between Northern and Southern Europe with regard to the importance of the religious factor and these differences are often attributed to the different religious traditions.

Orthodoxy is the dominant tradition in a number of Central and Eastern European countries. Orthodox theology provides people with the idea of 'sobernost', referring to 'sober' and 'community', and can be understood in terms of 'unity-in-freedom'. This idea of 'sobernost' is distinct from the emphasis on individual freedom in Protestant churches, but also from the Catholic idea of a community that is centralisticly directed from above. 'The principle of sobernost implies that the absolute bearer of truth in the Church is not the patriarch who has supreme authority, nor the clergy, and not even the ecumenical council, but only the Church as a whole' (Demey, 2003: 2). A key notion in this theology is 'theosis', which is 'the mystical transfiguration of man in divine glory. It is an ontological 'link', a universal connection between the human world and the divine one . . .' (Naletova, 2001: 111). Although this orthodox theology suggests a kind of 'all-including' religiosity, the consequences of former Soviet ideology and policy of religious suppression should also be taken into consideration. This policy of suppression is likely to have had severe consequences for the degree of secularization. Consequently, *Catholic societies will be more religious than Orthodox societies, and both will be more religious than Protestant countries.*

The expectation, therefore, was that a Catholic religious pattern would be distinctive from a Protestant or an Orthodox pattern. To this can be added that the religious pattern should depend upon the 'religious economy' of a country. Analogous to mainstream economic theories, Finke and Stark argue that religious competition results in substantially higher levels of institutional religiosity and church affiliation. They use economic metaphors to describe the changing shape of religious life in a country. The market share of a denomination has, according to this view, important consequences for the religious commitment of the members of the denominations. A pluralistic religious situation is conducive to 'a wide range of alternative faiths well adapted to the needs of the consumers' (Iannaccone, 1992: 128). Therefore, a key variable for explaining high levels of religious commitment and religiousness is the degree of competition among the suppliers of religion. In mono-religious cultures, there is no competition. In religiously pluralistic cultures, the members of the various religious groups are likely to emphasize their distinctiveness, in order to compete effectively with the other religious groups. Therefore, in more religiously pluralistic societies, people will be more active and more religious than in less pluralistic societies. The hypothesis is the following: *the more religiously pluralistic a country is, the more its people will be religiously active and religious.*

Martin (1978a, b) investigated secularization in Europe and demonstrated that it takes place in different ways. According to Martin, the European religious landscape can be approached from two different angles: 1) the relation of religion to national, regional, and subcultural awareness (center/periphery)'; and 2) power and countervailing power. 'The relationship of religion to power arises because it is not only the bearer of identities but a source of legitimacy and of philosophies supporting legitimacy' (Martin, 1978b: 235). He further argued that different forms of religious pluralism can be distinguished. 'Complete pluralism' results from competition among various denominations, which are independent of authorities and cultural elites. 'Civic religion' is one of appearances (e.g., the US). 'Complete pluralism' can be distinguished from 'qualified pluralism', which is characterized by competition between a state church, associated with a specific cultural elite, and other societal groups, as is the case in England. 'Qualified pluralism' appears in another form also: e.g., in

Scandinavia, where there is competition within the state churches themselves. Another distinct form of pluralism is 'segmented pluralism', referring to a situation in which rival groups of Protestants and Catholics live in territorially separated areas.

Martin's analysis illustrates that a conglomeration of factors affects the tense pluralism-monopoly positions. He refers among other things to historical, geographical, political, ideological, and theological aspects, and his clustering of countries clarifies that some constellations facilitate secularization, while others seem to hinder these processes.

Since Martin's publication in 1978 however, the European political and religious landscape changed dramatically and his theory failed to accurately address these changes. The far-reaching political and ideological transformations in Central and Eastern Europe are assumed to have had a profound impact on the position of churches and denominations in the countries involved. The situation in Western Europe has also changed. An increasing proportion of the Europeans no longer regard themselves as belonging to a denomination, and these people are likely to display lower levels of (traditional) religious beliefs and practices. Thus, we expected that *in countries where a majority is unchurched, the levels of religiosity would be lowest.*

Inspired by Martin's theory, we considered it likely that in countries where the majority is churched, the levels of religious beliefs and practices would depend upon which denominations are present in the society (Catholic, Protestant, Orthodox people) and the degree to which denominations are present (monopoly position or not). The traditional doctrine of the Catholic Church is assumed to impose a stronger collective identity upon its members, while Protestant culture is assumed to be more conducive to religious individualism. Therefore, *levels of religiosity will be lowest in Protestant countries, in countries characterized by a mix of denominations, and countries with a mixed population of (diverse) denominations and unchurched people.* Further, owing to the developments in the recent past, we expect that *former USSR influenced countries with a dominant Orthodox tradition can also be situated in this second group* because the ideological influence of the former USSR is still moderating the significance of Orthodox churches. Finally, *countries with a strong Catholic majority or monopoly will be most religious.*

Inglehart argues that the religious decline is a result of not only increasing rationality, functional differentiation, and specialization but also and most importantly, of increasing levels of security, produced by the establishment of the modern welfare state and material wealth.

In economically less advanced countries, we expected religion to have remained an important determining factor providing people with certainties and the assurance of salvation (Inglehart, 1997: 80). In economically more developed areas, existential security is assured and thus we expected the need for reassurance provided by religion to have diminished. Thus, *the more economically advanced a society is, the less traditionally religious its population will be.*

Another phenomenon that has entered the discourse on modernization is the globalization of human society. Globalization has been defined 'as the intensification of worldwide social relations which link distant localities in such a way that local happenings are shaped by events occurring many miles away and vice versa' (Giddens, 1990: 64). One of the implications of globalization is that people are confronted with increasing numbers of opportunities and alternative options. People living in a globalized society are assumed to encounter a great variety of cultural habits, values, and norms.

In traditional societies, people lived in small local communities separated from other communities, and they were influenced and dominated by strong institutions, e.g., religion. Particularly the churches played an important role in these traditional settings. By contrast, it is assumed that people in modern and postmodern society pick and choose what they want from the global religious and cultural marketplace. The increased 'supply' of alternative world views and value systems, provided to a large extent by the ever-growing mass media and international information technologies, is a crucial factor. Mass media introduces new religious doctrines, books, knowledge and interpretations, practices and ritual codes, ideas, and ways of thinking. Religious modernity can be characterized as a situation in which 'the regulatory capacity of institutions is called into question by the autonomous capacity of individuals to reject 'ready made' identities and to construct for themselves, starting from the diversity of their experiences, their own course of identification' (Hervieu-Léger, 1998: 222). Such a situation is often regarded as conducive to a further decline of traditional religiosity and of adherence to the traditional beliefs expressed by the traditional institutional churches. Hence, *the more globalized a society is, the less traditionally religious its population will be.*

The expectations thus far were formulated at societal level, but also within countries, the degree of secularization may differ among people. Following the aforementioned arguments about the differences between Catholic, Protestant, and Orthodox theologies, we assumed that differences would appear not only between countries but also among the people who belong to the diverse denominations. We presumed that *Catholic and Orthodox people will be more religious than Protestants.*

It is generally assumed that older people are more religious and more pious than younger people. This relationship, which has been verified empirically in almost all research, is explained 'by one of three theoretical processes. The "traditional model" (. . .) focuses on developmental processes related to age per se. Alternatively, a life course model (. .) attributes change (. . .) to changes in social roles, particularly in the family. A third interpretation characterizes observed variations in religiosity by age as a statistical artifact associated either with cohort replacement or period effects' (Argue, Johnson & White, 1999: 423). Older generations have been raised in 'more religious contexts' and, assuming that orientations remain stable throughout people's lives, we predicted that older people would be more religious than younger people, who have been raised and socialized in more secular contexts. Therefore, *younger people will be less religious than older people.*

As far as gender differences are concerned, in most studies it was taken for granted that women are more religious than men, but this generally accepted statement is grounded in diverse arguments. According to the work force theory, participation in labor means that people have less time to be engaged in church activities and, above all, 'work force participation can provide alternative sources of identity, interests, values, legitimations, and commitments so that religion simply becomes less important' (De Vaus & McAllister, 1987: 473). More men than women were employed, and thus less involved in church and/religious activities, and thus likely to be less religious. A distinction is often made between professionally active women and women without professional activities. The latter are the most religious ones (Dobbelaere, 1984: 72, 83, 95, 104, 111; Dobbelaere & Voye, 1992: 124; 2000: 134–136, 142). Because more women became active on the labor market in Europe during the last decades, we expected the gender gap in religiosity to have become smaller in the sense that the levels of religiosity of women active on the labor market would be comparable with the levels of religiosity of their male colleagues.

Some authors focus on the family context. Research shows that women pray more than men, and that in their prayers, women ask for the well-being and happiness of their families. Therefore, it may by concluded that this family-oriented attitude leads women to have stronger feelings of religiosity (Dobbelaere & Voye, 1992: 131, 160; 2000: 139). Although there is much discussion about the value of the general statement that gender differences in religiousness are a product of differential socialization (Miller & Stark, 2002), in line with most presuppositions, we expected the following: *women who are not employed outside their homes will be more religious than women who are employed, who in turn will be more religious than men.*

Education means increasing cognitive skills, a more critical attitude towards authority, and an increasing emphasis on personal autonomy and individual judgment, and consequently, lower levels of religiosity. This hypothesis is based on Weber's idea of the absolute incompatibility of religious and scientific orientations. It is argued that people are either scientific or religious, but not both (Johnson, 1997: 232). Although the relationship may be more complex (see, e.g., Johnson, 1997: 233), most empirical evidence indicates a negative association between level of education and degree of religiosity: *the higher a person's level of education, the less religious he/she will be.*

Inglehart has argued that materialists emphasize economic growth, career certainty, and security. They are preoccupied by the struggle for survival and religion provides reassurance and certainties. Post-materialists emphasize the satisfaction of needs, such as self-development, autonomy, and emancipation, because their basic (physical) needs are satisfied. Post-materialists do not have to rely on religion for assurances and certainties in life because they have been raised and socialized in relatively secure economic circumstances and thus they take security for granted. Therefore, Inglehart found that a secular orientation 'is linked with Post-materialist values' whereby people describe themselves to a lesser degree as religious or believers in God (Inglehart, 1990: 189–192). In the light of this interpretation, it seems reasonable to assume an association between a post-materialistic orientation and religiosity: *Post-materialists will be less religious than materialists.*

3   Data, measures, and analytical strategy

Not all countries in the EVS were used in our analyses. Malta was excluded because the response pattern of this country was very specific, and difficult to interpret. Northern Ireland was excluded because it is part of the UK and thus these two societies would not be differentiated, while the religious situation in the UK is different from that in Northern Ireland, the former being characterized by Anglicanism, the latter by a clear Catholic-Protestant cleavage. Finally, Turkey was excluded because this country is the single representative of a Moslem society and we had no hypotheses on this religion.

3.1   *The dependent variables: Religious beliefs and religious practices*

The indicators in the EVS concern several dimensions of religiosity. One of these dimensions relates to religious ideology or religious doctrines. Each religion 'maintains some set of beliefs which adherents are expected to ratify' (Stark & Glock, 1968: 14), and the more of these beliefs people adhere to, they are said to believe stronger. Such a dimension of religious faith refers to institutional religion and does not indicate a more general religious attitude. A more general dimension does not include specific statements about the content of religiosity, nor does it refer to institutional religion or concrete rules and dogmas. Even people who do not belong to or feel attracted by one of the traditional religions or churches may be religious in a more general way (De Moor, 1987: 22).

In our analysis, *religiosity* refers to religious beliefs and not to practices or to membership or institutional religiosity. It was measured using the answers given by respondents to questions concerning:

a) the importance of religion in life;[1]
b) being a religious person;[2]
c) belief in religious dogmas: God, life after death, hell, heaven, sin;[3]
d) the importance of God;[4]
e) strength and comfort received from religion.[5]

---

[1] How important is religion in your life: 1 = very important; 2 = quite important; 3 = not important; 4 = not at all important.

[2] Independently of whether you go to church or not, would you say you are 1 = a religious person; 2 = not a religious person; 3 = a convinced atheist. This variable was recoded: 1 = religious, and 0 = not religious or atheist.

[3] 1 = yes and 0 = rest.

[4] How important is God in your life: 1 = not at all important; 10 = very important.

[5] Do you find that you get comfort and strength from religion? 1 = yes and 0 = no, or do not know, or no answer.

A factor analysis yielded one factor, and factor scores were calculated in such a way that high scores indicate high levels of religiosity and low scores low levels of religiosity.

Religious orientations measured in terms of beliefs are, of course, just one way of exploring the religious domain. Religion is, according to one of the founding fathers of sociology, 'a unified system of beliefs and practices relative to sacred things, that is to say, things set apart and forbidden—beliefs and practices which unite into one single moral community' (Durkheim, 1965: 62). Religious practices or 'acts of worship and devotion, the things people *do* to carry out their religious commitment' (Stark & Glock, 1968: 15) are other expressions of religion. This dimension can be measured in various ways, for example, by church membership and actual participation in church activities. We focused on acts of worship or religious practices, not on church membership because in, e.g., the Scandinavian countries, this would yield spurious results. Church affiliation in the Nordic countries is rather high. Almost all Scandinavians consider themselves members of the Lutheran church. These high levels of church membership are often explained from the connection between church and state in these countries. In Scandinavia, 'there exists an historically determined connection between church and state, and (. . . .) citizenship implied church membership' (Gustafsson, 1994: 21). People in the Nordic countries entered into the Lutheran church by birth (Lane & Ersson, 1996: 184), and being a church member is considered almost a citizen's duty in these cultures. Several reasons for this have been suggested, one being that church membership in these countries can be seen 'as a way of expressing solidarity with society and its basic values' (Hamberg, 2003: 50). However, since the level of actual participation in religious activities is rather low in the Nordic countries, church membership in these countries is a less meaningful indicator of religiosity than in other countries. Therefore, we did not include church membership, but focused on actual participation in religious activities.

Religious practice in our analysis is a combination of three characteristics. It is indicated first of all by church attendance based on the question 'Apart from wedding, funerals, and christenings, about how often do you attend religious services?'[6] A question on moments

---

[6] Answers ranged from 1 = more than once a week; 2 = once a week; 3 = once a month; 4 = Christmas/Easter; 5 = other specific holy days; 6 = once a year; 7 = less often; 8 = never.

of prayer is also part of this construct. The question was 'Do you make some moments for prayer, meditation or contemplation, or something like that?'[7] Finally, membership in and doing voluntary work for a religious organization is included.[8] Again, factor analysis was applied and factors scores were calculated in such a way that high scores indicate high levels of religious practice.

3.2 *Independent variables at individual level*

At the individual level, we included age, level of education, gender, religious affiliation, and, as a value orientation, we included post-materialism.

Age was measured using year of birth and recoded as age in years. Level of *education* was determined by age when education was completed.

Gender referred not only to the male-female distinction, but also to being employed or not. Women who were employed were distinguished from those who were not employed. For gender we included two dummies: one for women who were not employed, and one for women who were employed.

Religious affiliation was measured in two steps. The respondent was asked whether he or she considered him/herself a member of a religious denomination and, if so, which one.[9] These two questions enabled us to make a distinction between *Catholics, Protestants, Orthodox,* and *unchurched* people. These were included as dummy variables in our analyses and members of other religious denominations were the reference group.

For *post-materialism*, the original short scale (see Inglehart, 1977; 1990; 1997) was used. Respondents were asked to choose which of four goals mentioned their country should aim at for the next ten years. They were asked to indicate the most important and the second-most important goals. Two items related to materialist priorities: 'maintaining order in the nation' and 'fighting rising prices';

---

[7] 1 = yes and 0 = the other answers.

[8] If a person was neither a member nor did voluntary work for a religious organization, the person was given the score 0. If a person was either a member but did not do voluntary work, or the other way around, the person was given the score 1; while if a person was a member and did voluntary work, the person was given the score 2.

[9] Great Britain was the exception. Here, the filter question was not asked.

two items reflected post-materialist priorities: 'giving people more to say in important government decisions' and 'protecting freedom of speech'. The construction of the scale was as proposed by Inglehart (1977): if both the most important and second most important aims are materialistic, then the respondent was considered to be a pure materialist. If the chosen aims were two post-materialist aims, the respondent was considered to be a pure post-materialist. If a respondent prioritized one materialist and one post-materialist aim, he or she was considered to belong to the mixed group. Depending on the most important aim, the respondent could be mixed with materialist priority or mixed with post-materialist priority.[10]

3.3   *Independent variables at aggregate level*

We argued above that Martin's analysis, developed in the mid-'70's, does not do justice to the current European situation as it has developed in more recent years. In particular, the growing group of unchurched people in Europe, and the Central and Eastern European countries that were under the influence of the USSR, were underexposed in these analyses. Barrett et al. (2001) provide more recent data on denominations and religious adherence for all countries worldwide. Not only is church membership registered, but non-affiliation or 'no longer-affiliation' is also indicated, as well as the number of agnostics and non-believers. The classification developed by Barrett et al. resembles more or less the classification we proposed based on the EVS data.

Our classification distinguished 9 categories: a) *Protestant countries* (more than 70% of the population is Protestant): Denmark, Finland, Sweden, Iceland; b) *Catholic countries* (more than 70% is Catholic): Austria, Croatia, Ireland, Italy, Lithuania, Poland, Portugal, Spain; c) *Orthodox countries* (more than 70% is Orthodox): Greece, Romania; d) *Mixed Catholics/unchurched* (large parts of the people are Catholic, but a significant part of the people is unchurched (Belgium, France, Luxembourg, Slovenia, Slovakia); e) *Mixed Anglican/unchurched* (a large part is Anglican and a large part is unchurched: GB); f) *Mixed unchurched/Catholics* (most people are unchurched and many people

---

[10] The resulting typology was 1 = pure materialist; 2 = mixed with materialist priority; 3 = mixed with post-materialist priority; 4 = pure post-materialist.

are Catholic: Czech Republic, Hungary); g) *Mixed unchurched/Protestant* (most people are unchurched, a large minority is Protestant: Estonia); h) *Mixed unchurched/Orthodox* (most people are unchurched, but a large part is Orthodox: Russia, Belarus, Ukraine, Bulgaria); i) *Mixed unchurched/Mixed* (most people are unchurched, the groups of Catholics and Protestants are almost equally sized: the Netherlands, Latvia, Germany).

In our analyses, Estonia was the reference group because it has a particular religious composition and was the single representative of that curious mix. The same was true of Great Britain, which was the only representative of an Anglican society with a large part of unchurched people. As such, this country could have been chosen as the reference group as well.

Apart from the religious profile indicated by the typology based on the kind and number of denominations in a country, religious profiles can be obtained from what is known as the *Herfindahl concentration index*. This measure is based on the combination of 1) the number of churches/denominations in a country; and 2) the adherence to these churches. The more churches in a country and the more evenly distributed their market shares, the more religiously diversified the country is. The Herfindahl index is calculated using the formula Σs_i^2 where s_i is the proportion with value i. The maximum value of the index is 1.0, and it can easily be transformed into a pluralism index by subtracting the Herfindahl index from 1. Information on the numbers of people affiliated with religious organizations in the different countries was simply taken from the responses to the questions on membership in the EVS surveys. The larger the number of churches and the more even the distribution among them, the lower the Herfindahl index and the more pluralistic (less concentrated) the religious market.

A country's *welfare* was measured using GDP per capita (ppp). The data used in our study came from the Human Development Report (HDR) 2001 and referred to the year 1999.

Globalization refers to the increased exposure to modern means of communication and flows of information. The spread of such modern communication technology devices can be used as an indicator. Both the World Development Report and the Human Development Report provide comparable measures for the national numbers of newspapers, (mobile) telephones, and television and radio receivers, but also for the spread of IT market issues such as the number of

PCs, Internet use, and Internet hosts. Unfortunately, not all indicators were available for all countries and thus we confined our measure to the number of televisions, telephones, mobile phones, and Internet hosts in a country. The results of a confirmatory factor analysis of the various structural globalization indicators justified the combination of statistics for TV sets, telephones, mobile phones, and Internet hosts in one scale of IT market.

3.4 *Analytical strategy*

First, we conducted a number of bi-variate analyses at individual level on the pooled dataset to determine the relationships with religiosity and religious practice and the impact of each predictor variable. Correlation coefficients were calculated twice; not controlling but also controlling for 'country'. Next, we moved to the aggregate level and investigated the relationships in terms of simple correlation coefficients.

In order to establish the relative impact of each of these characteristics, a number of regression analyses were performed using the stepwise method. We started by using a model to test the impact of social demographic characteristics on religiosity and religious practice. In the second step, we included denominational affiliation, that is, whether the respondent was Catholic, Protestant, Orthodox, or unchurched. Next, post-materialism was entered, followed by aggregate characteristics. The first macro features were the religious profiles (Estonia being the reference group). Pluralism, measured using Herfindahl's index, was entered in a separate step because it was correlated with religious profiles measured using the typology. Finally, we included the countries' levels of globalization (IT market) and GDP.

4   *Results*

We tested our hypotheses in a number of bi- and multi-variate analyses. The results are described in sections 4.1 and 4.2. Since the clustering of countries was based on only two attributes, denominational affiliation and number of denominations, we examined whether such a clustering made sense in terms of levels of religiosity and religious practices, and we looked more closely at the category of unchurched people.

4.1 *Bi-variate analyses at individual level*

In Table 11.1, we display the correlation coefficients (controlled for country and not controlled for country) between the dependent variables, religiosity and religious practice, and the individual socio-demographic characteristics of education, age, and gender.

The associations did not differ dramatically if country was controlled for. Women appeared, as suggested, to be more religious than men in terms of both religiosity and religious practices, although the correlation was not substantial. Women who were employed were indeed less religious than women who were not employed, and their levels of religiosity were closer to those of men than those of women who were not employed. This was a general pattern found in all countries; see Figures 11.1 and 11.2. The work force theory thus seems to have been corroborated, at least partly. However, some differences were found between men and professionally active women, not only in Western Europe but also in former communist countries, where women's labor participation was the official doctrine.

Higher educated people appeared to be less religious while older people were found to be more religious. From a comparison of mean scores for men and women, and several educational categories and age groups, age seemed to be linearly related with religiosity. The older the age group they belonged to, the more religious people were. This was true for religiosity and for religious practice, although

Table 11.1 Pearson correlations between individual characteristics and religiosity and religious practice not controlling and controlling for country

	Religiosity		Religious practice	
	r	r (controlled for country)	r	r (controlled for country)
Education	−.123	−.106	−.027	−.032
Age	.202	.220	.159	.178
Woman at home	.213	.202	.168	.173
Working woman	.003(ns)	.016(ns)	.024(ns)	.024(ns)
Catholic	.366	.431	.335	.380
Protestant	−.008(ns)	.154	.080	.196
Orthodox	.176	.231	.037	.149
Other	.097	.116	.086	.111
Unchurched	−.565	−.537	−.494	−.482
Postmaterialism	−.076	−.090	.005(ns)	.046

** $p < .01$; all other correlations except (ns) are significant at $p < .001$

Figure 11.1   Mean scores on religiosity for men, employed women and non-employed women

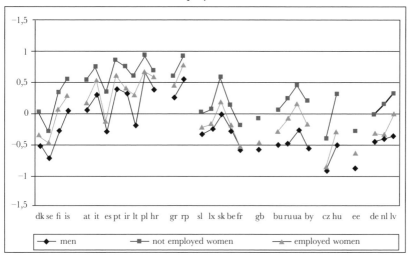

Figure 11.2   Mean scores on religious practice for men and employed women and not employed women

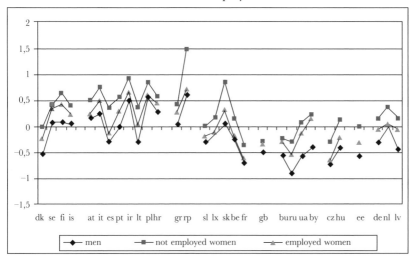

with regard to the latter dependent variable, it should be noted that the oldest age group (81–89) was less frequently involved in religious activities than the second-oldest age group (71–80). This may be due to the fact that these people are less mobile and, therefore, no longer able to go to religious services. Levels of education did not seem to be linearly related with religious practices. Whereas in general it was confirmed that higher educated people are less religious, this can be said to a more limited extent of religious practices. The higher educated groups appeared to be slightly more involved in religious practices than were the middle educational levels.

Religiosity and religious practices were also found to be related to belonging to a religious denomination or being unchurched, but were not associated with post-materialism at individual level. Thus, post-materialists are not less religious than materialists. However, not surprisingly, unchurched people appeared to be the least religious, while adherents of other[11] religious denominations were most religious, in terms of both religious beliefs and religious practices. Catholics and Orthodox people were found to resemble each other with regard to their levels of religiosity, while Orthodox and Protestants were closer to each other as regards religious practices. Both, Orthodox and Protestants, scored lower than Catholics and adherents of other denominations. Protestants were far less religious than adherents of other denominations, Catholics, and Orthodox people.

At this point of our analyses, we concluded that it seemed to make a difference for religiosity and religious practice if the respondent was a man or a woman, if women were employed or not, and if the respondent was older or younger, higher or lower educated, Catholic, Protestant, Orthodox, or unchurched. The only prediction that was not confirmed was that post-materialists are less religious than materialists.

4.2 *Bi-variate analyses at aggregate level*

At aggregate level, some of our hypotheses were not confirmed. Pearson correlations between predictor and dependent variables are displayed in Table 11.2.

---

[11] When at least 50 respondents indicated belonging to the same denomination, we included them in a category of 'other' denomination. Consequently, the group of 'other' was constructed using small denominations.

Table 12.2   Pearson correlations between a country's degree of religiosity, religious practice and some country characteristics

	Religiosity	Religious practice
Pluralism (Herfindahl)	−.631***	−.629***
Protestant	−.171	.075
Catholic	.623***	.526**
Orthodox	.382*	.344*
Mix: Cath + Unch	−.139	−.159
Mix: Prot + Unch + Cath	−.179	−.202
Mix: Unch + Orth	−.118	−.343*
Mix: Unch + Cath	−.291	−.269
Mix: Unch + Prot	−.294	−.175
Mix: Unch + Cath + Prot	−.210	−.111
It-market	−.201	−.025
Gdp	−.150	.065

*** Correlation significant at 0.001 level (1-tailed)
** Correlation is significant at the 0.01 level (1-tailed)
* Correlation is significant at the 0.05 level (1-tailed)

Religious pluralism did not seem to generate more but less religiosity and less involvement in religious practices. The religious tradition was found to matter as expected: Catholic societies appeared to be more religious than Orthodox countries, which were in turn more religious than Protestant countries. Also as expected, the results suggest that the more globalized a society is, the less religious its inhabitants. The same counts for welfare: the higher the GDP of a country and thus the more wealthy its people, the less religious the people are. We expected to find differences in the religious profiles of countries with respect to levels of religiosity and religious practices. Our analyses substantiated the view that dominantly Catholic societies as well as dominantly Orthodox societies are more religious and religiously involved than dominantly Protestant countries and countries with other religious profiles. The least religious countries appeared to be Estonia (Mixture of unchurched and Protestant) and UK (Mixed Anglican unchurched). The countries with the most mixed religious profiles (the Netherlands, Germany, and Latvia) appeared to be neither the least nor the most religious. Thus, to conclude, religious profiles seemed to make a difference, while religious pluralism did not generate the expected effect.

4.3 Multi-variate analyses

In the next section, we describe how these single variables at individual as well as at aggregate level were included in a multiple regression analysis to explore the effects of each of them when controlled for the others.

4.3.1 Religiosity

The results of the regression analyses are presented in Tables 11.3 and 11.4. Most important seemed to be the denomination the respondent belonged to: all denominational members as well as unchurched people were less religious than people of other (small) religions. However, the least religious appeared to be unchurched persons, followed by Protestants. Catholic and Orthodox people did not differ greatly in their levels of religiosity; both were more religious than the unchurched and Protestants.

As expected, older people were more religious than younger people, women more than men, and women who were not employed more than employed women. Level of education did not appear to be a significant attribute of religiosity, although the direction of its negligible effect was in line with our hypothesis. Post-materialism did not appear to be an important attribute of prediction levels of religiosity.

As far as country characteristics are concerned, our findings show that the more globalized a society, measured in terms of IT market facilities, the less religious the people in that country. This confirmed our hypothesis, although the effect was rather modest. Economic development did not affect the level of religiosity.

We found that the more religiously pluralistic societies are, the less religious the people in that country are. This contradicted the hypothesis. The effect of the societies' degree of religious pluralism on an individual's level of religiosity was slightly smaller than the effects generated by the religious profiles of countries (in terms of R^2: .407 and .417 respectively). In particular, living in dominantly Catholic and dominantly Orthodox societies seemed to produce higher levels of religiosity among citizens (note that Estonia, which is an unchurched Protestant society, was the reference group).

4.3.2 Religious practice

The religious denomination the respondent belonged to was an important predictor of religious practice (see Tables 11.5 and 11.6). Although,

Table 11.3 Results regression analysis regressing religiosity on individual and country characteristics and religious profiles

Religiosity	B	Beta	B	Beta	B	Beta	B	Beta	B	Beta
(Constant)	−0,301***		0,183***		0,240		0,113*		0,101*	
education	−0,014***	−0,074	−0,003**	−0,017	−0,002*	−0,013	0,000	−0,002	−0,001	−0,006
age	0,009***	0,145	0,007***	0,116	0,007***	0,113	0,008***	0,128	0,008***	0,128
not working woman	0,455***	0,203	0,332***	0,148	0,328***	0,147	0,330***	0,147	0,329***	0,147
working woman	0,269***	0,117	0,220**	0,095	0,218***	0,095	0,231***	0,100	0,232***	0,101
Catholic			−0,134***	−0,066	−0,131***	−0,064	−0,223***	−0,109	−0,235***	−0,115
Protestant			−0,560***	−0,215	−0,559***	−0,214	−0,429***	−0,165	−0,439***	−0,168
Orthodox			−0,157***	−0,054	−0,165***	−0,057	−0,366***	−0,126	−0,375***	−0,129
Unchurched			−1,463***	−0,653	−1,464***	−0,653	−1,439***	−0,642	−1,446***	−0,645
Postmaterialism					−0,028***	−0,028	−0,040***	−0,040	−0,033***	−0,033
CATHOLIC							0,293***	0,131	0,285***	0,127
PROTESTANT							−0,099**	−0,034	0,083*	0,029
ORTHODOX							0,484***	0,121	0,424***	0,106
MCU							−0,016	−0,006	0,005	0,002
MAU							−0,331***	−0,032	−0,231***	−0,022
MUC							−0,086**	−0,022	−0,120***	−0,031
MUO							0,113***	0,038	0,021	0,007
MUM							0,062*	0,019	0,102***	0,032
ITMARKET									−0,095***	−0,096
GDP									0,000	0,000
R	.080		.395		.396		.417		.420	
adj R	.080		.395		.396		.417		.420	
R change	.080***		.316***		.001***		.021***		.003***	

Table 11.4 Results regression analysis regressing religiosity on individual and country characteristics and religious pluralism (Herfindahl index)

Religiosity	B	Beta	B	Beta	B	Beta	B	Beta	B	Beta
(Constant)	−0,301***		0,183***		0,240***		0,522***		0,507***	
education	−0,014***	−0,074	−0,003**	−0,017	−0,002*	−0,013	−0,002	−0,009	−0,002	−0,008
age	0,009***	0,145	0,007***	0,116	0,007***	0,113	0,007***	0,125	0,008***	0,128
not working woman	0,455***	0,203	0,332***	0,148	0,328***	0,147	0,336***	0,150	0,333***	0,149
working woman	0,269***	0,117	0,220***	0,095	0,218***	0,095	0,223***	0,097	0,227***	0,099
Catholic			−0,134***	−0,066	−0,131***	−0,064	−0,192***	−0,094	−0,215***	−0,105
Protestant			−0,560***	−0,215	−0,559***	−0,214	−0,621***	−0,238	−0,492***	−0,189
Orthodox			−0,157***	−0,054	−0,165***	−0,057	−0,221***	−0,076	−0,321***	−0,110
Unchurched			−1,463***	−0,653	−1,464***	−0,653	−1,445***	−0,645	−1,460***	−0,651
Postmaterialism					−0,028***	−0,028	−0,037***	−0,037	−0,021***	−0,021
PLURAL							−0,640***	−0,110	−0,723***	−0,124
ITMARKET									−0,113***	−0,115
GDP									−0,001	−0,001
R	.080		.395		.396		.407		.415	
adj R	.080		.395		.396		.407		.415	
R change	.080***		.316***		.001***		.011***		.008***	

again, Catholics, Protestants, and Orthodox, as well as unchurched people, were less active than adherents to other religious groups, Catholics participated more than Protestants in religious activities, who in turn participated more frequently than Orthodox people, who participated more than unchurched people.

Gender differences also appeared to be important and were in line with our hypothesis. Women participated more than men in religious activities, and women who were not employed did so more than employed women. Also, older people were more active in religious activities than younger people, but level of education did not generate differences in levels of religious practice. The same counts for post-materialism.

The explanatory power of objective pluralism (the Herfindahl index) was less strong than the religious profiles (R^2 .303 and .315 respectively), as was also the case with respect to religiosity. People living in Mixed Catholic/unchurched countries and people in countries that are Mixed unchurched/Orthodox appeared to participate least frequently of all, while living in a more pluralistic country appeared to be conducive to less religious participation. Levels of globalization had the expected impact: the more globalized a country is, the less its people are involved in religious practices.

4.4 *Clustering of European countries*

In his cultural map of the world, Inglehart (1997) found evidence that religious traditions are important determining factors. Our classification of countries was less broad than that suggested by Inglehart, and was based on the ideas of both Martin and Barrett. It was unclear however, if such a clustering of countries would make sense when other criteria were used, i.e., e.g., degrees of religiosity and religious practices. The poor explanatory power of religious profiles[12] may be caused by the fact that the clustering of countries based on the criteria suggested by Marin and Barrett does not make much sense.

To address this question, we calculated the country means scores for religiosity and religious practices. These are shown in Figure 11.3.

---

[12] The multiple regression analyses demonstrated clearly that individual characteristics are more important attributes than countries' religious profiles.

Table 11.5 Results regression analysis regressing religious practices on individual and country characteristics and religious profiles

Practice	B	Beta	B	Beta	B	Beta	B	Beta	B	Beta
(Constant)	-0,586***		-0,169***		-0,215***		-0,017		-0,104	
education	0,003*	0,014	0,012***	0,065	0,012***	0,062	0,012***	0,064	0,012***	0,062
age	0,008***	0,138	0,006***	0,105	0,006***	0,107	0,007***	0,119	0,007***	0,119
not working woman	0,398***	0,178	0,305***	0,137	0,308***	0,138	0,308***	0,138	0,310***	0,139
working woman	0,261***	0,114	0,217***	0,095	0,218***	0,096	0,221***	0,097	0,220***	0,096
Catholic			-0,081*	-0,040	-0,083*	-0,041	-0,183***	-0,091	-0,194***	-0,096
Protestant			-0,290***	-0,112	-0,291***	-0,112	-0,295***	-0,114	-0,305***	-0,118
Orthodox			-0,416***	-0,133	-0,409***	-0,131	-0,520***	-0,167	-0,522***	-0,167
Unchurched			-1,258***	-0,567	-1,257***	-0,567	-1,280***	-0,578	-1,283***	-0,579
Postmaterialism					0,022***	0,022	0,007	0,007	0,009	0,009
CATHOLIC							-0,002	-0,001	-0,067*	-0,031
PROTESTANT							-0,207***	-0,072	-0,083*	-0,029
ORTHODOX							0,184***	0,037	0,133**	0,027
MCU							-0,273***	-0,105	-0,352***	-0,136
MAU							-0,662***	-0,067	-0,619***	-0,062
MUC							-0,269***	-0,070	-0,342***	-0,090
MUO							-0,276***	-0,093	-0,381***	-0,128
MUM							-0,088**	-0,028	-0,102**	-0,032
ITMARKET									-0,131***	-0,127
GDP									0,078***	0,071
R	.054		.296		.296		.315		.317	
adj R	.054		.296		.296		.315		.316	
R change	.054***		.242***		.000***		.019***		.001***	

Table 11.6 Results regression analysis regressing religious practices on individual and country characteristics and religious pluralism (Herfindahl index)

Practice	B	Beta	B	Beta	B	Beta	B	Beta	B	Beta
(Constant)	-0,586***		-0,169***		-0,215***		0,015		0,019	
education	0,003**	0,014	0,012***	0,065	0,012***	0,062	0,012***	0,065	0,012	0,065
Age	0,008***	0,138	0,006***	0,105	0,006***	0,107	0,007***	0,118	0,007***	0,118
not working woman	0,398***	0,178	0,305***	0,137	0,308***	0,138	0,314***	0,141	0,314***	0,140
Working woman	0,261***	0,114	0,217***	0,095	0,218***	0,096	0,221***	0,097	0,222***	0,097
Catholic			-0,081*	-0,040	-0,083*	-0,041	-0,136***	-0,067	-0,142***	-0,070
Protestant			-0,290***	-0,112	-0,291***	-0,112	-0,341***	-0,132	-0,305***	-0,118
Orthodox			-0,416***	-0,133	-0,409***	-0,131	-0,448**	-0,143	-0,473***	-0,152
Unchurched			-1,258***	-0,567	-1,257***	-0,567	-1,246***	-0,562	-1,250***	-0,564
Postmaterialism					0,022***	0,022	0,014*	0,014	0,019***	0,019
PLURAL							-0,512***	-0,089	-0,539**	-0,094
ITMARKET									-0,031*	-0,030
GDP									-0,005	-0,004
R	.054		.296		.296		.303		.304	
adj R	.054		.296		.296		.303		.304	
R change	.054***		.242***		.000***		.007***		.001***	

Figure 11.3   Country mean scores on religiosity and religious practices

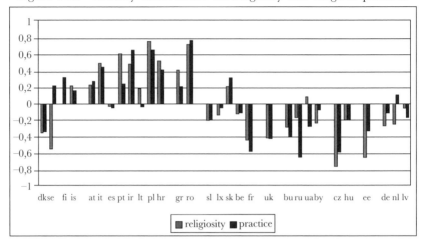

Using levels of religiosity and religious practices, it is clear that there
are major differences between the countries in one cluster. The
differences between Denmark and Sweden, on the one hand and
Finland and Iceland, on the other, are one example. Spain is a clear
exception among dominantly Catholic countries, even compared with
its neighboring country, Portugal. In the cluster of Catholic countries, Poland seems more similar to Orthodox Romania than to other
Catholic countries. Slovakia is a clear exceptional case in the cluster of Mixed Catholic/unchurched countries. The Czech Republic
is more similar to Estonia in terms of religiosity and church attendance than to the other country in this cluster, Hungary. France,
being a Mixed Catholic unchurched country, resembles the UK more
than the other countries in the cluster of Catholic unchurched countries. Thus, within each cluster, there were severe nuances and
differences, and the clustering based on the criteria suggested by
Martin and Barrett seemed to be less valuable for our analyses. This
is also revealed in Figure 11.4, in which we plotted the country
means scores on both dimensions.

It is obvious that the clustering of countries based on these two
indicators (dimensions) does not resemble our Barrett and Martin-
inspired classification of countries. Once again, the differences among
the Scandinavian countries, with Sweden and Denmark, on the one
hand, and Finland and Iceland on the other, are striking. The posi-

Figure 11.4   Country mean scores on religiosity and religious practice

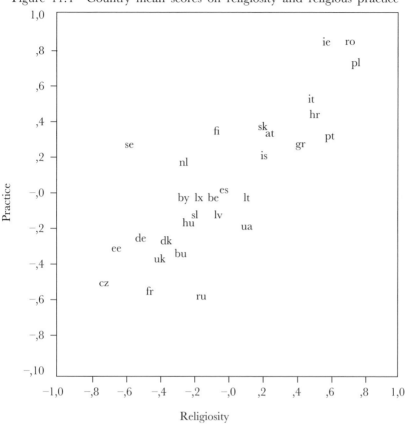

Religiosity

tion of France is quite different from that of Belgium, Luxembourg, Slovenia, and Slovakia, countries that are part of the same Barrett and Martin-inspired cluster. But Slovakia and Slovenia also appear to be quite different, though they experienced the same Soviet doctrine for many years. Spain seems to be more similar to Belgium and Luxembourg than to Italy and Portugal.

A cluster analysis demonstrated that the classification suggested by Martin and Barrett was not replicated when religious orientations were used. It seemed to be useful when based on the criteria of church adherence and pluralism, but not in terms of religious beliefs and practices. Poland, Romania, and Ireland clustered in our analysis, whereas these countries fell in different categories according to Barrett's classification. Austria, Slovakia, Iceland, Italy, Croatia,

Portugal, and Greece were also not in the same category according
Barrett's classification. Hungary, Slovenia, Belarus, Belgium, Luxembourg, Spain, Latvia, Lithuania, and Ukraine appeared to be highly
similar in religious beliefs and practices. The Netherlands, Finland,
and Sweden appeared as one cluster, while Germany, Estonia, France,
the Czech Republic, the UK, Denmark, Bulgaria, and Russia appeared
in the cluster of least religious countries.

4.5   *Belonging without believing and believing without belonging?*

It was clear from our analyses that the degree of religiosity and religious practices was strongly (strongest) affected by the respondents'
being churched or unchurched. It was not surprising that unchurched
people were less involved in religious practices and also less religious
than church members. However, the analyses revealed that the idea
that the religious situation of Europe can be characterized in terms
of 'believing without belonging' does not do justice to the actual situation. In fact, this characterization was found to apply to a small
minority (7%) in Europe. About 27% of European unchurched people declared themselves religious. Far more unchurched Europeans
considered themselves not religious (57%) while about 16% said that
they were convinced atheists. This pattern did not occur in all countries to the same degree. In Figure 11.5, we show the percentages
of people that are churched and religious, or churched and not religious, or unchurched and religious, or unchurched and not religious.

   In most countries, a majority was found to be churched and religious. In Poland, this was more than 94% of the respondents, and
in many countries, it was the vast majority. However, in Estonia
and Belarus, less than 25% belonged to the group of 'churched and
religious people' and also in France, the UK, the Netherlands, Sweden,
the Czech Republic, and Hungary, this pattern was found among a
minority of the respondents.

   About 13 % of Europeans appeared to be churched and not religious. This is typical of Sweden, a country in which religious profile
can be characterized by 'belonging without believing'. Forty-four percent of Swedes is churched but not religious. However, Great Britain
(43%) and, to a lesser extent, Belarus (34%) resemble the Swedish
case. In Denmark and Finland, majorities appeared to be not only
churched but also religious.

   The 'believing without belonging' situation was found to be par-

Figure 11.5 Percentages churched and unchurched, religious and not religious respondents in Europe

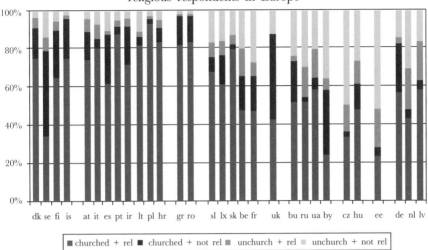

ticularly characteristic of the Netherlands, Estonia, and Latvia, where more than one in every four respondents did not belong to a religious denomination, but considered him/herself a religious person. Finally, the most secular societies in Europe according to the percentages of unchurched people in combination with those of not religious persons occured in the Czech Republic and Estonia, where about half of the respondents belonged to this category. In the Netherlands, Russia, and Belarus, this category was rather substantial: about one third of the respondents in these countries fell in the category of not belonging and not believing!

It is clear that if more and more people leave the churches in the (near) future, it will not result in people in all countries believing without belonging. People leave the churches not only because they no longer accept the rules and dogmas proclaimed by church leaders, but also, and perhaps mainly, because people's religious convictions and beliefs are on the decline.

5   Conclusions

In this chapter, we empirically explored the religious orientations and practices of contemporary Europeans. We argued that processes

of secularization, rationalization, functional differentiation, globalization, modernization, and post-modernization, have all changed the
role of religion and the churches in Europe. Although such processes
seem to occur through out Europe, they do not seem to occur at
similar speeds in all European countries. Therefore, differences in
the degree to which societies are secularized are to be expected.

We distinguished two dimensions of religiosity: one referring to
religious beliefs, the other to religious practices. These dimensions
are closely linked but are not the same. Although people who are
involved in religious practices are likely to be more religious than
people who are not involved in religious practices, people who are
religious are not necessarily involved in religious practices.

We made a distinction between independent variables at the individual and at the aggregate level. At the individual level, we included
age, level of education, gender (male-female and employed versus
not employed women), denomination, and materialist or post-materialist orientation. Religious profile, religious pluralism, economic
development, and degree of globalization were the independent variables at the aggregate level. In general, we conclude that the hypotheses concerning the individual level were more strongly corroborated
by our empirical findings and more unambiguous than the hypotheses at aggregate level.

As far as individual characteristics are concerned, the hypotheses
were more or less confirmed: women were found to be more religious and more religiously active than men, higher educated people
are less religious than people with lower levels of education, and
older people are more religious and religiously active than younger
people. The denomination a person belongs to was also found to
matter: Catholic and Orthodox people are more religious than
Protestants. Catholics participate more in religious activities than do
Orthodox and Protestant people. Our empirical findings did not support the hypothesis that post-materialists are less religious or less
involved in religious practices.

Further research into the gender differences is required. Although
gender differences with regard to religiosity and religious practices
were found, the associations were not strong. It seems that our ideas
of work as a converging factor need to be reconsidered. Important
in this respect is that, even in those countries that experienced Soviet
domination with its doctrine of women's labor participation, a clear
distinction exists between men and (employed) women in degrees of

religiosity and religious practices. What will happen in these countries if women's participation in the labor market declines?

The observation that there is no linear correlation between education and religious practice also requires further investigation. Why do higher educated people participate more instead of less in religious activities, as we predicted, whereas they appear to be less religious than less educated people?

Inglehart's hypothesis also requires more reflection and perhaps re-interpretation. We did not find much evidence for the idea that post-materialists are less religious in beliefs and practices. Perhaps post-materialists deconstruct, consciously or unconsciously, a functionalist interpretation of religion ('religiosity as a provider of feelings of security') and opt for a more substantial interpretation of religion. In order to decide if this statement is true, further research could focus on the content and significance that materialists and post-materialists attach to religiosity.

As indicated above, our findings at the aggregate level were not supportive of the hypotheses formulated, and were ambiguous. Theory suggests that, in more economically advanced societies, people are less traditionally religious. Our findings indicate indeed that the higher the GDP of a country, the less religious its inhabitants. The same is true for globalization. The more people can be confronted with an increasing number of opinions and ideas, by using TV, (mobile) telephone, and the Internet, the more their own traditionally accepted convictions come under pressure and lose credibility. The opposite can also be true: the more a person knows about diverse religious opinions and convictions, the more the person may rediscover his or her own traditionally accepted convictions. Our findings support the hypothesis that more worldwide communication possibilities in a country correlate with lower levels of religiosity, but the impact is modest. The idea that, as a result of worldwide communication possibilities, people will value their 'own' traditional religious convictions more strongly, was not confirmed by our findings. Nor did we find confirmation of the hypothesis stating that the more religiously pluralist a country, the more religious its people. The opposite seems to be true in contemporary Europe: religious pluralism correlates with a lower degree of religiosity and a lower degree of participation in religious activities.

Finally, the denominational situation of a country deserves attention. Theory suggests that religious monocultures make people lazy, while competitive religious cultures stimulate religiosity and religious participation. Our analysis did not offer much evidence for this hypothesis. Dominantly Catholic and dominantly Orthodox countries were found to be more religious than dominantly Protestant countries and countries with large numbers of unchurched people. Countries with various patterns of mixtures were neither the most religious, nor the least religious. The view that countries as Poland, Slovakia, and Romania are more religious than other Central or East European countries, as the social systems in these three countries were to a lesser degree dominated, reformed, and reorganized by Communism, must be revised. In Croatia, for example, proportionally higher levels of religiosity were found than in Slovakia, while the level of religiosity in Lithuania appeared to be comparable to that in Slovakia. Important in this respect is what will happen in Orthodox countries. The theological concept of 'sobernost', which should be understood in terms of 'freedom-in-community', can explain the importance of religiosity for Orthodox people. Given that former Soviet ideology will diminish, it seems likely that as soon as individuals have internalized the idea of 'sobernost', the influence of Orthodox religion will increase.

It is clear that characterizing Europe in terms of 'believing without belonging' does not do justice to the varieties that exist in the European religious domain. In some countries, the reverse is true, while in the majority of countries, 'belonging and believing' appears to be the dominant pattern. In some countries, a significant group of people who neither belong nor believe was found. It is, therefore, no wonder that the 'clustering' of countries according to the 'old dividing' lines no longer makes sense. The countries' levels of religiosity and involvement in religious practices did not yield a clustering of countries that resembled the clustering suggested by Martin or Barrett. Having analyzed religious developments in countries and clusters of countries, it is clear that one single explanation is insufficient. A combination of influencing factors, e.g., cultural and socio-economic heritages, should be taken into account. An interdisciplinary approach, which pays attention to, e.g., historical, cultural, and anthropological findings, may provide a more detailed theory to explain and enable understanding of the 'patchwork' pattern of religiosity and religious participation we observed in contemporary Europe.

References

Argue, A., D.R. Johnson & L.K. White 1999. Age and religiosity: Evidence from a three-wave panel analysis. *Journal for the Scientific Study of Religion* 38: 423–435.

Barrett, D.B., et al. 2001. *World Christian Encyclopedia. A Comparative Survey of Churches and Religions in the Modern World.* (Second Edition. Vol. I). Oxford: Oxford University Press.

Berger, P.L. 2001. Reflections on the sociology of religion today. *Sociology of Religion* 62: 443–454.

Casanova, J. 1994. *Public Religions in the Modern World.* Chicago: University of Chicago Press.

—— 2001. Religion, the new millennium, and globalization. *Sociology of Religion* 62: 415–441.

Davie, G. 2000. *Religion in Modern Europe.* Oxford: Oxford University Press.

—— 2002. *Europe: The Exceptional Case.* London: Darton, Longman and Todd Ltd.

Demey, P. 2003. *Theology of Orthodox Churches. Course notes 2002–2003.* Leuven: Faculty of Theology.

De Moor, R. 1987. Religieuze en morele waarden. Pp. 15–49 in L. Halman, F. Heunks, R. de Moor & H. Zanders, *Traditie, Secularisatie en Individualisering.* Tilburg: Tilburg University Press.

De Vaus, D.A. & I. McAllister 1987. Gender differences in religion: A test of the structural location theory. *American Sociological Review* 52: 472–481.

Dobbelaere, K. 1984. Godsdienst in België. Pp. 67–112 in J. Kerkhofs & R. Rezsohazy (eds.), *De Stille Ommekeer.* Tielt: Lannoo.

—— 1995. Religion in Europe and North America. Pp. 1–29 in R. de Moor (ed.), *Values in Western Societies.* Tilburg: Tilburg University Press.

—— 2002. *Secularization: An Analysis at Three Levels.* Bern, Brussels, etc.: Publishing Group Peter Lang.

—— & L. Voyé 1992. Godsdienst en kerkelijkheid. Pp. 115–162 in J. Kerkhofs, K. Dobbelaere, L. Voyé & B. Bawin-Legros (eds.), *De Versnelde Ommekeer.* Tielt: Lannoo.

—— & L. Voyé 2000. Religie en kerkbetrokkenheid: ambivalentie en vervreemding. Pp. 117–152 in K. Dobbelaere, M. Elchardus, J. Kerkhofs, L. Voyé & B. Bawin-Legros (eds.), *Verloren Zekerheid.* Tielt: Lannoo.

Durkheim, E. [1915] 1965. *The Elementary Forms of Religious Life.* New York: Free Press.

Giddens, A. 1990. *The Consequences of Modernity.* Stanford: Stanford University Press.

Gustafsson, G. 1994. Religious change in the five Scandinavian countries, 1930–1980. Pp. 11–58 in T. Pettersson & O. Riis (Eds.), *Scandinavian Values.* Uppsala: Acta Universitatis Upsaliensis.

Halman, L. 2001. *The European Values Study: A Third Wave.* Tilburg: EVS, WORC, Tilburg University.

—— & R. de Moor 1994. Religion, churches and moral values. Pp. 37–66 in P. Ester, L. Halman & R. de Moor (eds.), *The Individualizing Society.* Tilburg: Tilburg University Press.

Hamberg, E. 2003. Christendom in decline: The Swedish case. Pp. 47–62 in H. McLeod & W. Ustorf (eds.), *The Decline of Christendom in Western Europe, 1750–2000.* Cambridge: Cambridge University Press.

Hervieu-Léger, D. 1998. The transmission and formation of socioreligious identities in modernity: An analytical essay on the trajectories of identification. *International Sociology* 13: 213–228.

Iannaccone, L. 1992. Religious markets and the economics of religion. *Social Compass* 39: 123–131.

Inglehart, R. 1977. *The Silent Revolution*. Princeton: Princeton University Press.

—— 1990. *Culture Shift in Advanced Industrial Society*. Princeton: Princeton University Press.

—— 1997. *Modernization and Postmodernization*. Princeton: Princeton University Press.

Jagodzinski, W. & K. Dobbelaere 1995. Secularization and church religiosity. Pp. 76–119 in J.W. van Deth & E. Scarbrough (eds.), *The Impact of Values*. Oxford: Oxford University Press.

Johnson, D.C. 1997. Formal education vs. religious belief: Soliciting new evidence with multinominal logit modelling. *Journal for the Scientific Study of Religion* 36: 231–246.

Lane, J.E. & S.O. Ersson 1996. *European Politics*. London: Sage.

Martin, D. 1978a. *A General Theory of Secularization*. Oxford: Basil Blackwell.

—— 1978b. The religious condition of Europe. Pp. 228–287 in S. Giner & M. Scotford Archer (eds.), *Contemporary Europe. Social Structures and Cultural Patterns*. London: Routledge & P. Kegan.

Miller, A. & R. Stark 2002. Gender and religiousness: Can socialization explanations be saved? *American Journal of Sociology* 107: 1399–1423.

Naletova, I. 2001. Symphony re-considered: The Orthodox Church in Russia on relations with modern society. Notes on the social concept of the Russian Church. *Österreichisches Archiv für Recht und Religion* 48: 98–133.

Stark, R. & R. Glock. 1968. *American Piety. The Nature of Religious Commitment*. Berkeley: University of California Press.

Therborn, G. 1995. *European Modernity and Beyond*. London: Sage

Wilson, B. 1982. *Religion in Sociological Perspective*. Oxford: Oxford University Press.

CHAPTER TWELVE

NORMATIVE ORIENTATIONS TOWARDS THE DIFFERENTIATION BETWEEN RELIGION AND POLITICS

Loek Halman & Thorleif Pettersson

1 *Introduction*

Both religion and politics are difficult to define, and much has been written on the key characteristics of these phenomena. A common thought is, however, that in the world of religion, man is regarded dependent on supernatural powers, whereas in the political realm, people are assumed to govern themselves. Obviously, this difference does not prevent political concerns to operate in the world of religion, nor religious convictions to affect politics. To investigate such occurrences is a key interest for both religious studies and political science.

In sociological terms, the relationship between religion and politics refers to the degree of differentiation between the two systems. In less differentiated societies, the polity, the economy, the judicature, the education system, the health care, etc., are often said to have been under the presidency of religion. Then, due to differentiation, specialized roles and institutions developed in order to handle specific features or functions, which were previously carried out by one role or institution (Wallis & Bruce, 1992: 12). Alongside differentiation processes, religion became more institutionally separated from other spheres (Alexander, 1990: 1), and the religious organizations lost much of their impact on schools, hospices, social welfare, registry of births, marriages and deaths, social relations, organization of leisure (Dogan, 1995: 416). Thus, the relationship between religion and politics only concerns a specific instance of the much broader issue of general functional differentiation.

In this chapter, we focus on only one of the many relationships between religion and politics, namely whether people *want* religion

to have an impact on politics or not. In order to get a better understanding of peoples' views in this regard, we will investigate the simultaneous importance of both their basic value orientations and
socio-economic background, and the impact of a set of structural
factors in the countries they live in, such as the degrees of secularization, and religious and political pluralism, respectively. In this
sense, we will broaden the research on the relationship between religion and politics to include both micro- and macro-level factors. As
an introduction to these analyses, we present our theoretical arguments in section 2. Then, in section 3 we describe our data and the
measurements used. In section 4 we report on the results of our
analyses, and in a final concluding section (5) we discuss and evaluate our findings.

2   Differentiation or dedifferentiation of religion and politics?

It is beyond the scope of this article to review all of the research
on the many linkages between religion and politics. Rather, our
analyses are guided by three specific approaches to this problem.
The first is based on a kind of revision of general secularization theory. The second is the highly debated so-called 'new paradigm' in
the sociology of religion, which assumes that the degree of pluralism
in the religious sector has a profound impact on peoples' orientations
toward religion. The third approach is built on the assumption that
peoples' views on the relationship between religion and politics is
related to their basic value orientations.

    The secularization theory based approach to the relationship
between religion and politics is linked to Casanova's (1994) highly
noticed rejection of the so-called privatization thesis. This thesis,
which is founded on secularization and modernization theory, says
that contemporary religion becomes increasingly marginalized to
matters in the public sphere, and hence to politics. Contrary to this
thesis, Casanova finds the Islamic revolution in Iran, the rise of the
Solidarity movement in Poland, the role of Catholicism for the Sandi-
nista revolution in Latin America, and the increased political importance of North American Protestant fundamentalism to demonstrate
that contemporary religions refuse to accept the marginal and privatized role, which theories of secularization and modernization have
reserved for them. In line with such developments, Casanova claims

that contemporary religion turns *de*privatized and increasingly important to the public sphere.

Since Casanova's claim is contrary to general secularization theory, it should be noted that his rejection of the privatization thesis is not based on a general dismissal of secularization theory altogether. To the contrary, he regards differentiation as a primary distinguishing characteristic of modern society, and the differentiation between the religious and secular spheres is said to constitute the still defensible core of secularization theory (Casanova, 1994: 212). However, to assume that differentiation *necessarily* must entail the privatization of religion is said to be no longer defensible (Casanova, 1994: 7), and the privatization of religion is seen more as an option than as an inevitable structural trend. This view is built on the assumption that the privatization of religion is affected by various factors, which differ between different contexts. Religious rationalization, which is associated with developments towards pietism, religious individuation, and religious reflexivity, is viewed as one cause of religious privatization. General structural differentiation which constraints religion into a specific religious sphere is seen as another cause. Liberal categories of thought, which permeate the entire structure of modern Western thought, is said to constitute a third causal antecedent of religious privatization (Casanova, 1994: 215). In addition to these overarching causes, there are also some other circumstances driving towards the privatization of religion. A given religion is said to be less likely to assume public roles and to resist pressures towards privatization, the lesser its heritage of a public collective identity. Similarly, the more a religion has experienced notable declines, the less likely it is expected to be able to resist such pressures. And the less global and transnational a religious tradition is, the less probable its interference in the public civic society (Casanova, 1994: 225).

In accordance with these assumptions, religious privatization should primarily be seen as an option, and not as an inevitable structural trend, affecting all contexts in a similar way. In this regard, only public religions at the level of the civil society are seen as 'consistent with modern universalistic principles and with modern differentiated structures' (Casanova, 1994: 219). Thus, Casanova's rejection of the privatization hypothesis primarily is built on the assumption of a continuing and/or strengthening relationship between religion and the public civic society. Obviously, religious bodies have forwarded normative critiques of the actual boundaries between the private and the public spheres. This is at the heart of Casanova's claims of public religions at the level of the civic society. What he understands as the deprivatization of modern religion is the process 'whereby religion abandons its assigned place in the private sphere and enters the undifferentiated public sphere of civil society to take part in the ongoing process of contestation, discursive legitimation and redrawing of boundaries [between the public and the private]' (Casanova 1994: 65f.). By 'crossing boundaries, by raising questions publicly about the autonomous pretensions of the differentiated spheres to function without regard to moral norms or human considerations, public religions may help mobilize people against such pretensions, they may contribute to a redrawing of boundaries, or, at the very least, they may force or contribute to a public debate about such issues' (Casanova, 1994: 43).

However, this relationship between religion and the public civic society is primarily assumed to occur at the level of public discourse. Whether the religious actors have a real impact or not on peoples' understandings of how to differentiate between the public and the private is seen as less important. 'Irrespective of the historical outcome of such a debate, religions will have played an important public role' (ibid.). Undoubtedly, bishop conferences and church synods have launched—and very likely will continue to launch—a number of opinion building efforts with regard to various public issues, for instance concerning legislation and social practice related to reproduction, abortion and euthanasia, aid to developing countries and arms trade, mass media and public education, care of the elderly and sick, schooling and cultural programs. These efforts can certainly be said to demonstrate that religion in the modern world can (still) be involved in public and political issues. However, to the degree that such efforts have little impact, and people find them less relevant, we argue that differentiation between religion and the public civic society is a more adequate characteristic of contemporary society than de-differentiation. In this sense, the crucial matter is— at least as we see it—not whether religious spokesmen participate in and try to influence the public discourse on various matters in the public civic society, but whether their efforts have an impact or not. And quite regardless of what one finds to be the crucial matter in this regard, comparative analyses of how ordinary people evaluate the role of religion with regard to politics and public matters may offer an interesting complement to the kind of investigations presented by Casanova.

In order to get a better understanding of why people differ with respect to their normative views on the proper relationship between religion and politics, we will not only investigate the impact of the secularization-related factors which Casanova has pointed to, but also analyze the importance of the structure of the religious and political sectors in a society. This is our second theoretical approach. In recent years, the degree of pluralism in the religious sector is given increasing attention as an important predictor of religious involvement. According to some, higher levels of pluralism drives towards increased involvement (see e.g., Stark & Finke, 2000), while others see it as a cause of decreased participation (e.g., Bruce, 1999). The debate between the proponents of these two understandings has been lively, to say the least (Beckford, 2000: 491). Some relate the positive impact of religious pluralism at the macro level to *competition* between the various churches and denominations. The more competition they face, the more likely they are to adapt their supply to the religious demands, and thus the higher the religious participation (Stark & Finke, 2000). Others have seen the degree of pluralism as inversely related to the degree of *religious regulation* (e.g., Chaves & Cann, 1992). Since regulation is assumed to have a negative impact on the quality and diversity of religious supply, regulation and uniformity of the religious sector is expected to yield lower levels of religious participation. Yet others have argued that the positive impact of religious pluralism is moderated by the degree of *diversity in religious demands* (Hamberg & Pettersson, 2002). In line with these arguments, we simply assume that the more religiously diverse a society is, the greater the probability that people have found a religious voice to their liking (Hamberg & Pettersson, 1994, 2002). Therefore, the more diversified one's country is at level of churches, denominations, and religious organizations, the more likely one would be to accept a religious impact on public matters.

Similar arguments can also be forwarded with regard to the political system. Admittedly lacking support from previous research in this area, we therefore tentatively assume that the more pluralistic a country is in the political sector, the more likely it is that people will accept religion to have an impact on politics. In addition to the degree of pluralism in the religious and political sectors, we also assume that peoples' views on the religious differentiation depend on the general level of functional differentiation in a country. The stronger the general functional differentiation, the more likely people would be to prefer differentiation between religion and politics.

In this chapter, we will broaden the research on the relationship between religion and politics and assume that peoples' views on this matter also depend on a set of micro-level factors. With regard to these, we expect adherence to traditional values to foster a positive attitude towards a close relationship between religion and politics. Since these values are partly religious (cf. below), it follows that adherence to them is likely to favor a religious influence on public issues. On the other hand, we assume adherence to civic values to be associated with a positive attitude towards a differentiation between religion and politics. Since these values are secular in their basic premises (cf. below), adherence to them would be prone to reject such an influence. However, it should be noted that civic values also favor active social and political involvement according to each actor's personal convictions. From this point of view, there is reason to assume a positive relationship between civic values and e.g., political involvement by religiously committed persons.

With regard to peoples' socio-economic background, we expect the younger, the better educated and the males to be more in favor of a functional differentiation between religion and public matters. These assumptions follow from previous research on how people from different social strata are socialized into and acquire the two basic value orientations (see e.g., Inglehart, 1997; Pettersson, 1994). Further, some interaction effects between the micro- and macro-level factors can also be tentatively assumed. Thus, the traditional value orientation can be assumed to be more influential the stronger the degree of religious pluralism at the macro level. In a similar manner, the civic orientation can be assumed to be more influential, the stronger the degree of political pluralism at the macro level.

In summary, then, we expect peoples' views on the relationship between religion and politics to depend on both macro- and micro-level factors. Among the former, we assume lower levels of secularization and general functional differentiation to be associated with more positive attitudes towards a close relationship between religion and politics, and we expect the same for higher levels of religious and political pluralism. Among the micro-level factors, we assume adherence to the traditional value orientation to foster a positive view on a closer relationship between religion and politics, while adherence to the civic value orientation is expected to foster a negative view. We also assume older, female, and less educated people to demonstrate more positive attitudes towards a closer relationship between religion and politics.

3   Data and measurements

We rely not only on the survey data from the most recent European Values Study (EVS) surveys, but also on the data collected in the last wave of the World Values Survey (WVS). The empirical analyses are based on from 38 countries[1] being mainly influenced by Christianity in their religious traditions. This selection is made in order to obtain contexts with roughly similar understandings of the concept of religion.

3.1   Dependent variables: Views on the relationship between religion and politics

As already mentioned, our analyses will cover only one of the many dimensions of the relationship between religion and politics, namely whether people *want* religion to have an impact on politics or not. In the EVS/WVS questionnaire, these views are tapped by agreement-disagreement to following four statements: a) Politicians who do not believe in God are unfit for public office; b) Religious leaders should not influence how people vote in elections; c) It would be better for (one's country), if more people with strong religious beliefs hold public office; and d) Religious leaders should not influence government decisions. For these items, a 5-point response scale, ranging from 'agree strongly' to 'disagree strongly' was used.

Statements a and c tap the degree to which one prefers religiously involved people to be engaged in politics and to hold public office,

---

[1] The additional countries, their abbreviations and number of cases from the recent WVS wave are: Argentina (ARG) 1280, Canada (CA) 1931, Chile (CHL) 1200, Mexico (MEX) 1535, Philippines (PHL) 1200, South Africa (ZAF) 3000, United States (US) 1200, and Venezuela (VEN) 1200.

while statements b and d indicate the acceptance of religious leaders trying to influence political behaviors such as voting and government decisions. The more one agrees with statements a and c, the more one prefers religious people to be involved in public affairs, and the more one disagrees with statements b and d, the more one accepts that religious leaders influence politics. Two principal component analyses, one for the individual level data, and one for the aggregated level, verify that the four items can be used to tap these two different orientations towards the relationship between religion and politics. The results from these factor analyses are given in Table 12.1. It should be noted that the factor structure is almost identical at the individual and the aggregated level. However, there is also some reason to extract only one dimension including all four items. This general dimension then indicates views on the general differentiation between religion and politics. Therefore, we have calculated three different factor scores, one for items a and c, one for items b and d, and one for all four items.[2] With regard to our theoretical expectations mentioned in the theoretical introduction, we see no reason to differentiate between the three different measures of peoples' views on the relationship between religion and politics. Rather, we tentatively assume that our assumptions are equally valid for the attitude towards religiously committed people holding public office, the attitude towards efforts by religious leaders to influence political decisions, and the attitude towards a general differentiation between religion and politics.

3.2 *Independent variables*

In order to explain why peoples' views on the differentiation between religion and politics differ, several hypotheses have been forwarded. In the following, we will describe the measures we use to investigate these.

3.2.1 *Two micro-level value orientations*
Previous comparative research on the EVS/WVS data has focused on two basic value dimensions. The first is the 'traditional versus

---

[2] In order to facilitate the interpretation of the results, the responses to items b and d have been recoded. Therefore, a higher score on each of the three scores indicate a greater acceptance of a religious influence on politics and public matters.

Table 12.1   Results from a varimax rotated principle component analysis of four items tapping views on the relationship between religion and politics

	Factor 1:		Factor 2:		One factor solution	
	Indiv. data	Aggr. data	Indiv. data	Aggr. data	Indiv data	Aggr data
Politicians who do not believe in God are unfit for public office	**.90**	**.97**	.07	.20	.71	.83
Religious leaders should influence how people vote in elections	.09	.21	**.89**	**.95**	.62	.80
It would be better for (one's country), if more people with strong religious beliefs hold public office	**.88**	**.97**	.16	.17	.75	.79
Religious leaders should influence government descisions	.13	.16	**.88**	**.96**	.66	.77
Explained variance:	50%	66%	30%	31%	47%	63%

Data from the 1999/2000 wave of the EVS/WVS project in 38 countries. At the individual level, each national data set is weighted to yield 1.000 respondents and a total n of 38.000. At the aggregated level, the national mean scores for each item are analyzed (n = 38)

the secular rational value orientation', where 'the authority of God, Fatherland and Family are all closely linked' (Inglehart & Baker, 2000: 25; cf. Inglehart, 1997: Chap. 3). The second is the 'survival versus the self-expression value orientation', which taps a syndrome of 'trust, tolerance, subjective well-being, political activism, and self-expression' (ibid.). These two basic dimensions correlate with key macro- and micro-level characteristics (see e.g., Inglehart, 1997; Inglehart & Baker, 2000), for instance with economic development and the size of the industrial and the service sectors at the macro level, and with age and education at the micro level. Based on previous analyses (Pettersson, 2002, 2003), a modified version of these two value dimensions has been developed. These can be shortly described as follows.

The traditional value orientation taps attachment to religious and traditional family values together with experiences of national identity. The measure of religious values is assessed by a composite score from two components, once concerning the importance of religion,[3] and the other whether one thinks that the churches are giving adequate answers to man's moral, spiritual, social, and family problems.[4]

---

[3] The importance of religion was measured by a rating scale with response alternatives ranging from 'not important at all' (value 1) to 'very important' (value 4).

[4] Respondents were asked whether the churches give adequate answers to 'the

The two components of religious values (the importance of religion, and church adequacy, respectively) are then added into a single measure of religious values.

The measure of traditional family values is calculated as a composite score from two components, one concerning the importance of the family,[5] and the other whether one adheres or not to a set of traditional opinions on family life, for instance strict parent-child relations, formal marriage as a basis for family, etc.[6] The two components of family values (the importance of family, and traditional family values, respectively) are then added into a single measure of traditional family values.

The measure of national identity taps one's sense of national pride and national belonging.[7] The two components of national identity (national pride, and national belonging, respectively), are added into a single measure of national identity.

The civic orientation is measured by a postmaterialism index, a social capital index, and an index tapping protest proness. Even if a number of definitions of civic culture and the civic society have been proposed (see e.g., Inglehart, 1997: Chap 6; Weintraub, 1997),

---

moral problems and needs of the individual', 'the problems of family life', 'people's spiritual needs', and 'the social problems facing our country today'. From the answers to these four questions, a church adequacy score can be calculated (cf. Halman & Vloet, 1994). Those who find that each of the issues is given an adequate answer receive a score of 4, while those who find that none of them is given an adequate answer receive a score of 0.

[5] Answer categories ranged from 'not very important at all' (value 1) to 'very important' (value 4).

[6] Respondents were asked whether they thought that 'one must always love and respect one's parents, irrespective of their qualities and faults', that 'it is the parents' duties to do their best for their children, even at the expense of their own well-being', that 'marriage is not an outdated institution', that 'a child needs a home with both a father and a mother in order to grow up happily', and whether they disliked of 'a woman who wants to have a child as a single parent but she doesn't want to have a stable relation with a man'. Those who adhere to each of these 5 views receive a score of 5, while those who support none of them receive a score of 0.

[7] National pride was decided from a question about how proud one is to be 'Swedish', 'Mexican', etc. The answers are given on a four point rating scale, ranging from 'not at all proud' (value 1) to 'very proud' (value 4). The second component is assessed from two questions on whether one feels that one belongs first of all or in the second place to 'the locality where one lives', 'the region', 'one's country', 'the continent where one lives' (e.g., Europe, South America etc), and 'the world as a whole'. Those who choose 'one's country' in the first place receive a score of 2, those who choose 'one's country' in the second place receive a score of 1, while those who don't choose this alternative at all receive a score of 0.

these three aspects are often regarded as key dimensions of civic involvement. The postmaterialism index taps the degree to which the respondents prefer materialist or postmaterialist views on the way society should be organized (Inglehart, 1990, 1997).[8] The social capital index is built on two components, one concerning social trust, and the other involvement in social networks, formal as well as informal (cf. Putnam, 2000). The component of social trust is measured by the questions whether most people can be trusted, or if one needs to be very careful in dealing with others and whether it is important to encourage children to learn tolerance and respect for other people. The answers to these two questions are combined into one measure for social trust.[9] The component of social networks is measured by two indicators, one for informal social connectedness, and one for the formal. The indicator for informal connectedness is based on four items, which ask how often one spends time with friends, with colleagues outside the workplace, with people belonging to one's church, mosque, or synagogue, and with co-members in clubs and voluntary associations.[10] The indicator for formal social relations is assessed by a set of questions which ask whether one does voluntary work in 14 different organizations and social movements. The score for formal social relations is simply calculated as the number of organizations in which one is doing voluntary work. In order to get a combined score for social networks, the measures of formal and informal civil connectedness are then added.[11]

The measure of protest proneness taps the willingness to engage in various forms of social protests. The question was whether one 'has done', 'can imagine to do', or would 'never do' each of these five

---

[8] The postmaterialism index asks the respondents to choose the most and the second most important from the following four opinions: maintaining order in the nation, fighting rising prices (materialist items), giving people more say, and protecting freedom of speech (postmaterialist items). The index ranges from materialist views (value 1) to postmaterialist views (value 4).

[9] With scores ranging between 0 and 2.

[10] The answers are collapsed into one single measure, ranging from 0 to 4. Those who say that they meet regularly each month with each of the four categories, receive a score of 4, while those who say that they do not, get a score of 0.

[11] Since the score for the formal relations can reach a substantially higher number than the score for informal connectedness, the two scores are given equal weight by transforming each to a simple dichotomy, with values 0 and 1 and above. In order to achieve an over-all measure for social capital, the scores for social trust and social networks are then added. This score ranges between 0 and 4.

acts: sign a petition, join a boycott, attend a lawful demonstration, join an unofficial strike, and occupy a building or factory. The measure of protest proness captures how many of these acts the respondents has been involved in or can imagine to do.[12]

The results from two principal component analyses of the six indicators for the two basic value orientations, both at individual and aggregate level, are presented in Table 12.2. The results demonstrate that the six indicators relate as expected to the two value dimensions.

In Figure 12.1, the aggregated factor scores for the two basic value dimensions are plotted against each other. Many of the post-communist countries score low on the civic orientation, and also comparatively low on the traditional values. This is the case for Russia, Estonia, Lithuania, Latvia, Belarus, Ukraine, Hungary, and Slovakia. The Northern European Protestant countries of Sweden, Denmark, Finland, the Netherlands, and the UK score high on the civic orientation and low on the traditional values. A third group of predominantly Catholic and Orthodox poorer countries score low on the civic values, and high on the traditional values. In this group is found for instance Romania, the Philippines, Poland, Mexico, Argentina, Venezuela, Portugal, and Greece. A fourth group consists of the two North American countries of USA and Canada,

Table 12.2   Results from a varimax rotated principle component analysis of six items tapping traditional values and civic involvement

	Factor 1: Indiv. data	Aggr. data	Factor 2: Indiv. data	Aggr. data
Religious values	**.74**	**.85**	−.09	−.12
Family values	**.70**	**.86**	−.21	−.29
National identity	**.55**	**.67**	.15	.44
Postmaterialism	−.09	.01	**.66**	**.88**
Social capital	.25	.02	**.68**	**.88**
Protest proness	−.24	−.36	**.69**	**.83**
Explained variance:	28%	31%	21%	45%

Data from the 1999/2000 wave from the EVS/WVS project in 38 countries. At the individual level, each national data set is weighted to yield 1.000 respondents and a total n of 38.000. At the aggregated level, the national mean scores for each item is analyzed (n = 38)

---

[12] The index ranges between 0 and 5. The index has been used and validated in previous value research (cf. Halman & Vloet, 1994).

Figure 12.1   Scatterplot of the aggregated means for the two basic value
orientations for 38 countries

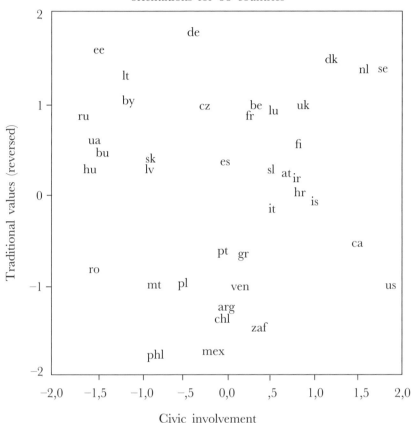

which score high on both the civic and the traditional value dimensions.
These results parallel the findings from previous research on earlier
EVS/WVS data (see e.g., Inglehart, 1997; Inglehart & Baker, 2000).

Previous research on the 1990 EVS and the 1996 WVS data from
about 60 countries has demonstrated that each of the two basic value
orientations are correlated to the degree of economic development
(GDP per capita), and that in addition the traditional values are negatively related to the size of the industrial sector, while the civic orientation is positively correlated to the size of the service sector
(Inglehart & Baker, 2000). Similar relations can be found for the
1999/2000 EVS/WVS data analyzed in this chapter. The traditional
values are positively related to the size of the agricultural sector (the

agricultural production as percentage of the GDP), and negatively
to the GDP per capita (World Bank figures for 1998). These correlation coefficients are .22 and −.28, respectively. By contrast, the
civic orientation is positively related to both the GDP per capita and
the size of the service sector (the service sector as percentage of the
GDP). The correlation coefficients are .75 and .45, respectively. In
this sense, the civic orientation seems to be related to the logics of
the growing service society, and the traditional values to the logics
of the shrinking agricultural sector. It should also be noted that at
the individual level, traditional values are positively related to age
and negatively to education, while the corresponding relations for
the civic orientation are reversed.

As independent variables at the micro level, we will also use age,
education and gender. Education is measured by one question asking at what age one finished/will finish one's education. Admittedly,
this is a very crude measure of the degree of education. However,
more nuanced measures, taking each country's specific education system into account, would infringe on cross-country comparability.

3.2.2   *Macro level variables*

As already mentioned, we assume the degree of pluralism in the religious and political sectors, respectively, to influence peoples' views
on the relationship between religion and politics. In order to measure the degree of religious pluralism, two different dimensions of
the religious sector deserve attention. These are the number of
churches and denominations, and the distribution of 'market shares'
among them, respectively. The more churches and the more evenly
distributed their market shares, the more diversified and plural the
religious sector. This kind of pluralism is often measured by a pluralism index, which is based on the Herfindahl concentration index.
The concentration index is defined as $H = \Sigma s_i^2$, where s_i is the market share of church i, that is the number of persons affiliated with
church i divided by the total number of persons affiliated with any
religious organization. Data on the number of people associated with
the various religious organizations in a country is simply taken from
the question on this issue in the EVS/WVS questionnaires. The
larger the number of churches and the more even the distribution
of memberships among them, the lower the Herfindahl index and
the more pluralistic (less concentrated) the religious sector. Therefore,

the religious pluralism index can be calculated as 1—the Herfindahl concentration index for the religious sector.

For the political realm, we have calculated a similar score of political pluralism. The score is based on the respondents' answer to a question of political preferences. The question asked 'If there was a general election tomorrow, which party would you vote for?' The larger the number of political parties in a country, and the more even the distribution of party preferences among them, the lower the Herfindahl index and the more pluralistic the political party sector. Therefore, the political pluralism index can be calculated as 1— the Herfindahl concentration index for the political sector.

We also assume the degree of secularization to have an impact on peoples' views on the relationship between religion and politics. The degree of secularization is measured by the national means for the factor scores from a one-factor principal component analysis of three items in the EVS/WVS questionnaire. These three items tap how important religion is in one's life, how often one attends a religious service, and how important God is in one's life. In a previous study (Halman & Pettersson, 1999), we have found this factor score to be an efficient measure of the general degree of secularization. Finally, as an indicator of the degree of modernization and general structural differentiation in a country, which we also assume to have an impact on peoples' views on the relationship between religion and politics, we will use the GDP per capita (purchase power parities) for the year 1998 (data from Johansson, 2000). Admittedly a rough indicator, the GDP has nevertheless in many studies shown to be a potent proxy for the degree of modernization, and hence for the degree of general functional differentiation.

4   Results

Figure 12.2 presents a scatterplot of the national means for the two dimensions of peoples' views on the relationship between religion and politics. Several aspects of the scatterplot deserve attention. First, it should be noted that the means for the two items saying that religious leaders should influence political decisions (the vertical dimension in Figure 12.2) are comparatively low, ranging between 1.47 (France) to 2.40 (US). This indicates that in each country, it is only a small minority who both accepts that religious leaders try to influence political decisions and how people vote in general elections. This minority ranges from 2.2 percent in Portugal to 15.8 percent in Mexico. Accordingly, in each country vast majorities seem to reject the idea that religious leaders should influence politics. This finding is certainly not in line with the dedifferentiation thesis, which by and large would assume the opposite. By contrast, the means for the two items saying that religious people should hold public office are somewhat higher, ranging from 1.58 (Denmark) to 3.89 (Philippines). This kind of relationship between religion and public matters is therefore seen as more acceptable. In the Philippines, it is even a majority of about 60 percent who agrees with each of the two statements saying that religious people should hold public office. In Argentina, Mexico, Ukraine, Chile, the US, Venezuela, Malta, and Greece, comparatively strong minorities between 20 to 40 percent are of the same opinion, whereas in a majority of the countries, this minority is considerably weaker, ranging below 10 percent. For all countries except Sweden, the preference for religious people to hold public office is higher than the readiness to accept that religious leaders influence political decisions. As expected from the varimax rotated factor analyses, the correlation between the two mean scores is low (at the individual level .25; at the aggregate level .39).

The scatterplot illustrates some further interesting differences between the 38 countries. One group of countries (Denmark, Belgium, and France) score low on both dimensions, while another group (Sweden and the Netherlands) seems to dislike that religious people hold public office, but to be comparatively less critical towards religious leaders who try to influence politics. A third group of countries (the US, South Africa, Venezuela, Ukraine, Greece, and the Philippines), score comparatively high on both dimensions of the relationship between religion and politics, whereas a fourth group (Romania and Malta) demonstrate comparatively high likings for religious people to hold public office together with a certain dislike for religious leaders who try to influence political decisions.

As already pointed out, our basic research hypotheses concern the relationships between on the one hand peoples' views on the relationship between religion and politics, and on the other their basic value preferences, their socio-economic background, and the structural characteristics of the political and religious systems in the countries they live in. In order to investigate these hypotheses, multi-level analyses are required. For these analyses, we have applied the HLM

Figure 12.2   Scatterplot of the aggregated means for two dimensions of the relationship between religion and politics

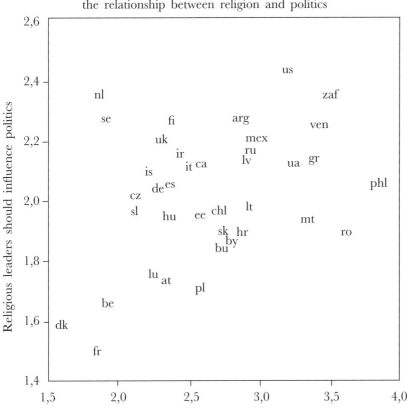

program[13] which enables the estimation of the simultaneous effects of both micro- and macro level independent variables (see e.g., Raudenbush & Bruk, 2002; Hox, 1995). The results from these analyses are presented in Table 12.3.

The results for each of the two components of the relationship between religion and politics are in most instances similar to the results for the general measure of attitudes towards the differentiation between religion and politics. In the following, we will therefore only comment on the results for the general measure. As can be seen from Table 12.3, our theoretical assumptions are mostly confirmed by the results. The traditional value orientation is associated with preferences

---

[13] We have used the HLM program, version 5.01.2067.1.

Table 12.3   Results from a set of two-level hierarchical linear regressions of factors affecting people's views on three dimensions of the functional differentiation between religion and politics

	Religious people should be involved in politics	Religious leaders may influence political decisions	General differentiation between religion and politics preferred
Micro-level factors			
Traditional values	.42***	.17**	−.44***
Civic orientation	−.24***	−.09*	.22***
Age	.00***	−.00*	−.01**
Gender	.09***	.04**	−.09**
Education	−.01***	.01	.00**
Macro-level factors			
Political pluralism	.25	.26*	−.36[a]
Religious pluralism	.12	.43**	−.73**
Secularization	−.33***	−.06	.34***
Gdp/capita (ppp)	−.01**	.00	.00
Macro-micro interaction			
Tradit values-tradit values	.03	.08**	−.08*
Polit plur-trad values	−.16**	−.08	.17*
Relig plur-trad values	−.00	−.00	.04
Civicness-civicness	−.09***	−.09*	.04*
Polit plur-civicness	.18***	.09*	−.18***
Relig plur-civicness	.04	.04	−.04

a $p < .10$, * $p < .05$, ** $p < .01$, *** $p < .000$

Entries are unstandardized multi-level regression coefficients. Results for the 1999–2000 EVS/WVS data for 40.449 respondents from 38 countries

for a closer relationship between religion and politics, while the contrary holds for the civic orientation. Furthermore, the older, the lower educated, and the females appear to favor a closer relation between religion and politics. Of the macro-level factors, higher levels of secularization are positively related to a preference for a differentiation between religion and politics, while higher levels of pluralism in the religious and political systems seem to foster acceptance for a religious impact on public matters. Of the macro-level factors, it is only the general level of functional differentiation which seems to be unrelated to peoples' views on the relationship between religion and politics. It can not be excluded that this negative finding is caused by a less relevant indicator for the general level of structural differentiation (i.e., the GDP per capita).

With regard to our tentative expectations on the interaction effects of the micro- and macro-level predictors, the results are partly in accordance with our expectations. The impact of the civic orientation seems to be stronger, the more pluralistic the political sector. In contrast, the impact of the traditional value orientation does not seem to be conditioned by the degree of pluralism in the religious sector. This finding is not in line with our tentative expectations.

5   Conclusion

We have reported on a set of comparative analyses of peoples' normative orientations towards the differentiation between religion and politics. Our analyses were based on three theoretical perspectives: A modified secularization approach, the 'new paradigm' in the sociology of religion, and studies on the impact of peoples' basic value orientations, respectively. With regard to the latter, we assumed the traditional value orientation to foster a negative view on the differentiation between religion and politics, and the civic orientation a positive view. We also assumed the older, the less educated and the females to be more in favor of a closer relationship between religion and politics. With regard to the 'new paradigm' in the sociology of religion and the positive impact of religious and political pluralism, we assumed positive attitudes towards a closer relationship between religion and politics to be more prevalent, the more pluralistic the religious and the political sectors are. With regard to the modified secularization theory approach, we assumed preferences for a close relationship between religion and politics to be primarily found in the less secularized societies.

The results from a set of multilevel regression analyses of the 1999/2000 EVS/WVS data from some 40.000 respondents living in 38 different countries were in accordance with our theoretical expectations. The traditional value orientation appeared to be associated with a negative view on the differentiation between religion and politics, while the civic orientation was related to a positive view. The younger, the more educated and the males were also found to be more positive towards the differentiation between religion and politics. Such positive attitudes were also more prevalent in the more secularized societies. If the latter result seems self-evident and maybe trivial, the finding that pluralism in the religious and political systems was associated with a positive view towards a closer relationship between religion and politics, has to our knowledge not been demonstrated in previous research. It should be noted that this finding was expected from the much debated rational choice theory influenced by the so called 'supply side theory' of religious involvement. In this regard, our results have demonstrated that this theoretical perspective has bearings in areas which have not been targeted by previous research.

Casanova's well known thesis on the rising involvement of religion in public matters served as one of our main theoretical entries. Our analyses did not demonstrate any widespread preference for religion to be a potent actor in the political and public realm. Rather, in a general sense, the results demonstrated that in most countries, people seemed to reject a religious influence on politics and public matters. This general pattern is also supported by another dataset. When the so called RAMP project[14] asked people in Belgium, Denmark, Finland, Great Britain, Hungary, Ireland, the Netherlands, Norway, Poland, Portugal, and Sweden, whether the main religions should have an influence on politics or not, large majorities were of the opinion that they should not. However, since Casanova's thesis claims that the preferences for a religious impact on public matters has increased over the last decades, our cross-sectional findings that comparatively small minorities hold this opinion, cannot be forwarded as a rejection of this part of his thesis. Nevertheless, these results deserve attention. Of course, one important aspect of the relationship between religion and politics relate to the substantive social and political orientations of the various minorities who argue that religion should have an impact on politics and public matters, for instance with regard to their views on democracy and policies of extraction and distribution. Should these orientations show to be markedly different in comparison to other groups, the issues we have discussed in this chapter become even more interesting and important.

One key part of Casanova's thesis states that the privatization of religion should be understood not as an inevitable structural trend, but rather as an option depending on a variety of factors. In this regard, we have found that the acceptance of a religious impact on politics and public matters seemed to be related to the degree of secularization. In this sense, we have demonstrated a new set of

---

[14] Data are from another survey project on Religious and Moral Pluralism (RAMP). For more information on this project, see Dobbelaere & Riis, 2003.

findings which add to the general knowledge of such secularization processes. However, it should also be noted that we have found support for the so called supply side theory, which is often forwarded as an alternative to secularization theory. Therefore, our results suggest that secularization theory and supply side theory should not be seen as so mutually exclusive as is often claimed, at least when it comes to the relationship between religion and matters in the public realm (cf. Hamberg & Pettersson, 2002).

In methodological terms, several aspects of our investigation need critical examination. For instance, analyses of other sets of data, based on different surveys and questionnaires, may yield different results. The questions we have used do not distinguish between attitudes towards a religious impact on *different kinds* of public issues. Rather, they asked for views on a religious impact on politics and public matters in general. Should one for instance have asked specific questions for the so called policies of regulation (e.g., divorce, abortion, euthanasia, etc.), people may very well be in favor of a strong(er) religious impact (cf. Minkenberg, 2002). Furthermore, should one have asked the question 'Generally speaking, do you approve or disapprove that people base their political decisions on their own religious beliefs?', quite many can be imagined to approve. If the matters were put like that, it is hardly unlikely that people would appear more prone to accept a religious influence on political matters. In contrast, the questions used in the EVS/WVS surveys focus on the general religious influences exerted by a religious collective or a super-ordinated religious authority (religious leaders, highly religiously committed persons). Therefore, our data may to a certain extent tap attitudes towards the political influences of authorities and large collectives in general, irrespective of whether these are religious or not. It might also be illuminating to ask people about the political influences of other kinds of ideological leaders than the religious ones. Such questions might demonstrate that the reluctance to accept a religious influence on public matters is by and large a token of a more general reluctance in such regards.

Therefore, in order to arrive at safer conclusions about peoples' normative views on the relationship between religion and public matters, a whole range of future investigations are needed. The results we have found suggest that such investigations can be worthwhile. Thus, the interaction of religion and politics remains a challenging issue to the social sciences.

References

Alexander, J. 1990. Differentiation theory: Problems and prospects. Pp. 1–16 in J.C. Alexander & P. Colomy (eds.), *Differentiation Theory and Social Change*. New York: Columbia University Press.

Beckford, J. 2000. 'Start together and finish together'. Shifts in the premises and paradigms underlying the scientific study of religion. *Journal for the Scientific Study of Religion* 39: 481–496.

Bruce, S. 1999. *Choice and Religion: A Critique of Rational Choice Theory*. Oxford: Oxford University Press.

Casanova, J. 1994. *Public Religions in the Modern World*. Chicago: The University of Chicago Press.

Chaves, M. & D. Cann 1992. Regulation, pluralism, and religious market structure. *Rationality and Society* 4: 272–290.

Dobbelaere, K. & O. Riis 2003. Religious and moral pluralism: Theories, research questions, and design. Pp. 159–172 in R.L. Piedmont & D.O. Moberg (eds.), *Research in the Scientific Study of Religion Volume 13*. Leiden, Boston: Brill.

Dogan, M. 1995. The decline of religious beliefs in Western Europe. *International Social Science Journal* XLVII: 405–418.

Ester, P., L. Halman & R. de Moor (eds.) 1994. *The Individualizing Society. Value Change in Europe and North America*. Tilburg: Tilburg University Press.

Halman, L. 2001. *The European Values Study: A Third Wave. Source book of the 1999/2000 European Values Study Surveys*. Tilburg: EVS, WORC, Tilburg University.

——— & T. Pettersson 1999. Differential patterns of secularization in Europe: Exploring the impact of religion on social values. Pp. 41–65 in L. Halman & O. Riis (eds.), *Religion in Secularizing Europe. The European's Religion at the End of the 20th Century*. Tilburg: Tilburg University Press.

Hamberg, E. & T. Pettersson 1994. The religious market: Denominational competition and religious participation in contemporary Sweden. *Journal for the Scientific Study of Religion* 33: 205–216.

——— 2002. Religious markets: Supply, demand, and rational choices. Pp. 91–114 in T. Jelen (ed.), *Sacred Markets, Sacred Canopies: Essays on Religious Markets and Religious Pluralism*. Lanham, MD: Rowman-Litttlefield.

Hox, J. 1995. *Applied Multilevel Analysis*. Amsterdam: TT-Publikaties.

Inglehart, R. 1977. *The Silent Revolution*. Princeton: Princeton University Press.

——— 1990. *Culture Shift in Advanced Industrial Society*. Princeton: Princeton University Press.

——— 1996. *Modernization and Postmodernization*. Princeton: Princeton University Press.

——— & W. Baker 2000. Modernization, cultural change and the persistence of traditional values. *American Sociological Review* 65: 19–51.

Johansson, L. 2000. *Dokumentation till databasen Länder 01*. Lund: Lunds Universitet, Statsvetenskapliga institutionen.

Minkenberg, M. 2002. Religion and public policy. *Comparative Political Studies* 35: 221–247.

Pettersson, T. 1994. Individualización, secularización y cambio de valor moral en la Escandinavia contemporánea. Pp. 483–498 in J. Díez Nicolás & R. Inglehart (eds.), *Tendencias mundiales de cambio en los valores sociales y políticos*, Madrid: Los libros de Fundesco.

——— 2002. Individual values and global governance: A comparative analysis of orientations towards the United Nations, human values and social change. Pp. 209–234 in R. Inglehart (ed.), *Findings from the Values Surveys, International Studies in Sociology and Social Antropology*. Leiden: Brill.

—— 2003. The United Nations between Islam and the secularized West. *Temenos* 37–38: 163–180.

Putnam, R. 2000. *Bowling Alone*. New York: Simon & Schuster.

Raudenbush, S. & A. Bryk 2002. *Linear Models. Applications and Data Analysis Methods*. London: Sage.

Stark, R. &. R. Finke 2000. *Acts of Faith: Explaining the Human Side of Religion*. Berkeley: University of California Press.

Wallis, R. & S. Bruce 1992. Secularization: The Orthodox model. Pp. 8–30 in S. Bruce (ed.), *Religion and Modernization: Sociologists and Historians Debate the Secularization Thesis*. Oxford: Clarendon Press.

Weintraub, J. 1997. The theory and politics of the public/private distinction. Pp. 1–42 in J. Weintraub & K. Kumar (eds.), *Public and Private in Thought and Practice. Perspectives on a Grand Dichotomy*. Chicago: The University of Chicago Press.

CHAPTER THIRTEEN

CIVIC MORALITY IN STABLE, NEW, AND HALF-HEARTED DEMOCRACIES

Ola Listhaug & Kristen Ringdal

1 Introduction

The formation of a strong civic morality is important for the development of a well-functioning society. If citizens freely accepts state regulations, pay taxes, and contribute to the common good, government will have less need of enforcing supervision and control of citizens—and more effective governance is possible. The argument for civic morality does not need to be framed in economic terms, although civic morality and political trust may have beneficial consequences in creating a well-organized state and contribute to efficiency in markets. Civic morality is also part of the wider normative fabric that contributes to the integration of citizens into the polity. Such integrative functions, supplied by civic morality, trust, or other democratic attitudes, might be seen as especially important for democracies that are in the making (Mishler & Rose, 2001a: 30–31). But contrary to what is needed, many observers would argue that societies that are in a transition from totalitarianism to a full-fledged democracy would be least likely in creating conditions that are favorable for the development of a morality for the common good.

In this chapter we compare the strength of civic morality across 33 countries that include stable democracies, new democracies, and transitional democracies. The stable democracies in the material are countries in Western Europe with at least twenty years of continuous democratic experience. The countries that started to establish a democratic system following the breakdown of communism in Eastern Europe and the Soviet Union after 1989 are classified in two groups, new democracies and transitional regimes. New democracies have been relatively successful in achieving the political freedom that we associate with democracy; while transitional regimes are lagging in the development of freedom, and have at least partly fallen back into an authoritarian mode of governing (Mishler & Rose, 2001b).

2   *Theoretical framework*

It is fair to say that civic morality has not been at the core of scholars' research interests when they study the state of democracy. Despite the lack of such research, there are a large number of recently published comparative studies of democratic attitudes that are highly relevant for our work.

The output of empirical research on problems of democracy has been through a strong growth cycle in the last ten years. Two factors account for this. First, the wave of democratization in the last decade of the twentieth century has led to a renewed interest for the study of how democracy is possible, and of factors that can contribute to viable democracy. Second, as a result of the democratic process a large number of countries became accessible for the collection of systematic social and political data. This has been particularly important for the study of mass attitudes and behavior. Several large programmes of survey research are launched to monitor citizens attitudes and behavior in the former communist countries of Eastern Europe. With data from these collections we can investigate trends in democratic attitudes, compare elites and mass, and also evaluate findings across a large number of countries in East and Central Europe and the former Soviet Union. These studies were designed to monitor the situation within a region that had left communism behind. The larger comparative picture which include established democracies can be filled in with data from the European Values Study. This survey includes many of former communist countries and the major mature democracies in Western Europe.

With data from the Values studies we can compare the status of democratic attitudes in both groups of countries. This is important for at least two reasons. First, it is always useful to have comparative frame of reference when we want to answer the question if democracy is succeeding or not. This is probably more true for mass attitudes than for other aspects of democracy, because it is very difficult to find absolute standards for trust in government, confidence in institutions, or a sound level of civic morality. Second, it seems fair to say that scholarship has focused on the problems of mature democracies almost to an equal degree as the worry for the situation in new democracies.

Indeed, concerns for the state of established democracies are at the heart of major research projects that are completed in the last few years. The largest by far is the Beliefs in Government study of the European Science Foundation, which reported its findings in five volumes in 1995 (see Kaase & Newton, 1995 for an overview). A somewhat smaller effort, with a more policy-oriented focus is the Harvard project on Visions of Governance (Nye, Zelikow & King, 1997; Norris, 1999). Pharr and Putman (2000) have edited a volume of articles that take stock of the fate of the predictions of a prominent *crisis* volume from the seventies (Crozier, Huntington & Watanuki, 1975)—to see what happened to the gloomy view of the future. The conclusions of all these projects are neither broadly negative nor strongly optimistic about the state of democratic politics in mature democracies; instead they strike a middle ground—but leave enough questions of skepticism to keep the focus on these issues alive. A quote from one of the chapters in the Pharr and Putnam book could sum up much of the conclusions of the three projects: 'This chapter has reviewed a large body of evidence to demonstrate that over the quarter century since Crozier and his colleagues issued their report, citizens' confidence in governments, political parties, and political leaders has declined significantly in most of the Trilateral democracies. . . . [But t]hese criticisms of governments and leaders do not necessarily translate into a "crisis of democracy" that threatens constitutional representative government' (Putnam, Pharr & Dalton, 2000: 27). The three studies have distinct analytical perspectives but they share much of the same data (including data from the first waves of the Values studies). This somewhat limits their significance as independent confirmations of the same underlying empirical patterns.

The unease about the situation for democratic politics in stable democracies and the less than perfect transition from dictatorship to democracy in Eastern Europe, constitutes a strong argument for the inclusion of both groups of countries in the study. Moreover, some of the most interesting and challenging scholarship has looked across the bridge between the two groups, as done by for example Mishler and Rose (2001b) and chapters in Norris (1999). In general we will hypothesize that civic morality is weaker in new democracies than in stable democracies. Many factors can account for this, like weak economic performance, incompetent elites, and relapses into authoritarianism in government, just to mention a few of the variables that are commonly mentioned. But civic morality should also be assessed more broadly to take into account cultural and social factors that work alongside the effects of the economy and current political events.

To analyze civic morality in a wider setting we propose four hypotheses that cover some of the important factors that influence civic attitudes. We see these hypotheses as relevant for both stable and new democracies, but their strength might be different in different systems. To account for the latter possibility we will test for inter-action effects in the statistical model to see of some factors are par-ticularly important in new democracies or transitional regimes when compared with stable democracies.

2.1 *Interpersonal relations*

In line with the arguments of Putnam (1993; 2000) we expect that civic morality is strengthened by factors that bring individuals into a wider network of people. This process is facilitated by interpersonal trust and voluntary activism. A person who is trusting toward others will also be likely to develop positive attitudes toward the larger com-munity and to accept rules and regulations that are set by government.

Putnam aims at understanding the problems of Italian democracy in the longer historical view (Putnam, 1993) as well as what as he sees as negative trends in contemporary American society and polity, and possible in other advanced countries (Putnam, 2000). The analysis of Italy seeks to explain the basis of effective government, and why this has succeeded better in the north than in the south. His main argu-ment is that democratic success or failure is related to the existence of 'vibrant networks and norms of civic engagement, while others are cursed with vertically structured politics, a social life of fragmenta-tion and isolation, a culture of distrust' (Putnam, 1993: 15). Similar themes are echoed in his analysis of contemporary United States: Civic virtues are declining as a consequence of an excessive individu-alism and weaker beliefs in community and the common good (Putnam, 2000).

Putnam's thinking stands in some contrast to a prevailing view that political support best can explained by political factors, and that cultural and social factors are of less importance (Holmberg, 1999; Newton, 1999; Newton & Norris, 2000; Mishler & Rose, 2001b; Listhaug, 1995a, 1995b). Recent scholarship has attempted to test

Putnam's hypothesis of a positive link between activity in voluntary associations, interpersonal trust and political trust and confidence in institutions, but do not find that this link is of any significant size (Newton, 1999; Newton & Norris, 2000).

2.2 *Performance*

A well-functioning democracy that solves problems and delivers the goods to citizens will have a positive effect on citizens' morality. This effect can be assumed across all types of institutional performance but may be most easily illustrated by economic examples. If tax collection is efficient and tax revenues are used for good purpose, citizens' tax morality will be strengthened. If tax avoidance is prevalent and government wastes a large share of what is collected, tax morality will suffer.

In an early comparative study based on EVS data, Listhaug and Miller (1985) test the hypothesis that restrictive attitudes toward tax avoidance is related to the size of tax revenues: Citizens should be less likely to accept tax evasion in countries with a low level of taxation. They found no support for this prediction. The reason for the negative finding could be that attitudes toward tax avoidance are determined by a much more complex assessment of institutional performance where taxation level is less of importance than a more comprehensive evaluation of the equity of taxation and how the income from taxation is spent. The degree of governments' fairness and efficiency in use of tax money maybe more important than tax level in determining public attitudes towards taxes. Similarly, the amount of corruption may have detrimental effects on public attitudes, as suggested by Richard Rose: '. . . the longer corruption persists at the elite level, the greater the likelihood that the mass of the electorate will become indifferent to dishonesty, or decide that the only way to deal with a corrupt state is to benefit from lawbreaking oneself, whether in the form of avoiding taxes, smuggling, or corrupting civil servants and elected representatives' (Rose, 2001: 105). His focus is on post communist societies, but he also see sees the fight against corruption as the biggest obstacle to creating European unity.

Evaluations of political and institutional performance can be absolute or relative to the preceding regime. Mishler and Rose (2001b) make a strong case for the argument that citizens in new democracies or regimes that are in transition will use assessments of how well the current regime performs only when it is compared with the previous regime. The Mishler and Rose idea is that this contrast is most important in countries that have changed regime from a totalitarian state to democracy. Relative comparisons of performance in stable democracies will be less dramatic as governments come and go in an orderly fashion, without making much of a break with the past. The policy changes that result from change in government may be important enough for the groups that are most strongly affected by policy shifts, but these shifts would be minor when compared to what have happened to citizens who have seen a one-party state being dismantled virtually over night. It is important to note that the contrast effect needs not necessarily be a strong positive number, a negative balance is also possible. This is more than a theoretical possibility as many countries that abolished communism in favor of a market economy and electoral democracy, have experienced significant reactions against the new regime primarily fueled by frustrations over economic problems and the failure of the new regime to fulfill the expectations of the revolution.

2.3 *Culture*

The impact of performance on civic morality is primarily an influence from above as it measures the success or failure of governments in creating favorable evaluations among mass publics. The influence of culture and social structure is primarily an effect on civil norms from below and is rooted in citizens' past socialization and experiences. There are many social and cultural roots of civic morality. In all societies religion is a major source of norms about what is right or wrong. We expect that individuals with a strong religious attachment will show a stronger civic morality than citizens with a weaker religiosity. It is also entirely possible that religion can be a source of uncivil behavior, both within and between societies. History as well as contemporary events—not least September 11, 2001—remind us about this. In general, however, we expect that religion will strengthen civic morality in society.

Values that tap into the left-right dimension are important in most societies. The left is associated with support for state intervention in the economy and social welfare. Right is associated with support for individual responsibility and competition. We expect that collectivists will have a strong sense of civic morality because tax evasion, claiming state benefits that one is not entitled to, and similar forms of behavior, will undermine the power of state and government to implement collectivist policy positions.

2.4 Moral behavior of fellow citizens

Finally, it is likely that civic morality will be influenced by perceptions of the moral behavior of others. If a person observes that others claim benefits that they are not entitled to or cheat on taxes, hers or his support for moral principles will likely suffer. It is difficult to stick to principled behavior when fellow compatriots not only break norms and the law, but also may benefit in economic terms from such behavior.

3 Model and measurement

Our measure for civic morality is created from a set of moral acts that the respondents are asked to assess if they can be justified or not. This is measured on a ten point scale where 1 is labeled never and 10 always. Among the 18 acts that were listed in the questionnaire we see four as tapping into the concept of civic morality: Claming state benefits which you are not entitled to, Cheating on tax if you have the chance, Someone accepting a bribe in the course of their duties, Paying cash for services to avoid taxes. Public opinion on these acts is moderately restrictive when we compare them with all 18 acts. Three of the items fall in the most restrictive half, with bribery as the most restrictive. The somewhat less precise act of paying cash for services to avoid taxes, falls in the permissive half of the distribution.

The four items load on the same dimension in a factor analysis with varimax rotation. The only other item that loads on this dimension is lying in your own interest. We see this act as conceptually different and will not include the item in the index for civic morality. The four items satisfy the conventional criteria for scalability. We have created a simple additive index by summing the score on the items after we reversed the scale so that 10 is he most restrictive value, indicating that the act can never be justified. The additive index has a theoretical range of 4 to 40 and a mean of 34.8 and a standard deviation of 6.4 for all countries combined.

For interpersonal relations we have measures of interpersonal trust and civic activism. Interpersonal trust is a dummy variable where 1 says that one cannot be too careful in dealing with people and 2 says that most people can be trusted. The measure of civic activism is constructed by counting the number of voluntary organizations that a person is active in. The scale goes from 0 to 15 where the count is from a list of organizations. We expect that interpersonal trust and membership in voluntary organizations is positively related to civic morality.

Performance is divided in two classes, institutional and personal. We measure institutional performance by three indicators, confidence in parliament, confidence in civil service, and relative rating of current system compared to the communist system. For stable democracies we compute the relative rating by subtracting the evaluation of the current system of governing minus the rating of the system as it was ten years ago. Confidence in parliament and civil service is measured on a four point scale where a high value indicates confidence. Difference rating is the difference between current and past regime and goes from –9 to 9 where a positive value means that the current system is evaluated more positively than the old system. For all indicators we expect that positive performance evaluations will have a positive effect on civic morality.

We measure religiosity by how important people say God are in their life (measured on a 1–10 scale, where 1 means not at all important and 10 is very important). We expect that religiosity is positively correlated with civic morality.

In our model left-right values are measured on a 4–40 point collectivism scale where a high value is the associated with collectivism and low values are associated with individualism. The scale is constructed by summing four items that measure support for individualism vs. collectivism. On each item the most extreme individualist position is coded 1 and the most extreme collectivist position is coded 10. In line with the arguments presented above we expect a positive relationship with civic morality.

We have constructed an index for how people perceive the behavior of their compatriots for three of the items that are included in the civic morality index: Claiming state benefits to which they are not entitled, cheating on tax if they have a chance, and paying cash for services to avoid taxes. The score for each item goes from 1 (almost all) to 4 (almost none). We sum the scores of the items to create the index, where a high value indicates that people see their fellow citizens as having a strong civic morality. We expect that positive perceptions will strengthen morality.

Age and education are also in the model. Both are statistical controls, but have a substantive meaning as well. Age can be seen primarily as a proxy for factors that are associated with socialization effects that are not specified in the model. This can be illustrated for religion. Older people are more religious than younger persons. In a model not including religiosity some of the positive effect of religiosity would have been picked up by age. It is likely that some of the assumed positive effect of omitted religiosity variables beyond the one that we measure, is included in the estimate for age. The same is probably true for other variables that tap into norms and values that get stronger with time.

Education is an ambiguous variable. Education is a cognitive resource that may increase political support by way of increasing the internal efficacy of citizens, or education may stimulate critical reflection that in at least some cases may have a negative impact on political support and other democratic attitudes (Listhaug, 1995a). This might also be the case with civic morality, and we keep the question open.

4 Empirical results

We return to the first research question: Is there any systematic variation of civic morality across countries? To attempt an answer to the question we arrange the countries according to the mean value on the index in ascending order. The results are laid out in Figure 13.1.

The results from Figure 13.1 suggest that there is no straightforward correspondence between strength of civic morality and type of country. The countries with the weakest civic morality are Belarus, Lithuania, France, and Belgium. On top of the list are Malta, Bulgaria, Iceland, Italy, and the Czech Republic. We observe that post-communist states are all over the continuum. Other countries that we also tend to see as one group, for example the Nordic countries, are relatively dispersed in the distribution. We could see this as a disappointing finding if we want to establish a link between system performance and morality. It is evident by just eyeballing the distribution that politically unsuccessful countries are located at both ends of the civic morality distribution. Before we look more closely at the relationship between performance and country we need to establish a classification of the countries.

We group the countries in three categories: Stable democracies, new democracies, and transitional regimes. This classification is based

Note: Data are weighed

Figure 13.1   Civic morality by country

on similar categorizations by Klingemann (1999) and Mishler and
Rose (2001b). Table 13.1 shows the empirical distribution of the
countries. We use the same theoretical criteria as Mishler and Rose
(2001b). The state of democracy as measured by the Freedom House
index. Regime change is counted when a country has experienced
a system change of regime in the last twenty years. Countries are
counted as free when their score on the Freedom House index is
2.5 and lower. Countries with a score above 2.5 are classified as
partly free or not free. In our material no countries fall in the category stable non-democracies. Mishler and Rose (2001b) had five
countries in this group: India, Mexico, Taiwan, Turkey, and Venezuela.

In contrast to Mishler and Rose (2001b) we count Spain as a stable democracy. We do the same with Portugal and Greece. This follows from the applying the criteria of twenty years since regime
change. A more detailed examination of these countries would probably have given strong empirical support to the decision to classify
the countries as stable democracies. The former communist countries fall in two groups. Eleven countries in his group are classified
as new democracies. Among these countries only Bulgaria (2,3) and
Romania (2,2) have scores on the Freedom House index (Freedom
House, 2000–2001) that bring them close to the cutoff point between
free and partly free. We include East Germany among new democracies but we are aware that many of the political characteristics of
this unit are the same as for Germany. For example Freedom House
gives only one index value for Germany after 1989.

The Freedom House scores at the time of data collection are for
Ukraine 3,4, Croatia 4,4, Russia 4,5, and Belarus 6,6. Belarus is the
only of the country that is classified as not free. The trends for Ukraine
and Russia are negative. In the year after the EVS survey the two
countries received ratings of 4,4, and 5,5, respectively. Croatia is on
the move in the opposite direction: In 2000–2001 the score for this
country is 2,3, passing the threshold to free, and moves the country
into the new democracies group (but this is after our data collection).

As expected from the distribution in Figure 13.1 we find that the
scores on the civic morality index do not show much variation across
the three categories of countries (Table 13.2). The mean is 34.4 for
stable democracies, 34.3 for new democracies, and only marginally
lower, 32.6, in transitional democracies.

We have worked under the assumption that the civic morality is
influenced by political performance, and a weak performance in new

Table 13.1   Classification of countries by change of regime and freedom

	Free Freedom House index le 2.5	Partly free/not free Freedom House index gt 2.5
	Stable democracies	*Stable non-democracies*
No regime change last twenty years	France Great Britain West Germany Austria Italy Spain Portugal Netherlands Belgium Denmark Sweden Finland Iceland Ireland Northern Ireland Greece Luxembourg Malta	
	New democracies	*Transitional regimes*
Regime change	East Germany Estonia Latvia Lithuania Poland Czech Republic Slovakia Hungary Romania Bulgaria Slovenia	Croatia Russia Ukraine Belarus

Note: The classification is based on Klingemann (1999), Mishler and Rose (2001b), and the freedom scores for appropriate years as published by Freedom House (2000–2001)

Table 13.2   Civic morality by state of democracy in country.
Means and standard deviations

Stable democracies	
34.4 (6.0)	
(N = 17141)	
New democracies	*Transitional regimes*
34.3 (6.5)	32.6 (7.6)
(N = 9885)	(N = 3387)

Note: Data are weighted and N for each country is set to 1000 cases

democracies and transitional regime would undermine civic morality in these countries. The finding that civic morality is pretty much constant across the three groups of countries, leads us to examine this assumption. First, we must check if evaluations of the current political system is consistently more negative in new democracies and transitional regimes than in mature democracies.

While civic morality does not show much variation across the three classes of countries, the pattern for evaluation of the current regime is clearly different (see Figure 13.2).

Italy, Greece, France, and Belgium are among stable democracies which have the lowest ratings. Malta, Luxembourg, Netherlands, Iceland, and West Germany have the highest scores in this group. The variation ranges from 4.3 for Italy to 6.8 for Malta. Among new democracies the lowest scores are for Lithuania, Romania, and Slovakia. East Germany, Estonia, and Bulgaria are in the top end. The variation goes from 3.2 for Lithuania to 6.0 for East Germany. East Germany is in a league of its own in this group. We observe that Bulgaria and Estonia, the countries that are closest to East Germany would have ranked near the bottom of the distribution for stable democracies, with only Italy and Greece below them. The four transitional regimes have low ratings. Russia is at the bottom with a mean of 2.6. Croatia and Ukraine are at 3.4, and Belarus has a score of 4.4. The data produce fairly strong evidence for the conventional view that the satisfactions with government are lower in the countries that abolished communism than in stable democracies. This should weaken civic morality in these countries, but it does not. But evaluations of current conditions may carry less weight in these countries, what may

Figure 13.2   Rating of current system of governing by type of country

A. Stable democracies

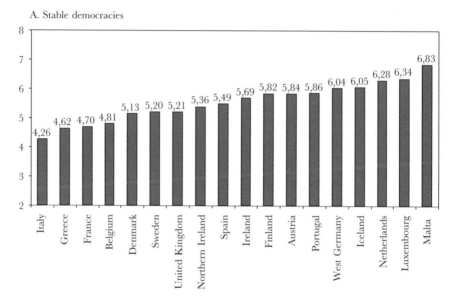

B. New democracies

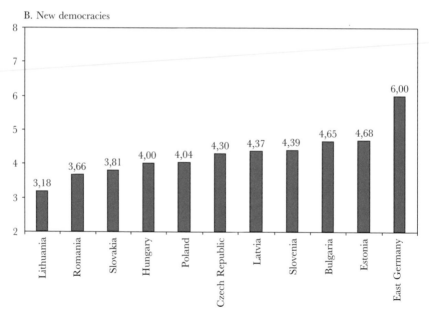

C. Transitional democracies

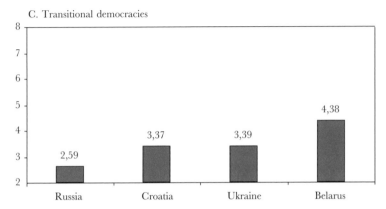

Note: Data are weighted

count is the evaluation of the current condition when compared with life under communism.

Is it support for the hypothesis that the publics in post-communist countries see the current situation in a more positive light when they compare it with life under communism? The data in Figure 13.3 and Table 13.2 tell us that the answer to this question is no. For stable democracies the baseline for comparison is the situation ten years ago. Stable democracies divide in two groups of equal size. Eight countries rate current system lower marks than the situation in the past, ten countries rate the present system higher than the past alternative. We note that the differences are fairly small as the range goes from −.7 (Greece) to .9 (Portugal). New democracies have a negative balance; seven countries have negative differences, and four countries are on the positive side. Especially the negative differences in this group are markedly larger than in stable democracies.

All four transitional democracies have negative differences. Russia is at −3.2, Ukraine −1.6, Belarus −.9, and Croatia −.5. Overall, the patterns for relative assessment of present vs. past is similar to what we found for ratings of the current system. To see this more clearly we present the means for the two types of measures in Table 13.3.

The mean rating of current system is 5.5 in stable democracies, 4.3 in new democracies, and 3.4 in transitional regimes. The same rank order holds for difference ratings, .0, −.4, and −2.0.

If mass publics' assessments of the political performance of political systems vary so much across countries and civic morality does not, maybe civic morality is less dependent on performance than we

Figure 13.3   Difference of current political system vs. previous regime

A. Stable democracies

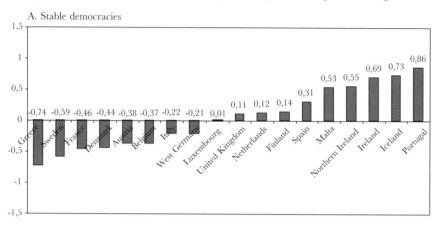

B. New Democracies

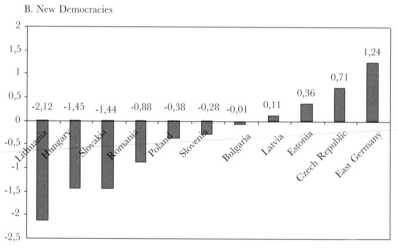

C. Transitional democracies

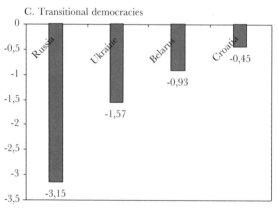

Note: Data are weighted

expected? To answer this question we now turn to an analysis of the explanatory variables. We have pooled the data and set each country to equal size. We use stable democracies as the reference category and include dummy variables for new democracies and transitional regimes. The results are presented in Table 13.4.

Table 13.3 Ratings: Current system of governing and difference between current and previous regime by state of democracy in country. Means and standard deviations

	Rating of current system	Difference in rating of current systemand the system ten years ago
Stable democracies	5.5 (2.0) (N = 17412)	.0 (2.3) (N = 15721)
New democracies	4.3 (2.1) (N = 10480)	−.4 (3.6) (N = 9835)
Transitional regimes	3.4 (2.1) (N = 3778)	−1.5 (3.5) (N = 3506)

Table 13.4 Regression analysis of civic morality

	b	beta
New democracies	.427	.031***
Transitional regimes	−1.005	−.050***
Age	.066	.171***
Education	−.190	−.027***
Life satisfaction	.180	.067***
God important in life	.233	.121***
Collectivism	−.032	−.036***
Voluntary org activism	.048	.008
Interpersonal trust	−.028	−.002
Confidence in parliament	.121	.016
Confidence in civil service	.609	.073***
Difference rating of system	.035	.017
Perception of state of civic morality in society	.322	.090***
R square	.091	
(N=)	(19588)	

Note: Data are weighted and N for each country is set to 1000 cases. See the text for the description of variables. The dummy for stable democracies is the reference category for the dummies for new democracies and transitional regimes. *** p< .001

We find that new democracies as a group has slightly stronger civic morality than stable democracies (the reference category) while transitional regimes are slightly below this group. Compared to the bivariate results (Table 13.2), the group effects have become stronger. But the message is the same; civic morality is not markedly stronger in stable democracies than in post-communist countries.

The expected impact of systems performance shows up only for confidence in civil service. Confidence in parliament and difference rating of system of government (present vs. past) is not related to civic morality. Life satisfaction has the expected positive impact. The hypotheses about activism in voluntary organization and interpersonal trust are not supported. Religiosity is, as expected, important for civic morality. Collectivism is weakly negatively related to civic morality. This goes against the hypothesis that argued that those who held leftist (collectivist) values should have a self-interest in a strong civic morality. The strong effect of age supports the hypothesis that socialization effects are important. Since the model includes religiosity, this result suggests that the effect of socialization goes beyond the impact of religious norms. Finally, citizens who perceive that their fellow citizens behave according to the law, are more likely to have a strong sense of civic morality.

The model in Table 13.4 does not inform us about how the various independent variables operate in the three groups of countries. We have above discussed a few possibilities that the effects of independent variables will be different in post-communist countries when compared with mature democracies. This discussion is primarily related to the impact of relative performance evaluation of the political system. The analysis up to this point has not given much support to the notion that ratings that compare present with the past should carry more weight in these systems than in stable democracies. We now proceed with a more rigorous statistical test in a model with interaction effects (see Table 13.5).

We continue to use stable democracies as the baseline and include interaction effects for the two post-communist groups. If an interaction effect is significant for either of the two groups we include the other as well, even if this effect is not significant. Before we discuss three of the most interesting interactions, we observe that the main effects for stable democracies are in line with the hypotheses for all variables except voluntary activism and interpersonal trust (no effects) and collectivism (the effect is negative, which is contrary to the hypothesis).

Table 13.5 Regression analysis of civic morality.
Model with interaction effects

	b	beta
New democracies	3.251	.237***
Transitional regimes	−5.028	−.251***
Age	.048	.124***
Education	−.211	−.030***
Life satisfaction	.288	.106***
God important in life	.312	.161***
Collectivism	−.035	−.039***
Voluntary org activism	.049	.008
Interpersonal trust	−.054	−.004
Confidence in parliament	.535	.069***
Confidence in civil service	.387	.046***
Difference rating of system	.102	.048***
Perception of state of civic morality in society	.300	.084***
Newd*Age	.033	.116***
Transi*Age	.076	.166***
Newd*Lifesat.	−.269	−.134***
Transi*Lifesat.	−.001	−.021
Newd*God imp.	−.220	−110***
Transi*God imp.	−.033	−.011
Newd*Conf.parl.	−1.203	−.201***
Transi*Conf.parl.	−.787	−.085***
Newd*Conf.civil	.694	.121***
Transi*Conf.civil	.363	.042
Newd*Diff.rating	−.042	−.013
Transi*Diff.rating	−.193	−.037***
Newd*Perception	−.024	−.013
Transi*Perception	.278	.104***
R square		.104
(N=)		(19588)

Note: Data are weighted and N for each country is set to 1000 cases. See the text for the description of variables. The dummy for stable democracies is the reference category for the dummies for new democracies and transitional regimes. The interaction terms are the product of the dummies and one of the other variables in the models as indicated by the label witch includes the first part of the name of each variable. *** p< .001

We demonstrated above that citizens in post-communist countries are more negative to the current system when they compare it to the past than are citizens in stable democracies when they compare the situation in their countries ten years ago. The interaction results add further weight to the rejection of the hypothesis of the importance of comparisons with the past for these countries. The signs for the interaction effects of difference ratings are negative and significant for transitional democracies, and negative, but not significant, for new democracies. This means that the positive effects of the difference ratings of the political system that we observe in mature democracies are strongly reduced in post-communist states. In fact the net effect is negative for transitional democracies (tables not shown). We find much of the same for confidence in parliament. The interaction effect for this variable is negative and significant in post-communist countries. The effect is especially strong in new democracies, but is also of considerable size in transitional regimes. The resulting net effect is negative in both groups, but significant only in new democracies (tables not included). The negative interaction effects of confidence in parliament stand in marked contract to the positive interaction effects of confidence in civil service. The net effect for confidence in civil service is actually higher in post-communist countries than in stable democracies. We thus have a conflicting result for performance evaluations. For assessments of public bureaucracy, post-communist states follow the same logic as mature democracies, and even to stronger degree: Civic morality is strengthened when citizens feel that bureaucracy is doing a good job. For political evaluations (relative rating of the system of government when compared with the past and confidence in parliament) the positive link is missing in post-communist societies.

The interaction effects of age are positive in both groups and suggest that socialization effects are more important in post-communist societies that in mature democracies. The effect of socialization is probably related to values that go beyond religion as we observe that the interaction terms for religiosity (God important in life) have negative signs.

We observe that the perception of the morality of fellow citizens carries a stronger weight in transitional regimes. This is the category of post-communist countries which has met with less success in the years after the fall of the totalitarian state. It may make sense that citizens in these countries look more to their fellow citizens than to the political system when they form their morality about how to relate to the state.

5   Conclusion

The formation of a strong sense of civic morality is important for the development of a well-functioning society, and may be seen as exceptionally crucial for countries that are going through a transition from dictatorship to democracy. With data from the 1999 EVS study we demonstrate that levels of civic morality are quite similar in mature democracies and in post communist countries. This probably comes as a surprise to those who see civic morality as driven by institutional performance as most scholars will agree that the political systems in post-communist states have done badly in recent years. This is also what our data show. Ratings of the current system of governance are much lower in new democracies, and especially in transitional regimes, than in stable democracies. The same is true if we compare the present with the past. But the multivariate regression analysis fails to establish a strong link between political performance and civic morality. This is especially the case in post- communist states. Instead we observe that social and cultural variables are important. Age is by far the strongest correlate of civic morality, but religiosity is also of importance. These findings suggest that norms and values that get stronger as people are aging, also work to strengthen norms for civic behavior. Since the effect of age is stronger in post-communist countries, and especially in transitional regimes, we may speculate that past socialization effects from the totalitarian regime may still be at work so that older people may be more likely to obey the rules.

We observe that there is a consistent impact on perceptions about the behavior of ones fellow citizens. This effect is strongest in countries with the least developed democracy. If people see others as sticking to the rules, civic morality is strengthened. This finding suggests that the horizontal dimension is important. Civic morality may be influenced from above, how elites perform, from below, by socialization effects that are rooted in the cultural, social and political structure of the past, or in the horizontal dimension: how citizens perceive the behavior of others. The mix of these explanatory factors may be different in mature democracies and post-communist regimes and explain why civic morality shows relatively small variation across systems.

References

Crozier, M., S.P. Huntington & J. Watanuki 1975. *The Crisis of Democracy: Report on the Governability of Democracies to the Trilateral Commission*. New York: New York University Press.

Freedom House 2000–2001. *Freedom in the World Country Ratings 1972–73 to 2000–2001* http://www.freedomhouse.org

Holmberg, S. 1999. Down and down we go: Political trust in Sweden. Pp. 103–122 in P. Norris (ed.), *Critical Citizens*. Oxford: Oxford University Press.

Kaase, M. & K. Newton 1995. *Beliefs in Government*. Oxford: Oxford University Press.

Klingemann, H.D. 1999. Mapping political support in the 1990s: A global analysis. Pp. 31–56 in P. Norris (ed.), *Critical Citizens*. Oxford: Oxford University Press.

Listhaug, O. 1995a. The dynamics of trust in politicians. Pp. 261–297 in H.D. Klingemann & D. Fuchs (eds.), *Citizens and the State*. Oxford: Oxford University Press.

—— 1995b. The impact of modernization and value change on confidence in institutions. Pp. 163–178 in R. de Moor (ed.), *Values in Western Societies*. Tilburg: Tilburg University Press.

—— & A.H. Miller 1985. Public support for tax evasion: Self-interest or symbolic politics? *European Journal of Political Research* 13: 265–282.

Mishler, W. & R. Rose 2001a. What are the origins of political trust? *Comparative Political Studies* 34: 30–62.

—— 2001b. Political support for incomplete democracies: Realist vs. idealist theories and measures. *International Political Science* Review 22: 303–320.

Newton, K. 1999. Social and political trust in established democracies. Pp. 169–187 in P. Norris (ed.), *Critical Citizens*. Oxford: Oxford University Press.

—— & P. Norris 2000. Confidence in public institutions: Faith, culture, or performance? Pp. 52–73 in S.J. Pharr & R.D. Putnam (eds.), *Disaffected Democracies*. Princeton: Princeton University Press.

Norris, P. (ed.) 1999. *Critical Citizens*. Oxford: Oxford University Press.

Nye, J., P.D. Zelikow & D.C. King (eds.) 1997. *Why People don't Trust Government*. Cambridge: Harvard University Press.

Pharr, S.J. & R.D. Putnam (eds.) 2000. *Disaffected Democracies*. Princeton: Princeton University Press.

Putnam, R.D. 1993. *Making Democracy Work: Civic Traditions in Modern Italy*. Princeton: Princeton University Press.

—— 2000. *Bowling Alone: The Decline and Revival of American Community*. New York: Simon and Schuster.

——, S.J. Pharr & R.J. Dalton 2000. Introduction. Pp. 3–30 in S.J. Pharr & R.D. Putnam (eds.), *Disaffected Democracies*. Princeton: Princeton University Press.

Rose, R. 2001. A Diverging Europe. *Journal of Democracy* 12: 93–106.

CHAPTER FOURTEEN

GENDER ATTITUDES TOWARDS RELIGION IN SIX POST-SOVIET STATES

LARISSA TITARENKO

1 *Introduction*

The third stage of the European Values Study was conducted approximately ten years after the collapse of the communist system. These ten years make it possible to identify some preliminary, still vague features of the 'second great transformation' (Burawoy & Verdery, 1999) that destroyed most of the pivotal features of the Eastern and Central European communist world. There are no predictions as to whether the new trends will prevail in the long run. Neither do these trends suggest that East and West have become very much alike. What we want to do is to look at gender attitudes toward religion in some European republics of the former Soviet Union. By comparing present-day gender attitudes toward religion in six former Soviet states (FSS) with similar values in Western Europe we will make progress toward answering the major research question formulated by Halman (2001: 2): 'did Europeans share a homogenous and enduring set of values at the end of the millennium?'

The six European post-Soviet countries that are included in the 1999/2000 EVS—the three Baltic republics (Estonia, Latvia, and Lithuania) and the three so-called Slavic republics (Belarus, Russia, and Ukraine)—have some specific cultural features in common. Before 1991 they were part of the Soviet Union, so that in their pattern of development, including values and attitudes, they differed greatly from the other European regions. During the post-Soviet years of independence they have changed a great deal, but their Soviet legacy remains strong; hence some new post-Soviet social and political trends are similar to such trends in Western European countries, while other trends are opposite. For example, the level of religiosity in Western Europe has decreased (Ester, Halman, & de Moor, 1994), while in the FSS it is rising (Novikova, 2001). In Russia the number of believers has grown in all age groups in the 1990s in comparison with the previous decades. Almost 60% of Russians identified themselves as believers in the mid-1990s (Volkov, 2001: 190). In Belarus the number of registered religious communities in 2000, by Kruglov's estimate, increased by a factor of 3 compared to the end of the Perestroika period (Kruglov, 2002: 14). The new political regimes do not discourage religious celebrations or church attendance, and the new political leaders are even keen to demonstrate their closeness to the predominant denominations in their countries.

In general, the role of religion is growing in the FSS owing to the processes of national renaissance and the need to foster new national identities (Volkov, 2001). However, this growth is not linear.

Gender patterns differ considerably from country to country: while women prevail among those who belong to religious denominations or identify themselves as religious, men predominate among the non-religious and non-affiliated. In social and demographic terms, the majority of believers are older females, unemployed, poor, and less educated; the non-affiliated are mostly young and middle-aged males, better educated, employed, and with higher incomes. Overall, there are greater differences among women regarding religion than among males, whose attitudes towards religion are more uniform, regardless of age, country, and education. In evolutionary terms, the FSS are currently shifting from an official mass atheism to a spontaneous growth of various kinds of religiosity.

This chapter will address the question of what factors determine who was religious in the FSS at the turn of the millennium and who was not and why. Findings from the 1999/2000 wave of the EVS will be presented to show whether gender differences influenced the choice of religious values in these countries and if so, how and why. Furthermore, we will determine whether other social and demographic factors also played a part in the choice of religious values. We will analyze the findings using pooled data for all six FSS countries, and, if expedient, data for each individual country.

2   Theoretical framework

In order to explain current gender attitudes towards religion in the FSS, we need to place religiosity as a social phenomenon in a relevant theoretical framework. To this end, it is necessary to take into account several factors influencing religiosity in selected countries and world wide.

First, the process of globalization affects the FSS as it does other parts of the world. For example, with the strong support of the global community (mainly, Western Europe and the USA), the Baltic republics have undergone many political and economic reforms, so that the Baltic population now enjoys a much higher standard of living than their former compatriots in the Slavic republics. At the same time it is safe to assume that the post-Soviet population's values are influenced by the Western phenomenon of individualization (Ester et al., 1994; Inglehart, 1990). If, like Western countries, the post-Soviet countries are undergoing individualization, we should find different types of religious beliefs replacing the previously typical Soviet homogeneity in opinions, norms, and the models of behavior.

Second, as the FSS are still undergoing a dramatic transition from Soviet style communism to democracy and market economics, several social groups have not adjusted well to the new reality. They feel deprived because of social and economic instability and are suffering the effect of a badly deteriorated standard of living. As Maslow earlier showed, such groups often seek religion (or a new ideology) in order to escape psychological deprivation and meet their basic needs (Maslow [1962] 2002: 126). That is why the sociological paradigm of social and cultural trauma as described by Sztompka (2001) is useful to explain the situation in the FSS. The Baltic republics have managed to adapt to social and political changes better: they have become democratic states and have turned toward Europe. In contrast, as Castells explained, the Slavic republics have destroyed communism 'without much apparent benefits to their people' (Castells, 1998: 64). Consequently, now they are far behind the Baltic republics both economically and politically. While the Baltic republics are among the new members of NATO and the EU, the Slavic republics still strongly bear the heavy burden of a Soviet spiritual legacy that affects the population's values and everyday life.

An important part of the post-Soviet transition has to do with the formation of new national identities to replace the former Soviet identity. In the Baltic republics Soviet identity has never been strong, so that the people (at least those belonging to the titular nations) have quickly restored their national and cultural identities. In contrast, in the Slavic republics many people had truly internalized Soviet values and therefore have suffered from value uncertainty after the Soviet collapse. In many cases it was easier to find a new identity if one was affiliated with a predominant religious denomination. For that reason, ethnic (national) and religious factors are among the most influential cultural and political phenomena in the FSS. Religious renaissance is not closely associated with the current political regimes; rather, it reflects a broad interest in the historical heritage and the sincere desire of the people to go back to their 'deep national roots,' to restore the cultural traditions of their predecessors, which are generally viewed (whether that is true or not) as genuinely relevant for democratic development. Hence, religious renaissance can be described within the framework of ethnic (national) renaissance and the search for authentic historical traditions and norms intended to replace Soviet norms and traditions.

The search for a new religious identity is important primarily for those who were socialized under the previous Soviet regime and therefore have lost their values and norms after the Soviet collapse. Of course, some of these middle-aged and elderly generations socialized under communism, have retained their atheist world outlook (that is why there are many religiously non-affiliated persons in the FSS as well), while the rest look at religious values as a possible substitute for former communist beliefs and values, especially in the moral sphere. Religion makes their lives meaningful and gives them hope for the future. That is why such people currently hold religious values in very high regard. As for the younger generation, it had no 'previous values' to lose; the young did not experience post-Soviet social and psychological trauma, and their socialization has been influenced mainly by other, non-religious factors. Some young people are very open to new religious cults and practices, but their interest in religion is lower than that of the old generations. With this theoretical explanation in mind, the following statement is taken as the main hypothesis for the observed period of time in the six former Soviet republics:

H1: After the Soviet collapse, the level of religiosity of the FSS population has differed from country to country and within each country, from one social and demographic group to another.

On the country level, we suppose that Lithuania, being the only one pure Roman Catholic country in this group, will demonstrate the highest level of religiosity. The Baltic countries taken together may also have a higher level of religiosity, than Slavic states: they belonged to the USSR for less than 50 years and therefore they did not destroy their previous cultural legacy, religious norms, and the like.

Let us look at the numbers of those in six countries who are affiliated with one denomination or another and who identify themselves as religious.

The levels of religious affiliation and religious identification shown in Table 14.1 confirm the fact that a lot of people in the FSS currently identify themselves as religious. While during the Soviet period, in accordance with the official ideology, the majority seemed to be atheists (or at least non-religious), a few years later more than half of the population (except for Estonia) identified themselves as religiously affiliated, and two thirds (except for Belarus) identified themselves as religious.

These two exceptions are worth noting. The fact that Estonia is the least religious country in the sample can be explained by its history, cultural traditions, and openness to new models and norms. One may assume that fewer Estonians are affiliated with traditional Christian denominations than people in other FSS. On the other hand, Belarus

Table 14.1   Belonging to religious denominations and personal religiosity in the European states of the former Soviet Union

States	Belong to Denomination	Religious Person	Non-Religious Person	Atheist
Orthodox:				
Belarus*	52.2	27.5	63.1	9.3
Russia	50.5	65.7	29.4	4.9
Ukraine	56.4	75.3	21.9	2.8
[Sub-Total]	53.0	59.2	38.1	5.7
Mixed Catholic-Protestant-Orthodox:				
Estonia	24.9	41.7	51.6	6.6
Latvia	59.3	76.9	20.3	2.8
[Sub-Total]	42.1	59.3	36.0	4.7
Catholic:				
Lithuania	80.5	84.5	14.1	1.5
[Total]	54.0	61.9	33.4	4.65
European	72.2	66.7	28.2	5.1

Note:* Belarus question on religious identification was not similar to other countries

is a rather traditional country and the exception in her case is due
to the way the question about religiosity was translated. Belarus
respondents were asked whether they are 'religious,' 'not very religious,'
or 'atheist;' and many respondents selected the second answer, identifying themselves as 'not very religious,' rather than 'non-religious'
as did people in other countries where the options were 'religious,'
'not religious,' and 'atheist.' As a result of this inconsistency, we cannot adequately compare Belarus with the other five countries on the
basis of this question. However, according to other surveys on religiosity
in Belarus, as Novikova, Ivanyuto and Tarnavskiy (2001) stress, up to
80% identify themselves as religious (Novikova, Ivanyuto & Tarnavskiy,
2001: 327).

Taking into account these additional data, we can assume that at
least more than half of the population in the FSS currently consider
themselves as affiliated or religious. This is a substantial shift towards
religiosity within the short post-Soviet period. Because this shift reflects
a growth in a broad interest in the historical heritage, as well as
people's search for new spiritual values and for a new identity, it
may be considered significant.

One more confirmation of a growth in religiosity in the FSS is
given in Table 14.2: according to these data, currently, more attend
religious services regularly (at least once a month) than they did it
when they were 12. Conversely, fewer say they never attend services
than they did when they were 12.

Catholic Lithuania and religiously mixed Latvia (more precisely,
the Catholic part of its population) are different: more attended religious services there when they were 12 than they do now. The explanation is cultural: as Cipriani described (1994), the Catholic population
in the communist countries used to associate political resistance to
the communist regime with religious affiliation, so, high church attendance under communism was also a political anti-regime phenomenon
whose importance decreased after the collapse of communism. The
Catholic Church has now lost its previous enormous political influence,
so that those who used to go to church only for political reasons
have lost their close affiliation with the Catholic Church. As for the
countries where the Orthodox denomination predominated, there
were no direct links between Orthodox church attendance and political resistance. These facts show a complex non-linear relationship
between the former Soviet regime and different religious denominations
in the FSS: in some countries, people attended church more than
they do now, and the political regime was unable to prevent it.

Table 14.2   Attendance of religious services in
six European former Soviet states

| States | More than once a month: | | Never attend services: | |
	now	when being 12	now	when being 12
Orthodox:				
Belarus	14.5	10.9	27.8	49.3
Russia	9.2	5.6	50.1	75.4
Ukraine	16.9	8.1	30.5	57.3
[Sub-Total]	13.5	8.2	36.1	60.7
Mixed Catholic-Protestant-Orthodox:				
Estonia	11.1	8.6	37.8	55.3
Latvia	15.1	19.7	34.6	52.3
[Sub-Total]	13.1	14.2	36.2	53.8
Catholic:				
Lithuania	31.5	49.0	16.0	13.7
[Total]	16.8	17.0	32.8	50.6
European	31.6	56.5	29.5	23.8

Source: EVS 1999–2000

If we compare church attendance in the FSS and the Western European countries, it is still higher in the West—32.6 percent on average versus 16.4 percent. However, church attendance is visibly declining in the West, while it has definitely increased in the FSS. This trend toward religiosity has the strong approval of post-Soviet national political elites because they are interested in national and cultural renaissance and consider the growth in religiosity as part of this renaissance.

A number of other economic and political factors should be mentioned that are contributing to the rise of religiosity in the FSS: (a) the high level of political uncertainty and instability during the first years of independence (it motivated some to search for psychological equilibrium in the religious domain); (b) the demise of the social safety net that used to help one cope with everyday social and moral issues under the previous regime; and (c) the growth in economic inequality and the concomitant decline in standard of living for the majority of people in the FSS. As a UNICEF survey stressed ('After collapse,' 1999), in 1998–1999 GDP and output in all former Soviet states were still lower than in 1990 under the Soviet regime (p. 4). Such a situation also drives the most alienated population groups toward religion as their only hope and comfort.

As a result of religious growth in the FSS, more people currently value religion more than politics in their lives. Although the difference between the value attached to politics and religion is not large—the religious (mean) value is 2.7 while the political (mean) value is 2.8 on 1–4 scale—this is a sign of a shifting interest in mass consciousness from politics and ideology towards spiritual religious values. Political leaders also approve of this fact. For example, Russian President Vladimir Putin, as quoted by House (Commentary, 2002), stressed that religion is very important for Russians, because, 'after the previous dominant ideology—Communist ideology, which essentially took the place of religion [in Russia]—ceased to exist as a state religion, nothing can replace universal human values in a human soul as effectively as religion can' (Commentary, 2002: 1). This explanation is equally applicable to other predominantly Orthodox countries in the FSS.

Having explained the causal links between the current social and political situation in the FSS and religion, and having shown the reasons for the growth of religion, we may assume that the current

Figure 14.1   Importance of six values (means) in six countries

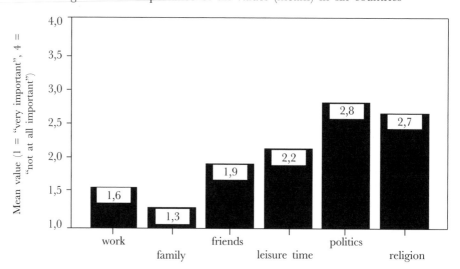

Cases weighted by WEIGHT

level of religiosity in the FSS is significant, and that it differs from country to country.

These considerations lead to another hypothesis that explains gender attitudes towards religion among the population of the six post-Soviet states in greater detail:

H2: In post-Soviet states women's religiosity is higher on average than men's. The older the women, the more religious they are.

If this hypothesis is correct, females would attend church services more often than males, they would pray oftener, more of them would identify themselves as religious than men, and they would have higher confidence in the Church than males.

Indeed, while the former Soviet ideology proclaimed that Soviet citizens had to be atheists, the present-day post-Soviet states are relatively more open towards religiosity in their population. Freedom of religion is not only declared in the Constitutions, but has become a practical issue. According to sociological data, many women identify themselves as religious while far fewer males do the same (Kruglov, 2002: 17). Such a situation creates a variety of religious attitudes among the population of the post-Soviet region and increases individualization of religious beliefs and models of religious behavior.

On the individual level, we would like to analyze which demographic categories are correlated with the most positive and most negative gender attitudes towards religion. As the second EVS wave showed, age is a significant factor for religious values (Ester, Halman & de Moor, 1994: 63). We hypothesize that older females with a low level of education, unemployed, and having a low income, are the core members of the most religious group. If these social and demographic factors are significant, the above-mentioned group of elderly females will show a high level of religiosity. We also assume that young men are the least religious group among the FSS population.

We can mention several factors as the basis for H2. The ongoing post-communist transition in the FSS has already brought an enormous increase in inequality, which leads us to expect a significant deterioration in the social status of women. According to UNICEF data ('After collapse,' 1999), the social and economic indicators of women's status decreased: females constitute 60% of the unemployed, women are last hired and first fired, their representation in political life has dropped, and they lost many of their previous social benefits (pp. 29–33). Elderly women with small pensions and restricted public contacts are suffering even more than other age groups, as they lost the official Soviet values, adequate state support, any hopes they had, and do not have enough life time left for re-socialization. Under such conditions women clearly need something that would replace their Soviet values and help them survive. In search for such beliefs many females have simply returned to pre-communist traditional patriarchal values, where religion played a significant role. In contrast, fewer males have done the same, because men are more often involved in work for pay and political life, leading to another hierarchy of values among them. One should also keep in mind that widespread male alcoholism, at least in the Slavic republics (Gilinskiy, 2000), has been an obstacle to males becoming religious.

3   Data and operationalization

All the data used in this chapter are from the recent European Values Study surveys (Halman, 2001). When other sources of information are used, it is so stated in the text.

Before discussing the empirical data on religious values and gender attitudes towards religion it is necessary to mention some limitations regarding the research findings.

First, the fieldwork was conducted in 1999–2000, shortly after the acute financial crisis in Russia and countries related to its economy, Belarus and Ukraine. Consequently, the population of these countries was mostly concerned about the economic situation and faced hard issues—unemployment, inflation, low wages, and wage arrears. The previous optimistic expectations regarding a post-Soviet 'better life for all' had been shattered again. Under these conditions some respondents likely were experiencing a high level of frustration and depression, so that their answers might be more pessimistic and religiously-colored than before the crisis. It is therefore necessary to explore dynamics of religious views in order to reveal the long-term trends with regard to religion in the FSS.

Second, one of the key questions about religion ('are you a religious person') was slightly reformulated in the Belarus survey, so that the number of those who identified themselves as religious turned out much smaller than expected. Because of this glitch, the Belarus data is not fully comparable to the other data based on this key question. We should keep in mind this data inconsistency in our further calculations of indexes of religiosity.

Third, as the absolute majority of believers in these countries are Christians, we chose to discuss only Christian denominations and to ignore variants of non-Christian religiosity. Actually, according to the data from EVS, non-Christian groups are significant only for Russia and not for the other selected countries (Halman, 2001: 75).

Fourth, research data did not take into account cultural differences between the several Christian denominations. Thus, the Orthodox Church which is predominant in the Slavic countries does not require any official affiliation with a particular church or even regular church attendance—it is enough for one to be baptized or to identify one-self as an Orthodox believer. Catholic traditions are different, so as is culturally expected of them Catholics always attend services more often than Orthodox believers.

Fifth, one has to mention the different historical backgrounds of the Orthodox, Catholic, and Protestant denominations in the FSS and earlier in Tsarist Russia. The Orthodox Church was officially connected with the Russian monarchy, while the other Churches enjoyed no such privilege. In general, the Roman Catholic Church has not been officially welcomed either in the Russian Empire or the present-day Slavic countries. Under the Soviet regime, the Roman Catholic Church was involved in the anti-Soviet national struggle, especially in the Baltic republics and Western Ukraine. Consequently, the rapid growth of Orthodox communities after the Soviet collapse did not preclude the growth of Catholic communities as well: for example, as Kruglov showed, in Belarus alone the number of Roman Catholic communities increased by a factor of 3.5 in the 1990s (Kruglov, 2002: 14). However, Roman Catholic communities operate under different conditions and have more problems getting registered in the Slavic republics, especially in Russia.

It is difficult to say to what extent these factors could negatively affect data quality. However, such problems are typical for any cross-cultural research: they make any research results not definitive, but open to further revision. At the same time, there is no other way to collect data and do cross-cultural analysis. To minimize possible errors, it is necessary to use latent comparable constructs and longitudinal analysis.

In this chapter we use some complex latent variables related to several important manifested variables. The relationships between the manifested variables within each country and within the post-Soviet region as a whole are primarily tested using the chi-square technique (the most sensitive in this case). After the existence of correlation between manifested variables is proved, we can construct three new latent variables to clearly evaluate gender differences in each country and in two regions (Baltic and Slavic). These latent constructs measure different attitudes, norms, and existing patterns of behavior related to gender religiosity.

1. *External religiosity*: a set of manifested patterns of behavior, such as attendance of religious services, celebration of 'rites of passage,' belonging to a denomination, and having traditional Christian beliefs. The key (filter) question is 'belonging to a denomination,' so, it makes sense to measure the external religiosity of those who belong to one denomination or another. We assume that those who regularly attend services (at least once a month), accept major Christian beliefs (in God, heaven, hell, life after death, and sin), and accept the importance of celebrating 'rites of passage' (birth, death, and marriage) are religious in the eyes of the public. The complex variable called 'external religiosity' which combines the above-mentioned ten questions, will indicate the level of publicly observed involvement in religious services and people's manifested acceptance of religious norms and beliefs. We assume that those who selected less than five out of ten above-mentioned questions demonstrate a relatively low level of external religiosity, while the rest (those who selected 5–10 questions) demonstrate the high level of external religiosity. They are the core church members in the FSS.

However, there are always people who are not affiliated with any Church but who still believe in God and identify themselves as religious. We refer to this kind of religiosity as 'intrinsic religiosity.'

2. *Intrinsic religiosity*: a set of religious beliefs and positive personal attitudes toward the idea of God. The key question in selecting this kind of believers is a person's self-identification as religious, regardless of whether he or she belongs to a denomination or not. Thus, we include five positive answers to the following questions (we divided all answers in a 'yes'—'no' dichotomy) in order to construct this complex variable:

• Are you a religious person?
• Does religion give you comfort and strength?
• Do you pray regularly (at least once a month) outside of religious services?

- Is God important in your personal life? (a 1–10 point scale was also divided into two possible 'yes'-'no' answers)
- There is a personal God (this belief is important to distinguish between intrinsic religiosity and a spirituality, also on the rise in the FSS, that is more amorphous and primarily stresses the existence of a Supreme Being, or Spirit, without the notion that it plays a role in an individual's life).

A group of people selected according to these criteria have probably not been baptized. However, they believe in God and pray regularly outside religious services; therefore, they can be considered sincere believers whose religiosity has intrinsic (not manifested) nature. According to Novikova et al. (2001), the number of intrinsic believers is growing because present-day Christian religiosity in the FSS is for the most part 'not connected with institutionalization of beliefs' (Novikova et al., 2001: 318). Usually such believers do not attend church regularly and therefore it is impossible to have any statistical calculation of their number—the scholar is forced to rely only on self-identification on the basis of these subjective indicators of religiosity. As with the external religiosity, we assume that those who selected at least two out of five above-mentioned questions demonstrate a relatively low level of intrinsic religiosity, while the rest (those who selected 3–5 questions) demonstrate the high level of intrinsic religiosity.

3. *Confidence in the Church*: a set of positive evaluations of the role the Church plays in society as a social institution. Actually, we assume that religious persons always hold the Church in high regard. However, some non-religious persons also do so, so that this complex variable can be higher than the previous two variables if the population displays general positive attitudes towards the Church. When the population has no confidence in social institutions generally, confidence in the Church is low as well. Chi-square showed a correlation between confidence in the Church and confidence in the most powerful institutions (police, armed forces, and social security system), and Pearson coefficient ($r = 0.15$) shows that this correlation is necessary to take into account.

This construction is based on respondents' positive answers to the following questions: (1) Is the Church giving adequate answers to an individual's moral problems and needs? (2) Is the Church giving adequate answers to the problems of family life? (3) Is the Church giving adequate answers to people's spiritual needs? (4) Is the Church giving adequate answers to social problems facing the country today? (5) Do people have 'a great deal' or 'quite a lot' of confidence in the Church? Again, those who selected at least two out of five above-mentioned questions demonstrate a relatively low level of confidence in church, while the rest (those who selected 3–5 questions) demonstrate the high level of confidence in Church.

Comparing these three new variables by countries we shall discover in which country people are more religious. Chi-square calculations proved a correlation within the questions selected for each new variable and between new three variables as well.

On the basis of three new constructs we can reformulate H2, giving more details on religiosity: women have a higher level of confidence in the Church regardless of denomination and country than men, and their level of external and intrinsic religiosity is greater than for males. Statistical analysis and graphs below will demonstrate gender religious differences in the FSS.

4 Analysis of data on religiosity

First of all, we shall check the data for the reformulated H2 (that females have greater religiosity and higher confidence in the Church than men). Statistical data analysis proves this statement about difference in gender religiosity. The mean score of women's external religiosity is 0.78 calculated on a [0–1] scale, while the same score for males is 0.68. The assumed significant difference of this variable is 0.1, so the above-mentioned gender difference is significant.

If we divide the people, who expressed external religiosity, by gender and age for each country, then Lithuanians will be the most religious without any significant difference for age groups of women: all of them are very religious. There is no age difference for men's external religiosity in Russia and Ukraine, and for Belarus men the correlation is the opposite: older men are less religious than men below 60.

If we divide the population into two separate groups—the Baltic and Slavic republics, then external religiosity for the Baltic countries will be higher than for the Slavic countries (0.79 versus 0.72), with the same gender proportion: females prevail in both country groups. It seems than the Balts show a higher level of cognitive and practical aspects of religiosity regardless of gender than Slavs, who are more oriented toward religious emotions.

Figure 14.2   External religiosity, by gender and age

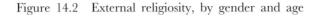

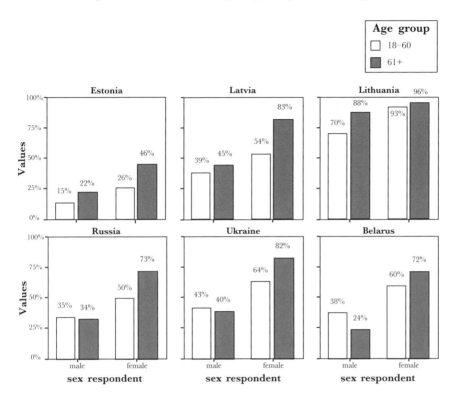

Intrinsic religiosity (emotional dimension) is a little lower, but gender distribution is similar: 0.70 mean score for females and 0.57 for men (with the same significance at 0.1 level and above). Intrinsic religiosity for the Baltic countries is generally lower than for Slavic countries (0.63 versus 0.70), but gender distribution of intrinsic religiosity within the regions is similar for each country and for the region as a whole.

If we divide those people in each country, who expressed the intrinsic religiosity, by age and gender, then again Lithuanians will be higher than others: both men and women demonstrate the highest proportion of religiosity of this type. Statistics proved that elder women (61+) are more religious than the rest of women (18–60). However, statistics did not prove the significant religious difference by age among the men in Ukraine, Latvia, and Belarus regardless of the fact that the sample showed the age difference for men in Belarus and Latvia.

Figure 14.3   Intrinsic religiosity, by gender and age

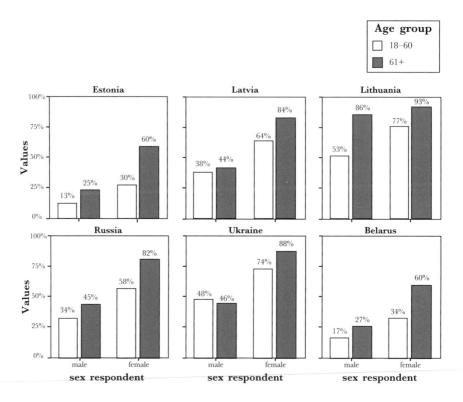

It is worth mentioning that Orthodox Christian beliefs are also cor-related with gender ($r = .262$): more females have traditional Christian beliefs than men. However, this issue is not so straightforward, as many in the FSS have non-Christian beliefs or mixed traditional Christian and non-traditional beliefs. Pearson's coefficient ($r = .270$) indicates a direct correlation between traditional Christian and non-traditional beliefs (in reincarnation, telepathy, and lucky charms), and therefore confirms the existence of a fragmented, non-coherent pat-tern of beliefs in post-Soviet countries. In general, almost two thirds of the respondents selected at least one non-Christian belief, and more than 25 percent among them selected both Christian and non-Christian beliefs. We may conclude that present-day Christian reli-giosity in the FSS is far from traditional religiosity: many accept non-Christian beliefs and do not need official institutional affiliation.

Confidence in the Church is the third component of a multi-dimensional analysis of religiosity, as explained earlier in this chapter. It was expected that women's confidence in the Church would be higher, and our calculation supports this fact. Overall, the mean score for the confidence in the Church is 0.63 for females and 0.49 for males, without any significant differences between Baltic and Slavic regions. On average, the Church is among the institutions in which people have confidence in the FSS.

One of the reasons the Church is held in high regard is that ordinary people do not associate the Church with the previous communist regime: in Soviet times religious practice was effectively prohibited for those who cared about their professional career and social status. Recently, the Church as an institution has been associated with the process of transition from communism (in one way or another). That is why, unlike many other social institutions, the Church is among the most trusted institutions: very high in Ukraine, Latvia, Russia, and Belarus. In fact, the level of confidence in the Church is one of the highest: only education has an even higher rating in Belarus, and education plus Army in Russia (Bashkirova, 2000: 56), while in Ukraine the Church is the most trusted institution. In total, the level of confidence in the Church in the Slavic republics is higher than the average European figure: 26.8 percent versus 19 percent express 'a great deal' of confidence in it.

The situation in the Baltic republics is culturally different: Latvians and, especially, Lithuanians also express a good deal of confidence in the Church. As for Estonians, their confidence in the Church is the lowest among the six countries.

Not surprisingly, those who identify themselves as religious have higher confidence in the Church than the non-religious (Pearson's correlation coefficient = .496). This correlation is significant.

While looking at different kinds of religiosity in different countries, we identified one more latent variable based on analysis of three key questions on religiosity. We converted the answers to these keys into a 'yes'—'no' dichotomy. This procedure led to results that showed quite a similar interrelation and hierarchy between affirmative answers to the above-mentioned three questions in the six countries.

With the exception of Belarus (the data inconsistency on religious self-identification there was mentioned earlier), in the other five countries and in the region as a whole a general trend has been found: more identify themselves as religious than belong to any religious denomination, and even fewer agree that religion is very important in their life. These results also confirm that present-day religiosity has less to do with religious institutions, so that many identifying themselves as believers are not connected with any particular denomination or Church (they are not necessarily core or modal members).

All three selected variables are closely connected ($r > .5$). The biggest gap between these variables is in Latvia, and the smallest difference is in Estonia. These results demonstrate an imbalance between (1) the number of those who clearly identify themselves as religious, (2) those who belong to a religious denomination, and (3) those who hold religion in high regard. Having this trend in mind, we can analyze only the third (smallest) group of respondents in order to describe the major socio-demographic characteristics of those (both men and women) whose attitudes toward religion are the most positive and strong (so called the core religious group).

5   Socio-demographic categories

Previous research on religiosity in the FSS, especially in the Slavic countries, demonstrated that the religious persons are most likely to be female, elderly, poorly educated, unemployed, and living in the country rather than in big cities (Novikova et al., 2001: 318). The most significant categories seem to be a combination of gender and age. Quite often, in a transition society middle-aged groups, usually

Table 14.3   Several indicators of religiosity, by gender

States	Religion is important		Affiliated		Religious persons	
	men	women	men	women	men	women
Belarus*	32	57	41	61	17	36
Russia	34	54	39	60	52	77
Ukraine	42	64	43	67	62	86
Estonia	16	27	19	30	32	50
Latvia	22	45	53	64	65	86
Lithuania	47	71	72	89	72	94
[Total]	32	52	45	62	50	72

*Note: Belarus question on religious self-identification was not similar to other countries, so that these particular data are not comparable with other countries.

employed and better educated, are less religious than the elderly, who need religious beliefs for establishing a new social network and enjoying the benefits of social welfare and moral support from the Church. Religion helps the elderly find a new identity—as a believer, or a member of a church community. The most successful in the FSS currently rely upon themselves and business, while the least successful believe in religion because it can provide them with spiritual equilibrium. Religious values provide protection against social injustice and economic inequality for poor elderly people in the FSS.

Our first research task was to check the previous analyses by examining new EVS data on the socio-demographic background of those who agree that religion is important. Pearson's coefficients confirm a significant correlation between the question about the importance of religion and two socio-demographic variables: age ($r = -.194$) and gender ($r = -.225$). Figure 14.4 shows that the older the people, the more religious they are. This correlation is especially significant for females: the mean difference between groups of young and elderly women is 0.57, while the mean difference for similar groups of males is half as much (0.26).

When two extreme age groups, divided by gender, are compared, the differences between countries become very clear. The mean value of religion for young men in all six countries is close to 3 ('not important'), while the mean value for elderly females in Ukraine, Belarus, Russia, and Latvia is close to 2 ('quite important'). It is even higher in Lithuania, but significantly lower in Estonia. Probably,

Figure 14.4   Intrinsic religiosity, by gender and age

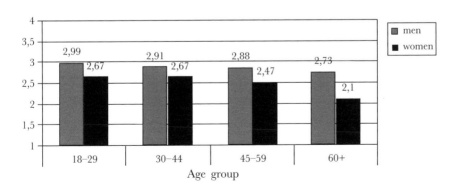

Age group

Figure 14.5 Importance of religion (means), for two age groups in six countries: young men (18–29) and old women (60+)

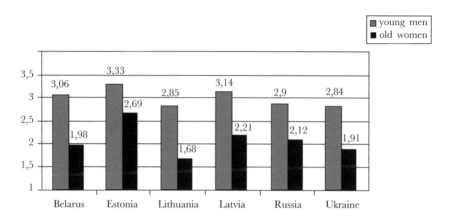

these differences show that the young generation in Lithuania is much more secularized than previous generations. As for Estonia, it seems that the young generation follows the same secularized pattern of socialization as the generations of their parents and grandparents. However, as Figure 14.5 shows, elderly women in each country value religion more highly than young males do, even in the most religious country Lithuania.

Our second research task was more special: to examine sociodemographic differences between two groups selected as the most and the least religious. The first group included those who demonstrated the high level of external and intrinsic religiosity and said religion is very important. The second group included those respondents who negatively answered questions about the importance of religion and religious affiliation, and did not identify themselves as religious.

Table 14.4 shows the overall profiles of the most and least religious in the FSS. As expected, gender patterns provide the strongest contrasts. Females are significantly better represented among the most religious than among the least religious. Age differences among the two groups are also prominent: older people prevail among the most religious; however, the least religious also include a large number of people aged 18–29 (21 percent). The employed are over-represented among the least religious (43%), and people with the low-income among the most religious. Better educated people are more likely to

Table 14.4   Differences in socio-demographic categories of the most religious and the least religious people in the former Soviet states

Categories	Most religious	Least religious
Gender (women)	77	30
Age (60+)	45	24
Income (lowest)	25	9
Size of place of living (big: more than 100.000)	38	49
Employment (not)	62	43
Education (primary)	30	7

be least religious. Size of place of living is not significant: people of both groups used to live in any place, however, there are more least religious people in big cities. In general, these results support the earlier expectations concerning the socio-demographic characteristics of the most religious.

6   Conclusions

The general conclusion is that the current level of religiosity in the FSS differs significantly from country to country. As has been argued in this paper, the main factors that determined the growth of religiosity in the 1990s in the Slavic republics include the collapse of the Soviet Union and its communist system. One could mention, for example, the social and economic deprivation affecting the old (Soviet) generations, the psychological discomfort of the population caused by value uncertainty, and the failure of Soviet beliefs. In the Baltic republics the main factors include the building of new identities and the restoration of pre-Soviet national traditions.

Gender differences have a significant effect on religion in all six countries. Data analysis has confirmed that women are more religious than men in all the countries, regardless of historical and cultural background and dominant religious denomination. Other socio-demographic characteristics that have the most significant effect are age and employment. The social profile of the most religious and the least religious is generally similar to the profile found earlier in West European countries. However, the younger generation's socialization makes young people less religious, so that the proportion of non-religious among youth in all the countries is bigger than among the elderly, especially among males.

Most striking are national differences: Lithuania shows the highest level of religiosity in the FSS. Ukraine, Russia, and Latvia show an average level of religious belief and religious practice, while Belarus is a bit lower on this scale, and the Estonian pattern is the lowest. However, the emotional dimension of religiosity (intrinsic religiosity) differs greatly from the cognitive and practical dimensions (external religiosity), and both contrast with confidence in the Church as a social institution. Analyzing current Christian religiosity from the standpoint of Orthodoxy, one can find that religious beliefs are becoming less traditional and more mixed with non-Christian beliefs, self-identification as religious does not correlate with church membership and church attendance, and the public role of the Church is mostly restricted to spiritual needs. It is also worth mentioning that the growth of religiosity in the FSS notwithstanding, the proportion of the non-affiliated and non-religious is still significant among the middle-aged generation, as well as among young and elderly males.

References

After collapse 1999. Florence: UNICEF.

Bashkirova, E. 2000. Value transformation in Russian society. *Political Studies* 6: 51–65. [in Russian]

Burawoy, M. & K. Verdery 1999. *Uncertain Transition*. New York: Rowman & Littlefield.

Castells, M. 1998. *End of Millenium*. Volume 3. Oxford: Blackwell.

Cipriani, R. 1994. Transitions and Transitions: Reflections on the Problems and Prospects for Religion in Eastern and Central Europe. In W. Swatos (ed.), *Politics and Religion in Central and Eastern Europe: Transitions and Transitions*. Westport: Praeger Publishers.

Ester, P., L. Halman & R. de Moor 1994. *Individualizing Society. Value Change in Europe and North America*. Tilburg: Tilburg University Press.

Gilinskiy, Y. (ed.) 2000. *Deviation and Social Control in Russia (19th and 20th centuries): Trends and Sociological Interpretation*. St. Petersburg: Aleteya. [in Russian].

Halman, L. (2001). *The European Values Study: A Third Wave*. Tilburg: EVS, WORC, Tilburg University.

House, K. 2002. Russia's Leader: Smart, Modest—and an Enigma. *Commentary* 1–2.

Inglehart, R. 1990. *Culture Shift in Advanced Industrial Societies*. Princeton: Princeton University Press.

Kruglov, A. 2002. *Fundamentals of the Study of Religion*. Minsk: TetraSystems. [in Russian]

Maslow A. [1962] 2002. *Towards a Psychology of Being. Religious Values and Peak-Experiences*. Moscow: EKSMO-Press. [in Russian]

Novikova, L. 2001. *Religiosity in Belarus at the Turn of the Century: Trends and Features*.

Minsk: BTN-Inform. [In Russian]
——, O. Ivanyuto & A. Tarnavskiy 2001. Major characteristics of ethnic and religious relations in present-day Belarus. In *Selected Papers of Belarus State University*. Minsk: Belarus State University Press. [in Russian]
Sztompka, P. 2001. Social change as trauma. *Sociological Studies* 1: 6–16. [in Russian]
Volkov, Y. (ed.) 2001. *Sociology of Youth*. Rostov-on-Don: Feniks. [in Russian]

ABOUT THE AUTHORS

Helmut K. Anheier is Centennial Professor of Social Policy at the London School of Economics and Political Science, and Professor and Director of the Center for Civil Society at UCLA's School of Public Policy and Social Research, Los Angeles, USA.

Wil Arts is a Professor of General and Theoretical Sociology and Director of the Research Institute of the Faculty of Social and Behavioral Sciences at Tilburg University, The Netherlands.

Jerzy Bartkowski is an Assistant Professor at the Political Sociology Section in the Institute of Sociology, Warsaw University, Poland.

Jaak Billiet is a Professor in Social Sciences at Catholic University Leuven, and head of the Centre for Datacollection and Analysis at the Department of Sociology at Catholic University Leuven, Belgium.

Hans De Witte is an Associate Professor at the Department of Psychology at Catholic University Leuven, Belgium.

Veerle Draulans is an Assistant Professor of Practical Theology at Tilburg University and an Associate Professor of Gender Studies at Catholic University Leuven, Belgium.

Tony Fahey is a Research Professor with the Economic and Social Research Institute, Dublin.

Aikaterini Gari is an Assistant Professor of Social Psychology in the Department of Psychology, The University of Athens.

John Gelissen is an Assistant Professor of Social Science Methodology and Statistics at the Faculty of Social and Behavioral Sciences at Tilburg University, The Netherlands.

James Georgas is a Professor Emeritus of Psychology at the University of Athens, Athens, Greece.

Paola Grenier is a Dahrendorf Scholar at the Centre for Civil Society at the London School of Economics and Political Science.

Loek Halman is an Associate Professor of Sociology at the Faculty of Social and Behavioral Sciences at Tilburg University, The Netherlands, secretary to the Board and Steering Committee of EVS and program director of the 1999/2000 EVS study.

Aleksandra Jasinska-Kania is a Professor of Sociology in the Institute of Sociology, Faculty of Philosophy and Sociology, Warsaw University, Poland.

Marcus Lima is a Professor of Social Psychology at the Universidade da Baía, Portugal.

Ola Listhaug is a Professor of Political Science and Chairman of Department of Sociology and Political Science, The Norwegian University of Science and Technology, Trondheim, Norway.

Diniz Lopes is an Assistant at the Instituto Superior de Ciências do Trabalho e da Empresa (ISCTE), Lisbon, Portugal.

Kostas Mylonas is a Lecturer on Research Methods and Statistics in Psychology in the Departmernt of Psychology, The University of Athens.

Penny Panagiotopoulou has been teaching Psychology of the Consumer at the University of Athens, Greece.

Thorleif Pettersson is a Professor in the Sociology of Religion, Uppsala University, Uppsala, Sweden.

Kristen Ringdal is a Professor of Sociology at the Norwegian University of Science & Technology (NTNU).

Emer Smyth is a Senior Research Officer with the Economic and Social Research Institute, Dublin.

Sally Stares is a research student in the Social Psychology Department of the London School of Economics and Political Science.

Larissa G. Titarenko is a Professor of Sociology at the Department of Sociology, Belarus State University, Minsk, Belarus.

Jorge Vala is a Professor of Social Psychology at the Instituto Superior de Ciências do Trabalho e da Empresa (ISCTE) and Researcher at the Instituto de Ciências Sociais of the Universidade de Lisboa, Portugal.

Leen Vandecasteele is a PhD student at the Catholic University Leuven, Belgium.

Malina Voicu is a Senior Researcher with Research Institute for the Quality of Life, Romanian Academy of Science, Bucharest, Romania.

AUTHOR INDEX

SUBJECT INDEX

EUROPEAN VALUES STUDIES

ISSN 1568-5926

1. P. ESTER, L. HALMAN & R. DE MOOR (eds.), *The Individualizing Society*. Value Change in Europe and North America. 1994. ISBN 90 361 9993 X
2. R. DE MOOR (ed.), *Values inWestern Societies*. 1995. ISBN 90 361 9636 1
3. L. HALMAN & N. NEVITTE (eds.), *Political Value Change in Western Democracies*. 1996. ISBN 90 361 9717 1
4. P. ESTER, L. HALMAN & V. RUKAVISHNIKOV (eds.), *From Cold War to Cold Peace?* A Comparative Empirical Study of Russian and Western Political Cultures. 1997. ISBN 90 361 9737 6
5. L. HALMAN & O. RIIS (eds.), *Religion in Secularizing Society*. The Europeans' Religion at the End of the 20th Century. 1999; 2002. ISBN 90 361 9740 6 (1999), 90 041 2622 8 (2002)
6. W. ARTS, J. HAGENAARS, J. & L. HALMAN (eds.), *The Cultural Diversity of European Unity*. Findings, Explanations and Reflections from the European Values Study. 2003. ISBN 90 04 12299 0
7. W. ARTS, L. HALMAN (eds.), *European Values at the Turn of the Millennium*. 2004. ISBN 90 04 13981 8